D0231710

WITHIN THE SHADOWS

Ernest Tarrant

authorHOUSE®

AuthorHouse™ UK Ltd.
500 Avebury Boulevard
Central Milton Keynes, MK9 2BE
www.authorhouse.co.uk
Phone: 08001974150

© 2009 Ernest Tarrant. All rights reserved.

No part of this book may be reproduced, stored in a retrieval system, or transmitted by any means without the written permission of the author.

First published by AuthorHouse 11/17/2009

ISBN: 978-1-4389-5716-6 (sc)

This book is printed on acid-free paper.

Within the Shadows
by
Ernest Tarrant

This short biography takes place between February 1942 and September 1944 during which time I assumed the identity of a French boy who had been killed in an air raid on Lille where he was working as an apprentice in an engineering company

On hearing of his assumed death, and because no body was recovered, his very loyal parents volunteered his identity to De Gaulle's office in London to be used in anyway for the defeat of the Germans

At this time the conflict between Churchill and de Gaulle was emerging as a problem because Churchill did not believe de Gaulle's claims that the French people were ready to rise up against the occupiers and drive them out

The Germans had only occupied part of France, the unoccupied part being allowed to remain independent as Vichy France. The resistance activity in occupied France led by diverse groups, each with their own objectives, was heavily suppressed by the Germans and resistance members caught by the Germans were tortured, imprisoned and worse in order to penetrate the resistance organisations further

In Vichy France the situation was quite different. The little resistance activity that did exist had little support from the general population who were essentially apathetic. The view was that the well organised Germans backing Marshal Petain's government could not be any worse that the constantly changing governments and policies France had endured in the immediate pre-war period

Churchill recognised Vichy France would remain independent only as long as it was convenient to the Germans and he needed to have reliable information as to the attitude of the people and to establish resistance activity in Vichy France

With this objective in mind he sought out available French identities which could be used either by members of the French section of the SOE, or specially sought out volunteers, who could establish themselves in Vichy France prior to the Germans moving in

Thus an intense search for suitable persons to replace a series of available identities began

Henri Dufour, the young man killed in the air raid on Lille was just starting the fourth year of his apprenticeship, He had not been recruited by the French army because he had a club foot on his right leg, surgically corrected, but nevertheless he failed the medical examination. He was nineteen years old, fair complexioned from his Flemish mother, not at all bright which resulted in his being transferred to a special school for retarded children. He obtained his apprenticeship due to the influence of his grandfather who was a senior manager at Precision Metal. By all accounts he made surprisingly good progress

In 1941 I passed the intermediate science examination. I was also liable for military service within the next year but wanted deferment to continue studies for a full science degree and applied for deferment when I registered for military service. Deferment was granted as I was unlikely to pass the medical examination due to a club foot on my right leg. Shortly after deferment being granted I was 'required' to attend a meeting at a hotel near Victoria Station for a 'review of my deferment status' .After being required to sign a version of the Official Secrets Act, I was invited to volunteer for special assignment in Vichy France. Prior to this meeting my background had been investigated, especially my education. I had spent four half terms in French speaking schools, I had an 'A' in French, I was educated at a Catholic school and could pass as a Catholic, and. I bore a reasonable likeness to a certain young Frenchman but most important of all I had a surgically corrected club foot on my right leg. Could I please volunteer for this assignment and reply within a week. I must not discuss the assignment within any person

I did volunteer and after the training period the story begins

Within the Shadows

by

Ernest Tarrant

This book is dedicated to Lisette Mathilde and Robert

For their Boldness and Bravery in accepting me into their family

and also to

Patrice

for

his ultimate sacrifice

I am indebted to my wife for the title of the book and her encouragement to
biographically record the events occurring during my time in France

Chapter 1

Departure

Late one Monday afternoon in February 1942 several submarines were laying alongside at a naval base in Southern England. The usual buzz of activity was quietening down as the light began to fade, except for the outermost where it was increasing

Men in uniform and dock workers were going on and off. Those going on were carrying various packages, fresh food for the first few days at sea and stock for the freezers to be eaten thereafter. The latest amendments to the admiralty charts had already gone on board, as had torpedoes, ammunition, top ups for the medical chest and all the paraphernalia to keep the vessel at sea for many weeks, and to cater for her crew

The commander of the outermost submarine crossed the decks to the quayside looking at his watch somewhat anxiously. He went in to an office, used the telephone, returned and joined his number one who had also come ashore on the quay. "Still no news from the dock gates," he said. "Half an hour's the absolute limit or we'll miss the tide". "Blasted civilians never understand seagoing timekeeping," number one replied, "I don't think they are exactly civilians, not where they are going commented the commander. A man emerged from the dockside office, and called out, "Car's just entered the dockyard gates sir, be with you in ten minutes."

"Right," said the commander, get a couple of ratings over to handle their baggage, we sail in twenty minutes from now. Get clearance from the port duty officer, start the diesels and make ready." "Aye, aye sir." The lieutenant scurried off the Commander walked up and down stamping his feet. The temperature was not much over freezing; be warmer at sea he thought. A black limousine approached stopped, and two young men emerged each carrying a small piece of hand luggage

"Commander Ellis?" enquired the first, "At your service" replied the commander "Good," said the first, "my name is Max and this is Jean." They all shook hands. "Sorry we're a little late but the driver took a wrong turn entering the city and we got lost. It took four people, believe it or not, before anyone would tell us the way to the dockyard. They must have thought we were bloody foreigners"

Understandable, thought the Commander, your English is not perfect and I can smell the garlic from here. "Come along aboard, she's the third one out, mind the slippery decks"

All climbed the ladder to the top of the conning tower. "Will you please go below at once gentlemen, I am anxious to catch the tide;, my number two will show you to your quarters. Once we're clear of the port entrance you can come up for some fresh air." The last words Max and Jean heard as they went below were "Let go forrard; let go aft"

When we got to our quarters, a tiny shared cabin with only a curtain as a door, Max remarked "It's even smaller than last time." So you've done this before I asked," "Pass" said Max, "you know what we were told at dinner last night." It had been a magnificent meal. You could have been excused for thinking there was no war

Max and I met for the first time at that dinner table. "After simple first name introductions we were put on our honour not to discuss our missions. We were simply two passengers in a submarine going to somewhere in France together, and we would part immediately on landing and were unlikely ever to meet again

During the course of charcuterie, medaillons of venison with sauce Robert, an excellent plate of French cheeses and crepes flambe it became obvious that Max knew much more about French food and drink than I did and we agreed that this was a subject we could talk about without breaking the ground rules. That meal was also my first experience of Chateau Margaux, Margaux and Max again spoke with some special knowledge of French wines commenting most favourably on the 1928 vintage we had just enjoyed, so that was another subject we could discuss

I was intrigued with Max, only about twenty-five or so, nearly perfect English but I'm sure he was French. Our hand baggage had been taken by the crew to be sealed up so that it would not be tainted with the persistent smell of diesel fuel. We would get it back when we disembarked. All necessary toiletries needed on board were by courtesy of the Navy. It was clear to me that Max had just been on a visit to England to be briefed I think, on some project I was not to know about

2

We finished stowing our little bits and pieces provided by the Navy, mostly in silence not really knowing what we could say to each other. "Do you play chess?" Max asked, "Oh yes I said I enjoy the game "Then that's what we'll do after dinner tonight," and we'll be slumming it after last night."

A head appeared round the curtain, "Commander's compliments gentlemen, we've just left the port entrance, and you can go up the tower when you wish." "I'll not bother," said Max, "but you go it's quite an experience if you've not done it before." I followed the second mate to the foot of the conning tower and climbed

It was not quite dark and we were slowly turning to starboard. I thought it was Portsmouth when we arrived in the car, and now I was sure, with the hills of the Isle of Wight to port and the lower land of Hampshire to starboard

Commander Ellis explained to me that he expected to stay on the surface much as possible so we could make as much speed as the sea would permit. "We can make about eleven knots on the surface but only seven submerged, and when you have a deadline to meet, it's surface all night unless we see or hear somebody else about

If it's your first time in a submarine you'll find the air gets a bit rich after we've been submerged for a few hours, so we always keep on top whenever we can"

We chatted about the boat, I learnt that Max and I brought the number on board up to forty-two, that our dinner would be served at eight bells, that the crew were under instructions not to ask us any questions, and if they did the Commander would like to know about it.

"Are those the Needles over there?" I asked, "Pass," said the Commander, "that's classified information, but I can't blindfold you" As the Needles passed slowly astern the Commander invited Max and myself to join the officers for drinks in the wardroom, saying he would hand over to the first mate in a few minutes time and join us

On a small vessel like a submarine the wardroom was only a screened-off area at the end of the whole dining area. Nevertheless we enjoyed a convivial hour or so with the commander and most of his officers before dinner

After dinner Max and I borrowed a chess set from the crew's games cupboard and played some hard fought games stopping at an honourable two games all. We were in fact well matched

Max then showed me the heads, and warned me about getting my own back if I operated the valves in the wrong order. Both of us had passed a stressful few days prior to sailing so it was then to our bunks

Though tired I could not sleep, the noise of the diesels was an ever-present unfamiliar background and most of the other noises were new. I simply lay awake turning over in my mind the events that had brought me to this point. The interviews after my application for extended deferment of military service to complete a special degree in chemistry when, I had been tempted by proposition to use my education and physical disability in the war effort with a fair reward at the end, plus a guaranteed university placement at the end of the war

The very quick call-up after I had agreed, no time for mind changing. Then those terrible weeks of basic training by N.C.O.'s who could only, be described as animals

The only high spot was the rifle range. I'd done some shooting with a point twenty two shooting, rabbits and foxes usually putting up a creditable performance. As soon as I had mastered the heavier kick of the point three-o-three Lee Enfield I could match the instructor shot for shot. "I'll put you forward for a marksman's course," he said. "I won't need that," I replied. He did not understand, and added that the army would tell me what to do, not vice versa

A few days later, on a Friday, I was selected for OCTU, and given a forty-eight hour pass with instructions to report to Titsfield next Monday to start special training

Then the submarine dived, something must have been sighted or heard. The much quieter hum of the electric motors, with the crew now on silent routine, allowed me to fall asleep. I was woken again by the submarine diving, but this time it was six bells in the morning watch, and I could smell breakfast

On my way to the wardroom I paused to look at the charts and the trace. We were now in the western approaches and were routed to go round Ushant later in the day. I found it difficult to cope with predicting our progress because of the difference between submerged speed and surface speed

We must have been on the surface most of the night to reach where we were marked on the logging chart

After breakfast a conversation with Max revealed that he knew where we were bound and he had been this way before. "It looks as though we'll be rounding Ushant during the day" We won't exactly round Ushant," said Max. "We have to keep a good way out to sea because of vessels coming out of Brest and Saint Nazaire, and there are usually E-boats around. We never know whether they are crewed by German or French so we always take a course with plenty of sea room at this part of the trip"

Now he did talk a little more openly. "Once we are clear of Ushant we stay at least a hundred miles off the French coast until we get to forty-five degrees south. By that time we are well clear of vessels coming out of Brittany or the Loire estuary and any northbound vessels coming out of the Gironde estuary will be to the east of us, so that we can turn due east and go straight in towards the coast. If we do intercept the path of an outbound or inbound vessel we stop and

4

sit on the bottom until they pass. Because there are so many wrecks in the area, if their Asdic does pick up an echo they cannot tell the difference between a submarine and a wreck"

"There's really nothing to do but eat, drink and sleep" said Max, "This is the worst part of the journey. Two days thinking about what you are going to do and say when you arrive." "Today, I'm going to read this morning, we'll try and get two of the crew to make up a four for cards this afternoon, and this evening I'll get drunk, thoroughly beat you at Chess, and go to sleep"

Most of it happened but the boredom became as big a problem as the air. By 1600 I was suffering and could not read or concentrate on cards any more. The relief when we went on to diesels at nightfall was so, so refreshing

That night sleeping was again difficult. I'd had no exercise, plenty of food, and some alcohol, but the noise of the diesels again made sleep impossible

I thought again about what got me here. All the intense coaching on the part I was to play, my history with the family I was to join, my schooldays in a town I'd never been to, the apprenticeship in Lille living with my maternal grandparents, that terrible night when most of the family were killed by British bombs

And then my surgical history, treatment by Professor Elias in Vichy, twice, each time walking better, but back to that nun's school in Saint Flour, where all they did was to keep you quiet and happy, and pray for miracles. Another school, in Murat, Ecole St. Jean, a special school for retarded and disabled boys. At least that school made a conscious effort to equip you for life

There were things to do, workshops, gymnasium, laboratories, and they taught you about how things worked, and what to do when they didn't. There was one thing that hadn't worked for me and that was parachuting. With hindsight it was probably not the best idea, I naturally favoured my left leg because it was stronger, and therefore it always touched down a little ahead of my right

By this stage all training was being carried out in French. The Corsican parachute instructor training me had noticed this and had advised against training me for parachute drops into mountain regions, because it was always likely to be a rough ground landing, for which I was not physically suited. However, he was over-ruled and training continued until I made just the sort of rough landing he had foreseen, and badly wrenched my left knee. After all he really did know; he had already been parachuted into Corsica eight times on various special operations. In my view he knew what rough landings really were like and his advice should have been taken. So that is why I was now in this tin can, cooped up for some days instead of floating down to earth in cool fresh air hoping for a soft landing

5

We dived twice in the night, both times in a hurry, and each time at a steep enough angle to wake both of us. The crew told us in the morning that it had been a still, quiet misty night with bad visibility and each dive was made due to the sounds of vessels rather than the vessels themselves

Another day to read, play cards and chess, eat, doze, eat again, drink, take dinner with the officers after the course for the night had been settled down

Another misty night was developing outside with almost no wind at all. Dinner was disrupted by an emergency dive when a freighter and two E-boats passed quite close to us. As the Commander said if he hadn't been looking forward to his dessert he'd have sunk the buggers for disturbing his meal

Bedtime again, same problem about sleep, "Too much of most things and not enough of the other," as Max put it. I got a sight of the charts again on the way to bed and we were well into the Bay of Biscay and the sea was like a millpond.

Dozed and thought again, the letters left behind to be posted at intervals. The most difficult letters I had ever written, lots of bright chatter but saying nothing, I tried to make them different, almost impossible, and of course there would be no answers until leave time when all incoming mail was to be read before arriving home

The last forty-eight hours leave I had enjoyed in December, when for those two days I could flaunt a new uniform and repeatedly explain that I was a technical officer and going overseas to do work where technical training was more important than command structure involvement and I did not expect to be back home for some years. I am sure not everybody believed it

Then back to the final training, about my change of identity. Repeated coaching in the new and different family history I had committed to memory, about the family to whom I was returning after three years away, at least they would acknowledge me. With everyone else I had to re-establish myself. However I had a screen to shelter behind. I was not very bright but I was said to have improved while I had been away doing that apprenticeship, even if the Germans had finally tossed me on one side

Those intense Morse-code practice sessions, two hours at a time with the same two women as would be receiving my messages, so that we became intimately acquainted with each others 'hand' and they would recognise an impostor misusing my equipment this was stressed as exceptionally important and it took me several weeks before I realised just how important

All those sudden shock tests, such as being arrested leaving ones billet by men in SS uniform and being brutally interrogated using all the latest procedures known to be in use. Injections of Scopolamine to loosen one tongue, and how to resist it, and confuse your interrogators. Suddenly being woken out of a deep sleep and questioning in English to try to break you by making you speak English. The sudden slap across the face to try to get a similar result, I woke up with a start and lashed out but it was only Max shaking me, "Breakfast in fifteen minutes," he said, "You must have had a weird dream last night." I could not answer

At breakfast the Commander said, "We'll be at our rendezvous point by about 1500. We are due to try contact with the shore at 2000 and at thirty minute intervals thereafter until 2200. By that time the tide will be wrong, and if we are not successful we will try again tomorrow night." We agreed to be dressed in our smelly French outfits by 1930 with our small bags ready to go

There would be a rehearsal of the handling of the canoes and lifejackets at 1630 in the dining area which would be cleared for the purpose. We would wear oilskins over our clothes and lifejackets, and these were to be removed on shore and either given to the two pick-ups if they were there, or returned in the canoes

This was the first intimation we had that this was a dual purpose operation, and had obviously involved much planning and coordination

The rehearsals were routine, at 1930 we were ready. The submarine was already on the surface and inching slowly inshore on almost silent diesels. The canoes were inflated and on the deck. This time we went on deck via the forward hatch. It was easier with our bags and life-jackets. A small sea was running. We donned our oilskins. At exactly 2000 the signals to the shore brought no response, and at every thirty minute repeat the same result. By this time everybody was near frozen to the marrow and gratefully retreated below to hot rum grog.   Disappointment was natural and the crew resigned themselves to another day of boredom tomorrow. The submarine withdrew from the shore as stealthily as she had approached it until we were near to a submerged wreck with enough water under us to be able to submerge at will. "We'll have to spend tomorrow sitting on the bottom." said the commander, "and try again tomorrow night, same time, same spot on the ocean

"If we lay close to a wreck any passing ship using Asdic will expect an echo from this location and unless somebody coughs at the wrong moment, they won't trouble us." We actually stayed on the surface all night, there were no shipping movements and everybody got a good night's sleep

The next day was total boredom. As a basic precaution we went to silent operation. Sotto voce conversations with the crew showed how much they disliked this type of operation they were looking forward to putting us ashore, picking up two to go back to England and then getting on with the war

"Sometimes we waste four days and get no contact," said a leading hand. However there was one consolation, with the lower level of activity, the air

7

quality was good for much longer. A hastily arranged solo whist tournament reduced the boredom of the afternoon.

At 1930 we did it all again, more smoothly this time. At 2000 there was an immediate reply with the correct identification. Canoes launched at once oilskins on and away we went, two canoes of three men, two paddling, one passenger trailing a light line behind us back to the submarine. Fair visibility, I could just make out a low shoreline ahead and a spit of low land to the north terminating in a silhouette of a lighthouse. Looking all round I could just make out another silhouette of a larger lighthouse on the horizon to the south west. There was no moon. An occasional flash of light from the shore kept us on course. I guess it took about twenty minutes

Landing on the firm sand beach was clearly a well practised routine, Pass words exchanged, passengers ashore, oilskins and life-jackets off and passed to two waiting silent individuals who donned them at once. I made contact with Jacques and Pierre as instructed. Max made contact with two others. A quick handshake with Max and a whispered "bon chance" and he was off with his two escorts southwards along the line of bushes at the head of the beach

Jacques and Pierre helped the two unknowns into their canoes, one paddler had remained in each canoe. As soon as the second was in Jacques and Pierre pushed the canoes off and they were paddling away also being pulled by the lines they had trailed on the way ashore. Jacques and Pierre came up the beach with some scrubby branches brushing out the footmarks until they reached the dry powder sand. Max was already out of sight. I never saw him again but some of his exploits came to my attention from other resistance members. He had experience. By the time we were ready to move the canoes were already alongside the submarine. A final exchange of light signals, and it was all over

Chapter 2

Arrival

We headed inland directly away from the beach on a well trodden path. After about a hundred metres we stopped, and Jacques dragged some bicycles out of a thicket. I turned back to look at the submarine. All I could see was a trace of wake where she had moved out to sea

On the bicycle Pierre rode there was a tiny pinpoint of red light at the back of the saddle which I had to follow at a distance of fifty to a hundred metres. Jacques brought up the rear immediately behind me. If the red light stopped or went out I was to stop at once and hide with Jacques. Strictly no talking or smoking and to make the best speed possible, no problems, we travelled in silence surrounded by silence. We crossed a small road and a ditch. After some time we heard the occasional vehicle and it was apparent that we were nearing a larger road. We must have travelled at least eight kilometres by this time

Then the red light went out, I stopped and Jacques came up beside me. He whispered, "This is only because of the main road, Pierre wants see what the traffic is like, it's busier than usual." The red light appeared again. "Let's close up," whispered Jacques, "we have to cross a largish stream by a bridge along that road, it's the only crossing point for many kilometres." They had done this before, As we reached Pierre he set off to the right with the red light out, Jacques and I waited at the side of the road listening for vehicle sounds, Jacques was also watching the dark area where Pierre had ridden, that tiny red light appeared again, a final ear for vehicle noise and we set off fast over the bridge to where Pierre waited at the start of another footpath on the left

The paths were better now, and we made fair speed. Some of the 'bridges' over the ditches were only single planks with no handrail. "Just be sure you steer straight, aim straight, and keep pedalling," whispered Jacques. We kept going always generally Eastwards moving steadily inland for nearly an hour when again we stopped as the red light went out. Again Jacques was instantly beside me whispering, "The next problem is a small village, and another stream to cross, and there may be people about. Let's move up to Pierre and decide how we are going on"

We Joined Pierre. He was standing at the roadside in a deep patch of shadow. "I'm going to ride through the village to check who is about and come back for you, stay under the tree, if any vehicle comes turn your backs to the road so your faces don't show in any headlight, then they won't see you," whispered Pierre. He was back in less than five minutes

"No gendarmerie, police or Germans about," he whispered "Let's go." We rode off through the village. A couple of bars were still open and lights were showing in most of the houses. Over the stream, more like a small river this one, and back on to those seemingly endless footpaths. Now there was the first sign of contour in the land and the paths were drier, fewer ditches and planks and the moon rose giving us some help

We passed occasional habitations with dogs advising of our approach. We were now making excellent progress. Finally as we approached another habitation, our coming announced by another dog, I noticed three candles alight in an upstairs window which suddenly went out as we approached. For the first time Jacques actually spoke out loud, "It's all OK and now it's suppertime"

'The bicycles went into the barn and sacks were thrown over them. Madame, Jacques wife, I think, opened the door and at once sat us down at table, producing a tureen of a very rich and meaty soup with good farm bread and jugs of wine which with cheeses and more wine made a very hearty supper. The sudden drop in the tension of the journey made me realise that I was really hungry. I suddenly thought, nobody in England had asked me if I could ride a bike

"You will wait here for a couple of hours or so until another man, Raoul arrives. He will take you out of the coastal exclusion zone," Jacques explained to me, "It's essential you are out of the exclusion zone before daylight. Otherwise if any reports at all of our activities tonight reach the Germans they close off the coastal zone and search everywhere." And with that good news he left me to rest and doze

Raoul came out of the night at about two o'clock and that was the end of my dozing. He appeared to be senior to Pierre and Jacques. He ate the remains of the soup and drank plenty of some sort of brandy, I tasted it but did not like it. They said it was 'fine' but I did not understand the word

Raoul said, "It's about six kilometres to the border of the exclusion zone. Along the border there is a continuous barbed wire fence, after that it's about another nine kilometres to the safe house. I've already cut a hole in the fence and I do not think any German patrols will find it during the night. If we are unlucky enough to meet a patrol both the dog and the handler will be shot and we will have to run for it separately. Keep moving South and when it is light ask your way to Perignan. By the side of the church the priest lives in a small villa with a blue door, your usual password will get you inside. Tell them what has happened and wait there until somebody comes for you. They will shelter you until further arrangements have been made"

Jacques left with us; this time he rode the bicycle with the red light and acted as our advance scout. The moon was now high and about three-quarters full making the journey quite easy. We got to the wire without incident, found the hole, crawled through, and manipulated the bicycles through with us. I never knew there were so many points on a bicycle on to which the barbs of barbed wire could catch. Raoul's leather gloves were essential. We parted from Jacques, his job was to rejoin the two cut parts of the fence and remove our tracks as best he could, and go back home

We also did what we could on the Eastern side of the wire and removed our tracks for about thirty metres to the metalled road. Now we made good fast progress to the safe house on the outskirts of a small town

The house was large, three stories with large group of outbuildings. We were expected and all traces of our arrival were cleared away in a few seconds. Our bikes went into a shed with many other bikes, all sizes and colours imaginable

A young man in a smock took a light broom and brushed out our tracks from the gate to the main road. I was given a hot drink well laced with brandy, and sent up to the attic to sleep as long as I wished. I quickly drifted off into a deep sleep

I vaguely remember half waking to various sounds outside but all else was oblivion. After all it had been quite a night!

Around two o'clock Raoul woke me with a different set of clothes he wanted me to wear today, "I'll explain later when we're on the way," he said, "Pack your other clothes and they'll go into the van we use

By the way have you hurt your leg? I noticed last night you were riding your bicycle unevenly." No," I replied, "I have a club foot on my right leg which causes that leg to be a little shorter and thus I pedal unevenly." "That of course makes you unfit for military service and if your cover is ever suspect nobody would never think of you as an SOE (Special Operations Executive) member with that impediment, and it also exempts you from French military service", commented Raoul, "a very good idea"

"I got a message from Hector, no I mean Jacques, this morning, he closed the gap well and he thinks it will be a week a least before the Germans find it and your trail will be very cold by then. Jacques is very good at that sort of thing, they still haven't found the last hole and that was over a month ago

"Now about crossing into Vichy France, I have a permit to go to the Saturday market in St. Junien each week with my son. You will ride in the cab with me wearing those rather distinctive clothes which you are just putting on. My son will be tucked away in the back

Now as soon as you are ready there is some food for you in the kitchen, don't eat too much because we'll dine famously this evening, then come out into the yard to finish loading the van with me and to be seen in those clothes"

I found my way down to the kitchen where there was a plate of cold meats salad, bread and coffee waiting for me. As soon as I had finished I went out into the yard

"So you've finished stuffing yourself at last" was shouted at me as I emerged into the sunshine. "If you don't help me get this wagon loaded we'll never get to the border in time. It's the same every week; you leave it all to your poor old dad and just come along for the ride." I smiled inwardly at the play; some heads were turned to look at me as I tried to help. "Don't go putting those vegetables on top of that tray of jam, you idiot, you'll make the labels dirty and it won't sell," was the next outburst. And so it went on, I tried to help; every thing I did was wrong and was aired to anybody within earshot. Finally we got the last boxes on board, raised the tailboard, and tied the sheet firmly

The wagon was about a six tonner, a Renault, fairly new, only 28,000 Kilometres on the clock as I discovered when I got up into the cab. I almost made a mistake by going to the left hand door, just stopped myself in time, and continued round the front of the vehicle and climbed up into the right hand seat

Some minutes later Raoul joined me with a large folder of papers in his hand."You played your part well." he said quietly, and, louder," if we have missed anything it's your fault." was the final outburst, drowned partly by the start-up of the engine

After we got clear of the town, Raoul explained how we would get through the border. First of all his son Marc was an asthmatic which is why he was not in the French military. We would get to the Vichy French border between five and six o'clock, when it was always busy, mainly with people who crossed daily to and from their work. My distinguishing clothes were usually worn by Marc. Normally the border guards did not even speak to Marc. If they did speak to me I was to start panting and use the throat and nose spray on the dashboard in front of me, while Raoul explained about my asthma to the guards.

Raoul added that I was the eighth one to cross the border in this manner. "Don't worry about the spray," he added at the end, "it's only water"

During the journey Raoul was most informative about the attitude of the French population towards the Germans. "You must remember," he said, "it's hundreds of years since this part of France has been occupied by enemy troops, and if you remember your history you will recall they were English. So far the Germans have been very correct in their attitudes and behaviour. If they continue like this it will be difficult to raise much in the way of a resistance movement because they are bringing money, of a sort, into this poorer part of France"

"Does anybody listen to the BBC?" I asked, "Or to De Gaulle's broadcasts?" "De Gaulle is not known in this part of France and is not considered important, very few listen to the BBC. It is an offence of course, but difficult to detect unless a person is caught red-handed. The only punishments I have heard about were for repeating the BBC reports to another person"

"That is very different from what I was told in England," I said. "De Gaulle claims all loyal French men and women are ready to rise up against the Germans whenever he chooses to order it." "It may be different in other parts," Raoul went on, "but the average Frenchman in this region is totally disillusioned with politicians and past governments who have achieved so little for us

That's the reason why there is so much support for the communists at present. You do know, I suppose, that there is a Communist resistance movement especially in the remoter regions that are actually challenging the Germans sometimes"

"Do they also exist in Vichy France?" I queried, "Not in the parts that I know," Raoul replied, "but there are plenty of remote mountain regions in Vichy France." This was all new to me and something I needed to check, just in case it was one man's prejudiced opinion

It was a pleasant enough afternoon, warm for February, and quite sunny. Not much traffic and only an occasional sign of any German activity. At   the crossing point, which was a bridge over a broad river, the German control point was on one side and the Vichy French, the other. We joined the queue for the border. It moved steadily. "Doesn't look as though they are doing any searches today," Raoul remarked quietly. "We'll be through in quarter of an hour." The German inspection was cursory and we passed through, over the bridge to the Vichy control; a more thorough examination of our papers, and a few questions about when we would be returning. Any other thoughts they might have had were dealt with by Raoul's little bottles of farm distilled liqueurs

We stopped a few kilometres short of St. Junien at a hostelry well known to Raoul. "Here we have a safe parking place, real French food, cooked superbly, good wine, and comfortable beds," he said, "and people who are totally trustworthy. When I am doing a run like this the hotel and restaurant are closed to all other people, as a precaution

The place is run by Violette, her husband, Aristide is the Chef, and her three daughters who are all married and live locally; also there is a son but he is still missing in this war"

We parked the wagon behind the inn. Aristide came out to greet us. "Your boxes are just in the back with blue crosses on them," said Raoul to Aristide. "Then I'll let Marc out" and thus I met Marc for the first time. He was a good looking lad, nineteen or twenty I guess, but with terrible asthma

I apologised to him for taking his seat, but he claimed he had been comfortable and warm in his nest under the goods. I poked my head in. It did indeed look comfortable. "I can sleep quite happily in there, all the way," said Marc

As we settled down to some aperitifs in the corner of the dining room by a log fire, all seemed very right with the world. "This is a dinner to celebrate your arrival in the real France," said Raoul," Tonight we will eat as Frenchmen should eat and drink as Frenchmen should drink without any interference from anyone"

I am sure, apart from the departure dinner in England; this was the best meal I had eaten since the war started. During the meal tomorrow's movements were outlined. Raoul and Marc were to leave early to get a good pitch in the market and get the stall set up for business. I could sleep until about eight, and then I was to dress in my usual clothes, having passed the rather distinctive clothes back to Marc, when I undressed tonight. Another Jacques would be calling for me in the morning and I was to remain in my room until he arrived. Aristide would introduce me. We were to breakfast at leisure and then pass through St. Junien, simply to check that nothing was amiss

Dinner was not a rushed affair. Now our business was almost over we relaxed in the intervals between the courses. Aristide himself brought the food to the table and waited until we had approved each creation before retiring to put the finishing touches to the next. It was relatively simple food, a vegetable soup, but I'd never tasted its like before. It was followed by a plate of snails grilled in their shells with herbal butter, a veal escallop that dissolved in the mouth to meld with its sauce. Cheese to see the red wine off; then a longish pause until Aristide came in with his, very appropriate, as he said, "piece de resistance," the Tarte Maison. I had never seen a tarte like this before. I guess it was forty centimetres diameter. The thin pastry case, round the outside, was lined sliced peaches, in the centre were patterns of cherries, strawberries and raspberries. The whole thing was lightly caramelised on the surface, and served cold with thick cream

It was superb, each fruit type had retained it's own flavour, but its texture was more like that of raw fruit. I asked how it was done but this was something Aristide was not going to talk about. We simply could not finish it but Violette and Aristide came to our assistance accompanied by various brandies and liqueurs to go with the real freshly ground and brewed coffee. What a meal and what a welcome to the real France!

We lingered long at the dinner table. In spite of dozing at the dinner table, I did not sleep immediately. Who were these people? Aristide obviously knew something, I felt sure Raoul knew something of my mission, Marc probably not. Why was Aristide going to introduce me to another Jacques in the morning? Eventually, the brandy did its job, I did sleep

Chapter 3

Henri Dufour, Never be Late

Saturday morning and it was market day. As I dressed I noticed much more traffic on the road than yesterday and almost all going the same way. I watched the road going into St. Junien, guessing that is where Jacques would be coming from. An elderly Citroen, the same model as I had seen used by the police in Paris a few years ago, slowed down and turned into the yard and drove straight round to the back. That's him I thought. A few minutes later Aristide was knocking on my door I picked up my bag and went down to breakfast

We had the dining room to ourselves. "Jacques," said Aristide, "This is Henri Dufour." We shook hands. Jacques was another of these mature Frenchmen in their mid-fifties, too old to be of use to the French military and probably with service in the first war. Loyal, without a doubt, and truly trustworthy. Back to my thoughts of last night, but no fears because I came to the conclusion that I was now among friends who were all preparing to resist the Germans when they eventually occupied Vichy France. There was warmth in the way these people dealt with me. Up to now I had been a package to be protected and transported according to instructions, at some risk to the conveyor

Over a leisurely breakfast Jacques explained the next stages to me. "This is a travelling day and by tonight you will be in Clermont-Ferrand about two hundred and twenty kilometres away. First we must visit the market in St. Junien just to check that nothing untoward has happened to Raoul and Marc, and you should buy a few little things in the market, and get on the bus at a quarter past eleven to Limoges." "By the way you will need some money in your pocket

It will be better if you buy your own tickets, because most people do. Here is about three thousand Vichy Francs, that will be quite adequate to get you right through to Saint Flour no matter how you travel." Once again they seemed to know all about me and where I was going

16

Before we left I again asked Aristide just how he had made the Tarte Maison with that wonderful fruit in February. In answer, he took me into the kitchen and showed me his store of preserved fruits. Jar upon jar of what looked like fresh sliced fruit in a pale liquid, peaches, apricots, plums and whole fruits like strawberries, raspberries and cherries. Aristide explained

"When the fruit is in season we take perfect fruits and slice them into a clear brandy with just enough sugar to keep the fruits plump and leave them there until we need them. The secret lies in the strength of the brandy and the right amount of sugar for each type of fruit. After we have baked the pastry case we fill it with the fruit while it is still warm and return it to the oven. The alcohol burns off and just caramelises the surface to enhance the flavour. Then we immediately take the tart from the oven to the refrigerator to cool it quickly before the fruit loses it's fresh taste and texture"

Having had my first lesson in the Cuisine Francaise, we said our goodbyes to Violette and Aristide. Both of them hugged me; again the warmth of these people, so loyal to a France that was in danger of being overwhelmed into the mass of occupied Europe

We set off in the Citroen. The morning rush had subsided, the road was quiet until we crossed the Vienne and entered St. Junien by the railway station. "We'll drive right up to the market," Jacques said, "Some of the early birds will be leaving by now, and if we are lucky we can find a parking place." We were lucky and managed to park behind the large collegiate Church. "You wait here in the car for a few minutes. I'm just going to check with Jacques that there are no problems." He quickly returned

"All OK," he said, "I'm sorry it's not possible to drive you to Clermont, it is too risky and I don't have enough petrol. We would be sure to be stopped by the gendarmerie and then anything could happen. I'm going to get rid of the car and I'll be back at the west door of the Church at a quarter to eleven. You go and buy your few things in the market, toiletries and such as you will need in the next week or two, make sure you get a carrier bag so that you look like a shopper. If you see Jacques or Marc, do not acknowledge them. There are lots of strange eyes in the market and you are a stranger, and therefore suspicious"

I agreed. "When I come back I'll greet you as a friend and we'll walk off together to the bus station"

I bought a pair of shoe brushes, passed near to Jacque's stall which was busy, and allowed myself to be sold a rather nice leather belt embossed with a chain of Fleur-de-Lys. I had not seen a market quite like this before, you could buy so many things, and some of them were alive! To see chickens being sold and carried off by their legs up-side-down was new to me. Caged songbirds I could understand, but piglets carried in the arms of the purchaser, almost like a baby, or

17

a net full of baby rabbits being carried hurriedly to a car before they could nibble their way out struck me as bizzarre. This was a new experience so absorbing I was late for my rendezvous with Jacques

When I first saw him at the Church door, he was angrily looking at his watch When he spotted me approaching, he rushed towards me grabbed me by the hand and we dashed off to the bus station. We did have some time to spare but not much. The bus was slow and full, we sat apart. It stopped about every two hundred metres to set down people loaded with bags of market purchases. As the passengers thinned out, Jacques caught my eye and pointed to an empty double seat right at the front. We joined each other. In a low voice Jacques said, "Lesson number one, you are never, never, never late for a rendezvous. If you are early, slow down. It is permissible to be up to two minutes early or up to two minutes late, but fourteen minutes late puts others at risk. Always remember, people waiting about attract attention. I hope you did not stand and stare in the market; that would immediately mark you as a stranger and possibly a foreigner

I apologised most humbly

By now we were the only passengers left in the front of the bus. It was the custom to move towards the rear and exit as you neared your stop. Jacques went on, "Lesson number two, you will see many things you have not seen before but you must never let others know that you have never seen them before. You will taste things you have never tasted before, if you don't like the taste you must still eat it

It is perfectly permissible to refuse a dish saying simply, that is not to my taste. In France everyone can be an individual, so you must learn your dislikes."Lesson number three," said Jacques," When you said goodbye to Violette and Aristide this morning, you should have hugged Aristide as well just letting him hug you, and when you hugged Violette you should have kissed her once on each cheek, that is the French way"

The bus was beginning to fill again as we approached Limoges. "Enough for now," said Jacques. "We'll take lunch in Limoges, the restaurant will be busy, and I'll be watching you carefully, don't let me down." We rode on in silence. After all that intensive training, within twenty-four hours I had let myself down badly, several times. But was it really all my fault?

I could not recall anything about kissing a middle aged woman who hugged me, or hugging a man in response to his hug, which beggared the question, did my tutors know?

We arrived in Limoges, a city with a feel about it, a place of some importance with wider streets, better buildings. Eventually we reached the bus station, within sight of a large Cathedral standing up above the rest of the city. "We'll leave our bags in the left luggage office. I'll check the time of our bus for

Clermont, and then we will know just how long we have for our lunch." Jacques returned, "Clermont bus leaves at twenty past three, I've just got two reserved seats. They expect it to be full as it leaves here; it would be stupid if we could not get on for the whole journey because locals wanted to go a few kilometres down the road. After all there are plenty of other buses going on that road to other places, which they can catch"

We walked off skirting the mound where the Cathedral stood towards the shopping area. Jacques had a restaurant in mind where he was known and consequently we got a convenient table. I heard the head waiter address him as Monsieur Descartes was introduced as Monsieur Dufour and duly welcomed by the head waiter as a friend of Jacques. Aperitifs were brought with menus and a wine list. There did not seem to be any shortages. I commented on this to Jacques, and he told me that, nowadays portions were smaller and menus changed much more often depending on what was in the market, and prices rose almost every month

The meal was good and satisfying without being in any way notable. We had the time to linger over coffee and brandy. Two acquaintances of Jacques passed our table and stopped to shake hands with Jacques and exchange a few words of business chatter. Again I was introduced as Monsieur Dufour from Clermont, and Jacques told both that he was on his way to Clermont for a few days. "Don't worry," he said after they had left, they are completely trustworthy, and they know about the business in Clermont"

We left the restaurant in good time and strolled gently back to the bus station. The day was brightening after a gloomy morning, and even the sun might appear. We retrieved our bags and took our seats. This was a more substantial vehicle, the seats were angled and padded, which was just as well, we had nearly four hours journey ahead, "there will be a necessary break of five minutes at Arbusson, " said Jacques. The bus was full on departure with many standing, but within ten kilometres there were spare seats. "People don't travel much today, I wouldn't be surprised if we were the only ones going all the way to Clermont

We could have done the journey quicker by railway but there would have been controls at the stations and on the trains, whereas the buses are not controlled at all, so far. Tomorrow when you get all your proper papers you can pass any control, but until then we take the safer way." From this I deduced that he didn't think much of London's paperwork as well as their training. We chatted and I dozed from time to time, the day became warm and the lunchtime brandy was doing it's job. Jacques woke me at Arbusson for the necessary break

It was a pity it was dark long before we reached Clermont. The road was constantly hilly and the road wound its way between some high peaks. I woke

Jacques and asked, "These are quite high mountains, and some of them look like volcanoes?" "They were all volcanoes once," replied Jacques, "but there has not been any volcanic activity for about fifteen hundred years and it's thousands of years since the last real volcanic eruption"

This is some of the richest land in France, the sheep here produce the best wool, all the milk of the region be it goat sheep or cow makes some of our finest cheeses, the fruits are especially rich in flavour and make fine liqueurs and the walnuts are the best I've ever tasted" "That all sounds most interesting," I commented. Then Jacques spoke quietly in my ear, "And the hill farmers here are the most dishonest of all Frenchmen, but, make friends with them and you'll never be short of anything so it is worth taking the time to get to know them"

Quite suddenly after a specially steep and winding descent, we were in the outskirts of Clermont. The bus was stopping frequently. "We'll stay on to the bus station", said Jacques, "I don't know Clermont well after dark, and so we'll take a taxi at the bus station." By doing that we got to the Palmyra 'Restaurant with rooms,'for special guests' as Jacques put it. "And a totally safe house"

We freshened ourselves and smartened ourselves up; after all it was Saturday night, the greatest night of the week for eating out. Before we went down to the dining room Jacques told me about he menu here. "It is not an a la carte menu. There are various complete menus at a fixed price, you should order as the menu at a price, and then go on to choose, where a choice exists." Another thing my tutors had not mentioned. The dining room was almost full. Madame showed us to a residents table, brought us aperitifs and left us to study the menus

We were both hungry in spite of having done very little. The staff and the kitchen were busy and it was some time before Madame could take our order. The dinner started with a tasty soup served with plenty of bread, the other courses were quite small. Nevertheless with the wine it was a satisfying tasty meal but otherwise unremarkable. "You cannot do so well in the big cities as in the country. There are many more restaurateurs buying in the black market and they may have to go further afield, which takes time and money "Jacques explained

When Pascal joined us for coffee, Jacques asked Madame if we could have a private room for a business discussion. Fresh coffee and brandy arrived and when we were settled, Jacques introduced him as the resistance co-ordinator for the region reporting directly to De Gaulle's office in London

Pascal simply said he knew all there was to know up to the present about me. Pascal, who also exuded the warmth of feeling, clearly wanted to establish a good relationship. He explained his co-ordinating role for all sorts of resistance activities and asked me to agree to keep him informed of any offensive plans against factories producing for the German war effort, and eventually against

German forces when they eventually moved in. I immediately asked when he thought that would be

His opinion was different from that of my English colleagues of the SOE. Pascal did not think the Germans had enough troops to spare to do the job properly, and unless they were forced to occupy Vichy France, they would not do so. He agreed however that it must occur eventually and before any invasion of mainland Europe by the Allies took place

I asked Pascal about the strength of the resistance in the area. He explained that one of his problems was to convince De Gaulle that the resistance was not one body. There were many groups each with differing objectives, different names, some were equipped, others had virtually nothing, most had some political affiliation and none of them recognised any authority other than their own leadership

First there is the OCM an organisation of ex-army officers, mainly in the northern parts of occupied France, Very little activity to date but they are trying to recruit members in Vichy France total size unknown

Next comes Liberation Nord based on the members of some engineering trade unions. So far they have successes in disrupting production in factories where they have a dominant membership position and could rely on the workers support. They could be important because they can act quickly if necessary

In Vichy France there is a similar organisation called Combat Liberation, they appear to be better organised and already have some successes in factories working primarily for the German war machine

Next in importance come the communist inspired FTP, they make a lot of noise and claim to be the largest of the various resistance groups, they blame their lack of success on their lack of supplies and blame everybody else for that. Another group are the Maquis also communist originating from Corsica, and appear to be supplied by the Italian communist party out of northern Italy! They have been active in Provence and the southern Rhone valley with successes against power generation plants. Recently they are also reported to be present in the Auvergne but have not made any contact with me

Lastly and by far the smallest is the resistance inspired by De Gaulle and nominally led by him. Totally inactive so far, membership in whole of Vichy France is in the hundreds."I thanked Pascal for taking the time to explain the various factions, and had to ask him who I should consider supplying and how I should make contact with them

"When you arrive in Saint Flour one of the first people you will have to meet will be Sergeant Alexis Lescaut, he is the local police station's senior officer. He will be the one who will take your travel papers and use those to reinstate you in the local community, give you a new identity card and the other necessary papers"

"Lescaut reports directly to me on all resistance matters. He is completely trustworthy; you should take his advice entirely for the first few months, while you get the feel of the local situation. It will be quite different in Saint Flour from Clermont. The people are mostly fellow travellers they have suffered from many years of misgovernment ever changing and inconsistent. They are not naturally militants. Here in Clermont, there is militancy and we fear political rioting rather than properly controlled resistance." I left the subject at that, but was concerned, because London had told me nothing about this sort of thing,-did they know?

Pascal now talked about the family I was returning to in Saint Flour. "I went to see them personally when this idea was first discussed, they felt that they had lost their son but never been able to mourn because no body had ever been found. If in death he could still serve France, they would accept another as their son, doing his duty for France. I think of them as the truest most loyal people I am ever likely to meet"

I was intrigued at this; I thought the idea had originated in England, another false-conception? "If you have any problems with your new Mum and Dad you must contact me directly and urgently, I feel responsible for all of this"

By this time it was past two o'clock. Pascal went to the telephone and called for his car. When I saw the huge chauffeur-driven Citroen that came to collect him, I realised he must be a man of considerable power locally if not further afield as well

Sunday morning, and we slept late. Jacques finally called me about half past nine. We had the restaurant to ourselves so we could talk. "It's not exactly a busy day," said Jacques, "all we have to do is go to Vichy and meet the morning express from Paris, you will meet your alter ego, who has travelled from Lille in your name and got all the right stamps on your papers, so that Sergeant Lescaut can issue you with a new Identity Card when you arrive in Saint Flour. After you've got your new papers you must give him the identity papers they gave you in England so that he can destroy them." "What did really happen to Henri Dufour, I have to know," I demanded." "Please calm down," said Jacques. "Lille was heavily bombed by the RAF as you know. The Renaud family home suffered a direct hit. It was thought that Madame Renaud, her two unmarried daughters and Henri Dufour were in the house at the time. Monsieur Renaud was at the factory. Parts of Madame and her daughters were recovered from the wreckage and properly identified. No trace of any other person was found. Under French Law therefore with no evidence of death, Henri Dufour remains alive

If it ever becomes necessary Monsieur Renaud, your grandfather, will testify that you were out when the raid took place and that you eventually turned up at the factory some days later shocked by what you had seen and experienced. He took you to the flat where he had re-housed himself and kept you there until you recovered. Because you did not attend for work at the factory the new German controlled management of Precision Metal cancelled your apprenticeship and sacked you as an unsatisfactory apprentice. Thus without employment in occupied France you were entitled to travel back to your parents in Saint Flour, which is what you are doing this morning

I was specially instructed to tell you this additional part of your cover story, because this is what your Mum and Dad have been saying around Saint Flour."It is a tangled web I've got to live in," I said. Shortly afterwards we strolled round to the bus station and took a bus for Vichy

The bus and railway stations in Vichy are one and the same location. "Let's take a stroll around the station and see who's about," said Jacques. As we rounded the front of the building and entered the booking hall Jacques pointed out platform six, "You see that platform is completely fenced off, that's where the train from Paris will arrive, Vichy is the first stop after the border, so all passengers must leave the train and pass through our border point control which is just there," he said, pointing to a group of temporary huts blocking the way between platform six and the booking hall. When the train is empty it will be searched by our border police, passed out of platform six and shunted back into platform five, just here and all the passengers who are travelling further on return to their seats and new passengers may board because the train then goes on to Nimes"

"So how do I get to meet my namesake?" I asked. "You see that black doorway at he far end of the platform, well that's the superintendent's office, and the last coach of the train stops right outside that door. As the train pulls into the platform, you will be in the superintendent's office, when the passengers start to leave the train you will come out of that door carrying your small case and go to that seat just by the side of it, put your bag on the seat and start to retie your shoelaces, Your namesake will come to you and also place his suitcase on the seat. His first words to you should be, "Hello I'm Henri Dufour," and your answer must be, "and so will I be soon"

While this is going on he will be taking off his coat and folding it up to go over his arm, during this time he will slip you a bunch of papers which will include your travel permit, your train ticket, your identity card issued in Lille in 1939, your discharge letter from Precision Metal s.a. and the agreement of the Burgomeister of Lille that you may return to Saint Flour, as you are unfit for military service"

"But how will he get off the platform?" I questioned Jacques, "Don't worry he has a return ticket to Vichy and a travel permit to visit Nevers to see a sick Aunt but you don't need to know anything about that. Just you concentrate on getting your own clearance

Now listen again, I expect you'll get all your papers in a brown envelope, just leave them there and hand the envelope to the policeman at the control point. After he has read them and stamped them, he will ask you how you are going to get to Saint Flour, you will of course say, "by bus". Because it is Sunday he will pass you on to another desk to change some of the occupation Francs you will also have in the envelope, at least enough to get you to Saint Flour on the bus. I'll be waiting for you in the booking hall but look carefully, for me, because my appearance will have changed. Now we'll see when the train is due

"We went to look at the arrivals information, but nothing was shown regarding the Paris express. "That means she's running late as usual" said Jacques, We'll go and get some lunch in the buffet, it won't be much but it will keep you going until you get home"

We took the lunch in the buffet, Jacques was right it wasn't much. We could see the main area of the booking hall and platform six from the buffet. Eventually Jacques said, "There's some information just gone up on the arrivals board." People were beginning to crowd round the entrance to platform five and Jacques said, That's a sure sign she'll be in soon." We walked smartly to the information board, Paris express due at 14.25, "Only one and a half hours late," said Jacques, on a four hundred kilometre journey, now you must give me all the Vichy francs you have in your pocket, you'll get them back later but you must not have any such money on you as you pass control, just in case they search you. Now," said Jacques, "We go to the other way in to the superintendent's office on platform six. I'll show you the door, it will be locked, but you knock hard until they open and simply say "Pascal sent me", they will let you in and you wait until the passengers are getting off the train before you go on to the platform.

"We walked into the staff entrance to the station offices, after a few twists and turns we came to the locked door. "You're on your own now," said Jacques, "Good luck". I wrapped hard on he door, twice, I heard the key turn and the door opened a crack, "Pascal sent me," I whispered, the door opened wider and the man looked out to see if anyone was watching, "OK", he said pulling me inside and relocking the door

"You've been told what to do I hope " "yes," I replied. The train will be here in about ten minutes, you can watch out of that window, I'll go on to the platform as soon as the train is pulling in, you know when you've got to move, good luck"

He did not say another word we waited in silence. It was one of the longest ten minutes of my life. Then it all happened as planned, I moved to the seat and began to tie my shoelaces, within seconds somebody was saying quietly in my ear, "Hello, I'm Henri Dufour," I was so flabbergasted I forgot to reply. "Hello, I'm Henri Dufour," was repeated in my ear, "Oh yes," I replied, "and so will I be soon." He quickly gave me a brown envelope and a handful of occupation francs. Having finished the folding of his raincoat, he disappeared into the crowd. I stuffed the money into my pocket slipped the envelope into the inside pocket of my jacket and also mingled with the crowd moving towards the platform exit

The border policeman took quite a long time reading carefully all of the documents. He called an inspector over to look at the agreement from the Burgomeister of Lille, but all seemed OK and I was relieved when he proceeded to stamp all of the documents and returned them to me. He said I had to go to the police station in Saint Flour tomorrow morning to get a new identity card and be re-registered as living in Saint Flour. He asked how I was going to get there and I replied, "By bus". "OK", he said, "See my colleague there," pointing to another desk and he will change enough money for you to get your ticket, and you'll have to go to the bank in Saint Flour to change the rest." Money was changed with no problems and I passed out into the booking hall. I was almost the last person out. I looked all round for Jacques and eventually spotted him by the main entrance. I hurried across to him with my two cases

"The bus leaves in five minutes," he said, "we must hurry." We got to the bus with very few minutes to spare, Jacques having bought the tickets in advance. Once we were seated he said, "I really thought we were not going to make it, "was there a problem?" "Not really," I said, "Everything is now stamped, the delay was because they read everything very carefully, and there was quite a lot of it." I put my hand in my pocket to take out the envelope. "No, no", said Jacques, "leave it where it is, If they've stamped it all, that's what matters." Jacques took his opportunity to return the Vichy Francs I had passed to him for safe keeping. "Sometimes they search people at the control looking for such things as wrongful possession of currency"

"There's no direct bus to Saint Flour on Sundays, so we're going as far as Issoire on this one and I'm going to leave you there. I'll see you on to the right bus for Saint Flour but it is better that you arrive alone, anything else would look suspicious. Don't forget as you arrive that family greetings are much more effusive in France. It is quite possible that others might know of your arrival and be looking on"

We had about a fifteen minute wait in Issoire. During these few minutes I tried to express my thanks to Jacques for all he had done. He was dismissive of thanks, "My first loyalty is to a free France and if that involves making it possible for you to help me and my friends achieve our liberation then I do it. Now the last thing you must know is that as soon as your bus leaves with you on board I will telephone the Terminus with a prearranged message that will tell them you are on the bus." We shook hands, "We hope for great things from you, please do everything you can to help us"

Suddenly I felt alone as I walked the few metres across to the Saint Flour bus. I turned round and looked back. Jacques was not in sight

Chapter 4

Meeting my Family

There were few passengers and I had a seat to myself. I was Henri Dufour, with papers to prove it, coming home to rejoin my family after spending over three years with my grandparents in Lille

So much had happened in those three years, the war, the invasion of France, the take over by the Germans of the company where I was apprenticed and finally that dreadful night when the family home received a direct hit by a bomb dropped during an air raid on Lille killing all of my relatives except my grandfather who was working at the factory, which was the probable target of the air raid, the irony of it. I was going home to join the family business, a bar-cafe-restaurant I had been told, but I should have known

Not a prosperous business but a typical bus-terminus establishment like so many in France. Open all hours serving a wide variety of food and drinks to travellers and locals alike, but I knew all of that. I'd been there before hadn't I? Not a large family, just Mum and Dad and tante Mathilde who would all welcome me as a son and nephew returning home, but concealing the truth of the loss of a son and nephew in their loyalty to France. Could I live up to their expectations? They would all welcome me with open arms, but what about Sambo, the cat, very much my cat, I had been told, nobody had explained matters to him, and to him I would be just another human being

What was the Terminus like: my recollections of such establishments in Rheims, St. Denis and Louvain were vague? As a schoolboy I had never entered one. I remembered glass fronts, a smoky atmosphere, plus smells of food and drinks of all sorts. I had been told that the Terminus was the largest such place in Saint Flour. Important because of its commanding position overlooking the main square of the lower town, where the main weekly market took place every Friday, and where the buses discharged their passengers for both the upper and lower

27

town. It didn't sound at all like the places I had seen in the cities of Rheims, Paris and Louvain

With so few people on the bus nobody spoke to me after the conductor had checked my ticket. But in Saint Flour the context would be different. People would speak to me because they would be sure they knew me and I would not know whether or not I knew them. I would have to play for time, be tired; still distressed by the tragedy of Lille, and of course I was not a very bright lad at all

And what was Saint Flour like? At least I had been thoroughly briefed with up to date maps, and I had a good visual image of the layout of the town, essentially in two parts, upper and lower, the upper part originating as an ancient fortified hill top town so typical of the remoter regions of France. The lower part was simply the recent expansion as the population grew. All of the administration of the town was in the upper half and most of the employment was in the lower half

There was only one road to the upper town entering through a narrow gate in the old walls, just wide enough for a car to enter but nothing larger. In addition there were a number of stepped pathways passing through smaller gaps in the walls located essentially to meet people's needs

The work possibilities for people were a tannery, a lanoline extraction plant with an associated soap works, a slaughterhouse, a laundry, a spinning and weaving mill using local wool, a small transport company with an associated mechanical workshop for farm machinery, a bus depot and numerous smaller enterprises each employing just a handful of people. A family run brewery, making light draught beers for the local bars, completed the employment possibilities. There was not enough work for everybody and some bus loads of men were weekly commuters to Clermont. There was some seasonal work in catering for tourists but nowadays there were not so many of them

My parents and my aunt; what would they be like. I had seen good recent photographs of them standing in front of the Terminus during my coaching into the role of Henri Dufour. I had assurances from my instructors and Pascal that they would play their parts in my assignment. But they were on their home ground, it was easier for them. I was a new son replacing one who had been away for three years and was now dead. I had got to make it work. If I did not my life would be at risk and almost certainly their lives as well

The countryside was all new to me. Since leaving Clermont the roads had climbed steadily. I had seen several roadside altitude markers of over five hundred metres and the hills were much higher. After I left Issoire on my own, the road climbed even further and for a long time there were extensive views all round until we descended into a river gorge which was also spectacular with a road a railway and a river competing for the valley floor. But after about twenty

28

kilometres of the gorge and a little town called Massiac we climbed again and even higher, I saw several altitude markers of over one thousand metres. By now the daylight was fading and a drizzle of rain made the roads, which had been dry, slick with the mud of winter

We arrived quite suddenly, a longish gentle descent, over a railway bridge, houses, a workshop of some sort, some lights, round a left hand bend, more lights and houses, a sharper right hand bend and we were pulling up alongside the kerb right outside the Terminus

Mum and Dad had been watching for the bus to arrive and were at the door to greet me. A hug and kisses from Mum, duly returned, and a real hug from Dad. The photographs were proved good. I had no doubt about who was who among the group waiting when I got off the bus. Mum was taller and slimmer than most of the other women, her long and strong fair hair and her complexion confirmed her Flemish parentage. Dad was a typical Frenchman in size, but the loss of most of a lung due to the gas of the first war showed in the lines of his face and many movements were obviously a strain to him

Considering that Mathilde was his sister they were so different in size and stamina that the same parentage was near unbelievable. A hug from Mathilde was like being surrounded by three people, all at once, she was a big woman! Just as we were all moving into the Terminus Mum whispered to me that there was a girl in the cafe who used to teach me at school, Yvette, who now worked in the Terminus. My next test?

When I saw her, girl be blowed, Yvette was a real smasher, also tall about one metre seventy, chestnut brown wavy hair to her shoulders, smiling dark eyes, a well shaped young woman's figure. Yvette hugged and kissed me on both cheeks. I was surprised and showed it. "You have changed" was all I could say. I found out a few minutes later she had a baby in a playpen in the room behind the bar. In order to avoid too much exposure to Yvette and the locals in the bar, I pleaded a long tiring journey and Mum led the way up to my room

"When the bar has closed up I'll call you down to supper, in the meantime get some rest," she said, and I lay down on the bed. I dozed and wondered how many more 'Yvette like' incidents there might be in store for me However, thanks to Jacques advice I thought I had handled the greetings in a passable manner

It being a Sunday all the bus trade was over early in the evening, the drizzle continued and the locals did not linger long. Before nine o'clock I was called down to supper and looking forward to a good talk with Mum and Dad and a chance to see how Sambo would act towards me. Just then tante Mathilde returned

29

Tante Mathilde came with a list of items she wanted dealt with yesterday. I had to point out to her very strongly indeed that my role was to be low key, and I was expected to take some weeks settling in and ensuring acceptance as Henri Dufour by the townsfolk. "If you want to help, the most useful thing you can do is to act as my eyes and tell me immediately if you hear any expressions of doubt about my identity. When I have settled in I will be able to consider your requests". She took umbrage at this and left saying she would talk to sergeant Lescaut and Pascal about my attitude

I told my parents about my meeting with Pascal and I felt sure he would stand by me. My parents said they were sure sergeant Lescaut would also uphold my authority. We had supper and a good long talk, Mum had noticed my surprise over Yvette and said, "Pascal told London about Yvette and you should have been aware that you would meet her but London never answered." "It's quite a tragedy really, Philippe, her husband, was called to the colours in the 1938 crisis over Hitler's invasion of Czechoslovakia

He married Yvette when he was on leave about a month before the war started. He was on leave again shortly before the Germans invaded Belgium and left Yvette pregnant with her baby, Jean-Francois. In September Philippe was reported missing believed injured and a prisoner of war. Since then she has heard nothing, but about two months ago all her allowances were stopped and she had no income at all. Both of the families are helping her but they cannot afford to keep her completely, everybody's short of cash today. We needed some help, and she lives nearby, so we took her on, she's a great help and will do anything I ask, and she can just earn enough to keep herself and Jean-Francois with the money from the parents"

About now Sambo came in for his supper. After he had eaten he came over to me and after a sniff or two decided I was just another human whom he did not know. I tried to stroke him but he evaded me. This was clearly going to be a test, winning him over as a new friend. Mum said, "He doesn't remember you. After you left for Lille he always went to sleep on your bed for many months. You'll have to win him over again." "I'll try," I answered, "I have always had a cat and I like cats"

We talked more and I gained a deep respect for my new parents. They were risking their lives by accepting me into their home and acknowledging me as their son. I must never let them down. Then it was time for bed again

I lay awake for some time wondering about why London had not prepared me for the encounter with Yvette or was it just another test in their way of thinking? What would happen if I aroused Yvette's suspicions in any way? Was tante Mathilde just a big firework waiting to go bang? I must have slept in the end

30

I was woken soon after six by the sounds of the buses departing for Clermont. I dressed and went down to the kitchen to spend my first full day for three years with my family. Yvette was already there and said good morning with a hug and a kiss on each cheek. I was ready for her this time and returned the kisses. Jean-Francois was in his pram taking an interest in everything going on around him and munching something quite soggy and unappetising. I immediately found out that breakfast in the Terminus was a get-it-yourself affair. Of course I had forgotten where everything was kept, but Yvette came to my aid, chatting all the time, mainly about the Dufour family and I encouraged her with an occasional word or two

The Dufour family was small by French standards. Maurice and Bernadette Dufour only had two children, eleven years apart, Mathilde and Robert, now my putative aunt and father. The Terminus had been in the family for several generations, but was specifically left to Robert because of Mathilde's amorous adventures, four sons and no husband simply was not acceptable in pre-war France, and there were at least two fathers involved, and she still had the nerve to use the Dufour family name. Yvette was obviously closely acquainted with the Dufours for reasons I did not understand until much later

Yvette was an important and willing source of information about the Dufour family, not because I asked her, but because she chatted to me as one of the family, who knew all of these things anyway!

Mathilde worked as a part-time house keeper to a local widowed farmer. She had a good cottage with the job right next to the farmhouse, for herself and her two younger sons, Luke and Jean. Her two older sons, Andre and Pierre had been called into the French army at the time of the Munich crisis and were said by Matbilde, to be prisoners of war. Yvette said they were in prison somewhere in occupied France for looting. I learnt all of this before I'd finished my breakfast!

The Terminus was a large establishment. It occupied half of one of the shorter sides of the Place de la Liberte. The front was all glass with a double entrance door in the centre. The public area was L-shaped. as was the counter. To the right of the entry door was a bar area for the serious drinkers. To the left was a larger area with stone topped tables for those who couldn't take their drinks standing or who were eating bar snacks. The shorter arm of the L was screened off to be a restaurant area at lunch time with nicer tables and chairs. In the evenings this area was frequently used for card games, played for money if the police were not about. In general drinks were served from the counter opposite the door and food from the counter round the corner. A gap in the angle of the counter gave staff access to the public area. By this time I had to prepare for my trip up town to formally meet sergeant Lescaut and complete the formalities of arriving back in my home town

31

I had prepared my route in my mind. In the room behind the bar Dad went over this with me several times, it would not do to have to ask the way! I had to go first to the police at the Place de la Halle aux Bleds for all the formalities and then take my new identity card to the Hotel de Ville in the Place d'Armes by the side of the Cathedral for inscription in the town's register of residents

I set off up la rue des Tuiles-Bas. I had decided to speak to everyone I met even if only to say "Bonjour". It worked. Most people welcomed me back with handshakes and an occasional hug. I was only snubbed twice. Some clearly knew all about the family tragedy in Lille and expressed pleasure that I had escaped unhurt. As the rue des Tuiles-Bas became the rue des Tuiles-Haut I turned sharp right and almost at once entered the fountain gate turning sharp left into the Place de la Halles aux Bleds. The officer on the desk was very formal. He did not appear to know anything about what he had to do with my papers and was obviously worried by the letter from the burgomeister of Lille embossed with the swastika. He took all of the papers into the back office telling me to take a seat and wait. A few minutes passed and a sergeant came up to me hand extended, "Welcome home Monsieur Henri Dufour", and I knew at once I must have found sergeant Lescaut

Sergeant Alexis Lescaut, a good looking 40 year old had just missed being involved in the 1914-18 war. He had joined the police as an alternative to the military. He had done well for himself, a good record and steady promotion had now got him the senior police position in Saint Flour. He had been born in Aurillac so he was almost a local. He made me feel quite important by saying to the other police in the office, "I'll take care of Monsieur Dufour myself, his case is a little complicated," and to the young policeman who had originally seen me, "if you could please bring me the old file of Henri Dufour to my office it would help

We went into an inner office. The young policeman came in a few seconds later with an archived file on me. As the door closed Lescaut said, "Welcome to Saint Flour, Pascal has told me about your journey and I am most pleased to have you here"

He read through the envelope of papers carefully, "This all is perfectly in order; I can issue you with everything you will need straight away. After we've completed all the formalities and a new file has been opened for you, because you are now an adult, I am going to lose your old file because there will be a few small discrepancies between the two files and it is best if nobody ever discovers them." He proceeded with the necessary work, taking my fingerprints, and asking me to sign in several places.   "It's the signature that is really the problem," he said" I can see you've tried to copy the signature, but it is not really passable; anyone comparing the two files might ask some difficult questions. Fortunately juniors were not finger printed when you were registered. Now that you have a new adult file your old junior file has to be sent to the departmental archive in Aurillac

The transport is so unreliable today I'm sure it will never get there," he said as he rose from his desk walking over to the stove in the corner dropping my old file into it

We talked for a while. "Your parents have done a good job in preparing the town for your return, don't spoil their efforts please, we need you here"

I mentioned the problem of tante Mathilde, saying that, "I thought she was a big firework just waiting to go bang." "She's already exploded in this office this morning," he said, "but I assure you she does now understand your position. I don't think you'll have any further problems. If she does cause any, I have enough statements against her that I could arrest her for questioning and hold her in custody for months, and she knows that"

By the way you should have said it this way he said correcting my French. "You've been corrupted by the northerners and the Flemish influence." Thus he nicely gave me the perfect excuse for any minor slips in my style of French

"Try not to talk too much to too many people until they have had a chance to get used to the idea that you are back. Don't mistake my remarks about Mathilde's character. She is completely loyal and reliable on all matters related to the Resistance"

"Now take all these papers to the Mairie so that they can inscribe you in the town register, then you will get a vote; if we ever have an election. You'll need to be quick they close for lunch in twenty minutes." He led me to the door and we shook hands. I walked along the rue de la Rollandie to the Town Hall. No problems at all and ten minutes later the newest resident of Saint Flour was taking an almost confident leisurely stroll down to his home

Chapter 5

My New Routine

I arrived back at the Terminus in time for the second serving of the dish of the day. The portion served was huge. Today it was a casserole of lamb well spiced with beans carrots and turnips cooked all together. The gravy was thick from the beans and it was served with bread to mop up the surplus. When my plate went back with food left on it Mathilde came out from behind the counter demanding to know what was wrong with it. "It was absolutely delicious," I said, "but the quantity was far too much for me." "Don't think much of your appetite you'll have to do better than that if you want to get through the winter here. You've been spoiled by the fancy Flemish kitchen," she muttered as she returned to her kitchen

"She's a real tartar," said a voice in my ear. "Hello, I'm Manuel and I eat here most days." We shook hands. He was clearly not French. "I don't remember you",I said. "No you wouldn't, I arrived here after you'd gone to Lille, I come from Catalonia and I'm the comis-chef at the St. Jacques. There's no lunch trade at the hotel these days, so it's better to come here." There's only one way to stop her and that's to watch the amount she puts on your plate and stop her when it's enough. She probably thought you looked a little thin and wanted to fatten you up"

He was easy to talk to and we chatted for ten minutes or so. I learned that he trained as a chef in the Barcelona catering college and started working at hotels along the Costa Brava and Costa Dorada finishing up in Portbou at the end of 1939. Then he simply carried on into France to gain more experience

Quite how he got to Saint Flour wasn't too clear but he insisted he liked it here because it reminded him of Manresa where he was born. He did want to get to Paris eventually and work in one of the great hotels or restaurants there to extend his repertoire of dishes.   After the lunch period I helped with the

34

washing up and spent some time in the bar during the afternoon simply to find my way around and find out how everything worked

The routine of the Terminus was that Mum and Dad rose early and dealt with all of the trade up to the time tante Mathilde and Yvette arrived. The women went to the kitchen to prepare the dish of the day under Mathilde's guidance. The food was to be ready at noon for the first sitting. Dad ran the bar until about noon. Yvette prepared the tables. I was to assist Dad in the bar and to get to know the people who came in with Dad prompting the conversation as needed. The dish of the day regulars started arriving about a quarter to twelve and the first sitting was always full. By half past one the second sittings were all served and we could expect to get our meal. Dad went to rest as soon as he had eaten. While the women cleared and washed up I was to run the bar. The peaks and troughs of the trade were pretty regular, part controlled by the bus time table

Mathilde left for the day as soon as the clearing was complete. The afternoons were not busy. Between five and six trade picked up as the regulars called for a pre dinner drink and gossip. Dad reappeared about six as Yvette left for the day

The evening gossip was the time when all local happenings were thrashed over and the world put to rights. This was a valuable time for me to learn about the people and the events that controlled their lives. Mum got her rest in the evening, at least until she prepared supper for us. Dad and I ran the bar. Some evenings Mathilde returned to allow us to get our suppers at a reasonable hour. During the week trade died off soon after eight. At weekends we were busy up to about ten-thirty. Saint Flour didn't have any real night life under the Vichy regime

How Mathilde managed to get her supplies for the daily meals she prepared was a closely guarded secret. I noticed some of the regulars did not pay for their meals. Dad told me, "Bartering has always gone on in the country, it's simply tax evasion. Mathilde has her special arrangements with a number of farmers. Early on market days you will be surprised at the stuff that is delivered round the back of the Terminus, always provided there are no gendarmes about." Mathilde used the best of the outbuildings of the Terminus as her Larder. She had the only key and discouraged anyone else from entering

I watched Mathilde at Friday's market. She clearly knew the stallholders very well. I quickly recognised that she was as big a marketer as any three stallholders put together. Who was going to carry on this business when she moved south to Millau? I couldn't see London being impressed if I took it on! My first weekend in Saint Flour started on Friday evening. Mathilde came back to the bar with her two younger boys. They helped out with clearing and washing up of glasses to earn some pocket money. Mathilde circulated among the clientele and I heard her confirming many market deals she had made in the morning on behalf of farmers who did not attend the market

Alexis Lescaut came in towards the end the evening, not in uniform. This was clearly to tell everybody that he was definitely not on duty. There was discussion about who was staying where and who was going to move from one farm to another. I was bemused and asked why there were so many men working at the hill farms when I thought that most able bodied men were in the armed services or had been transferred by the Germans to war work elsewhere

Alexis took me to one side and said, "Here you see how we manage evading conscription. Many of the farmers did not respond to their conscription order. They now lead an itinerant existence moving constantly from one farm to another. If the Gendarmerie does call at their home farm they are never there and their family deny all knowledge of their whereabouts. Then there are the Maquis, the communists, who have taken to the hills for the same reason. The labour supply position at most of the hill farms is better that it has ever been

"I was told before I came that there was a quota system that France had to supply to the Germans," I said. "Yes there is", Alexis replied, "But the farmers simply don't meet the quota. The Gendarmerie has the task of collecting the quota but the farmers never have any food when the Gendarmes call." Dad joined in the conversation, "The Department of Cantal has never met even half of its quota and the sub prefecture of Saint Flour is proud that it has never met even one fifth"

At the end of evening Alexis joined us for supper. We talked over my situation. Alexis was satisfied that my initial acceptance had gone smoothly. He urged me to move about the town as much as possible to learn all about the odd little short cuts that existed and to be seen by everybody. Mum said she would use me to do some of the shopping she needed

Alexis talked about the persons who knew my real identity. So far only the Dufour family and himself The Maire of Saint Flour had been told that a British army officer was being placed in Saint Flour and had said that he did not want to know anything about it but agreed that he would find one of his town councillors to act as a cut out. This councillor would keep the Maire informed on a need-to-know basis of matters that might affect him

On Saturday morning Mathilde's two sons came with her. Both had bicycles and Mum sent me off on my first shopping trip on one of their bicycles. I found my way all right but the cobbles on most of the roads soon made me saddle sore. I felt the tyres and found them extremely hard. I learnt later that although there were plenty of outer tyres, inner tubes were almost impossible to find and that old wine corks were used to fill the space normally filled by air. The ride was just about comfortable on metalled roads but on riding on cobbles was very hard on the bum. Most of the shops did not charge me anything! When I offered money I was told that either Mum or Mathilde had 'arranged it'. Now I recognised the full meaning of Alexis' remarks about bartering

Sunday morning I went to Mass with Mum and Yvette. Dad baby-sat Jean-Francois, Yvette's son. He was only just walking and father Albert did not welcome young children at Mass. Mum had prompted me about father Albert. He had instructed me before my confirmation. I must therefore remember him. At the end of the Mass we spoke at the door. He was expecting me of course. Apart from welcoming me back to Saint Flour treated me just as any other member of his flock.   Another hurdle overcome

Sunday was a quiet day until the evening. Few buses, few customers, no dish of the day, and this was the day when Mum cooked a delicious family lunch, no shortages of anything. What a change from England. "Of course we can eat well," she said, "The farms still produce the food, they do not sell it to the markets because then it would be taken as part of the quota." In the evening some of the regulars were accompanied by their wives. Both Mum and Dad were in the bar and very much involved in the local gossip

I was a centre of attention and spent much time talking to people I should have known. After an hour or so I had to plead tiredness and retire. The last words I heard Mum say were, "He hasn't quite recovered from the shock yet," followed by sympathetic murmurings

I had not realised that Monday was a very long day at the Terminus. The weekly commuters to Clermont left on special buses at a quarter past five in the morning. They had their breakfast on the bus, Coffee and filled baguettes and some briocherie. The local bakery delivered the briocherie and baguettes at a quarter to five and in the next thirty minutes fresh coffee had to be made, over one hundred half baguette sandwiches made up with generous fillings. All packed on to trays ready to go on to the bus with trays of hot coffee in mugs. The bus company eventually returned all the empties later in the day. The noise of the buses woke me and I got down to the just in time to see the buses leave. "There was no need for you to have got up", Mum said, "We are used to the routine of Monday and you would only have been in the way"

Mum and Dad went back to bed until breakfast time. It was still completely dark and quite cold outside. Sambo was pleased to find someone to let him back in so early and to find him some breakfast. I even got a nuzzle and a purr from him

That morning I saw Saint Flour slowly wake up. As the day broke I saw the men on the early shifts on bikes going to work and the first of the regular bus crews cleaning out the vehicles parked behind the Terminus. The bus office next door to the Terminus opened at seven ready for the first departures soon after. I made myself some breakfast and coffee for everyone

Yvette arrived about eight with Jean-Francois. She was surprised to see me up. "Normally I have the place to myself for a while on Mondays," she said, as she helped herself to coffee, "This is much better to find everything ready"

Jean-Francois was toddling about all over the place until Yvette finally caught him and settled him in his playpen. "Too many hazards around to let him run free," she said. I apologised to her for being so gauche when we met as I arrived in Saint Flour. "I had spent the whole day travelling, being delayed, and I was not expecting to see her and although I recognised her, I could not recall where I had seen her before"

She laughed, "We all change as we grow up, if you had told me, when you left, that I should be married with a young baby when we next saw each other, I would have laughed for a week"

But now she was tearful. She told me about how her friendship with Philippe Pelletier had led to falling in love with him. Betrothal and wedding, followed quickly because Philippe was to be called up by the army. Then the dreadful news that he had disappeared in the fighting around the Belgian border and he was officially posted as missing believed injured and a prisoner of war. However a few months ago the Vichy government stopped paying her allowances saying it was the responsibility of the government of occupied France to pay her

Both sets of parents were forced into doing as much as they could to help her but she still had to work in order to live. Money was short and so were jobs for widowed mothers. "I feel in my heart that Philippe is dead and that Jean-Francois will never know his father and Philippe will never know he had a son. The letter I wrote to Philippe telling him I was pregnant was eventually returned undelivered"

The tears flowed faster now. Jean-Francois also cried in sympathy without knowing why. I hugged Yvette to try and calm her. Mum came down to breakfast and did the same for Jean-Francois.   She guessed what had happened. By the time Mathilde arrived to prepare her dish of the day everything was back to normal

In the afternoon when Yvette and I were left alone to manage the afternoon trade Yvette apologised for her outburst. "Without the job here at the Terminus I would be destitute," she said, "It is so convenient, just two hundred metres form home and your parents are so kind and understanding." It was a dull Monday. Both of us had some time for Jean-Francois. Soon Yvette had him addressing me a Monsieur Henri. Monsieur Henri was then expected to be a playmate

Around five o'clock some of the regular home time drinkers came in as usual and Dad came down to gossip, as usual. Yvette prepared to leave. She came and went via the back door as she lived in the street immediately behind the Terminus

"You have really changed," she said, "I always thought putting you in that special school was a mistake, your leg may be a handicap but the experience you have had in Lille has given you the competence to do almost anything," As she said goodnight she kissed me on both cheeks as usual and then full on the lips, "That one's from Jean-Francois"

When Mum came down I asked her about the special school. Mum led the way into the back room. "This is the sort of matter we must never discuss in with anybody else in earshot. You must know something about how disabling a club-foot is. Henri missed a lot of school and could not play any sports or games, so the teachers neglected him. Eventually he could not keep up with the other children so he was sent to the Nuns special school for retarded children in Murat and soon after you were placed there Yvette became an assistant teacher

Mum went to a cupboard and took out an envelope with photographs and school reports in it. Some of the later photographs included Yvette She was obviously younger and had long hair in two plaits. "I must remember to mention her plaits," I said. The reports were initially very non-committal. The later one mentioned an ability to use and understand machines and how to repair them. There were also photos of groups of boys. "I think all of those boys have now left Saint Flour either in the military or on compulsory war work for the Germans." "How far can I trust Yvette?" I asked. "Yvette is a loyal young Frenchwoman, all the more so because of what happened to Philippe," Mum replied

"Alexis Lescaut will be coming this evening after we close," Dad said quietly as I returned to the bar, "This lot will be gone about half past six and then there's only the last buses to come, not many passengers on Mondays"

Mum reappeared about eight and started the supper. By eight thirty the bar was empty. Over supper there seemed so much to say. I realised that talking time had to be won out of a busy work schedule when any confidential conversation might become public knowledge if overheard

Mum started off by telling me that Yvette had said how much the three years away in Lille had improved me and how much confidence I had gained. "We took Yvette on not just out of sympathy but because Mathilde will soon be moving to Millau. She is going there to form a new resistance group in the department of Aveyron. The former group were betrayed to the Mlice. Those that were actually caught have simply disappeared and we fear some at least have been executed"

"How will Mathilde explain her arrival there," I asked. "Mathilde is going back to live with the father of her two older sons. We don't know yet what will happen to Luke and Jean, something will have to be worked out. None of this is known yet in Saint Flour and must be regarded as secret for many weeks yet"

Several knocks at the back door announced the arrival of sergeant Lescaut. He greeted my parents in the French manner and I realised the relationship was indeed close. Lescaut said, "In this room now we have almost the whole of the trusted resistance members in Saint Flour, only Mathilde is missing." Dad added, "Anything we discuss here in these meetings must be regarded as completely secret"

"It won't be a long meeting tonight," said Lescaut," I have sent a message confirming your safe arrival and inscription to Pascal for transmission to London

When you have established yourself I have two radios for you and I hope you have the crystals with you." "Yes I have," I responded, "how long do you think that will be?" "Your parents and I will listen to all the gossip we can and when we are satisfied that you are accepted and not suspected in any way, I'll pass the sets to you and you are free to establish your own communication channel to London. This condition is laid down by Pascal and is not negotiable"

Speaking specially to me, Lescaut said, "You've made a good first impression build on it, get to know your way around thoroughly," and to Mum, "send him on all your errands, make him do the shopping, it'll take some of the burden off you and force him in to contact with the town as a whole." And again to me, "Your parents have taken a big risk in accepting you as their son, if you let them down, they may well pay with their lives, never forget that. I think you've got one of the best cover stories ever conceived, so don't waste it

I think that's enough sermonising for tonight, and I'm off to bed." In taking his departure Lescaut included me in a big hug

That night in bed I promised myself I would never let these people down, even to the extent of disobeying orders if necessary

Next day in the lull after the first buses had departed and we had breakfasted. Mum asked me to go and get a long list of shopping during the day when I had the time. I decided the best time would be when Luke and Jean came for their lunch and I could use one of their bicycles, which had huge baskets on the front and back. "I suppose you can ride a bike?" questioned Jean when I told I was going shopping on his bike. "I used to ride my aunt Maria's bike every day to the factory in Lille"."Oh but that was a ladies bike and they are easy to ride," teased Jean, "This is a man's bike and they are much more difficult, I pushed him out of the way and rode his bike out of the back yard and round the Place de la Liberte. The bike had the same cork filled tyres as before and was just as hard on the bum. When I got back into the yard I said, "We ought to be able to do something better than just corks inside those outer covers, let's think about it"

I managed the shopping easily and renewed acquaintance with many more persons. Everyone seemed aware of my return to the town. The baskets on the bike were a great help in containing the shopping although I could not ride with the baskets full and pushed the bike back home. Luke and Jean were waiting for me, and jeered as I entered the yard pushing the bike. "Told you wouldn't ride a man's bike, "shouted Jean, "Here then you ride it," I passed the loaded bike to Jean. He also found he could not get his leg over a loaded rear basket even if Luke helped him

"Can I have a look at how you fill those tyres?" I asked Luke. He led the way into one of the old outbuildings. This was their workshop, several buckets of corks, numerous outer tyres and some bicycle wheels bare to the rims. Luke described what they did, "We thread the corks on to two wire threads until we have enough to go right round the rim, then we twist the ends of the wire together as tight as we can. Then we mix some chopped straw with cow dung and half fill the outer casing with this mixture. Next we fit the outer cover to the rim in the usual way with tyre levers and leave lot to dry out for a few days." I thought about it for some minutes

"Well now I understand why I saw some bits coming out of the valve holes this morning." "That always happens," said Jean, "That's why we put the straw in, then; the tyres last for about six months before they lose the filling instead of a few weeks. We tried having the valve holes welded up but the welding distorted the rim and the wheels would not run true." "Anyway," Luke interjected, "It works and people buy them, and they never have to pump them up." "My instinct says you could find a better way," I said, "But let me think about it." Both the boys were rather resentful at my interference in their 'business.' What ever I thought of would have to be good

I talked to Mum about it in the afternoon. "Those two boys have grown up much better than their brothers, Mum said, "They are really quite enterprising"

In Saint Flour because some of the weekly commuters to Clermont work for Michelin, bicycle tyre outers can be obtained but there is no production of inner tubes in Vichy France and they are almost unobtainable"

"Used corks are plentiful in France and the only problem with the idea is that they have to have the whole wheel for some days to fit and fill the tyres but many bicycles in Saint Flour are running on their tyres today and the demand is increasing as inner tubes wear out and cannot be replaced"

While talking to Mum after lunch I asked if there was anything I could do about clearing up at the back of the Terminus. The yard was a total mess.

Mum admitted that; Dad was not strong enough to do much about it. Keeping the inside decorations in good condition was all he could manage

So I took on the job. Mum warned me about the one padlocked shed that was Mathilde's storeroom, "Better leave that alone or you'll never hear the last of it"

I also raised the matter of Sambo. He was supposed to be my cat. When I had approached him that morning ready to stroke him he simply swore at me and went out. When he came in again he did condescend to take one or two titbits from me, but that was all. I asked mum if I could be the person to feed him, she agreed so at least I started to buy his affection

Yvette spent most of the afternoon in the bar and was a little abrupt with me because I had done the shopping which was apparently one of her jobs. She was obviously worried that maybe her job was at risk. I tried to reassure her that I would have many things to do in the yard. However she was sufficiently aware that the finances of the Terminus could not stand another wage for me and said so. I had to tell her that some changes were coming which would make her position more secure

She clearly did not believe me. She left at her usual time without saying goodnight to anyone. Dad remarked on this when he cane in to take over the bar for the evening and I told him what had been said. "You forget it," he said, "this is for Mum and me to sort out"

The following day, after I had fed Sambo, which was much to his surprise and some suspicion, I started work on the outbuildings. Granddad Maurice had been meticulous in keeping the yard area neat and tidy and had always done the maintenance himself. The first building I started on was his workshop. Lots of items awaiting repair had been dumped in there, the feral cats from the yard had littered in there repeatedly, and there were some leaks in the roof. Many of the items to be repaired had deteriorated so far as to be valueless, I placed these outside to be carted to the dump

I repaired and re-felted the roof to keep the weather out and left the windows part open to dry the building out slowly. I had to net the windows to keep the cats out. Some of the tools had rusted beyond reclaim, but many were still usable. I spent several days cleaning and greasing and arranging things on shelves and in drawers so they could be found again. I couldn't work very late in the evenings because the electricity did not work

Just as I was about to lock up on Friday evening, Yvette came in, she had almost ignored me since our last talk over her job. She stood in front of me and humbly apologised saying Mum and Dad had assured her and she was sorry for her behaviour. What could I say or do. I was filthy with all the dirty work I had

42

been doing. She did not seem to mind; she kissed me on both cheeks and then full on the lips, and went off home saying, "forgive me"

Over the weekend I sorted out the workshop electricity supply. The wiring was old and the insulation had perished. When somebody had found the fuse kept blowing they had simply disconnected the circuit. I had found a new drum of cable in the workshop so I set to work and rewired the whole building and left spare connections to wire in the other buildings and for some yard lights

Sunday mornings were a quiet time in Saint Flour. Mum and Dad usually had a lie in until about eleven. I got up at nine, fed Sambo, who, was still somewhat surprised by my feeding him, but now he purred when I stroked him. Just before eleven there was a knock at the back door. It was Yvette with Jean-Francois, "Are you coming to Mass?" "Give me five minutes to smarten up, and I'll be with you," I replied

We left at about five minutes to eleven and were almost the last arrivals. Jean Francois was very well behaved for the whole of the service. When we were leaving the Church father Albert stopped us and said again how pleased he was to see me back in Saint Flour, and he would be calling at the Terminus to talk to me when he had the time. He knew Yvette and Jean-Francois as regulars of course"

The sun had come out while we were at Mass, Yvette took my hand and said, "I am so ashamed at the way I treated you." "Please, I've already forgotten it," was all I could think of to say. I walked home with Yvette. I had not seen her house before: she invited me in for a drink. I told her I had finished the electricity supply to the workshop

"Do you understand electricity?" she asked, "Oh yes I learnt all about that in Lille." "Could you do me a big favour and see if you can mend my iron, I don't know if it's the plug or the iron, it's just stopped working." "I'll take it with me and sort it out; it looks almost new, I should be able to fix it"

I returned to the Terminus. Sunday was the only day mum cooked the dinner and I was looking forward to a change from Mathilde's cooking. "I was surprised you went to Mass this morning," said Dad. "Yvette came to the back door just before eleven, and rather took me unawares, when she asked me to go with her. I can see you had a talk with her, she was quite apologetic." "We told her you would not be spending much time in the bar or restaurant as you were going to sort out the back yard and clear a lot of the rubbish. By the time you've done that Mathilde will have gone and that will mean more work for Yvette. The bar opened at twelve thirty for some regulars who wanted to be out of their kitchens while their wives cooked Sunday lunch

As they all departed to their homes, the bar was empty and we were able to enjoy our meal.   Mum had quartered a chicken, and overlaid it with ham and some spices and vegetables and baked it. Then she had taken the juices and made a sauce. It was served on a bed of rice, delicious

Mum said she got the idea from Manuel. Cheese and a tarte-tartin completed the meal. I told Mum and Dad about the tarte-maison that Aristide had served. "We used to do something like that here, but it was expensive to prepare and after Mathilde's lunches there was very little sale for any dessert, so nowadays we only serve cheese, and not too much of that"

During the afternoon I repaired Yvette's iron and put the finishing touches to the workshop electrics. Sunday was a lazy day, even though the sun shone most of the afternoon, very few people were about. The evening trade picked up a little, a few couples came in for a gossip and a drink or two. Listening to the people of Saint Flour talking in the bar, I did not hear a single mention of the war or French politics or even local issues, the people were totally inward looking

When sergeant Lescaut came in later as we were closing, I asked, "How do you expect to find enough people her to form a resistance groups."Lescaut waited until we retired to the back room before he gave any sort of answer. "I know it will not be easy, but the situation has been carefully weighed up. At present I have identified eighteen people in the town itself who I can trust, and I have their promises of active support when we are ready. Most of these men are ex soldiers of the 1914-18 war who have some weapon training in how to use normal infantry equipment. Out of town the situation is completely different. Most of the hill fanners are men who have been brought up with guns all their lives, they learned to shoot almost as soon as they walked, and most of them can hit a fly's eye while it walks up a barn door." "So these are the men we should also try to recruit?" I posed the question

"There are so many factors," said Lescaut. "First of all they are lazy and unless something is threatening their way of life, they won't do a thing, and so far nothing has touched them, they choose to ignore the quotas they have been told to supply to Germany, and the gendarmerie are not inclined to challenge them. Second they have been partly penetrated by the Maquis who often work with them for just their keep, but the Maquis have only minimal supplies of anything, and the hill men are not inclined to actively support them yet"

"What do you think will happen when the Germans occupy us?" I said. "The Germans will have exactly the same problem as the gendarmerie to enforce the quotas, and unless they saturate the area with troops, there is no way they can stop the hill men moving their flocks all over the place which frustrates any attempt at an accurate head count of the animals, and nobody believes that the Germans have such resources available." "You should take an early opportunity to go walking in the hills; unless you see the terrain at first hand you cannot

44

understand the problem." "By the way, changing the subject, I have a reply from London, which is why I actually came in. They emphasise that you must thoroughly integrate with the community and be accepted. I am required to confirm your statements when you are ready, and incidentally I hear you've already started, going to Mass with Yvette and Jean-Francois, not a bad idea that you know. By implication she is accepting you, and so is father Albert." I didn't mention the iron

Chapter 6

Making Myself Useful

The fine weather of the weekend continued and people started to talk about spring. I took advantage of this and got rid of two truckloads of rubbish to the town dump. This gave me space in the back yard to really sort out the remainder of the contents into some sort of order. There was a long roofed area right across the width of the Terminus building, the roof being built on to the stonework itself and the outer edge supported by five pillars. This gave quite a large reasonably dry area facing north-west. The roof was sound and the guttering was intact and the drains worked. I now managed to stack everything with a potential value under this to protect it from further deterioration. Just outside the north-east end of this sheltered area was a large cistern designed to be fed by a lift pump from the old well in the yard

I talked to Dad about this. "That was the old water supply for the Terminus until the law made it compulsory for all establishments serving the public to have a water supply from the local water company to a purity standard. Your grandfather had the supply connected about fifty years ago. The well water is good potable water unless l'Ander is running in flood and then it usually floods the well and then it is some months before the water is pure again. We used to use the cistern water for cleaning and laundry because we did not have to pay for it but when the pump went wrong I could not find anybody to repair it, and that's how it is today

"Could I try and repair it, I know how lift pumps work and there isn't very much that can go wrong, it's probably just a dirty valve or two." "Try it if you think you can do it, it could save us over two hundred and fifty francs a month, in water costs"

I disconnected the handle mechanism and borrowed Mathilde's two sons one lunch time to help me pull the shaft out. They were quite derisory about it

46

"You'll never get that old thing to work again." When we had got the shaft out and on to the bench in the workshop, it was every valve and every washer that needed attention. I explained to my cousins how it worked, they seemed impressed. I took me several days to clean the valves and get them working smoothly. The leather washers were too far gone to be any use, but when I cleared out the workshop I had found most of a hide with circles cut out of it and now I knew what it was for. I took me a while to find it again. I cut new washers and used grandfather's punches to cut the mounting holes. I was pleasantly surprised to find how well the punches sharpened up after almost twenty years of neglect. It was a struggle getting the old washers out. I had to heat and grease the old nuts and bolts before I could undo them

It was Friday afternoon before I had the pump's shaft ready to go back in. I had missed my chance to get my two cousins at lunchtime. I went in to the bar; Dad was there unusually early, talking to some of the hill men. The market had nearly packed up for the day. I asked dad if he could ask two of the men to help me. Two sturdy individuals passed through the back room and out into the yard. I had the shaft standing on end ready to be lifted and dropped into the pipe. The two hill men looked at the reconditioned shaft, "That's a very good job you've done there. Said one, "ought to work perfect," said the other. It took a few minutes only to lift the shaft and locate it in the pipe. It slid in very smoothly

After thanking them Dad invited them to take another drink in the bar. Although I had been working out in the back yard most of the week Yvette had never forgotten to greet me in the mornings or to say goodnight. When she was leaving that night I had just finished fitting the pump handle. "You can be the first one to try it," I said as she came in to the yard on her way out. "Will it work now, she said." She took hold of the handle and started pumping. After about twenty strokes, and following some peculiar noises from the pump shaft a steady stream of water flowed into the cistern. Yvette continued to pump for several minutes

When she stopped she clapped her hands and said. "That's wonderful; I don't know how you can do all these things." I picked up a piece of rag and started to clean my hands, walking to the workshop to find some soft soap. She followed me in saying, "First the electricity, then my iron and now the water pump." I was leaning against the bench, she came and stood very close, "do you think you could do something else for me, there's a terrible draught under the kitchen door and my feet get frozen when I stand at the sink"

"I'll have a look at it next week." she put her hands on my shoulder preparatory to kissing me goodnight. I raised my hands to show how dirty they were and that I could not hold her. She held me very close indeed for several minutes. She kissed me on each cheek and then very lingeringly on the lips." Until tomorrow," and she was gone

I finished cleaning my hands and went in to the bar. Dad was still drinking with the hillmen. They asked if it worked, "Yes, all I've got to do now is to clean out the cistern tomorrow and you can start using it." Dad poured me a brandy

On Saturday father Albert came to see me. He had been in the bar for some time talking to Mum and Yvette before Mum came out to the workshop to call me. I had just finished cleaning out the cistern and was filthy dirty. "I can't come in to the bar like this," I protested. Mum went back and the next thing I knew father Albert was there in the workshop, "I'm not frightened of a little dirt especially if it's in a good cause." "It's more than a little dirt," I said, "You can have no idea how much rubbish had accumulated in this back yard in the past few years, and I've sent two truck loads to the dump this week and I reckon there will be another soon." "I can see you've made a good start," he said, and turning the subject neatly, "as well as the one you made last Sunday." These clergymen never miss a trick I thought. He went on, "I was wondering if you knew all about Yvette"? "If you mean about marrying Philippe and the baby and Philippe being missing, yes Mum has told me." "Only I could not help noticing she seemed remarkably close to you last Sunday." "Well don't you remember," I said, "She was one of my school teachers at the Ecole St. Jean and she always gave me a lot of help." "Ah, that accounts for the closeness, but you must remember she is a married woman, and Jean-Francois must always have the first claim on her love and affection especially if the worst has happened to Philippe." "Thank you father," I replied, "But I feel now that I can repay the care and kindness she gave to me when 1 needed it. I learnt a lot in Lille and can make good use of that learning in Saint Flour especially now all the regular tradesmen are engaged elsewhere; I see it as my Christian duty and regard Yvette as a special case for help." "I hope I shall see you again tomorrow," was the parting remark

After I had cleaned up and tested all the taps in the laundry room. I pumped the cistern full of clean well water ready for the next laundry day I asked Yvette for the keys to her house so that I could see what was wrong with her back door. She was pleased I was acting so quickly. The problem was simply that the footboard at the base of the door was worn away leaving an uneven wide gap for draught to enter. A close fitting board added to the bottom of the door with some padding to close the gap dealt with the problem completely. When Yvette came to collect her keys at the end of the day I told her the job was done

"Did father Albert say any thing to you today,""Do you mean about us going to Mass together." "Yes but more than that, he told me 1 should not be seen too much in your company away from the Terminus." "Yes he said something similar to me, I told him you had helped me such a lot at the Ecole St. Jean, that I considered it my Christian duty to help you especially in your circumstances." "I don't suppose he liked that," she replied. "Nevertheless," I said, "I would be proud to have you and Jean-Francois acompany me to Mass at St. Benedict's tomorrow morning, will you come?" 'I'll have to ask Jean-Francois, but I'm sure he'll agree," She replied mischievously, "but can we please go to the ten o'clock Mass, there are always more people there"

She came close to say goodnight, I held her, and she kissed me and lingered in my arms. Suddenly she said "I must go," and gave me another kiss and was gone

I was ready the following morning, having fed Sambo and petted him awhile. He was starting to respond. When Yvette called we placed Jean-Francois between us, each holding one of his hands. Thus we arrived at Saint Benedict's to the surprise of many of the congregation, and thus we left without the approval of father Albert

The days slowly got longer and a little warmer, until it snowed one night, only about twenty centimetres but enough to cause chaos. The problem was the drifts on the hill roads, of over half a metre. The snow ploughs took a couple of days to reopen all the roads. The schools were closed for two days and the children were snowballing everywhere. Sambo didn't like the snow, his totally black coat made him a natural target for any passing child with a snowball. I made him a litter tray and put it under the canopy so that he did not have far to go. He got the idea immediately. Next Sunday morning when he was ready to go out he woke me by miaowing at my bedroom door, I went down and let him out and waited for him to return which he did in a very few minutes shaking traces of snow off his paws. I got his food ready while he was rubbing all round my legs and purring loudly, and left him feeding and returned to bed. When I awoke for the second time he was curled up beside me

The clouds lifted later in the day and the wind went round to the south west, and the thaw set in. On Monday everything was running with water and by the end of the day only a few drifts in shady corners were left

From the gossip over the sudden snowfall I found that this happened every three or four years, and that it marked the end of winter. This was certainly the case in 1942. More sunny days, warmer temperatures and only a little rain caused people to become more active. Most days I had some shopping to do for Mum and to enlarge my knowledge of Saint Flour. Sergeant Lescaut took an active interest in my progress

Out of the blue he would suddenly ask me, "When you turn from the rue Sorel into the rue des Jacobins, there is a large house opposite the church on the corner, what is the colour of the front door?" for example. In this way he made me observant and tested my knowledge of Saint Flour

Now that 1 had established myself as a competent repair man, Mum found lots of accumulated little jobs that needed doing round the Terminus. For over a week, I unblocked roof drains so that the terrace and the back yard became drier, re-washered taps that dripped, cleaned and oiled door locks that were stiff, checked and corrected endless electric switches, sockets, and light fittings. As a final job, Dad produced a very fancy Italian coffee machine that used to be his pride and joy on the bar. "It just stopped working," he said. We carried it out to the workshop. It was quite difficult to find a way into the machine. When I did manage to get the covers off of it, there were only two problems, it was rather dirty inside, and I think this was the reason why the heating element had burnt out. This was a real problem, I had no resistance wire. It was a well designed element and I found he wattage stamped on the casing, plus some other details of the supply voltage. Thus I was able to take some resistance wire out of an old electric fire and carefully coil it into the coffee machine element and replaced the sand that surrounded it, sealed it all up again and tested. It worked. It took me longer to put all the fancy trimmings back than it had taken me to repair it

That evening Dad and I carried the coffee machine back into the bar and set it up where it had been previously. Dad checked it and pronounced it "As good as new" Of course the next day everybody was able to see the machine in use again and the Terminus could again serve espresso and cappuccino coffee. When Dad told customers that I had repaired it there were many surprised expressions

The word went round the town like wildfire that I could repair electrical appliances. There had not been anybody in the town for over two years who could do the work. Dad took in at least twenty items and put them in the workshop in one day. When I went in there it was full, there was nowhere to actually do any work and there were no owner's names on any thing. I had to put a stop on any more repairs

Most of the jobs were simple taking less than an hour each, One or two were not possible because basically the appliance was worn out. The rest were large jobs where I put a price on the repair to be accepted by the client before I did the work. I cleared the first lot in a week or so. After that I told dad that he could accept two items per day and there must be a name and address attached to each one. After all I did have some other things to do! Nevertheless it became a steady business even after the two year backlog had run out. Other items turned up as well, often children's toys which I did the best I could with, it was often a broken spring. I became an expert a punching new holes in the end of clockwork springs

One quite important repair job came in one afternoon when Yvette was on in the bar. A neighbour of the Pelletiers, Philippe's parents, had heard about the repairs I was doing. A Monsieur Councillor Leman came in with his son and a spring wound Gauge O railway engine. This engine had been his son's special St. Nicholas day's present last year. M. Leman had made a special journey to Vichy to get the engine from a dealer who had charged him well over the proper price for the toy. It had worked for some days and then jammed and nothing would move. Monsieur Leman had no knowledge of clockwork mechanisms and felt he had been sold a dud. His son just wanted his engine working again and backed this up with a flood of tears

Yvette brought the engine through to me in the workshop and related the story. Leave it with me for a few minutes and I'll have a look at it. After I took the wheels and the bottom off the engine, the problem was obvious. A piece of walnut was jammed in the cog wheels. Twenty minutes work with tweezers and a fine brush and some oil and everything was working again. I replaced the bottom and the wheels, and carried the walnut and the engine through to the bar. "I suppose there's nothing you can do," said M.Leman. "I'm afraid not," I replied, "the walnut is completely destroyed," I said putting the bits on the counter, and bending down put the engine on the floor and let it run. His son squealed with joy as he chased across he bar floor

M. Leman then remembered that they had been eating walnuts on the day it jammed, but had not connected the two events. "The only way it could have got in there is down the funnel," I said, "it was either a very good shot or sabotage." I declined any payment for he job, and left Yvette and the Lemans chatting in the bar

Yvette was leaving early that evening to go to a friends birthday party, she came into the workshop to say goodnight full of how grateful M. Leman had been saying that if I ever needed any help to contact him, and what a useful member of the community I was in these difficult times. "M. Leman's a town councillor and a very close friend of the Maire, said Dad and is likely to be the next Maire of Saint Flour whenever the next election takes place." I gave Yvette her hair drier that I had repaired "Oh and you've even done this for me," she said as I handed her the drier

"I wish you could come to the party with me this evening." "But I don't have an invitation and I've already got things to do this evening, I think I'd better leave it." She hugged me and lingered willingly in my arms until she said I've got to go but I so wish you were coming with me," and kissed me passionately goodnight

I stood nonplussed for some minutes. Quite clearly Yvette was now a real and trusted friend, but she was also a married woman and she must have felt what she was doing to me when she was close in my arms. If one problem with Yvette was now solved, perhaps another was just beginning

Later that evening sergeant Lescaut came in as we closed for one of our private discussions. First of all he had heard of the engine repair because M. Leman had spoken to the Maire, who in turn had called Lescaut to ask, "who is this young man in the Terminus who does these repairs?"

Lescaut also brought news of the attack on the St. Nazaire docks by the Royal Navy and commandos. Vichy radio had reported it and was bitter in condemning the attack because of the very high civilian casualties and that nothing had been achieved by the attack. We tuned into the BBC French news later that evening. What a different story

Successful destruction of the dock gates, significant losses of men in the attack force and minimum damage to civilian installations and few civilian casualties. Of course nobody could comment on the truth or falseness of either report, but the difference was staggering

As the exaggerated civilian casualty figures became widely known there was much talk against the policies of the Allies towards France. Some past faults like the shelling of the French fleet at Oran by the Royal Navy were rehashed. Some views were expressed by the communist elements that now Hitler had invaded Russia and would certainly fail as Napoleon had failed, perhaps Russia should be France's principle ally. After all England and France had fought each other so many times in the past thousand years, why should they expect England to be a reliable ally now?

I talked to Mum and Dad about this. They were also concerned about the overall turn of events. Mum especially pointed out the long series of weak French governments there had been in the years before the war leading to poor administration, over taxation, poor control of labour and poor education. Many French people compared the state of France with the state of Germany exactly the same number of years since the Treaty of Versailles. Perhaps the people of Vichy France would be better under German administration?

Sergeant Lescaut also caught the mood of the people. He came in one evening at my request. I asked him about the progress of his list of reliable resistance members. The total after all his efforts was less than forty, although there were some impressive names among them. He also pointed out that the more loyal French people lived in the upper town and therefore used the upper town bars, whereas the less loyal people including most of the communists lived in the lower town and used the Terminus because it was the largest bar. He also said that there were nearly a thousand people who voted communist in the local elections and consequently we had nine communist councillors, out of forty-two, on the town council. One point of special interest emerged from his conversation was that Charles Pelletier, Yvette's, father-in-law and Dad had fought together in the 1914-18 war and were both key members of Leseaut's resistors

This was a crisis point and I had to say to Lescaut unless we could honestly report to London that there was a sufficient nucleus of trusted resistance members available to us we would not get the supplies or the extra support from London necessary to be effective against the Germans. I found no encouragement in Lescaut's reply. I doubt if you will find a very different result in any part of the Auvergne, and I know Pascal has much worse figures in Clermont unless you include the communists

I told Lescaut that I had to open contact with London and demanded his support. He agreed to advise Pascal that I was ready to start operations and ask for clearance. Two days later Pascal agreed

Suddenly it was Easter. I had lost track of the dates. If it had not been for seeing the people going into the Church for the Good Friday vigil I would not have known. There was little cause for celebration in Vichy France and little celebration other than the extra Church services.

While waiting for the answer from Pascal I had tried to put together my first report to London.   I agonised over saying too little to convince them of the apathy problem and verbosity to the point of boring them. Then there was the problem of transmission time limits. If we stayed on the air for more than twelve minutes it was possible for detector vans to triangulate the position of the transmitter to within one hundred metres. Basically I had decided never to remain on the air for more than 10 minutes. By the time I had got my message into a succinct form, coded it, and worked out the transmission time it meant eight sessions of ten minutes. I had two radio sets and two sets of crystals which meant two frequencies. I was out of practice at the Morse key and started working up my speed again while seeking advice from Pascal about long messages. He understood the problem and sent his number one wireless man over to help me. Cesaire was a Gascon, and a proud one. He reminded me of d'Artagnan the Three Musketeers character. He had been operating since August 1940 and claimed no one had ever detected him. When I asked him how he knew that, he had no answer

Nevertheless his practice made sense. He had brought with him a roll of suitable aerial wire. He worked on the principle that the detector sets could only detect the location of the aerial, so let's have many aerials and use them at random with both of the frequencies available. "It's all got to be part of your keep-fit campaigne, you get a bicycle with a big basket on the back to carry your radio and battery and you ride from one aerial to the other, send your message, and move on to the next aerial, wait for your time, send your message and so on until you are finished

The gendarmerie only has four detector vans in the whole of the Auvergne and a number of fixed detectors. When a fixed detector finds your signal he has to contact the nearest two vans so that they can get cross bearings and thus triangulate your aerial's position. Then they have to actually get to you, but of course you are no longer there, and the only thing that remains is a length of black wire that can be anywhere in a fifty metre radius," he explained, "and by that time, you could be on the air again using your other frequency from a differently located aerial." "We have never had any problems around Clermont. I have so many aerials I'm not sure I can remember where they all are but you must remember that if they repeatedly get similar locations for an aerial that is being used frequently they might set a trap for you. However I don't think the gendarmerie is very good at this detection, as far as I know they have not yet apprehended anybody in Pascal's area and we transmit about thirty messages a week." "I know there have been detector vans in this area," I said, "but of course, as far as I know, there has not been anything to detect."You should instruct all of your people to look out for the vans, they are very obvious, and have a central reporting point which you can talk to before, you go on the air. I should ask Alexis Lescaut to arrange that for you"

"However easy it is a this time to operate contact with England it will be more difficult when the Germans move in, I'm sure they will be much more active and efficient"

Cesaire spent two days with me going over Lescaut's maps of the area and finding places with a good northerly exposure, for siting our aerials. I finished up with twenty-seven sites, all within thirty minutes bicycle ride from Saint Flour, and I had a secret list of where they were as coded map references. So, at the end of the first week of April, just five weeks after I arrived I went on the air to London with eight transmissions over two days, and only one aerial gave a problem with variable signal strength The silence from London was deafening. I was expecting some reply within twenty-four hours. The message when it did come made no reference to my report. It required us to prepare to receive personnel by Lysander during period seventeenth to twenty-fourth April. Details of landing sites required by twelfth April latest

An emergency meeting was set up for the same night at the Terminus. Lescaut brought his detail maps and we found a number of possible sites. Next day Lescaut and I looked at all six, and of these two were most preferred. The best was about six kilometres out of Saint Flour to the north on the hills above Pagros. We proposed that the plane should approach Saint Flour from the north using the towers of St Etienne's Cathedral as a landmark, pass the Cathedral on eastern side and return on a bearing of 352 degrees and look for our recognition signals

By return came reply accepting location of landing strip and confirming four passengers to be met and escorted by members of Pascal's group who would make direct contact with us. Anticipated date seventeenth but other dates as fallbacks, actual operation to be confirmed by message on BBC. "Quartette on record tonight." Saint Flour was almost at the limit of the range of a Lysander, and any possible delay by weather could make the operation non-viable as would a slow turn round

Next day Pascal arrived unannounced to finalise details. Apparently both his Lysander strips were compromised and this operation was urgent. He was allowing it to be believed that the arrival would be at one of his strips and had even arranged for the BBC message to be leaked to the gendarmerie. He would have special transport laid on to be in Pagros village from one o'clock onwards. Just before this operation was due we got he news about the raid by British Commandos on the shipping in Bayonne harbour. This was a boost to our morale when we needed it most, especially as the following day Vichy radio announced that the civilian casualty figures in the attack on Nantes had been wrongly reported by the Germans and the revised figures were very similar to the BBC reports. Although we promoted much discussion over this, the bad feelings generated by the exaggerated first reports persisted

Chapter 7

Four Friends Arrive

The evening of the seventeenth was clear and bright and cold. "Warm clothes tonight," was Lescaut's whispered greeting when I met him outside the Terminus shortly after dark. "It will be several degrees below zero on the tops and the ground will be frozen hard." We went in to the backroom via the yard to avoid the customers in the bar. The BBC personal messages were due to start shortly. We tuned in keeping the volume low. Our message was in the first set, so we were able to switch off. A few minutes later the phone rang, and a very cheerful Cezaire confirmed that if we had the four parcels ready for him he could collect them at about one o'clock tomorrow. It all sounded quite innocent

This was getting exciting even Lescaut's blood was up. He said," we should leave at about eleven o'clock," "But its only about seven kilometres, and you've got the bicycles arranged," I protested, "and we've got to climb to over nine hundred metres," added Lescaut, "we'll all be quite warm when we get there, but have an extra coat to put on while we are waiting". "Who's going to be our third man I asked?" "Someone you already know, Councillor Monsieur Leman." We'll all meet in the yard of the Terminus at eleven"

At eleven it was still a fine night, no moon but bright starlight. We rode in silence with no lights. We did not see another person all the way there. The last two kilometres were very steeply up hill and most of it was walked. The strip looked different in the starlight, but we were pleased that we could see the silhouette of the Cathedral on the skyline to the south. We paced out the landing length and put our torches ready in position, checked the Aldis lamp, put on our extra coats and waited. It was bitterly cold.

At a quarter to one we thought we could just hear an aircraft but we could not, locate the direction, and then all was quiet again. Then we were all sure now to the south of us and getting louder, coming from exactly the right position. I picked up the Aldis lamp and flashed the recognition signal, immediately answered correctly and we ran to turn on the torches. The pilot acknowledged with two flashes of his landing lights and we stood back leaving a clear strip. There was no engine noise now, but soon we could hear a swishing sound, then just a short burst of engine noise and he was down and braking hard. He taxied back to the start of the strip and the door opened. Four persons dissemplaned and Lescaut and Leman led them to the side of the strip

I spoke briefly to the pilot asking him how he found the strip. "First rate, no problems, only four minutes late and that was because I took too wide a sweep round the Cathedral, do better next time." "Good luck safe journey," I called as I shut the door and locked it. Engines to full power and he was off. As soon as he was airborne, he reduced the engine power and within seconds he was out of earshot. I doubt if he was stationary for more than two minutes.

We picked up our torches, inspected the strip for any marks. There were distinct wheel marks that looked just as though an aircraft had landed.

Our four arrivals were led down the hill towards the lane leading down to Pagros.

There were some lights in the farm buildings of the little hamlet of Barrat and they had not been there when we went up. Lescaut, Leman and our four arrivals went on ahead and I started looking around. All of a sudden a voice spoke to me out of the darkness, "If you want I can put some sheep up there first thing in morning just in case there's any marks." So much for security, "Couple of hours of grazing "n dunging 'n nothing 'll show." I walked towards the voice

"Thank you very much; your cooperation is most welcome." He came out of the shadows, the moon had just risen over the rim of the hills, I recognised him as a Friday regular at the Terminus and he recognised me. "Just you let me know when you're doing it again and I'll be sure to have some sheep ready. Sergeant Lescaut knows me, tell him when you catch up with him that he can always count on Jean Chavent"

By the time I had caught up with the others the four arrivals were already in the back of the Pascal's van and about to leave. Pascal was pleased with the safe arrival

I told Lescaut and Leman about Jean Chavent. Neither was surprised at his attitude, but Lescaut said he had the reputation of charging for his favours. "Nevertheless I will make an early opportunity to go and thank him for his cooperation," then, talking to me," do nothing to encourage him until I give you the word. It just goes to show," he went on," nothing happens up there without somebody seeing something

On my next schedule I got a thank you for a good operation and an approval to use the strip as and when convenient

Because of the confusion over a number of matters I coded a message to London asking, 1. Status of Mathilde Dufour in organisation? 2. Any information on Yvette Pelletier nee Deville of Avenue du Commandant Delorme 7, Saint Flour bas, identity card No. 7621948-25. 3. How far geographically did my responsibility extend? 4. Was London aware of strength of communist resistance in area outside the towns and request instructions re contact and cooperation?

Reply by return. Mathilde currently reports to Lescaut but will shortly be moved South and then report to you re supplies and Pascal for all other matters. 2. Yvette unknown in London, rely on Lescaut's and Mathilde's opinions. 3. Geographical limits, as far as required but limit likely to be Le Puy to east, Millau to south, Clermont to north and Brive to west. 4. When supplies permit establish dumps in these directions. Communists in area considered of no significance. Do not cooperate. Lescaut has similar instructions.

The date on that reply reminded me it was only three days to Yvette's 'birthday, she would be twenty-two and already a widow. I badly wanted to do something to please her, but what can one do in such a situation without the risk of it being misunderstood by somebody or other. I asked Mum and Dad about it, their idea was close the Terminus early and have a surprise party for her, inviting some of her friends and both pairs of grandparents but then what about Jean-Francois, he should be asleep. Dad had a long telephone conversation with Charles Pelletier, they had also been talking about it over the weekend and had suggested to Yvette a luncheon party on the day at their home with Yvette's parents from Murat, but Yvette had declined because she needed to work to live

The outcome was that what Yvette needed most was money but any attempt to simply give her money would be misunderstood. I asked if there were any charitable funds in the town that could make a donation to her if the money for the donation was put up by friends and family, after all she was a deserving case, a war widow for whom no state funds were forthcoming. Then I suggested that if Monsieur. Leman was a close friend of the Maire he could arrange for the Maire to make a discretionary grant in such a case. Dad called Monsieur Leman who was sympathetic and agreed to press the Maire on this point immediately. He did so and called back in about half an hour saying the Maire was pleased to help in such a case, and if we gave him the amount concerned he would add something himself and make it a charitable grant

Mum and Dad were very generous and put up two thousand francs from all at the Terminus. Charles Pelletier promised five hundred francs as did M. Leman. It was arranged that I would collect the money in the morning and take it to the Town Hall. When I had the three thousand, because I was flush with cash from my repair jobs, I added a further two thousand and delivered the five thousand to the Maire personally. He was surprised at the amount but he added another five hundred and promised me that she would receive the cash from his assistant on the morning of her birthday

I had noticed Yvette wore two silver sleepers in her ears and I thought it would she might like some real earrings again so just as a special treat for Yvette. I called at the jewellers and bought her a pair of earrings, tiny gold stars, set with three emerald chips in the centre. Together with a card from Jean-Francois they were waiting for her when she arrived at the Terminus on her birthday morning

I was in the back yard when she came in. I gave her a special hug and kisses for a Happy Birthday. "You remembered," she said, "I didn't think you would"

Some minutes later, when she started to arrange the breakfast things she saw the card and little parcel from Jean-Francois. Mum came into the backroom at this moment also as Yvette opened the little box. "Oh, thank you so much" she said to Mum, "They are so lovely," and she put hem in her ears. "They are not from me," said Mum, "what does the card say?" "From Jean-Francois." "I think you'll find that is Henri's writing," said Mum

I was in the workshop when she came looking for me. "Look what somebody has given me," she said turning her head left and right. "I think they suit you perfectly, just the right colour against your hair." "Since when have you been taking my sons name in vain?" "Well I did help him choose them," I said. "He's been saving his pocket money ever since he was born to buy those." "What pocket money, "The pocket money I've just decided to give him."

Now that some real activity seemed to be starting I had to think about my sidelines. They were taking up more and more of my time. Although I had finished the yard at the back and done most of the little jobs Mum had asked for indoors, the number of repair jobs seemed never ending. Children's toys now made up most of the jobs. Most mechanical and electrical toys in France came from Germany or Czechoslovakia, these sources had stopped completely as had supply of any spares

I became quite expert at punching new holes in clockwork springs and refitting them in the toys. New brushes for tiny electric motors I made from the brushes of old starter motors which I begged from the local service garage was another speciality

Mum and Dad were more than happy with the increased drinks business when people brought or collected repairs. Mum, in particular, wanted me to continue because it was so much in character, and improved my cover. Of course I could start charging more, but that might lead to allegations of profiteering. In the end I made a huge effort over a week and reduced the backlog to almost zero, and put the charges up by fifteen per cent and limited the number of jobs

59

accepted per week to thirty. I wasn't popular but it made people realise that tiny repairs to toys could not be done for nothing

It was only just in time. At last here was a reaction to my long report on the attitude of the French population. Almost every message schedule brought questions and it became clear that my report was either not believed in London, or was being denied by, perhaps De Gaulle's office. The final sting in the tail was Advise what action you propose to take to correct situation

We sent a number of messages detailing differences in attitude of people in the lower town and the upper town, of how reaction to bad news first was not corrected by better news later even if the first bad news was stated to be untrue, of the effect the weak position of the Vichy government, seen as just another weak government like those before the war started We drew comparisons between Saint Flour and Clermont, drawing on Pascal for help, Clermont having a much larger proportion of political activists in its population than Saint Flour

Again the silence was deafening. Eventually a brief reply acknowledging our messages and repeating, Advise what action you, repeat you, propose to take to correct situation

One night Lescaut and two of his colleagues, all off duty were in the bar of the Terminus. I was looking after them and joining in their conversation Some news had been put out on the BBC about persecution of Jews in Vichy France. Lescaut said he had an instruction recently to keep a register of all Jews in the area. Vincent one of the other policemen, said, "There are two ghettos and one concentration camp in occupied France, ghettos at Compiegne and Drancy and the concentration camp at Natzweiller a remote location in Bas Rhine not too far from the German border

There had been many reports since the start of he war of persecution of Jews   in Germany and the occupied countries of Eastern Europe. Some horror stories had been leaked in Vichy France but only half believed. "Do we have any Jews in Saint Flour?" I asked he group in general. "There are only two families," answered Lescaut," the Bodanski's and the Salomanson's." I was surprised, "but Dr. Bodanski is my doctor, I never thought of him as a Jew" "Well he is," said Vincent, "and he's also the best doctor in town."

"I once tried to court Rosa, the eldest of Monsieur Salomansons grand-daughters," said Jean-Claude, the other policeman, "When she took me home to meet the family, they made it quite plain that if I did have any intentions which included Rosa, and my intentions must also include adopting the Jewish faith and entering the family business with a job for life." The Salomanson family owned a small chain of Jewellery and clock making shops and workshops throughout the region, all completely staffed by family members. Lescaut said, "At the last count there were twenty-seven of them, You have to keep an eye on them, they never bother to report new births until I have seen a new baby and threatened them if they do not register the birth"

The Salomansons were strictly orthodox Jews; they did not seek any contact with the general people of Saint Flour unless it was business matter. I never saw any of them in the Terminus and their shops were always closed on Saturdays and the Jewish festivals

Dr. Bodanski's family was much more conventional. He lived in the upper town with his wife and unmarried sister, who acted as his nurse/receptionist. He had three sons, two already qualified as doctors and doing their time as locums before finding a permanent practice. The youngest was at Lyon university studying to be a surgeon, he was said to be brilliant. The Bodanski's were really well integrated with the community. His wife and sister were active in local women's groups and he himself was always ready to help in matters outside his medical competence. His surgery was always busy, and his home visits, made nowadays in a pony and trap, were always late as he would make ad hoc diagnoses at the side of the road when hailed by patients.

Dr. Bodanski had been my doctor while I was undergoing the surgical corrections to my club foot in Vichy. He had already renewed our acquaintanceship when he stopped off at the Terminus for refreshment. He remarked on one visit how my walking had improved while I had been away, and I half expected him to ask to see my leg. Not that I should have anything to worry about because Mum and Dad had both said they could not see any real differences. I made a mental note to wear shorts sometimes in the summer just in case anybody had any doubts

During the spring I expanded my personal knowledge of the surrounding region. It wasn't easy because I was already supposed to know! Much of the exploration was done in the company of Lescaut because he always had transport available and I gradually got to know his colleagues. He assured me they were all loyal Frenchmen committed to resistance as and when it became necessary. None of them had taken up the financial inducements to join the expanding gendarmerie. Some of them were with us most of the time. Lescaut made no mention of my status simply saying he found me useful because I had direct experience of working with a Nazi management even though they eventually threw me out. The story was accepted but sometimes I saw some strange looks when I was explaining some complex plan or equipment Lescaut repeatedly said they could not talk about what they did not know I had to trust him. During these travels I got to know the hill men and soon recognised that they were probably the most important manpower resource we had. They had every excuse to be out anywhere, at any time, in all weathers with dogs, horses and sleds or travois

61

They could be looking for their stock, or their neighbours, and who could complain if they had not found any; it was their livelihood after all. Up to now my only experience of them was as customers, and frugal ones at that, in the bar after the Friday market making one drink last as long as the conversation

It was quite different in their own homes, they all made various quite potent liqueurs from all sorts of fruits and plants, and they had considerable stocks of them. French law permitted them to make for their own consumption but I saw many a little bottle changing hands in the market. Lescaut knew all about this of course and every now and then would issue a warning and very rarely a fine. Fines were paid with vociferous protestations, swearing and even threats

There was also significant production of cider by the farmers who had good apple trees, in the valleys. I never understood what the legal position was about this but you could usually buy some litres at a Friday market. I took comfort from the attitude of Jean Chavent following the Lysander operation. We had to have the support of these people, they would know about anything we did in the hills and we must not take any actions that would harm their delicately balanced economics. At present we were received as friends and very hospitably, but they were curious why the town police plus a local barman were visiting them in their homes. There was no precedent for this

Before we could reach any conclusion a message from London needed our immediate attention. A further SOE operative was being put into our area. He, code name Raymond, was to be accepted soonest when arrangements for his accommodation were settled. Lescaut was all for putting him to live on one of the hill men farms. I recalled Jean Chavent's offer of help. Lescaut sent me off to see him the next day

I thought long and hard about how to approach the question. I arrived at the Chavent farm in he middle of the morning. Madame Chavent sent me up towards the Sailhant waterfall where Jean was preparing some dipping troughs for the spring dip for sheep scab. It was a fair day and I enjoyed the climb. My arrival was announced by two dogs who rushed towards me, but I still could not see Jean. He eventually climbed up out of a trench he was digging. I think he was ready for a breather. I recalled his offer of assistance and told him we would be bringing in another man soon on the same strip and could we count on his help. He was very willing. Then I broached the question of where the man could stay. It was almost as though he could read my mind

"If he's prepared to earn his keep he can stay with us as long as needed." I added that, "this could be many months". "There's always work to done on a hill farm was the reply." He went on, "You must know that there are already several strangers staying with farmers up here. Rumour has it they are Maquis. I don't want to be involved with them and I am sure Lescaut's work is for the proper resistance, so I will willingly take your man. Do you know when he is coming?" "Not yet," I said, "but soon I am sure, probably depends on the moon I thanked Jean profusely, but he was quite dismissive, "It's time we did something to prepare for the time when he Germans move in, do you know when that is going to happen?" I've no idea," I said, "the rumour is that they haven't got enough troops available to occupy Vichy France." Taking my leave, we shook hands very firmly

"I think we will work things out well between us"

Lescaut was pleased with the arrangements I had made. "A good location only a few kilometres out of town and yet isolated with plenty of escape routes if ever needed." We agreed to advise London we could proceed at once. London responded by return with a first date just two days ahead and the usual fallbacks, using the same strip. The message stated, Raymond responsible to you alone, and should be prepared to act as your deputy. You are promoted Captain to allow for this. Raymond will advise you of his special knowledge of the area, and his special knowledge will doubtless be of value. Lescaut was intrigued by this message. After congratulating me on my promotion, he speculated on what the special local knowledge might be. "Perhaps he is a specialist in the design of sheep dipping troughs", I suggested

Over the past few days there had been frequent reports of units of the free French forces in North Africa holding out against the German and Italian forces at the oasis of Bir Hacheim. This was the first news we had of the free French forces in combat and had stimulated interest and a little pride in some of people of Saint Flour. The general commanding the forces had been born in the Auvergne. Some days later the reports were that they had been forced to withdraw Eastwards because of the overwhelming strength deployed against them. They managed to do this without loss during one night after having poisoned the water supply and leaving all the other stores booby trapped which inflicted some final casualties on the axis forces when they moved in

The next day we heard about the Commando raid on Boulogne and Le Touquet, but Vichy radio simply said the attack had been repelled with heavy casualties to the British and Canadian forces

The nights were shorter now and Raymond's arrival time was not due until thirty-five minutes after one o'clock. Once again we were lucky with the conditions on the first night. After confirmation with the personal message on the BBC everything moved into action. Lescaut produced a new man, Felix, to be our third man at he strip. We had given the text of the personal message to Jean Chavent so he knew as soon as we did. On our way up to the strip he had hot coffee and brandy waiting for us. This night's reception was not so cold inside or out!

The Lysander made a much better approach this time and landed early. The same pilot as before, "that was a better approach," he said when I opened the door," do it blindfolded next time." "By the way there are several little packages for you and one larger one. Your man's a bit queasy, turbulence over the Loire, should be all right in half an hour." Raymond was a bit unsteady as he disemplaned. As soon as I had the parcels off, I gave the pilot the all clear, closed the door and he was off again. Turnaround time was not more than three minutes

Then we made the introductions. After I had introduced Lescaut and Felix to Raymond, he said, "I was supposed to be met by Henri Dufour, "That's me," I said," but I heard you speaking perfect English with the pilot." "Nevertheless I am Henri Dufour" I said, speaking in French this time. We collected all our lamps and parcels and set off down the hill

As we were, going down I explained to Raymond that he was to stay with Jean Chavent on a semi-permanent basis and that we would be at the farm in about twenty minutes. "Get a good nights sleep and I'll call to see you tomorrow and we'll take a walk on the hills to give you an idea of the country." "But I already know the region," he said, "didn't London tell you?" "You've just had lesson number one," I said, "don't assume anything, and please don't discuss any matters with your hosts, they've agreed not to ask you questions, and I need to know if they do so." We'll have an exchange of information tomorrow while we are out on the hills"

We left him at the Chavent farm as soon as the introductions had been made "Do I understand London is not terribly reliable?" questioned Lescaut. "I am not happy with the communications," I said, "and I don't think it's our fault." We were now retrieving our bicycles and all of our lamps and parcels would not fit into the baskets on mine, so we cached some of the parcels under a straw pile for me to retrieve tomorrow

A fast downhill run back into town completed the night's work. I was up as soon as Sambo woke me on the morning. I unpacked some of the small parcels, each contained new crystals for the radios so now I had a greater range of frequencies at my fingertips. A quick breakfast and some whispered explanations to Mum and Dad and I was off for the day. I checked with Raymond that he was comfortable with the Chavents   . Jean was already out on the hills but Marguerite, his wife, assured me all was well. We set off towards Andelat as I had the intention of showing Raymond how close he was to Saint Flour

Once clear of the farm Raymond said, "Didn't London send you any details about me?" "Nothing other than your name and arrival time and that you would explain on arrival." "Did you listen to all your schedules?" "Of course," I replied, "I've only missed two since I've been here and that was over a month ago"

Raymond explained, he was the son of a French mother and an English father, born and educated in France, finishing at Toulouse university with a degree in civil engineering in 1934. When he was born his father registered his birth at the British Embassy, thus assuring him of British Citizenship. He was thirty-one years old and unmarried. His second job after leaving university was as maintenance engineer on the Truyere river dams from 1935-39

The family recognised that war was inevitable in the summer of 1939 and decided that England was a safer place than France. When he was engaged in the work on the Truyere dams he had lived in Entreygues-sur-Truyere thus accounting for his knowledge of the region. There was some risk of his being recognised hence the partly grown beard and moustache

When the family arrived in England Raymond was required to register for military service and was soon identified as a potential SOE operative because he was a qualified engineer with a of specialised knowledge of dams on the Truyere, and his perfect command of French. Like me he was made an attractive offer he found difficult to refuse

The Truyere river system drained a huge part of the Massif Centrale of France. In all there were six dams on the Truyere, four of them creating large lakes, before it joined he Lot. Following the success of the dam busters raid on the Ruhr dams similar operations were being planned as part of an overall strategy in the invasion of Europe by the Allies. Raymond's primary task was to assess how much damage would be done to the North-South roads and railways in the Auvergne and all points west

So now Raymond's presence with us was explained

By this time we had reached the hill above Andelat and it was a close run thing who could point out most landmarks to he other. Raymond asked me about my position in all of this as he had been told he was responsible to me. He was clearly expecting somebody considerably older." My role is quite different to yours and to any other operatives who come into this region. I have to keep a low profile, run the communications, and make sure everything needed is to hand when it is needed." "But what am I supposed to do while we are waiting?" he asked.   "Over the next few months we will all try and acquaint you with the problems we have here and believe me they are real because London chose to believe what De Gaulle says about the French people and their will to resist, rather than what we tell them. The most important thing you have to do immediately is to regularise your position here with Sergeant Lescaut who you met last night. He is the senior police officer in Saint Flour and is coming to see you this evening at the farm." "Do I have to take orders from him", he asked, "No," I said, "but you should listen very carefully to his advice and comply as far as possible with what he asks. Any problems must be referred to me." "The most probable status you can use is to be a deserter from the French forces who has taken to the hills to avoid having to serve the Germans in any way. Believe me, Lescaut is a friend in every sense"

Then I told him it had taken me a month to find my feet and to know about the problems, most of which remain unsolved. "As you become fully aware of the real situation here we would welcome your input, but please don't jump to conclusions." We were nearing the Chavent farm again by now. "I'm going to retrieve the parcels I couldn't carry last night and get back to my base. Lescaut will advise me of the results of your meeting this evening and doubtless I will contact you again soon Any help you can give to Jean Chavent I know will be welcome and it will occupy your mind too You could also spend some time up on the hills. It will darken your complexion and you can expand your knowledge of the local area. Make only a few acquaintances at this stage and only use Jean Chavent as your introduction. If you need to contact me you can always leave a message at the Terminus but only with Robert, Lisette or Mathilde. The girl who helps in the bar, Yvette, knows nothing"

Raymond's task was clearly an independent one until he had his plans prepared

I didn't think it would be good for any of us to be seen together, there was always a chance he could meet somebody who would recognise him. When his moustache and beard has grown more and his complexion darkened so he looked the part he was playing, the chances of recognition would reduce After we had parted I wondered how he would fare. Language was not a problem, even his accent was not that different from the local one and he even knew enough of the Auvergnat vocabulary to pass as a near local. When he had changed his appearance, he might look like a local and sound similar, but would only be known to a very few locals. How perilous was that? I had no answer

Lescaut, Felix and myself had already put together a provisional list of arms and munitions we thought would be a starting point for equipping the local farmers. Now we had to consider what Raymond might need. We considered this at our next evening together and decided that we could not even guess at what he would need and left the matter open. Then Lescaut surprised me saying, "Your shooting is marksman standard, so I've been told, and there are certainly some crack shots amongst the hill men, you should include some snipers rifles, the hill men have nothing heavier than their point two-two's." My estimate of the load was eighteen containers allowing for a fifty percent loss on the drop. London doubled that saying eighteen containers was not worth the effort. So on the night of second of May we were ready for our first drop of thirty-six containers

The need to find a drop zone became urgent. I decided to involve Raymond using the Barrat farm as a base We searched the local maps and found so many possible sites that we simply did not have time to look at them all. Then Raymond came up with a sound idea. "On the southern slopes of the Auvergne volcanoes there are some valleys with plenty of caves in the slopes, quite remote, so that although transport would be a problem, we could conceal the stores as soon as they were dropped, and collect them at our convenience for dispersion." Back to the maps

Raymond pointed out the area he had in mind and his local knowledge came to the fore. We immediately arranged to borrow Vincent, Felix and a police van from Lescaut and drive over there the following day. Although it was over twenty kilometres from Saint Flour, the advantages were so obvious that we decided at once to use it. Vincent remarked, "It's far enough from Saint Flour that the aircraft noise will not be heard especially if we bring the planes in over the Plomb du Cantal which is a good landmark even at night and if it is necessary a small fire near the peak could guide the planes in followed by a line of flares to mark the drop line"

When we got there we could see exactly how this could work. I said, "As far as I can see this place meets all the criteria I have been instructed to find." "The caves in this valley are over there among the trees," said Raymond. We left the van at a sharp turn in the road where there was room for it. There was nobody in sight. Vincent and Felix were in uniform. "If any of the locals show up, we are investigating complaints about sheep rustling," said Vincent. There were sheep dotted about all over the valley. "What happens to the sheep during the drop", I asked. "Oh they'll just go away up the other side of the valley, they don't like fires or strangers," said Felix. "Then let's go and look at these caves," I said. The caves were not easy to find. "We'll need to have some markers to get to find these caves," said Raymond, "but that is also an advantage because anybody will have difficulty in finding the caves." "There is another road at the top of this slope above the trees but we'll have to haul the munitions up the slope," said Felix. We explored the woods. It was about three hundred metres to the road mostly up hill and rough going. "We could use sleds to drag the stuff up the road and leave them in the caves after ready for the next drop." said Raymond. We returned to the edge of the trees above the valley

"Time for a smoke and a talk," I said. We settled down on the grass. "At the moment it all looks very possible. What I want each of you to do now is to go off in different directions and see if you can find any problems we have not yet considered and if there is a problem, look for a way round it. Vincent, will you go back to the road we have just looked at and explore in both directions to see if there are any houses where the people might be a problem. Felix will you go off to the south west where there is another small road and make a similar survey as well as seeing how we might get the stuff to that road. Raymond, find out what is over that hill to the south west and whether we could use that route. I'll look at the possibilities of getting the stuff down to the road where the van is parked now." All ways out were possible

Raymond reckoned his was the best because immediately over the ridge there was a good track way where we could even get the police van to a point which was reached by an all grass route from the caves so that dragging sleds would be easy even though it was somewhat further. The problem on my route was a bog where the stream turned to pass under the road. During wet weather, and for some time after, the bog would be more widespread and we would have to manoeuvre sleds around it. Our final conclusion was that we should use this valley for our first drop and try all four routes out at various times as a test. From the maps we could see no other site offering better prospects

The location of the drop zone was passed to London with approach instructions. Our next meetings were taken up with planning the dispersion of the goods after the drop. Alexis Lescaut had quietly been working out four suitable locations for stocking the munitions at or near appropriate farms where he could trust the farmers to protect them and only issue on instructions. There would eventually be a fifth for Mathilde's use when she had moved to Millau. "What do we do with the containers?" Was Dad's first question, how big are they? and what are they made of?" followed soon after. "They are metal, about one metre eighty high and round about half a metre diameter. "I replied but that is a guess, I've actually only seen one once." "Have you got to get rid of them?" asked Mum, "Yes I replied and the parachutes," I replied. "Can we have the parachutes to make underclothes." asked Mum. "Not until after the war," I replied. "But nobody will see them," protested Mum. "What about the washing line, "I said and that was the end of that one

"There is that bog you mentioned," said Dad "There are also the volcano craters." said Alexis, "but that is not so convenient or so close." "Suppose we hide them deep in those caves, how long would it be before anyone found them?" I asked. How long is a piece of string? Was the only conclusion "The bog wins." I said

Some days later Alexis and I went to see Raymond at the Barrat farm. He proudly showed us two sleds he had made. "How did you manage to do this without Jean Chavent knowing," asked Alexis. "Of course he knows what you are doing, he's not the least bit surprised that there will be an air drop soon, I don't think he knows where or when and he hasn't asked." "Do you trust him," I asked. "Yes I do." was the reply

Alexis supported Raymond but cautioned that although Jean Chavent's loyalty was never in doubt his honesty was suspect by many of the people who dealt with him. "I saw him in action yesterday," said Raymond, "over dipping some sheep for a neighbour, he drives a very hard bargain but it was an honest one." I had been favourably impressed by the way he so simply said he could put some sheep on the Lysander landing strip when that was exactly what we needed; and he had never referred to it since. We took the decision to include Jean Chavent and his wife Marguerite in our planning

We stayed at the farm until Jean came back from his day's work. Alexis went straight to the point. "You've guessed that we plan to bring in an air drop soon and you've seen the sleds that Raymond is making," Jean nodded. "Can we trust you to keep that confidential." "Yes," was the monosyllabic reply, "But he need not make any more sleds, there's another four in the small barn you can use. I don't suppose you'll need more than that." "Are you sure that there's enough space up there for an air drop?" Jean asked, "and I don't think I'll have enough barn space to store the stuff." "the drop will not be here," I said, "this is too close to Saint Flour and using the Cathedral tower as a marker means the planes would have to come in directly over the tower. One Lysander with a silenced engine is not a problem but some fully loaded bombers is a different matter"

"We have found a site in one of the valleys of the Plomb de Cantal which we will use." said Alexis, "and store the stuff in some caves until we disperse it to other places." "So that's why you want the sleds, you're going back after the drop to disperse the stuff in small lots in vans carts and so on." it was as though Jean had been in on the plan from the start. "The valley we are going to use is the one that runs down to le Che," I said. "That's the one with the bog at the bottom," said Jean, "You'll need to be careful in the dark, that bog is treacherous, I saw a sheep go in there once, only about thirty seconds and it was gone. Should be fenced off really but its cheaper to train the dogs to keep the sheep away from the bog"

"We were wondering if the bog might be the place to get rid of the containers," said Alexis, "You'll never see them again if you drop them in there, assured Jean. Another problem solved and another problem recognised how to keep away from the bog at night?

"When is this going to happen?" asked Jean. "We will have a planned date about ten days ahead of time and the actual date the evening before in the personal messages on the BBC," I replied. "Yes I've heard those and wondered what they were all about." "Who's going to do the hard work when you move the stuff from the drop to the caves?" was the next question. "We'll use two vans to bring ten people out from Saint Flour," replied Alexis. "I know who could find you eight men used to handling heavy goods from among the strays in the hills, I know exactly who to talk to." said Jean. "Can we trust them," I had to ask

"Well they won't talk," he said, "but they might borrow one or two things, I don't know if any of them will have guns to fire your ammunition, if they do have you'll lose some, we're all getting short of powder and shot and there's none available." "I think that's a small price to pay for what they are doing, if they say anything to you about it, you may quote me as saying I can't count very well"

Considering the haste with which this drop was planned, it went remarkably well. Only three containers missing and we saw one of them drop into the bog. "If we change the line of the flares so the North-East end is further North then we would reduce the chance of another going to the bog." I suggested. Raymond returned to the valley at daybreak the following morning and reported that there was no trace of container or parachute visible from the one that we know went in London considered this a good result, the drop plane pilots were both complementary about the location and marker fires

It took us a further week of carefully planned movements to move the stores on to the four outpost depots planned by Lescaut and our main stockpile on the outskirts of Saint Flour. I was uneasy about this; it seemed to be too much in one place and too near home

A very useful spin off from this last operation was two conversations in the bar of the Terminus, after the next Friday market. The conversations were virtually identical. Two of the heavy brigade who handled the dropped stores for us spoke to me separately, after taking me on one side, saying if I had other men I wanted to put in place they would agree to a similar arrangement as I had with Jean Chavent, and both for the same reason, they were worried about the presence of Maquis in the area and that they felt safer cooperating with the resistance rather than the Maquis. I wondered afterwards why they had spoken to me about it rather than Alexis Lescaut. I had been sending regular updates on the question of the morale of the local people, with the usual silence following. Now I felt I could send a message stressing the very positive assistance we had received from the hill men and that if we worked with and through them, positive results could be obtained. I stated that I would be making a proposal about this shortly after further talks with them. This got a reply, 'Expect your proposal re hill men soonest

Chapter 8

Co-ordination

I asked Lescaut if he could set up a three way meeting with myself and Pascal as I wanted to put a proposal about the hill men to them. He did so and we met the next Sunday afternoon at Brioude in a safe house. I had decided I had got to run the meeting, and this was embarrassing because of the age gap. Here was I at least twenty years junior to the others

I spelled it out in the simplest terms. "The hill men have demonstrated that they will help us if asked. Whatever we do they will know about any actions we took in the hills. Eight of them have already committed themselves by their actions in the past week. Two of those have committed themselves yet further by offering accommodation to other men we may want to put in the area. Thus the first question for discussion is; how many in numbers and proportion can we count on? If this number is judged satisfactory should we call a meeting of those we feel confident about and ask for their help?

Alexis made the first response. "After the ease with which we got cooperation for this last job I have thought very carefully about their help and my exposure of my position to them, I wasn't in uniform but they all knew me and recognised the risk I am taking. I don't believe they will let me or any of you down. I am not sure that the remarks about the maquis are the general opinion. I know that several of those who helped us employ maquis members who I never see should I visit their farms. I think we should trust them and not be too critical about political matters

Taking this into account I would expect more than half of them will work with us and that is just one hundred and eighty in the sub-prefecture of Saint Flour. Pascal commented, "Clermont is totally different, the communists have over thirty percent of the vote in our area, you cannot run a business without making some accommodation for their views. They are not unreasonable and provided they are not ignored they will cooperate with an otherwise right wing management. Ignoring them and working without their involvement could be a disaster even in Saint Flour." Turning to me he said, "I know you are under instructions not to supply them with anything but I would suggest to you that you should not enquire into the politics of the matter and proceed to get the best results you can. That should satisfy your superiors in England and it will certainly satisfy us here because we will recognise that you are following the best way to get results"

I came out of that discussion feeling that I had a clear direction to follow and in the future I would just ignore the politics of the matters in hand. On the way back to Saint Flour Alexis complimented on the way we had reached the right decision

Yvette had noticed how occupied I was getting with Lescaut. "Do you think you could find the time to do a little job for me?" she asked one morning, "I can always find time for you." I replied. Jean-Francois was getting ever more active and when he was loose in the house he went straight to all the odds and ends stored under the stairs, pulling them all out and turning the hallway into an obstacle course and of course putting things back was something he had yet to learn. Yvette had seen this area, in a neighbour's house, turned into a cupboard closed by a lockable door. "Could you please make one for me?" "I'll sort through my stock of timber this afternoon and see if I have the right timber and if I could borrow your keys I can measure up the job and get on with it. Not only did I have the right timber I even found hinges and a brass lock amongst the odds and end sends

When I looked at the space concerned it really was a simple job. I needed to make a frame to screw to the floor and underside of the stairs with two upright struts for the door opening and closed off with some light panelling. I made the frame that afternoon and went round and fitted it in the evening. "I'm busy most of morning," I told her when she came home from the Terminus, but I'll finish the door some time during the day and come round and fit it tomorrow evening." She was pleased and demonstrated it

I had many transmission schedules the next day as a result of our Brioude meeting, but I was lucky, conditions were good and I finished earlier than expected. I borrowed Yvette's keys and told her I was going to fit the door and she would find me still there when she went home. The door didn't fit perfectly the first time and I had some trimming to do. Yvette came home while I was still trimming the door. She went off to put Jean-Francois to bed and after he was sleeping she took a bath. I finished the job and I was pleased with it, all fitting properly and locking firmly. I even put a hook for the key; well out of the reach of Jean-Francois

Yvette came downstairs after her bath in a light dressing gown. She made some coffee and found a bottle of brandy. We sat side by side on the sofa simply talking about nothing in particular. She leaned across me to refill my glass. My arm went round her back and I did not let her return, she responded immediately with hugs and kisses. We remained like that for some minutes

The warmth of her body through the thin robe was exciting me beyond any previous experience. She broke off from the embrace. "I think that I owe you so much for all the things you do for me," "It's nothing really." I said, "I think I'd better go now," "You don't have to." she said. "Yvette," I replied, "I am extremely fond of you and Jean-Francois, and I respect you as a very special friend and companion." I have to go before I do something we may both regret." I slipped away as quickly as I could

I felt I needed a better understanding of these people called the Maquis and I went to the police headquarters with the express purpose of finding out all he knew about them. "Is the Maquis simply another name for the communist resistance?" "I am not sure and I am confused," was his reply. "The word Maquis is a Corsican word with two meanings, if you ever visit Corsica especially in the summer you will probably smell the island before you can see it. Most of the mountain land is covered by a mixture of low growing shrubs and bushes including many herbs which seem to grow very profusely and has this characteristic spicy smell. This mountainside growth is called Maquis. The other meaning is some of the Corsicans themselves. They are a very tough independent people and have often fought against imposed authority

They would attack suddenly from the hillsides and then disappear leaving just the smell of the herbs growing on the slopes. There are similarities between them and our hill men, but the important point is that the Corsican Maquis used to attack suddenly and then disappear into the hills so nothing remained but the smell. And that is how the word Maquis came to be applied to the Corsican resistance

"Well, are the Maquis also communists?" I had to ask. "I think so," said Lescaut, "but they are not the same as the French communist party. I think the Italian communists are as divided as our resistance movement. I have even heard that the communists in the Alps Maritimes along the Italian border who are the resistors in that area, are in fact mostly Italian defectors financed and supplied from Turin, which I find hard to understand." I pondered these statements for some minutes

"So the Maquis are attacking both the Germans and the Italian Fascist party, both of whom are our enemies." That sounds right," said Lescaut My next proposal to Lescaut was that he should try and encourage some of our known supporters to visit the Terminus sometimes and provoke an argument over the support for resistance. "I think that would be too transparent was the immediate reaction, you see our regular clients mostly live in the upper town and are known to live in the upper town. If you encourage our known supporters to come here in the evenings our regulars would immediately ask, why they are here." I had to agree

I could not get the idea of pub teams for darts, cribbage and shove ha'penny out of my mind. It took a bit of time to explain pub teams to Lescaut. He had heard of darts and seen it played in some bars in Bordeaux. Then he asked me, "Have you ever seen Petanque played but you might call it Boule." "Yes I've seen that played in the parks in Rheims and St Denis, but I don't understand the game." "Well there are some pitches for Petanque in the Princes gardens opposite the Chamber of Agriculture, why don't you go and have a look and see if you get any ideas. They should be playing by now, it's essentially a summer game"

On the next sunny day I went up to the Princes gardens, these were right on the western edge of the upper town. I watched the game for a while and immediately saw the similarity to English bowls, but it was played on a rough imperfect surface and that the roughness imperfections were part of the challenge of the game. Significant amounts of money seemed to be changing hands in some of the games

Lescaut with the help of Charles Pelletier and Councillor Leman agreed to try and stimulate some Petanque competitions between the patrons of the various bars around the Princes gardens, there were plenty of them. I started looking round the lower town and there was a possible place almost on my doorstep. Just behind the bus park off the Place de la Liberte, there was piece of waste ground that was only ever used on Fridays as a parking place for market trader's vehicles

I started asking questions about the land but nobody seemed to know who owned it. It was nothing like the smooth pitches of the Princes gardens but as Dad said, "It will be a more exciting game on that patch." So Dad, Felix, Manuel and myself scrounged some sets of boules from friends and started playing Petanque to see if any one objected. We played for a couple of hours one evening until it was dark and adjourned to the Terminus for refreshment. Just two days later there were six people playing throughout the evening and when they came into the bar afterwards, they were unanimous that it was a good idea to use the ground and that it was an extremely challenging pitch. In a week or two Petanque was played there every fine day. The time was ripe to encourage some competition

The momentum of the game increased, and in the bar afterwards we encouraged the idea of forming some teams with matches between them. It was good for business too. It wasn't long before the Terminus Ticklers challenged the Hautville Bouncers to a four-a-side match to be played after next Friday's market at about five o'clock. The Terminus Ticklers were bounced well and truly into second place and the players celebrated or otherwise in the bar afterwards. The competitive spirit was now working for us. After just three weeks a challenge was issued by the upper town to play the lower town an eight-a-side match on a Sunday afternoon in the Princes Gardens at three o'clock

Lescaut briefed his trusted people in the upper part of the town about what was expected of them during and after the match. Much to our surprise the lower town just won the match, and the post mortem afterwards was full of fierce arguments which were gently led to the lesser controversial issues of the war situation. Other less competitive matches took place in both halves of the town and we encouraged the same discussions afterwards. By the end of July we were satisfied that, taking the population of Saint Flour town as a whole about thirty-five percent would support a resistance movement against occupying Germans but there was little support for resistance against the current Vichy regime. I duly reported our conclusions to London and Pascal advised de Gaulle's London organisation through his channels. Our conclusion had to be that if London wanted action in the Auvergne before the German occupation the only way forward was to use the hill men on the conditions we had outlined

There was a very busy time on transmissions and receptions over the next week or so. The radio schedules worked better now when shared with Raymond. In the middle of this period we got information that a target had come to our notice in Ussel where a factory was making cylinder heads to Luftwaffe specifications and we proposed an urgent attack. London replied, Target agreed

The Vichy news service that evening reported that a British task force was attacking Diego Suarez capital of Madagascar and was making much propaganda out of the attack that the British were trying to extend their empire by taking over French colonies loyal to Vichy France. They reported heavy fighting and assured the French people that they would repel the invaders. The BBC broadcasts later that same evening confirmed the liberation of the capital of Madagascar after only token resistance the local commander surrendering after a few hours of patchy resistance

Chapter 9

Mathilde Commands Millau

The time for Mathilde's move South was near. The situation in Millau had calmed down, and it was time to start a resistance group again in that town

Millau was strategically important. It had the only road bridge over the Tarn capable of carrying armoured vehicles for over seventy kilometres east and west. It was astride the best of the three rail routes entering the Auvergne from the South, and a junction of four important roads. Denying access to Millau by opposing forces in a crisis situation was of no mean significance. Creating the organisation that could do it at a few hours notice was to be Mathilde's first priority

Millau was much bigger than Saint Flour, about five times as many people and much more industry and employment. Millau had started a resistance movement soon after the collapse of France. It was rather loosely arranged and consequently penetrated by the gendarmerie and mlice at an early stage. Direct contact with De Gaulle's office was in place, and their first supply drop was made in December 1941. The gendarmerie and mlice swooped the day after the supply drop, securing all the supplies and arresting almost all the members, who were sent to forced-labour camps in Germany or worse. The decision to put Mathilde in place in Millau was not taken lightly, but she had local contacts and had previously lived there and a woman as head of the resistance group would not expected by the opposition

Tante Mathilde was a big woman in every sense of the word. At least five foot ten tall she weighed well over a hundred and twenty kilos, arms like hams and presumably thighs to match. She got her own way largely by bullying, especially men. If you did not stand up to her you had lost any argument at the outset. Tante Mathilde standing arms akimbo in the doorway of the Terminus was enough to put even the most determined toper off his drink

However there were other sides to Mathilde. She was a practicing Catholic in many respects, a regular communicant usually attending one of the sung masses, where she joined the singing with gusto if not musical accuracy. If father Albert made an error in the service Mathilde was the first to point it out to him and if she did not approve of his sermon he was ill advised to come into the Terminus for a week or so. She could, and frequently did, quote large passages of Scripture in support of her contentions in any argument. I never saw her lose an argument even if her adversary started quoting back at her

It was some time before I realised that her four sons were named in order of the first four disciples called by Christ. I mentioned this casually to Manuel one day which drew the remark, "She probably intended to have her own twelve disciples," he said

On another occasion when Mathilde was being talked about, Dad intervened with the remark that she was probably the most generous person in Saint Flour, and Yvette added that when she first had the news about Philippe, tante Mathilde was of more help and comfort to her than anyone, including her own family

Tante Mathilde's impending departure raised several problems. Not the least of which was who was going to take over the Dish of the Day in the Terminus. As soon as Manuel heard about her going he came up with the suggestion that, because the St. Jacques dining room no longer opened at lunch times, could he take over the Dish of the Day, and go back to the St. Jacques in the evenings. Dad went and discussed this with Madame Belmont, owner of the St. Jacques

The idea was received with pleasure, she was becoming concerned about Manuel and the fact he was not fully employed or fully paid. Mathilde was consulted and had a long talk with Manuel about the economics of the dish of the day. She obtained much of her supplies by barter and exchange deals. Manuel had guessed at this because of the price charged for the meals and he had also seen some meals not paid for

He agreed to do it on the basis that he took half the cash taken for the food as his remuneration. He would continue the supply arrangements Mathilde had built up and honour her barter deals. He was the first person I had seen Mathilde let in to her store at the back of the Terminus

I also managed to get a look inside, it was unbelievable. An opportunity also came my way out of Mathilde's imminent move. Luke and Jean tried to sell me the idea of taking over their bicycle wheel business now I had the workshop going. They told me they were doing between twelve and fifteen wheels per week, I had no idea it was as high as that; it wasn't any wonder people were already asking what was going to happen about it because the filled tyres were so much better than corks on their own.

With the build up of my real reason for being in Saint Flour I could not see how I could possibly find the time to do it. I talked it over with Dad, he was keen to have the work done at the Terminus because it would further boost the drinks business, but of course he did not have time either

I wasn't keen to have it done in the workshop because it was a quite messy and smelly business and there would always be four or five wheels in process taking up space. We resorted to asking Jacques and Jean if they had any friends who would want to take it on, if we provided one of the outbuildings for them to work in.

It worked, we had three fifteen year olds who had about two weeks to learn what Mathilde's boys had perfected over a year or so I cleared another outbuilding for them, put a secure lock on the door and left them to it

The day of tante Mathilde's departure was a Friday. On the Thursday all her possessions had been loaded on to a large truck which left as soon as it was loaded. The Terminus closed as early as we could for a family farewell party. It wasn't easy to close so many people lingered on simply wanting to talk to her

We did not want to be too late going to bed that night because Mum and Dad were going to Millau on the bus with her to help with the settling in. While they were away I was left in charge of the Terminus with Manuel and Yvette. Two of the holiday reliefs were coming in at various times to help out as well. Friday morning was our normal start, all the passengers for the early buses were served as usual and the market traders were busy as ever. Mathilde and the rest of the party were leaving on the ten thirty bus for Millau. This bus was never so crowded as the earlier one. Even though there had been a large gathering the previous day to say goodbye to her, by nine thirty there were quite a number of the leading personages of Saint Flour on the terrace waiting to see her off

The Maire himself, about half the police force, father Albert, both the doctors, several solicitors, many of the shopkeepers, some with parting gifts. Most of the market traders brought a box of their own produce of and left it on the tables for her. While all this was going on outside everybody was getting ready inside. Yvette and I were busy in the bar

Suddenly, Mathilde took me firmly into the back and through to my workshop. "I need a few words in private with you," she said speaking much more quietly than usual. "I know you are very fond of Yvette and Jean-Francois, and I know Yvette thinks very much about you. Whatever happens between you, be as honest as you can be with her, I know your problems, but treat her with love and respect or where ever you are and whatever you are, you will have me to deal with."   "I promise you I will," was my reply. She hugged me and kissed me, "I trust you'" she said. I went back to the bar rather disturbed. But it was too busy to remain disturbed

A special place had been cleared in front of the Terminus for the bus to pull in. Some other passengers were already on board. All the boxes of presents were being loaded and the bus company waived any charge for the extra baggage

Getting Mathilde her sons and Mum and Dad into the bus was a very drawn out affair. Everybody wanted to give her a hug, a handshake or a kiss as the relationship dictated. The Maire made a speech but nobody listened. When the bus was about twenty minutes late leaving the police cleared a way through the crowd for the bus to pull away. Cheers and waves all the way. Even tough Mathilde was wielding a handkerchief

Well it was all good for business. Nobody could remember a busier Friday morning and it stayed that way through the afternoon. Even with the extra help we were rushed off our feet. Manuel was on trial for his first dish of the day, but it was, of course what Mathilde had planned for the day, all he did was to cook it

It looked different, the sauce was lighter the vegetables had been cooked separately and there was a side salad, already a difference.   However   lunch didn't happen for Yvette and me, we were so busy. When we did get a quiet spell mid-afternoon I went through into the back and Jean-Francois was missing. I dashed back into the bar and grabbed Yvette, "Oh, it's all right, he's gone to stay with his grandparents for the weekend, I simply haven't had time to tell you. I arranged this so I could work as late as necessary without worrying about him. I did remember that Mum had arranged rooms for both Manuel and Yvette to live in for the week or so while they were away, and they both had keys

It started to rain late in the afternoon and the market packed up. Nobody much lingered. Manuel kindly prepared a meal for us and took over in the bar while we ate. Then he had to go off to his dinnertime job at the St. Jacques

The excitement was over and soon after the last buses had come and gone we were able to close. Yvette went off to bed. I had to cash up and make up the books. The dish of the day had produced its usual amount, but the drinks were over two and a half times our normal Friday take. No wonder we were tired. I finished the washing up of the glasses and left them all to drain overnight. I locked up and went to bed. I lay reading for a while with Sambo beside me making up for the neglect he had felt during the day and fell asleep

Chapter 10

Yvette commands Henri Dufour

I always left my bedroom door slightly ajar so that Sambo could go and get food and drink without waking me

I don't know what woke me; Sambo jumping off the bed, or somebody in bed with me. Yvette was hugging me tight and smothering me with kisses. "What do you want from me?" was all I could blurt out between her kisses

In response she ran one hand down my body pulling my nightshirt clean up and over my head in one swift movement. Then I realised she was naked beside me. We made love repeatedly if somewhat ineptly on my part. When the ardour was spent, I again tried to talk to her. She was simply desperate for love and affection. I believe I can trust you, you have shown yourself to be a special friend and I need something special from you and your promise that this remains between us alone."

"You have my promise of that and more if you need it. I believe I am in love with you, not because of what has just happened, but because of the feelings I have developed for you since my return, I am sure you must have felt something of this." I hoped that was so," she replied, curling up ever closer to me. We dozed and then slept a little. I think we woke mutually during the night with passions aroused again, and sated before we slept finally, until that dreaded alarm clock woke me. I felt I had enjoyed the best night's sleep since I had arrived in France

Yvette was still fast asleep naked beside me. I didn't want to leave her but the morning noises outside were telling me I had to get up. I just got down into the bar in time to take in the first baguette delivery. Switching everything on took just a few minutes and the first customers were in. Manuel appeared and coped with the orders for cafe complet and I dealt with the rest

There was the usual lull after the first buses had departed, and Yvette appeared, very bright and cheery and got some breakfast for us. Manuel went off shopping for some items for today's dish, giving us some time alone before the next rush. As soon as we were alone Yvette came behind my chair putting her arms around me saying, "Should I be ashamed of myself for what I did last night?" "I think you were sincere, I certainly was, and if you were sincere, then we were both being honest with each other. The problem is what happens if Philippe is alive? and what happens if I make you pregnant?" And that was when the day started to become busy. Saturday was an unpredictable day for trade. The rain had cleared overnight and the sun was already on the terrace drying everything off after the rain. It was clearly going to be a bright and busy day. As soon as the extra staff came in all the outside chairs and tables were wiped over and tidied up. Manuel returned and worked on the dish of the day. This was his first entirely solo effort and he was out to make a good impression. He had one of the extra staff working solely for him Yvette was a different girl that day, very bright and cheerful, singing occasionally. Manuel noticed and commented. "She's probably had a goodnight's sleep without Jean-Francois to disturb her." "I knew nothing about Jean-Francois going to the grandparents for the weekend until they came to collect him," said Manuel. "Then you knew before me." I replied, "Yesterday was pretty hectic, I was pleased to see you sold all your lunches, what is today's dish I asked."Today will be different," announced Manuel. "First there is a little hors d'oevres, just to clean the mouth, then a savoury rice with kebabs of lamb, onions, tomatoes, peppers and a special Spanish sauce." I'm looking forward to that;"I said, "please be sure you keep two back for Yvette and me"

Our lunchtime came, I went and found a special bottle in the cellar, a 1934 Gigondas. "What are we celebrating?" said Yvette, when she saw the label. "I shall tell Manuel it is for his nouvelle cuisine, but if you do not know the real reason I shall be desolated." She came and hugged me. Manuel's nouvelle cuisine was very tasty indeed, when he came in to see how we liked it, I gave him a glass of wine and we all drank to his success

Manuel finished his day at the Terminus after lunch: he still had his dinnertime work at the St. Jacques to do

We did not know where Manuel was going to sleep that night. When mum and Dad discussed the split employment with Madame Belmont she learnt that Manuel frequently went out late after the dinner service was over and he was believed to have one or more paramours amongst the lonelier ladies of Saint Flour. He was not allowed a key at the St. Jacques so he had to ring the night bell to get in on his return, and sometimes he did not return at all

Manuel had his day off on Sunday from both the St. Jacques and the Terminus because neither served lunch or dinner. If you wanted to eat out in Saint Flour on a Sunday you had to go up town for a very limited choice. What concerned us most was that Manuel had volunteered to start early with me on Monday to do the breakfast baguettes for the early bus

After we closed on Saturday and having cashed up and locked up, I went up to bed to find both Sambo and Yvette already there both feigning sleep but. Yvette was waiting to talk. I listened to what you said earlier today about Philippe, I am certain in my heart of hearts that he will never return

I have dreamed horrible dreams about him being mutilated beyond recognition, and I really believe that is what has happened. We were passionately in love, believe me, but I will never see him again in this life. I will always care for Jean-Francois and caring for him is my life for the next twenty years or so until he marries and, please God has his own life. But I have so much love to give that I might smother him with it and that is not good for a child. I need someone else in my life too, to love; can you be that one to me?" I took her in my arms, "I believe that I am in love with you, because I have never felt like this before about anyone else

I am also fond of Jean-Francois but what will I feel if I make you pregnant and we have two children one with Philippe as a father and one of mine and what will you feel." "I don't want any more children until this bloody war is over. I will take the necessary steps to prevent it You remember the teaching we had at school about a woman's safe period. Well my safe period started on Friday, so we are safe at present, on Monday I will go to Madame Blasé who makes pessaries that we can use outside my safe period. I know what you are thinking about what the Church says about contraception but I believe it is wrong to bring children into a world at war"

We loved each other and slept close and naked. No alarm clock on Sunday morning and I slept and slept. Yvette had been up and came back in to the bedroom with a tray of coffee to wake me. She slipped of her dressing gown and came back into bed, I pretended it was the coffee that stimulated me, much to her annoyance

She asked me if I was going to Mass that morning because she thought we had too much to do. She teased me and then showed me how and where to touch her and excite her. I realised how clumsy I must have seemed in my loving of the last two nights. My ecstasy reached new heights and that morning I learned more about a woman's body than any schoolteacher in England had ever taught me

Sunday was not too busy, the weather was good and most people had work to do outside their homes. The spring was well advanced and all the work I had put in to the back yard was paying off. Now the drains were working properly again the whole area was slowly drying out, and this included the wine cellar under the Terminus. So I was able to find another bottle of something special for our supper on Sunday

It also meant that we could use the stocks of house wine that dad had laid down in previous years but which he had not been able to reach because of the flood in the cellar and the whole of the back of the bar area became less damp

When we went up to bed on Sunday night we were both very tired and I had a four-thirty get-up time on Monday. Yvette said we ought to go straight off to sleep. She snuggled up against me and we both felt warm and happy. But the double bed worked its magic. Soon she was slipping a thigh in between mine and feeling my readiness against her. We made gentle love that night and fell into a deep contented sleep. I managed to wake at four-thirty just as the spring of the alarm clock ran out

Yvette slept on

Monday morning, absolutely hectic, Manuel was supposed to be in at five but wasn't. He didn't arrive until after the early bus had finally left about twenty minutes late. I didn't ask him whose alarm clock had let him down, or who wouldn't let him out of her bed. He did compensate for it by making breakfast for all of us

The rest of the day went well; we had two extra staff in all day. So I was able to get to my listening schedules and got a message saying four more SOE personal were on their way to us by a roundabout route and should arrive in Saint Flour in about one month's time. Code names Victor, Sebastian, Simon and Patrice

Please arrange to lodge them as Raymond. They are all trained armourers and should teach your hill men how to shoot and carry out demolition work. Jean-Francois had of course returned during Monday morning, and was requiring his usual attention from Yvette. I had been too busy to really notice what was going on. Unbeknown to me, Yvette had moved a small cot for Jean-Francois and fixed it to her bed in her room at the Terminus. She whispered it to me just as she was leaving to put Jean-Francois to bed, and came down later with a mischievous smile on her face

Of course I had to meet up with Alexis urgently. He came in late on Monday evening and waited until we had closed up. Yvette went off to bed. Alexis had been meeting up with a number of the hill men on their farms as we had agreed. "We have four new arrivals to accommodate in about a month's time," I told him, "they are armourers and are to teach the hill men how to shoot." Alexis laughed, "They will arrive just about shearing time so they will be taught how to shear sheep in exchange for learning something they know already. Perhaps you should tell London an essential qualification for the Auvergne is to be able to shear sheep

"I think I've thought of a job Raymond can do," I said, "we need a reserve Lysander strip near to Saint Flour, I can tell him the requirements he has all the necessary understanding for the job let him find us another strip. It will occupy his mind and he will feel he is doing something useful." Alexis agreed. Some days later a message from Raymond told me he had found a suitable site

On a visit to a friendly farmer at la Cham he had seen a flat upland pasture with a clear approach from the South East, "In fact," he said, "the pilot can use the same Cathedral landmark and simply a different bearing to bring him in sight of the strip. It is a little further away but a better access. The Mathis family are nationalistic and anti German. They have two sons in the French army in Algeria and two daughters active in running the farm. You ought to come and see them"

Some days later I met him at the farm and looked at the site, if anything it was better than the Barrat farm strip. Perhaps too good, any spotter plane looking for a potential landing site would spot this one. Raymond had an answer, "If we strew a few boulders all over the strip it would appear impossible to land a plane there. If our boulders are dummies on skids we could clear the strip when required and replace afterwards. The skid marks could be dealt with by the sheep in the same way as the landing wheel marks." "But where are these mobile boulders coming from?" I questioned. "I'm sure I can make them with a hollow cement shell on wooden runners with lots of small stones stuck into the surface to match the local outcrops." I liked the idea. "Do it," I said, "if not here the idea is good for any site"

We walked down to the farmhouse. Sylvie opened the door and immediately recognised Raymond who introduced me. "Yes we've heard about you coming back from Lille but if you want to see Laurent he's out with the sheep down by Coltines and won't be back until about six o'clock. But come in and have a coffee." We went into the kitchen of an obviously spacious house

Coffee was prepared and the topics of the day talked over. "Have you heard if Mathilde arrived in Millau safely?" "Not yet," I replied, "but Mathilde will always survive." "I think she's very brave to go and set up a new group in Millau after what happened before," said Sylvie." She saw the expression on my face and said, "Don't worry we know all about the resistance here and we support you one hundred percent. Anything we can do, we will do

"I was going to ask Laurent if we could use the high pasture to bring in a plane one night." "Of course you may, we are both heavy sleepers and won't hear a thing." "Well there's a little bit more than that," I said, "We would like some sheep put on there immediately afterwards to tread out the wheel marks." "Oh you mean the same as Jean Chavent did last time, but we'll need to know a few days before so the sheep are in the right place." We enjoyed our coffee and took our leave to ride down to Coltines and find Laurent

"You see you can't do a thing in these hills without everybody knowing about it," I said to Raymond as soon as we were out of sight of the farm. "Do you think they know that it was me who arrived on the plane that landed at the Chavent farm?" "We must assume that they do"

We found Laurent Mathis without any difficulty and told him Sylvie had agreed to use his pasture as a landing strip. "I'm pleased to help and putting sheep up there when needed is never going to be a problem unless it is January-February time," he said. "Whatever help you need, if we can do it we will?"

A most satisfactory day

Next day I met with Alexis, told him about the strip, explained about the disguised boulders, and reverted to the subject of accommodation for our new arrivals. He had also done some thinking, "I think we should place two with your friends at la Cham," he said smiling, "and the other two at a farm you don't know yet at Saint Laurent de Veyres."I had to go there when you were at la Cham over a sheep rustling matter." They also knew about Jean Chavent and the landing, and have also offered us all possible assistance specifically accommodation for non locals who might do some work for them, they are terribly short of labour." and that was another problem solved, two could go there

The attempt to disable the Montupet factory at Ussel took place the next night. I knew it was imminent because Pascal had recently drawn the necessary explosives and detonators from our stock some days previously. Nobody from Saint Flour was involved and we did not know the detailed plan except that the action was being taken by a group of the workforce who objected to producing anything for the Luftwaffe. The damage done was minimal and production was only delayed for a few days and not months as was the intention

The attack was investigated by the mlice and the Gendarmerie but no arrests were made but uniformed guards were installed at the gatehouse and all persons entering and leaving were controlled. There was much disappointment as this was a wasted opportunity. Any repeat would not be so easily done. Pascal was quite dismayed at the poor result and was trying to find out the reason for the failure

That same evening I reported the attack to London as well as the confirmation that we could accommodate Messers Simon, Patrice, Victor and Sebastian. When I went up to bed Yvette asked me straight out if I was involved with Lescaut in resistance matters. I told her I was and that all loyal Frenchmen should be, she agreed

85

The time passed quickly while Mum and Dad were away and Manuel and Yvette with the two extra staff worked well together. I thought a lot about our recent encounters with the hill farmers. Their attitude was so completely different to the townsfolk and decided I had to write a much more detailed report to London that was too long for radio encodement and our radio schedules. It would have to be handed to the next Lysander pilot or should a courier pass through our area he might take it. So far we had not been visited by any courier

I asked Alexis to arrange a visit for me to the farm at Saint Laurent de Veyre urgently he did so and the next day I took the early bus to Funnels where Fernando Mousier had promised to meet me. He was a man in his fifties, well built and bronzed as most of the hill farmers. He was surprised to see someone so young and asked why I was not away at the war. I explained about my leg. I waited until we were safely inside the farmhouse before talking about the real matter of the visit

"Thank you for offer to accommodate some resistance men and I would like to enlarge on the talk you had with Alexis Lescaut." Madame Mousier came in with coffee at that moment plus a bottle of something more interesting. Monsieur Mousier said, "We should soon be getting some help from this young man," "Not me personally," I interjected, "but we expect several men to arrive in about a month's time and I would like to lodge two of them here." "Is this to be on the same basis as you've agreed with Jean Chavent?" asked Fernando. "Quite similar I replied, they will be expected to earn their keep, but when they have to carry out their duties they may be away for some days." "Let us know a few days before they arrive please," said Madame Mousier, "and everything will be ready. You'll be staying for lunch of course." "With pleasure," I replied. Coffee over and we went to look around the farm

As we were going round the outbuildings a neighbouring farmer joined us. Fernando introduced Dominique Lequy and the conversation broadened to the farmers problems. Dominique said, "It doesn't matter what you do the war won't change the fact that sheep eat grass, they produce wool and meat and lambs to keep the whole thing going. You can't run more than the same number of sheep on the hills because there is not enough grass to feed them."If the government want meat to meet the quotas for Germany they will have to pay for it with real money," added Fernand

"Then there's the vermin," Dominique said, "I've only got enough powder and shot to get through this year and there is none to be had anywhere in Vichy France"

From this I learnt that these prudent hill farmers filled their own shotgun cartridges from stock they bought in nineteen thirty eight when they considered war inevitable, and they had the same problem with shells for their rifles

More neighbours arrived. I met Regis Armengaud from Local and Fabric Bezeault from le Vedrinel. "Now you've got all the farmers who run sheep on these hills present," said Fernand "I thought it was only right that they should all be here because if there are any problems we're all in it together"

I heard all about their worries, the grass was late this year because of the late snowfall and there was probably not going to be a second cut of hay for the winter feed. Did I know if the soap works was going to close because if it did then the lanoline factory would shut and there would be no local facility for cleansing their wool? They with the Maire of Saint Flour had made representations to their deputy, but no answer, and it wasn't going to be a good summer was it?

By now it was time for lunch. The hospitality offered to us was most generous and the fact that I was ready to listen to their problems weighed heavily in my favour and I decided to ask how much storage space they could find for storing the munitions from another supply drop on their land

I had noticed signs of the usual Auvergne caves and said they would be quite suitable. The immediate objection was that they matured their cheese in the caves. "What, in all of them," I exclaimed, "You must be cheese millionaire"

"Some of those caves can be very damp," said Domenic, "and access is not always easy." Fernand said he was sure they could find enough storage in the large caves in the woods on the northern slopes and it was all downhill from those caves to the road. I suggested that I might be able to arrange for some powder and shot to be included in the next drop. That got immediate attention

They started talking in Auvergnat amongst themselves in great detail. I could not understand the talk but this was clearly going to be the little extra that would get their whole hearted support. "I'm prepared to put this request to De Gaulle's office in London if you can give me the exact specification of what you need and I will stress that we need the help of people like yourselves."Their response was quite explosive. "This jumped up army captain is no use at all, what had he ever done for the farmers or any other bloody politician for that matter," said Domenic. "I can't understand why the British let him speak for France and he was once indicted for deserting his post in the face of the enemy." said Fernand. I assured them that I would try to get all of their needs when they gave me the list. Once more they resorted to Auvergnat and finally Domenic said, "We re not convinced you can deliver on your promise but if you can get also some Antilles Rum for us we'll give you whatever help we can"

The argument had taken us right through a most generous lunch and well into the afternoon. We all parted as good friends with promises to be kept on both sides. Fernand. drove me down to Funnels for the bus back to Saint Flour. "How long before you have an answer," he asked. "I will have an answer before your visitors arrive"

Back in Saint Flour I left a message for Alexis that I needed to meet him urgently. He came into the Terminus at closing time and we decided we must have a meeting with Pascal as soon as possible in Brioude. It was arranged for the next Sunday. This was going to be a difficult meeting because I had decided that our case was not being helped by any association with De Gaulle. Alexis was inclined to sit on the fence. However when the meeting got under way and the facts were weighed, Pascal and therefore Alexis, as well, agreed to ignore the De Gaulle connection and commit the British to the agreement with the hill men

Pascal also commented on the failure of the Montupet attack. He concluded that the charges placed on the machines were probably too small and that he was sure that the packing placed over the charges was insufficient

"We need an expert to do this sort of work who can reliably instruct our people exactly how to position the charges." he said, "but all the charges detonated properly so very little evidence was left for the Mlice to work on."I returned much happier from Brioude. On the return journey Alexis complimented me, "I could never have dared to put such a proposal to ignore De Gaulle's office before Pascal"

Chapter 11

More Landing Strips

We had an urgent message to arrange to receive a number of packages for onward distribution to surrounding areas. The operation was top priority and take place within five days. There would be twenty packages each weighing about twelve kilos. A list of destinations would be sent when we confirmed we had the packages. Distribution must be completed by mid August. A second message stated that the skills of Victor and Sebastian, if used, would avoid any repetition of the Montupet failure

In view of the urgency and the number of packages we decided to use our second Lysander strip for this delivery, near la Cham, because the Mathis family farm had so many caves nearby that we could spread out these parcels widely and lessen the chance of all of them being found if searches were made. It was also apparent that some of them might be there for a month or two before collection or delivery. Alexis went straight over to la Cham and completed the arrangements

Message sent to London with new coordinates for strip and approach by Saint. Flour Cathedral and a bearing of 294 degrees to strip. London replied by return giving details of personal message to confirm which night for operation. I included in this message the fact I would send a detailed report via the pilot for immediate consideration and reply. This meant that I had very little time to prepare the report. I worked late into the night with help from Alexis. With the good weather that had set in the personal message came the next day

Vichy radio was reporting greatly increased air activity over France during the hours of darkness. We had some reports from neighbouring regions about failed drops and even requests to know if drops had been made in our region by error. We had no reports of such events but in a region like the Auvergne containers could easily disappear, and may never be found. Coupled with this development we noticed the mlice starting to use spotter planes to make daylight surveys of our region

Pascal reported that they were German Storch planes specially built for such work. Two of them were now based on the airstrip just outside Clermont.

We knew that the nights were now getting too short for Lysander operations as far south as South as Saint Flour due to the low cruising speed of the Lysander. However Pascal had heard that specially equipped Whitley bombers were able to make container drops, and were even landing on some deserted airstrips, discharging supplies and taking off again while the local resistance groups sealed off the area

Pascal was anxious that we should have such an arrangement in our region. He had an excellent small airport in Clermont itself but due to the existence of a large gendarmerie force, controlled by the Mlice, in a barracks barely three kilometres from the airport he reckoned it would take a small army to isolate that area

Pascal brought this matter up at our next meeting at Brioude. Raymond now attended our meetings because of his local knowledge. The problem was that our area, the Auvergne comprised seven or eight departments of France, depending on how one thought what the Auvergne was and they were among the most sparsely populated areas of France. So who was going to invest in airstrips let alone airports? We knew of a number of places where light aircraft landed on an occasional basis. These were all grass strips of doubtful quality and reliability.

Raymond said, "there is a gliding club a few kilometres out of Rodez, I went there once with one of my colleagues who is an enthusiast but it's only a grass field although it is flat and quite high so it should drain well." "Rodez should be a good town," said Alexis, "The Police in Rodez are pro-resistance and the local gendarmerie has refused to join the mlice. When the mlice from Millau tried to impose their authority on Rodez there was an exchange of gunfire and the Millau mlice were forced to withdraw." "I will contact my friends in Rodez and make discrete enquiries"

Alexis and Raymond were nominated to explore the possibility of using the gliding club. Raymond would provide several names of members of the gliding club, as a result of having had friends there, but he declined to visit or make any approaches for his own security

On Friday Mum and Dad came back from Millau on the last bus. Everybody was pleased to see them again. Both of them spent the evening in the bar greeting customers and passing on the news from Mathilde. We all learnt that Mathilde had set up home with Alain, the father of Andrew and Pierre. Alain was staunchly anti German and anti Vichy. In general Mum and Dad were happy with the arrangement, but they were cross at not being told in advance. All

Mathilde's possessions arrived safely and now the house was reasonably comfortable

Alain was employed as a carpenter/cabinet maker in one of the local furniture factories and Mum and Dad thought I would have a lot in common with him. He had very willingly agreed to work with Mathilde in the resistance, but had no security clearance! Mathilde, jumping the gun,   again. Fortunately Dad had remembered to get his full name, date of birth and get a sight of his identity card so we could get both London and Alexis via De Gaulle's office to check his background and credentials

The good news was that he had been accepted by Luke and Jean after a few minor battles when Alain convinced the two younger boys that he knew more than they did about most things

During the time Mum and Dad had been at Millau, Jean-Francois had learnt how to climb out of his pram. In the midst of the excitement when he saw Mum and Dad again he demonstrated his new skill much to Mum's alarm. She immediately said that if I went up into the loft I would find my old play-pen which had better be used for Jean-Francois. So that became my Saturday job. After I had sent the necessary enquiries re Alain to London and Pascal, Yvette had planned to stay on in the Terminus over the weekend, but I did not know what intentions she had about where she would sleep. Fortunately Mum and Dad were tired after their journey and when the last customers had gone Yvette and I offered to cash up and lock up for the night. So they went off to bed and early to sleep

After Yvette had finished the glasses she kissed me goodnight and went off to bed. I brought Sambo in and finally locked the doors. Yvette was of course in my bed and feigning sleep again. We tried to be quiet and hoped that Mum and Dad were fast asleep+

We were up sharp on time the following morning and no comments were made. When I got up into he loft as well as my old play-pen I also found my old push-chair which I brought down and cleaned up. The play-pen needed repainting so Jean-Francois had to wait a few days, but the push-chair was in good condition and only needed a clean and oiling. So on Saturday afternoon he was taken out by Yvette into the sunshine firmly strapped into his new chariot

Mum and Dad reviewed the proceeds for the time they had been away. They were pleased at the smooth changeover Manuel had made with the dish of the day He had not lost any customers and there may even have been a slight increase. The bar takings on the day of Mathilde's departure had been exceptional and most days while they had been away we were above average. So there were no complaints about the business and the comment was made that Mum and Dad might even have a few days holiday now we had shown we could manage without them

Saturday evening was the one time Mum and Dad regularly spent in the bar with their customers and simply gossiped. There was no early start on Sunday. That Saturday night was a late one. People wanted to hear over and over again about Mathilde and Alain getting back together and all about the house they had bought. It was well after midnight when the last of the customers left. I offered to cash up for them but they sent Yvette and I off to bed and settled down to do it themselves

Yvette went into her room and waited until Mum and Dad had gone up to their room on the floor above us. Then she came in with me. She was not the least bit tired. "What do you really remember about me at school?" she asked, I laughingly said, "two lovely long chestnut brown pigtails that I always wanted to pull, but didn't dare, laughing brown eyes, some puppy fat round the waist, bands on your teeth and a giggle, but without a doubt the best looking teacher in the school." She burst out laughing, "and now?" she asked. "I find that teenager, who always attracted me, is a married woman with a son, but tragically widowed, but is still the most attractive woman I have ever met." and quickly before she had time to reply, "so what do you remember about me?"

"A skinny boy," she said," very shy, very nervous, but much brighter than the teachers thought. You should never have been sent to that school, it was the worst thing they could have done. After all look at what you are now, the shyness and nerves have all gone, you're faster at arithmetic than anyone else I know and you seem to know how everything works and what to do about it when it goes wrong." I took her in my arms, "there is one thing I still don't know, and that is what I am going to do about you Yvette, you know how I feel about you and Jean-Francois." "We must wait until this war is over," she said, "none of us know what will happen when the Germans occupy Vichy France

For now we must remain as loving trusting friends, each satisfying the others needs for loving and caring. It can only be that way." Eventually we got to sleep. Yvette woke before me when Sambo demanded to be let out, and came back to bed with a tray of coffee and a freshly changed Jean-Francois. After a good romp on the bed, Jean-Francois settled down to play with his toys on the floor. Yvette slipped her robe off and came back into bed with me, warm and naked. We cuddled and dozed

We were woken by Mum knocking at he door and coming in to find us naked together. Mum was an understanding French woman, there was no anger in her voice, and she was concerned. "Yvette are you taking he proper precautions against pregnancy?" "and you Henri, you're not forcing yourself on Yvette or taking other advantages?" Yvette said straight away, "I made love to Henri because I knew I could trust him to give me stability and balance so that I could properly care for Jean-Francois." "We have both developed very deep feelings for each other and need the physical comfort, but we cannot do anything further about it until the war is over"

"You know that you are younger than Yvette and it is usual for the man to be older than the woman." Mum said, speaking to me, but it was Yvette who answered, "We are so perfectly compatible age difference is not of importance." Later in the day mum spoke to me alone

She wanted to hear direct from me that I was happy with what was happening, I told her of my standing instructions regarding female entanglements, and that I had neither told Yvette of my real identity and could not do so, or my status. She agreed for Dad as well. Mum then took a very constructive attitude. She said she would not judge us, after all we had known each other almost from infancy and a relationship between us was quite normal and she saw it as adding to my cover

Then she said, if I wanted to convert the first floor rooms at the end of the building into a place for the three of us to live together that would be the best arrangement, and then Yvette could let her house to give her some more income. She then asked me to convince Yvette that this was the best solution

After the Monday morning rush had subsided I asked Yvette to come up to the first floor and taking her to the end of the corridor said "Mum has suggested we could take these three rooms and that bathroom and convert them into a self contained apartment for all three of us live there together

You could then let your house to provide you and Jean-Francois with more money. How would you feel about that?" She stopped dead absolutely amazed at the idea. In the end she said, "I've got to think long and hard about this, it's quite a good 'idea." "I can only think of one problem," I said," and that is that we would have no cooking facilities up here, and it would be difficult to bring a gas 'supply up to this floor." We left it at that for the time being

Alexis dropped in late the next evening to bring me up to date. He had finally managed to recruit Charles Pelletier, Yvette's father-in-law, as a group leader for the Saint Flour resistance group. He needed to advise me about this because Charles might talk to his daughter in law. Question one, had I told Yvette about my involvement with the resistance, "yes," I said," and she approves." "Have you told her about your true identity?", "No," I said, "I dare not" "O.K., "said Alexis," and then Charles Pelletier must not know either"

"Have you been told about Yvette and me?" I asked. "Well I've seen you together and nothing would surprise me." "I have asked her to marry me but she will not consider it until after the war is over and of course provided Philippe does not return, although she is convinced Philippe is dead"

The important thing is that Mum and Dad have suggested we have some rooms in the Terminus as our home and that Yvette lets her house to provide some income for her." "Those are all very sound ideas," said Alexis, "It improves your cover, but will you be able to keep your coding and decoding secret from her?" "Up till now I've done it all in the workshop and had the door jammed shut so I couldn't be disturbed. I wasn't going to change anything"

A few days later Lescaut had a long talk with Yvette. He told her how pleased he was that we had chosen to share our lives and that he completely understood why we had done it. He said, "Henri is going to be trained to use Morse code and radios so that I could deal with communications with the French authorities in England, and act on resistance matters. So when you see him with papers and pencils using strange looking lists of numbers and letters, don't ask questions or interrupt because it is so easy to make a mistake and you are very distracting when you choose to be

By the way if you do decide to let your house I do know of a family who would like to move to Saint Flour and might be interested in your house. I can guarantee that they are trustworthy and reliable"

In all the contacts I had with Lescaut he was always very correct and somewhat distant and I did not know if he was a friend or just a necessary contact. Now I saw him in a new light, not just a sergeant of police I had to deal with but as a truly considerate compassionate and helpful friend. I told him so. He responded expressing his pleasure at the way I had integrated myself into the community and he felt sure that 1 would be a real asset to the resistance movement. We shook hands and from that time on we were Alexis and Henri in all circumstances. Furthermore, as I discovered later, Alexis must have been sending good reports on my activities to Pascal and thence to De Gaulle's office

Chapter 12

Holiday in the U.K?

The taking of holidays on the religious festivals was actively discouraged by the Vichy government who stated the loss of production on those days was contrary to the public interest. Thus the lead up to Pentecost also passed virtually un-remarked

On the Saturday before Pentecost, Vichy radio announced that a strategic factory in Montlucon had been sabotaged by a local resistance group. There had been some damage to production equipment but many of the explosive charges had failed. The mlice were investigating the source of the explosives and early arrests of the saboteurs were expected

Next day we had an urgent visit from Cesaire acting for Pascal. Cesaire reported that the factory attacked was the Dunlop tyre plant. Explosive charges had been placed on all the tyre building machines timed to explode together during the night shift. At the last minute a telephone call to the factory advised all the workers to get out at once. Almost all of them did so. But most of those who remained behind were injured in the blast. The mlice stated that the unexploded charges and their detonators were of British manufacture. Pascal was concerned because the resistance group in Montlucon had denied responsibility and he believed them because they had no supplies of explosives. What did we know about it?

We were interrupted at this point by news that there were four wireless detector vans in the vicinity of Saint Flour and two spotter planes active over the volcano region where we had taken our last supply drop. I had to assure Cesaire that all of the containers we found and their parachutes had been disposed of down a crater with plenty of rock on top of them. There were of course the two missing containers plus the one in the bog. I had made a reconciliation of what we received against what we expected. I excused myself from the meeting and went to check. I was able to report that the missing items were plastic explosive, three-o-three ammunition and grenades

All the detonators were accounted for. So it did not seem possible that of our supplies were involved. Alexis asked if there were any communist or maquis involved in Montlucon. Cesaire said, "no," but Alexis said, "now we know it is the Dunlop factory and the workers were warned to get out, and we know that the rubber factories around here are well penetrated by communist trade unions, my guess is that it is a communist inside job in the factory." he added, "Pascal ought to be able to find out about this in due course because as you know, Pascal has his informers in the trade unions"

There were still a lot of unanswered questions but we could go no further at this moment. We all agreed on a radio silence until the detector vans withdrew. The one bit of good news in all of this was that our reporting system for wireless detector vans actually worked, and that some of the reporters linked the presence of the spotter planes with the vans

Although we had advised London of our radio silence and they understood we continued to receive normally from them so that when the transmission silence ended several days later there was quite a backlog of messages to be answered, including a rebuke from London about the attack made at Montlucon without the approval of London. Please explain

Most of the messages continued the exchanges about the attitude of the Vichy French people. During these exchanges questions were raised about my, written report and could I have a reason to be absent from Saint Flour for a few days to visit the UK, for a face-to-face talk about my reports and reasoning

The conclusions we had reached about the Montlucon incident were of course included in these exchanges and accepted without comment. Because relations with Alexis had improved so much over the last few weeks I felt I could talk more openly to him over most subjects. So one night after the bar had closed I asked, "Can you explain to me why Saint Flour of all places was chosen as a centre for resistance activities, and how did you become deeply involved?" "It's a long story," he said. "When I left school I went to work in one of Pascal's factories as a trainee inspector. I made some progress and was spotted by Pascal as somebody with management potential. I got a lot of special training and was sent to college at the firm's expense. Unfortunately that would have been interrupted by military service, if I had not chosen to join the police." "I enjoyed my training in the police, especially the discipline and when I completed the training I decided to make my career in the police rather than go back into the factory environment. I got rapid promotion to sergeant and an appointment to the departmental headquarters in Aurillac

Soon after that I was given special responsibility for the Saint Flour district. Then when the former station officer for Saint Flour retired in 1937, I was appointed as his successor and came to live in Saint Flour. After the fall of France and its partition in 1940 Pascal had contacted him to assess his loyalty and he eventually gave his commitment to Pascal to support De Gaulle's resistance. Pascal's instructions were to find a suitable location for receiving supplies and personnel

The location must not contain any resistance targets, be remote from major conurbations and have a nucleus of loyal French people." Alexis said," your father, I mean Robert of course, Charles Pelletier, and Cornelius Leman all served together in the 1914-18 war. They were all gassed together, all hospitalised together and all discharged together and they have remained firm friends ever since even though Robert spent some years in Lille

They were the sort of group that Pascal was looking for as a nucleus to build on, and that's how Saint Flour was short listed as a possible location. After your mother offered her son's identity for use, the possibility of replacing Henri Dufour with an English officer was picked up by one of De Gaulle's planners in London, and that made Saint Flour pre-eminently the best location. So you see, it's your entire fault."   But went on to add, "Your cover story is possibly the best ever conceived, and I believe that the only way the Germans would find you is if you are betrayed, and even then they may not believe it!"

Yvette decided that letting her house and moving to the Terminus was the best option. She had also thought about the prospect of being in the house on her own with only Jean-Francois, when the Germans occupied Vichy France and imposed a curfew

"You are probably the most attractive woman in Saint Flour and alone in the house, what could you do if a German decided to force his attentions upon you?" I said, "If you reported him it would be your word against his." "Well I could suggest several Saint Flour women who would be willing to oblige a rampant German," she said. "I think you'll be much safer in the Terminus where there would be witnesses if the matter got out of hand."

"Do you want me to pass the news to Alexis," I asked, "so that his proposed tenants can come and see the house?" "Please do". I made a point of calling on Alexis the same day. He was pleased. "In confidence," he said, "they are a married couple, the man is nominally a bus company employee but in fact he is an undercover policeman, and his wife is also a plain clothes policewoman. They are both members of the resistance and Pascal will be very pleased to see them located in Saint Flour. From this you will no doubt gather that the owner of the bus company is also a member of the resistance as are many of his employees, and he knows them all"

So Monsieur and Madame de Boni became Yvette's tenants near to the Terminus and Monsieur de Boni in the employ of the local bus company. A most convenient arrangement

"While we are talking," Alexis went on, "I'm aware of London's request for you to go and I think I've got the perfect cover plan for you. We will let it be known that you are going to spend some days with Mathilde in Millau to deal with some electricity problems in her house. Your Mum and Dad will know the true reason of course, and I will tell Yvette that you have gone to be trained for radio transmissions, and will spend a few days with Mathilde afterwards just so that you are seen in Millau with Mathilde"

It sounded ideal and I agreed."The other good news," continued Alexis, "is that the landing field near Rodez has already been used by Whitley's landing personnel". "I wonder why London did not know about that" I asked. "Now I am quite sure that SOE and De Gaulle's office do not talk to each other," said Alexis

"OK," I said, I will confirm our plan to London and tell them about Rodez and that Rodez is a satisfactory location for us to work with, and can you, Alexis, advise your people in Rodez of our plans"

I confirmed to London as agreed. The non-committal reply by return, demanded to know the source of my information re Rodez as this was classified information far above my security level. I replied that we considered it our duty to be fully informed regarding all covert activity in the Auvergne, and that one of group was aware of the use of Rodez by Whitley's and it was a far better option than anything else we could find, unless of course, London had some more classified information that was beyond our reach!

Messages became decidedly frosty. Dates were proposed and accepted with fallback arrangements in case the weather intervened. I did not know for sure the cruising speed of the Whitley but my calculations showed that flying time over France needed to get from he channel coast to Rodez and return exceeded the hours of darkness on the proposed dates even if turnaround time was zero. This worried me and I spoke to Alexis about it, he in turn, spoke to his contacts in Rodez. The reply was that Whitley's had operated into Rodez several times last summer without loss as far as Rodez was aware, but the point of entry into French controlled airspace was not known. At least there was some comfort in that reply

My departure was scheduled for a Tuesday night. Because there were no buses going South from Saint Flour on a Tuesday I had to travel by train. There was no direct service to Rodez and the connection at Severac-le-Chateau involved a wait of nearly one and a half hours. This was judged too risky because strangers waiting around at railway stations attract the attention of the mlice. So a police

98

van was laid on to meet me off the train at Severac. The journey to Severac-le-Chateau was enjoyable. It was a beautiful summer's day, bright sunshine barely a cloud in the sky and only a light south wind to move the trees. How different from when I arrived in Saint Flour

Only a few people on the train, which stopped at every station and the passengers, were constantly changing. The scenery was spectacular, we were following roughly the route of the National highway nine which is the main North-South road through the Auvergne and frequently we shared a valley with the road and a small river

When we passed Mories our small river ran into the Lot, a much larger river that had spent several thousand years carving out its valley. The Lot was running very high swollen still by the winter's rain. The scenery became even more spectacular as road rail and river intertwined their way along the gorge like valley, the river being for ever topped up by tributaries. Then quite suddenly after we passed le Viala we crossed the river one last time and started to climb, at first by easy stages up the side of the gorge and then more seriously via a mixture of tunnels and viaducts, to an upland area clearly a watershed between the Lot and the next river to the south. The climb was slow and the opportunity to view wide expanse of the Causse de Severac was welcome

At the high point of the crossing we stopped for many minutes to allow the engine to take on water before a very picturesque descent into Severac

The waiting police van driver, Max, knew Alexis well and spoke highly of him. He apologised saying he would have to put me in a cell when we arrived at Rodez for safety. "When they have an 'operation' on the station sergeant arranges the rosters so that only the trusted men are on at night, which means that when we arrive a Rodez there will be a number of policemen on duty who were not known supporters of resistance and the only way to keep you out of their reach is to put you in a cell under arrest and awaiting questioning, following further enquiries. During the evening when enquiries were complete, the police will find their suspicions were unfounded and you will be released without charge." It all happened; when the duty men changed at eight o'clock Max and I went out to dinner at a local restaurant. It was an interesting meal, not because of the food, but because neither of us knew quite what we could talk about. Max was clearly thinking I might be an Englishman, but dare not ask. Eventually his curiosity got the better of him and he simply asked "Are you going to visit De Gaulle's group or the French section of SOE?" "I'm afraid I don't understand the question," I said, and Max let it go at that. We took our time over dinner and the drinks thereafter; my pick-up time was not until after two in the morning

So a gentle introduction to Rodez by starlight was in order. I remember being most impressed by the grandeur of the Cathedral and especially the bell tower. We were just in time to hear the last peal of the day at eleven

Back at the police Station all was ready for the 'operation'. The message had been broadcast by the BBC and the manager of the flying club confirmed that he would lodge a complaint about his phone being out-of-order at one o'clock, when of course nothing could be done until the morning. Soon after one o'clock two car loads of police left to be in position to close the main road that ran alongside the airfield as soon as the plane was on the circuit. It was really quite a slick well practiced operation. As soon as the plane had signalled and passwords exchanged, the main road was closed, I left for the airfield by car, the two trucks to collect the delivery were moved on to the airfield from a neighbouring farm where they had been concealed earlier in the day

The ride to the airfield took barely ten minutes. During that time the plane had landed and unloaded into the two vans, which were leaving as I arrived. I thanked Max and was aboard; within five more minutes, plane closed up, engines were started, no warming up necessary, and we were away

The night was still clear and a quarter-moon had risen. I sat up front with the pilot and navigator. The navigator explained, "We will climb steadily so that when we cross the German controlled coastal strip we'll be high enough to be undetected by their anti-aircraft systems." We would cross the French coast around Rocheport and fly well out over the Atlantic before turning north-east for Cornwall

The pilot said the outward journey had been uneventful, heavy cloud over the channel and northern France. He came below the cloud to get a fix as he crossed the Loire, "you can't completely trust these navigator chappies, don't you know." Then the further south he flew the better the weather. He told me he had flown a lot over France before the war and could usually recognise his position if he could get a sight of a large town or river or mountains. He struck me as the ideal man for the job; he didn't ask a single question; as distinct from his passenger, who never stopped

Chapter 13

On Holiday

We landed in Cornwall at about six-fifteen. There was a hearty English breakfast waiting for us. I had almost forgotten how good bacon and eggs tasted

The plane was refuelled and we flew on to Tempsford where we were expected. A bath followed a shave, fresh clothes and uniform all ready and with the extra pip. Gas mask and a small kit of toiletries and change of underclothes were added and I was taken by car to a short debriefing session somewhere in north London and then told I could sleep for the rest of the day and relax in the evening. I was sent by car to the Strand Palace in London with instructions to make no contact with anyone not even by phone. The programme for my visit was to be: Thursday; conference at SOE headquarters, Friday; liaison meeting with members of De Gaulle's staff, Saturday and Sunday I was on leave until the Sunday evening. At ten o'clock a car would call for me to go to a meeting with a senior government official who had made a special request to meet me. Then I was to return to the Strand Palace ready for a six-thirty departure on Monday; to a future planning meeting at a location in southern England. Return to France would be from a nearby airstrip. It was a pretty full programme for which everybody else would have had time to prepare and I had not even seen an agenda!

The Thursday meeting was devoted entirely to the situation in Saint Flour. Alexis had clearly reported to De Gaulle via his network that I had integrated successfully into the local scene. I was asked for my views. "The arrangements to get me from the landing place to Saint Flour were fine except for the fact that within five minutes of landing I was expected to ride a bicycle in the dark and nobody had asked me before I left if I could ride a bicycle. The escorts were kind efficient and helpful

101

The real shock was meeting a young woman who had been an assistant teacher at my school in France. I have been told that this information was sent via Pascal to De Gaulle's office for onward transmission to you." Blank faces all around. "Is there a full exchange of information between SOE and De Gaulle's office?" I asked. Now there was some embarrassment. The chairman said that De Gaulle's office only received a summary of the information received by SOE. I was then instructed that if I especially wanted De Gaulle's office to know about anything I should send that message via Alexis to Pascal and repeat it to SOE Headquarters, but never to send a message to Pascal without copying it to SOE. A neat evasion of the real issue

Then I was questioned about the use of the hill farmers as members of the resistance, and especially why could they not attend meetings in Saint Flour, say on a Friday after they had been at the market. The temperature of the meeting began to rise. "Many of these men can only get to the market on horse-back with their goods on pack animals or in a light cart." I was clearly not believed. "Some of the hill farms are only served by footpaths or tracks that are not passable to vehicles," again I was met with blank expressions of disbelief. "Do you understand that the two Lysander landing strips we use are three thousand five hundred feet and three thousand three hundred feet above sea level and the drop zone for our container drop is almost five thousand feet high?"

"The usual means of transport in these areas away from the roads is a sled or a two-pole travois because wheels do not last long in that terrain." I had to explain the travois, "It is simply two wooden poles fixed to the halter of a horse one on each side that are joined at the back by a net or with a tarpaulin to form a trough in which goods can be carried. The back ends of the pole simply drag over the ground. It is the same as the North American Indians use, but I never expected to see it in Europe." "Although I am not a military tactician I do not believe that any occupying force could ever control the upland areas of the Auvergne unless they saturated the area with troops. Controlling the towns and the villages on the major roads is one thing but control of the upland area and its small hamlets is something else. If you have reliable maps of the area I can illustrate some of the points I have been making"

No maps were available

I saw I had their attention and went on, "If I can just illustrate a point, when we take in a Lysander at Barrat above Pagros, the planning is simple at first site, only nine kilometres, say twenty five minutes by bicycle, but after the first eight kilometres you leave the bicycle under a hedge and start to climb two thousand feet in the next kilometre and that is an average gradient of about 1 in 2! Getting supplies up and down that section is hard work. Similarly bringing new persons, just arrived, down safely, in the dark, takes time and care. I don't want to appear negative, we can deal with these problems, but you gentlemen need to be aware of our problems when making proposals about what we should do"

The chairman cut the meeting short at that stage saying that they had learnt a lot about a region they did not appear to understand and thanked me for being so blunt about the misconceptions. I was not looking forward to the liaison meeting with De Gaulle's staff one little bit after the SOE conference. I was still tired from the journey and took an early dinner. I did get to sleep quite early, but had several long periods of wakefulness later in the night. I needed Yvette

I was ready and waiting when the car arrived for me next morning and feeling much better. The meeting was on almost neutral ground in a room at the Ministry of Defence. The French exercised their right to be some minutes late

The meeting was to be chaired by a French Colonel because the meeting had been called at the express request of one of De Gaulle's advisers. The meeting opened with an expression of complete satisfaction at the way I had integrated into the Saint Flour community. Alexis had even repeated his opinion that the only way any German would penetrate my cover was if I was betrayed

Accordingly access to my real identity was to be restricted as far as possible. Even on Sunday when I was to meet a senior government official I would be introduced as Captain Henri Dufour, and I was assured that no record of my true identity existed in General De Gaulle's offices

There had obviously been a report of yesterday's meeting to this meeting. I was also pleased to find out that the Colonel chairing the meeting knew the Auvergne and totally supported my statements of yesterday regarding the terrain and accessibility. There was a marked disagreement, as expected, over the support for the resistance

Politically the French wanted the figures to be as favourable as possible and there was some activity to bring the various factions together. There was also some difficulty because some factions existed only in occupied France or in Vichy France. The general view was that bringing the factions together would be easier when the Germans had occupied all of France

I pointed out that we had made some progress in bringing the two sides together in Saint Flour by getting the lower town and upper town people together somewhat more and provoking discussion, but no real swings had been detected yet, and that we would persevere with this matter. At this point the chairman intervened to say he had a positive move to make to bring the two sides together, "Lets adjourn for lunch." Arrangements had been made at a nearby hotel for lunch in a private room. News of my liking for French food had preceded me and the Ritz lived up to it's reputation

Exchanges continued over the lunch tables. I was interested to note that I was seated with the chairman on an all-French table thus isolating me from the SOE group. I was asked some very pointed questions and had to give some disloyal answers but also criticised the French for not making their position better known to SOE. The reply was that SOE did not listen

Little was achieved at the afternoon session, only lip service was paid to the real need for greater exchange of information and better liaison. I was relieved when the meeting broke up early, after all it was Friday and I actually got home to start my leave in time for tea

I was not expected, and only my mother was at home. She was so surprised and happy. I had to tell her that as I was in England there was a chance of a forty-eight hour pass so I took it

It was only five months since I had last been at my English home and it was all I could do to remember to call her Mum instead of Maman and I had to stop myself kissing her on both cheeks. She admired the extra pip on the shoulders and was again surprised. I played it down as far as possible saying it had nothing to do with command structure and it was simply to justify pay and allowances. However she said time and time again I must have done something to deserve it. She could not understand how my uniform was so perfect; she said it had hardly been worn. I dared not comment

She said my breath smelt of garlic and I admitted to having lunch with some French officers at the Ritz. That was about as near to the truth as I got that weekend

Family news was that Charles was still based at RAF Lyneham and was home about every two months or so. Ernie was working up at Leyland and was due home later tonight. Dad was on late duty and would be in about midnight Mum said how well I looked and wherever I'd been it was good for me, she was still fishing. Mum said I was lucky this weekend. She'd just been down to Handcross on Thursday and come back with all sorts of extras and the refrigerator was quite full

Ernie came in about eight and we sat down to a meal. He didn't have much to say as usual, except that he was being transferred back to Coventry in a month's time on a new project

Once more I realised how deeply I was imbued into the French life

Although my mother was a good cook with some French influence compared to the average Englishwoman, her food was bland by comparison with what I had become used to

I waited up to see Dad when he got home and he was another surprised person. "Can't understand why you didn't tell us about your promotion?" "It only happened a week or so ago and I knew then I might get a pass while I was in the UK." He knew better than to fish for more detail

I made a point of being up early on Saturday morning. I wanted to get out to the bank and make sure all my pay and allowances were being banked properly. The bank manager was also surprised and congratulatory; there had never been so much money in my account. I drew a modest amount to cover some cash for Mum and belated birthday presents for both Mum and Dad.

It was really difficult to find something suitable in the shops. In the end I found a scarf for Mum and a tobacco pouch for Dad. The rest of Saturday was spent talking to all and sundry, and we had plenty of callers as soon as it was known I was home. So many questions asked and so many lies told in answer. It became quite sickening.I took a decision that any further visits to the UK would only have a twenty four hour pass attached

Sunday morning was a sleep late morning. Everybody in the UK seemed to be getting disturbed nights due to the air-raids and Sunday morning was the time to catch up on sleep. I was not short of sleep and was up by eight. I kept quiet and laid the breakfast table and had the Sunday papers all to myself until almost noon. When I heard stirrings I put the kettle on and made the tea

Inevitably I was asked when I was leaving. I said a car would be calling for me at ten o'clock tonight, from which all assumed I was taking a night flight to somewhere. I did not disillusion them

The car was early so the goodbyes were short and sweet. Even at the last moment Mum tried to get an idea of where I was flying to that night. The driver said an air raid was expected and his orders were to get me under cover as quickly as possible

We sped into London straight up the main London to Brighton road only turning off at Kensington towards Westminster. I lost my bearings in a number of short-cuts the driver used and did not really recognise our location until we passed under Admiralty Arch and stopped. The sirens were just sounding the warning. I was hustled out of the car and through a small door into a guard room. My papers were all checked and I was searched. Then into a lift and I made a considerable descent. At the bottom I stepped out into a brightly lit foyer. Again my papers were checked and another more thorough search. Then I was shown into a waiting room, offered coffee, real coffee, and told that I was somewhat early and would I kindly wait

The total quietness of this underground area was un-nerving. There was probably an air raid going on, but I could hear nothing at all. Eventually I was summoned by a civilian to follow him and a door was knocked upon at which a deep voice said "Enter" and I was announced as Captain Henri Dufour

Winston Churchill was seated behind a large desk with many files within his reach. "Come in and sit down", he said indicating a strategically placed chair. There was a strong smell of cigar smoke but during the interview he did not smoke. "I'm having a lot of trouble over France he said and I am asking SOE and De Gaulle's lot to let me interview as many of their people from the field as possible and that is why you are here. I have to make up my mind about what is the real situation of the French people because all of what I am getting from my experts is conflicting reports. Everything you tell me will be in the strictest confidence, there are no hidden microphones and you must tell me the truth as you see it"

He picked up a file. "I have copies of all your signals and your written report regarding the attitude of the French in Saint Flour, and I have copies of other people's signals on the same subject," he said indicating the other files. "Now I have a series of questions I want you to answer if you can, take your time, I may ask you to explain something, remember I have never been anywhere near Saint Flour

"How many times have you been in France before the war?" "Twice," I replied, "once in Rheims in 1935 and once in St Denis in 1939" and I explained about our school interchanges each year. "Did you have any contact with people outside the school?" "Not a lot I said because we were always with some of the brothers and French pupils. Then I told him about our nights out from St. Denis and going into Paris on the metro" "After your last visit in 1939 did you form any opinion of French politics?" "Not really, but there was a feeling of unease about German intentions and some discussion by the brothers over the situation in Germany

I went on to say that our school interchange in 1938 had been to Stuttgart and how I had noticed the difference between Berlin in 1936 and Stuttgart in 1938" He referred to my file "Yes I see you were educated by the Christian Brothers, and of course they are Catholic and supposedly a-political"

"Why do you think support for the resistance movement is so poor in Saint Flour?" "You have most of the detail in my reports, but in summary I believe the Vichy government is seen as just another of the long train of short-term French governments and not of real significance, and possibly a German administration when they occupy Vichy France will be better for the people

There are two points of view, but those who voice support for the resistance are usually shouted down.""What have you been doing about changing the opinions of the people?" "There is little we can do except get the fact that some people do support the idea of resistance, recognised by all." I went on to explain about the population distribution in Saint Flour and the preponderance of left wing support in the lower town against the right wing majority in the

106

upper town. Also that we intended to continue this campaign throughout the summer months" "Do you think there is adequate support from the people of Saint Flour for us to use it as a supply base for the region and even beyond?"

"Before I answer that question, can I explain about the other people who are available to assist and who do not feature in the figures for Saint Flour. If we talk round figures, the population of Saint Flour is about four-thousand five hundred of whom about thirty percent are either strongly pro resistance or could become so if stimulated. Outside Saint Flour up in the hills there are another fourteen hundred people comprising the hill farmers, their families and their workers in the area that is about a twenty kilometre radius from Saint Flour and who use Saint Flour as a market for both buying and selling. Almost without exception these people are for resistance, but we must recognise that they are the least vulnerable to any reprisals. But add these people into the equation and I believe the answer is a firm positive"

I went on to explain the nature of the terrain and the difficulty I had at the SOE conference of convincing those present that it would need saturation by occupying troops to curtail the activities up in the hills, however firmly they might control the towns and villages on the main roads. I explained the problems of the hill farmers over their ammunition supplies for their sporting guns, and how we might buy their support and loyalty to the resistance. In addition I mentioned the rumoured penetration of the hill communities by the maquis, and the probability of the hill farmers working with the maquis if we did not secure their support for our cause. "Have you any idea of the strength of the maquis?" "How do you measure the strength of a smell on the hillside?" I asked. He saw the joke. "I believe we are talking tens of people as far as the Auvergne is concerned but in the Alpes Maritimes rumour has it there are many hundreds but that they are poorly provisioned

"Do you have personal contact with any other groups?" "No, my only sources of information are what is said in the bar of the Terminus, which is clearly of low level reliability, and what comes to me via Pascal and Alexis which I have found to be generally true, the information on the Alpes Maritime maquis came direct from Pascal"

"Do I understand you to say that the resistance operations in the Auvergne should better be mounted from outside the towns?" "Yes, because that's where our strength is. If a few resistance people go out of town to be with other resistance groups, they are not at risk. If some hill farmers come into town they have a few friends around but the majority are not in sympathy with them. That is not too important now, but when the Germans have occupied Saint Flour, it will be very different situation. I believe also it is better to store our supplies up in the hills. At present I have four small lots stored near to the site of probable

107

operations but the bulk is in Saint Flour On reflection I think that was a bad decision. Supplies stored in town can be concealed in many different places but searching a town for munitions is possible and will get a result if the search is thorough enough. Now consider the problem of searching an area of five hundred times that of Saint Flour where the supplies may be, buried?, bidden in a cave?, concealed on a farm?, down a crater?, in some thickets?, when you don't know where the caves are, or where it is buried, or which crater to look in, or on which farm they might be hidden. Then if you find some of the supplies how do you know if you've found them all?

Small groups of people searching the hills would be vulnerable to attack, so some armed support would be necessary, which brings us back to saturation by occupying troops and do you think the Germans have enough troops to do that even if they succeed in recruiting all of the gendarmerie into the mlice. The hill men are proud of the fact that no government in France has ever controlled the uplands of the Auvergne"

"Do you think the Germans will actually occupy Saint Flour when they move in to Vichy France?" he asked. "There are many reasons why they should. Saint Flour is at a cross roads of the main North-South road through the Auvergne with an important East-West road. I am told that one of the reasons why Saint Flour was first considered is that it is possible to cut all the North South rail routes through the region with a group of saboteurs working out of the town. The last reason is that there is a disused gendarmerie barracks which is maintained in a certain state of readiness for emergencies so that brick-built accommodation exists for about three hundred men, an important point during the winter"

"You have made out a convincing case for Saint Flour and I must thank you for your candidness over the attitude of the French people, which I am sure you know is different from other 'reliable information' that is laid before me by other advisors

I want you to keep on providing information on the French attitude as you see it and especially if you note any changes and to what those changes might be attributed

Any reports of this sort please keep entirely separate from other matters and have them directed to me. Then send me a message via Pascal asking me to read message number, whatever it is. Then I can ask for it just in case somebody decides it is not really important enough to come to my desk, will you do that for me?"

"Yes, I will"

"Now let's see if I can do something for you, do you have any needs that are not being provided by SOE?" "Yes, two; first I consider it imperative we reach the agreement with the hill farmers and this involves what some people would call a bribe, but I don't see it as a bribe at all, as far as I am concerned we need them on our side and if they cannot run their farms properly they won't have time to resist," I had his attention.

"And your second point?" "Radio communications out of Saint Flour are not easy because of the proximity of the high ground, so that I am, for ever, having to move my two radios. At present if I am seen carrying a little case it does not matter. But when we have German forces in the town somebody will recognise the cases. I have requested six extra radios and batteries so that I can keep them at farms on the fringe of Saint Flour and use them to transmit from the farms or move them elsewhere to confuse the opposition. I have no response to my request and I need those sets now not after the Germans have moved in. What is your expectation of when the Germans will occupy Vichy France?"

I don't know any more than you do, but be sure events will occur before the end of this year that will force the Germans to occupy Vichy France and that information is for your ears only. You will have your radios and batteries very soon. Now I have one other matter for you, I do not want to hear of any more about British munitions being used by the communist resistance groups. I am of course referring to the attack on Dunlop in Montlucon"

"Following the request from SOE Headquarters I have made checks. As far as I can ascertain we did not provide any material for that operation. Pascal believes it was a strictly local job. I have checked our lost containers from our only supply drop and none of the missing containers carried any detonators. It is just possible that maquis people might have found one of our lost containers which did carry explosives."

"I will try and see you when you are next in England, and I wish you good luck which is the most important thing you need, Good night." He must have rung a bell from somewhere on his desk because the same civilian was at my elbow to escort me out of the room

I was escorted back to the waiting room and offered a brandy and told the air raid was still going on and I should wait until it was finished before the car would take me to the Strand Palace. I looked at my watch I had been with Winston Churchill just about forty minutes and I thought I had achieved more in those forty minutes than in the last four months because I believed he was determined to understood the true position in France

I sat daydreaming, at least, perhaps even snoozing, to be awoken by a voice saying," your car is waiting the all clear will sound in a few minutes." The lift again, with a difference, I was saluted as I went to the lift, and saluted again as I arrived at ground level. I wondered what strange military convention required that they did not salute me when they were examining my papers and searching me, and yet the same men saluting me on the way out! I was too tired to work that one out. Back to the Strand Palace and a reminder that a car would be outside for me at six-thirty sharp in the morning. Just four and a half hours to sleep

The drive south from London was all quite familiar to me. Being full daylight gave me a chance to see some of the bomb damage. At Streatham Hill the main road was closed due to damage in last night's raid causing a small diversion. We continued South straight down the Brighton Road as far as Crawley, then a turn towards Horsham and on to the Worthing road at Horsham. By this time I was exercising my mind as to where the planning meeting was to be. Soon after we entered the coastal zone we turned left along the back of the downs and shortly right into what I knew to be the grounds of Wiston House. I guessed right that this beautiful mansion had been requisitioned by the Military

We had arrived in good time for a nine o'clock start. There were more than twenty people in the French planning team, I was not told the name of any of them and I was simply introduced as Captain Henri Dufour a liaison officer to the French resistance. There was a very large map of France on the wall with the inevitable celloglass overlay so that plans could be made and wiped as required

I took a few minutes to study this map before the business of the meeting started. Although there was a colour code for height in the background of the map, I could find no key to the heights indicated by the colours. There were already some wide arcs drawn on the celloglass that I rightly guessed were the limits of operation of various aircraft over France under some conditions not specified

The meeting opened with a statement by the Chairman that a ruling had been made recently that Saint Flour, which he wrongly indicated with his pointer, was now established as a supply centre for central France and would meet requests from adjacent groups when fully stocked, and that it was the stocking programme that was the first item to be dealt with by this meeting

We were to work on the assumption that all supplies would be dropped by container on to pre-designated sites in lots of up to four hundred containers. It should be understood that losses of up to twenty-five per cent might occur. I was asked to comment on these assumptions and to indicate on the map the approximate position of the dropping zones we would use

"On our last drop we received, thirty-six containers were dropped, of which we recovered thirty-three. We know that one container fell into a bog and was seen to disappear together with its parachute. The remaining two have not been found. A theory has been put forward that two parachutes may not have opened and the containers undershot the drop zone which would take them into dense woodland, the woods have been searched with dogs but no result. Based on our experience of that drop we will advise a modified vector to keep containers clear of the bog

But the bog has its uses. We unpack the containers in nearby caves and the bog is a useful place for the containers and surplus packing. The locals assure me that the bog never gives anything up. Eleven men were used to handle that last drop and we could have handled more containers but nowhere near four hundred"

I put a ring round a map location. "That, gentlemen, is where we took our last drop of thirty-six containers. I wonder if any of you would like to tell me what you can about the terrain from this map"

There was a fair period of silence but I noticed one of the team was being nudged to give an answer, a shy voice asked, "May I come up to the map?" "Of course," said the chairman. The shy voice continued, "The location is clearly an upland valley quite wide with a line of trees on the north-western side and a small stream running almost straight down the centre. No habitations are shown so I anticipate the area is remote from any dwellings. Can anybody tell me what the scale of the map is?" No reply. I said, "The length of the valley is about three and a half kilometres"

A man in air-force uniform got up, "A Whitley flying at 140 miles per hour which is a typical speed for such a drop could only drop about 30 containers in that length of valley, so gentlemen four-hundred containers means twenty aircraft, each arriving overhead the dropping zone at say one and a half minute intervals." I do not think that is an operation that the RAF would be prepared to contemplate. "The arguments ranged too and fro over longer dropping zones, bigger aircraft dropping containers at closer intervals until the chairman intervened with a question."What is going happen to the contents of these containers if there are no facilities nearby?" I answered, "Our last lot of thirty-three recovered containers were all unpacked and stored in dry caves that are concealed in that line of trees shown. It took a team of eleven men over three hours to get the contents of the containers into the caves and over a week of carefully planned transport to move the supplies to their permanent storage locations"

On the same scale four hundred containers will require around two hundred men to deal with them and the nights are shorter now and nobody wants to be caught on an open hillside with their hands full of munitions;! and, gentlemen we don't have two hundred men. I have now reached the same conclusion as I reached at a conference on Thursday, you simply have no idea of the problems of the terrain. I have waited patiently for somebody to comment on the altitude of the drop zone." The shy voiced map reader intervened, "There's nothing over fifteen hundred feet" I broke in again, "The figures are in metres, the average height of that drop zone is around four thousand feet. Gentlemen you have to recognise that the Auvergne is not just a higher version of the South Downs. It is an area of extinct volcanoes some active as recently as fifteen hundred years ago. The hills are steep the terrain too rough for wheeled transport. The farmers use sleds or travois to move goods, and horses to move themselves." Travois had to be explained again. I'm sorry Mr Chairman, Saint Flour is there, not where you indicated earlier, "I said taking a marker and correcting the location of "Saint Flour. Saint Flour itself is about the same height in metres as Chanctonbury Ring, up there, is in feet," I said pointing to the hill overlooking Wiston House, "and everywhere you go out of Saint Flour is uphill to over twice the height of Chanctonbury before it even starts to level out

"Gentlemen I can appreciate why you must be wondering about the positive decision to use Saint Flour as a base, and that is all it is, a base, a name if you prefer to attach to the stocking location. Only a minority of the population will currently support the resistance movement but when you add in the hill farmers, their families and employees in the area centred on Saint Flour the balance changes

The Germans will almost certainly occupy the town of Saint Flour, they are likely to impose a curfew, especially if they suspect any resistance activity in the area, but can they impose it outside the town without saturating the area with troops?"

"The business of being a hill farmer means you have to be anywhere at any time, day or night, to care for your flocks of sheep, there are no fences on the hills. The farmers always have dogs with them who give adequate warning of any strangers active in their area. Fodder has to be moved on sleds or travois"

The farmers have already been most cooperative in disguising the marks inevitably left when a Lysander lands and takes off, but a few hundred sheep moved on to the area immediately afterwards soon graze and dung away the marks left by the wheels. So it is our intention to store our supplies out of town, because the numbers of people needed to search the upland area is vast and if they are not protected they may well come to some harm. Movements made outwards from Saint Flour would have to be made in small lots of less than one hundred kilos, by sled or travois from a remote location they can be moved for many kilometres without ever crossing a major road and passed on from one farmer to another. The Auvergne farmers claim that no French government has ever controlled the upland areas of the region and I believe them"

We broke for lunch at that stage and I was surrounded by questioners and many apologists for their total misunderstanding of the limitations and strengths of the region. The kitchen at Wiston House lived up to its reputation

Two of the RAF personnel approached me after lunch thanking me for making it so clear to them that this would always be a little and often supply situation. I made them a promise that we would soon have other drop zones worked out and further Lysander strips because we saw the need to change the sites as often as possible

The afternoon session was much more harmonious, and constructive. It was agreed that the size of the drop in containers would be a Saint Flour decision based on our ability to handle goods, on the proposed drop zone. On the other hand we promised to adjust our container numbers to be multiples of a full plane load as far as possible

All sides recognised that the occupation of Vichy France was only a short time away and conditions after that event would be at least as difficult as current supplies into occupied France. I was told in confidence later that losses recently had been in the seventy percent region with sales of munitions to the mlice by the resistance featuring ever increasingly

After the meeting broke up I had some considerable waiting. The car eventually arrived and I was driven to a house somewhere in the Petworth area behind the downs. The ATS girls from Tempsford were waiting with my French outfit and to take away my uniform and any other traces of England. There were some special parcels to be delivered to Max personally. Some messages for Pascal being sent via me so that De Gaulle's office could not 'edit' them, plus several small packets for me. A verbal caution to Mathilde re security, and not yet to involve Alain, who was still a question mark. We went through all the paper formalities before dinner, served early as my departure was at 2045

After a short way into the drive I found my bearings. We had crossed the South downs and were nearing Arundel. We arrived at Ford airfield just in time to see the Whitley land and the fuel bowser drive up alongside. As soon as the plane's fuel tanks were topped up was I was emplaned and we took off without delay into the sunset. I tried to sit up front again but was refused as we were going to fly as high as possible and oxygen would be used for the first part, at least, of the journey, so I had to sit in a cold draughty fuselage with only an oxygen bottle for company. And I needed Yvette

Chapter 14

Back to Mathilde

It was a clear night and the visibility was excellent. I had a reasonable view out of the port side of the plane. Darkness came slowly as we crossed the Channel. I had no idea of our course. Eventually I could see some searchlight activity ahead and the shape of the land slowly emerged. We were flying directly into St. Michael's Bay passing over the Channel Islands and thus extending our penetration into the French area by some significant distance before we actually crossed the coast

Our landfall must have been close to St. Malo but I could not recognise the town. We flew on and the visibility deteriorated. I had nothing to do but wait. When we did begin to descend I could see some lights ahead in Vichy France

The navigator came back to tell me I could come off oxygen and come up front if I wished. I did and we slowly descended further and the form of the land became visible again. I was surprised to find the same pilot as brought me to England taking me back again. You've got quite a lot of kit back there, and I guess you've got some mischief planned. I had seen the load in the fuselage but only a very little of it was mine. "Hardly any of that is mine", I said, "doubtless that will all disappear in plain vans when we land"

The last part of the journey was without incident and we landed some minutes early. Everything was ready. I was first off with my small packages and straight into a plain police van, not even time to thank the aircrew

Max again was my driver. "These are for you," I passed him his parcels, which he put under the seats out of sight. My packets were on the back seat. The roads were almost deserted and the journey to Millau without incident. We approached the house very quietly. Strange arrivals at that hour of the morning would attract attention from anyone. Tante Mathilde was expecting me and after a whispered "Thank you Max," I moved rapidly inside with my case and packets

Tante Mathilde was her usual domineering self but I was tired and declined to talk that evening. I got several good brandies and a good sleep for the rest of the night. The following morning I was up and about early. Tuesday was one of the market days in Millau and the market was a good place to see and be seen

Clearly Mathilde had already established good relations with many of the market traders. I was widely introduced as her nephew from Saint Flour so that people would remember having seen me there After lunch we got down to business. I was completely amazed at what she had achieved in a couple of months, and she was able to prove it by letting me attend a meeting on Thursday when I saw first hand that there were still some very enthusiastic loyal Frenchmen who clearly knew Mathilde and trusted her in spite of last December's disaster

I met Alain, the father of Matthew and Marc, Mathilde's two eldest sons. He was fiercely pro-resistance as his two boys were now confirmed as prisoners of war and who continued to be held prisoner because they would neither volunteer for the French regiments of the German army nor agree to go to work in the German war machine. I took an immediate, liking to Alain, but was disturbed about his knowing my true identity and cautioned him especially on this point driving the matter home with the comment, "Not even Winston Churchill knows my true identity." I also had a serious talk with Mathilde on the same subject conveying the reprimand of General de Gaulle. She was not impressed

However I was most favourably impressed at the meeting on Thursday, when I had the chance to speak with many of her recruits without Mathilde breathing down anybody's necks. There was here a will to succeed with any task put before them. I promised them that they would shortly be called upon to submit suggestions for local sabotage operations directed solely against any support for the German war effort being carried out locally. While this was going on I promised to establish a storage point for supplies, under their control, but located outside Millau for exactly the same reasons as at Saint Flour

When I had my final talk with Mathilde and Alain, I expressed some doubts that they could hold back some of the enthusiasm until truly worthwhile targets had been identified. I asked Mathilde to construct a list of targets for her group and to consider the supplies to satisfactorily attack those targets, turn the whole matter into request to me and I would try to provide either with our next drop, or if she could satisfy me about her own drop zone, then perhaps direct

I returned to Saint Flour on the late morning bus from Millau. It was a glorious day again and the journey uneventful except for the pleasing scenery. As far as Severac the road followed a similar path to the railway. When we came to the crossing of the Causse de Severac the road took quite a different route, much more open and probably higher than the railway. From la Mothe onwards I saw the same valley from the road as I had enjoyed from the rail journey south. I arrived in Saint Flour as the market was packing up for the day later than usual because the trade had been good on such a fine day. The bar was busy and Mum and Dad could only spare a minute or two to welcome me home

Yvette waited in the room behind the bar for a greeting that would have been quite out of place in the bar. She hugged me and kissed me saying, "Oh how I've missed you, I couldn't believe how I've missed you," "Believe me I've suffered too in the same way," I replied

Even Jean-Francois was pleased to see me, he greeted me with a sloppy kiss and trying to say' M'sieu' Henri. Madame Pelletier came in the midst of all this to take Jean-Francois for the weekend. Although he was excited I don't think he really wanted to go. As the trade quietened down Mum served supper for us and said we could have the rest of the evening to ourselves

Yvette wanted to get out into the fresh air and I didn't object having been many hours sitting in a hot bus. It was beautiful summer evening, clear and still. We followed the Ander river bank out of town. As we left the outskirts of the town the silence of the country descended upon us. Only an occasional bird call and the rippling of the river disturbed the tranquillity. We passed through the hamlet of Bellegarde greeting a few of the locals and then into complete isolation. As we approached the start of the gorge of the Ander the trees closed in on the path. Yvette led me into the trees and we hugged and kissed in a highly exciting way. We wound our way farther into the wood and found a small clearing where we could settle down on soft grass completely alone

The few days we had been apart had left both of us with needs that had to be satisfied as a matter of urgency. Clothes came off and bodies entwined in sheer ecstasy. When the ardour was spent and relaxation was taking over, Yvette remarked cheerfully, "Well that'll keep me going 'till bedtime"

We tidied ourselves as best we could but when we looked at each other we both thought exactly the same thing, "I know exactly what you've been up to." We tried again, taking grass out of hair and picking bits of leaves off of clothes. I found a comb in my pocket and that made the biggest improvement. Yvette said, "There is a lane on the other side of this wood and it will be quicker to go back that way." We found the lane and drifted slowly back towards Saint Flour. The sun had set and the light was going rapidly from the lower part of the valley. It was almost dark as we went round to the back door of the Terminus. As Yvette said, "If we go through the bar looking like this, the secret will be out"

116

That was night when I realised that I was without any doubt completely in love with Yvette and I told her so. She responded and eventually we both fell into a dreamless and wonderfully deep sleep. As soon as we were downstairs next morning Alexis was in the bar with Raymond

There were also lots of other people so we went through into the workshop for a talk, messages had been coming in thick and fast since I had left England and although I had left Raymond to keep the listening schedule he did not have access to all the codes and replies were needed urgently. I had to lock myself away for all the morning decoding, and encoding some replies after lunch. Then a late evening meeting with Raymond and Alexis at his home to bring them up to date and get their agreement to some of the replies. I did not get back to the Terminus until after one in the morning. Sambo was waiting for me at the back door and was pleased to be let in. I crept upstairs to our room and found Yvette still awake and worried at my absence." Don't you want me any more she questioned?" I had to tell her about the large number of messages that I had to deal with and that I had been at the home of Alexis, and then we settled down to console each other

On Sunday morning we had our weekly long sleep. Yvette woke me about ten-thirty with coffee and some briocherie. Soon after we had eaten I asked her if we could be serious for a while. She was immediately alarmed and thought she had displeased me in some way. I calmed her down and told her that I was worried about how much money she had to live on. She was always making and mending for Jean-Francois and was very frugal with her own expenditure. Jean-Francois was now walking better every day and his needs would grow rapidly. I told her that I had plenty of money coming in from my repair work, but I could not of course tell her that I had only to ask to have any money I wanted from Alexis and Pascal. I went over to my trousers and peeled off four thousand francs notes from the money in my pocket, rolled it up tight and gave it to Yvette saying, "Look I have far more money than I need, please take this and use it for whatever you and Jean-Francois need," Yvette was clearly embarrassed and more so when she realised how much I had given her. It took me a long time to convince her that I was not paying her for her favours. I had to insist repeatedly that any favours she gave me were beyond price and that she had always done so much for me with the special attention and encouragement at school and now she needed help and I was able to help her and Jean-Francois who were without doubt the most special people in my life.

Eventually she calmed down completely and we did have our first serious discussion over money. She did eventually accept that she could call on me for anything she needed. She knew of course that I was earning significant money from my repair jobs but had no idea how much because I never charged her for the jobs I did for her. 1 also tried to explain what might happen when the Germans occupied Vichy France. It was likely that Vichy Francs would become worthless and be replaced by some sort of occupation money as in occupied France at present. I also told her that I was going to use most of my Vichy Francs to buy gold from the Salomansons, and give it to her for safe keeping so that whatever happened to me or to Vichy money she would always have something she could sell to provide for her and Jean-Francois in whatever was the currency of the moment. I do not think she really understood but she did agree to hide the gold and to use it as necessary, one piece at a time

From that time on Yvette's life became a lot less stressful and it showed in her features, the strain lines around her eyes disappeared even when she was asleep.

Chapter 15

Gold

The arrangement with Manuel over the dish of the day was working out so well that he needed to spend more time at the Terminus than at the St Jacques. With imminence of the German occupation it was unlikely that the St. Jacques would have many summer visitors. In a talk between Mum and Madame Belmont it was agreed that Manuel could move into the Terminus but on the understanding that he was always available on any evening when the St. Jacques needed him. Manuel was approached over this. It was quite clear that the attraction to Manuel was that at the Terminus he had his own key to the back door so that if a particular liaison did not come up to expectations he could return to his own bed without having to wake someone at the St. Jacques to get in

He was given one of the guest rooms on the first floor as part of his wages. Manuel had become an attractive proposition to several of the young and not so young widows and lone women of the town and slept away quite frequently. I teased him about this but he simply said, "I am doing an important service, I promise nothing but companionship and satisfaction." My guess is that at any one time up to eight women were depending on Manuel

I spent much of my time on Sunday coding and transmitting and I had a further meeting planned in the evening with Alexis, Felix and Raymond. Monday was going to be the start of a busy week. While I had been away a further two arrivals by Lysander had been arranged via Pascal and using our Barrat strip.

The two arrivals were simply to be passed on to the safe house in Brioude, whence Pascal would take over. They would finish the night of their arrival at the Terminus and leave for Brioude on the first bus of the day. Night of arrival planned for Wednesday with Thursday and Friday as fallbacks. The same

Lysander would bring my extra radios and batteries and this message was sent on the Wednesday after I had met the senior government official, he meant what he said

It was our usual pilot again. I quizzed him about his range and hours of darkness. "It's simply a question of weight, speed, engine-power and fuel capacity. I've got extra tanks of fuel instead of cargo, a supercharged engine to use the fuel and that means more speed and you can guess the rest. See you again soon"

Now we had the extra radios, Raymond and I could completely rearrange the send and listen schedules between us, and the pressure of the communications was much reduced. Our four new friends coming by the roundabout route were expected to arrive in Millau in six weeks time and would be passed into the tender mercies of Mathilde by their courier. They could rest up in Millau for several days while arrangements were made for their onward travel to the Saint Flour area

Now I had got the agreement of the senior government official to bribing the hill men with their sporting gun needs we had to get exact details of what they wanted. I asked Felix and Raymond to share this task and get me a final list by the next weekend and to be sure that the amount they asked for would cover their needs until the end of 1945. Pascal had also requested supplies for the sabotage of the Montupet plant in Ussel as a matter of urgency. Prototypes of the cylinder-heads made at Ussel had been approved by the Luftwaffe and full scale production had started. Pascal had the cooperation of a section of the workforce who could lay charges alongside the production lines during the nightshift I agreed to Pascal drawing whatever he wanted from our northern stock and advised Claude Bonnefoy, at Orphanges, to release supplies to Pascal on request and to advise me of what was used so it could be replaced

Alexis and I handled the reception of Messieurs X and Y on Wednesday without incident. After the exchange of passwords I don't think they said another word except yes and no and please and thanks until they got on the bus at seven-forty in the morning. Each of them clasped a small case which they never let out of their hands. We fed and rested them at the Terminus and they boarded the bus exactly two minutes before it departed

Two mystery men

I finally went shopping at the Salomansons Friday lunchtime. I looked at a number of items but none of them were quite what I was looking for, not heavy enough and too much gold smiting to pay for. After much contemplation time one of the sons came out into the shop, I think he had been listening to the conversation. "Would you really be looking for something like this," he said picking out a small gold ingot from a draw, "there's really quite a demand for them nowadays." "What weights do you have," I asked. "From ten grammes to one kilo," he replied, "but when you come to sell them you would probably not want to sell more than fifty grammes at a time, I would recommend you think in terms of twenty and fifty gramme ingots." "Thank you for your advice," I replied, "Can you tell me the price and the fineness of the gold?" "The fineness is always 990 and the price is as set out at the Vichy bourse on the day of purchase plus our commission of two to five percent depending on how much you buy. I advise you to think carefully about this purchase because the price has been rising steadily for over a year and we believe it will continue to rise until the Germans occupy Vichy France, but after that it may fall because that is when people will start to sell. Today's price is 228.16 Vichy francs per gramme plus our commission as I explained." "Thank you for your advice", I replied, "and I will consider the matter over the weekend and return on Monday

My next port of call was the police station where I was lucky enough to find Alexis and he was not so busy as to send me away. When we were alone I asked, "Is there any limit as to how much funds I can draw on you for?" "Not really," he replied, "I was wondering when you were going to ask for some money, you've been here over four months and not drawn a centime, all you have to do is to tell me if it is to come from your account in England or if it is for resistance work which would of course include your subsistence." "Well I need a hundred thousand francs on Monday and it should be against my English account." "You should have been drawing about five thousand francs a month while you have been here you know so I can provide say thirty thousand francs to cover your first six months here without any question whatsoever, so I would suggest you take advantage of that and take the remaining seventy thousand from your England account." "Thank you Alexis," I said, "As always your advice is sound and I accept it." "Well," he said," if you call here after say eleven on Monday morning the money will be ready, what size notes do you need?" "Eighteen at five thousand and ten at one thousand will be fine".

"Changing the subject now we have the opportunity," Alexis continued, "Felix and Raymond have finished their list for the hill men and I want to discuss it with you, but not now, can we meet at closing time this evening at the Terminus?" "Yes please do, I'll keep some supper back for us

When Alexis arrived that evening in addition to all the details of the needs of the hill men he had also received through his usual channels Mathilde's list. We reviewed the hill men's list first. Felix and Raymond had contacted over a quarter of them and multiplied up from that figure. It was quite considerable. Some of the hill men wanted to know how they were going to have to pay for these supplies and this was an issue with some of them. We hadn't even thought about that one. We made a policy-decision, all supplies were to be regarded as a

121

present from Saint Louis of France. When we examined the list in detail, it seemed completely reasonable."What contingency should we put on?" Alexis asked, "I think twenty percent should be ok" so we simply increased the list by a twenty percent just in case

Mathilde's list was another matter. If she had added in a few personnel carriers and other heavy vehicles it would have been enough to equip a brigade. I reminded Alexis of my reservations about their over enthusiasm. We decided to bring in about one third of her requests, and to sweeten the blow by giving her immediate access to the stock at Tremouloux under the control of Frederic Brenot for urgent needs. We promised to get supplies into Saint Flour for her and to establish an extra stock point nearer to Millau for her exclusive use. Alexis under took to communicate this to her. Alexis did not have any particular hill farm in mind and said he would have to make some careful enquiries because the proposed location was strictly in the police region controlled out of Millau

Things were moving apace now and I was in for a busy time complicated by the fact that there were now four mlice radio detector vans operating around Saint Flour. I arranged for Raymond to come into the Terminus late on Saturday afternoon and asked Alexis if he could bring Vincent and Felix as well

I was determined to try and confuse these detector vans

By now it was almost two in the morning. "It's just as well my wife trusts me said Alexis as I let him out the back door." And just a few minutes after as I was finally tidying up Manuel let himself in. "Did I see Lescaut just leaving?" he asked. "Do you think if I did not see you coming in you could forget you saw anybody just leaving?" "Of course", he said reassuringly Fortunately Yvette and Sambo were both sound asleep and I managed to creep into bed without disturbing either of them. The morning was different matter. Sambo woke Yvette to let him out. She came back to bed and woke me requiring attention. "What time did you finish last night," she demanded, I replied, "very late and I'm going to be busy all day today and if you can prevent disturbances I would appreciate it, and after today it will get better, I promise"

The four radio detector vans stayed around the area all the weekend, and appeared to be active in so far as they homed in on four locations during the day according to the sightings we had reported, but none of the locations had any connection to us. I was puzzled we never transmitted for long enough for any detectors to home in on our transmission points. They seemed to be quite slow in their movements taking over half an hour to close in. When they did close in they did not take any action. So what were they doing?

We started our transmissions on Sunday at the proper times limiting each contact to ten minutes. Our start up of transmissions did not appear to concern the detector vans at all. They preceded in just the same manner as when we were silent and we experienced no interference with our schedules which we completed comfortably on Sunday

Monday morning was its usual chaotic self. Later in the day I explained to Yvette that I would be collecting some gold to be hidden in the Terminus and that only she and I would know the hiding places. I think she understood why and that whatever happened to me, the gold was hers to use as and when she needed it and that it could be sold for whatever money she needed at the time

Shortly before lunch I called at the police station and Alexis had an envelope for me. I went away from the police station and carefully checked that I was not followed, and made my way to the Salomanson's shop. The same son, Ezekiel came out to serve me. I told him I wanted five fifty gramme ingots and ten twenty gramme. He suggested I came with him into the back of the shop just in case anyone else came in while we were making the business. He left me sitting in his office and came back a few minutes later with his scales and the ingots

He weighed each one in front of me and showed me the fineness mark. The weights were exact in all cases. He packed the gold into a compact little parcel and telephoned someone to find out the days price. "That is four hundred and fifty grammes at two hundred and twenty seven Francs ninety-four making one hundred and two thousand, five hundred and seventy-three francs exactly, plus our commission. How do you propose to pay?" "I will pay cash," I replied. But before that I may also like to buy that butterfly brooch I saw in the counter display, could I have a closer look at it please?"

He went and brought the brooch to me. I had noticed that Yvette wore the earrings Jean-Francois gave her for her birthday quite regularly and I was looking for something to complement them. When I looked at the brooch it was a charming, design and beautifully made, set with tiny stones in the wings and eyes and fitted with a loop of gold at the back so that it could also be worn as a pendant. Ezekiel said, "The brooch is expensive, the stones are only tiny but they are real and well cut as you can see, and of course there is much work in claw setting those tiny stones so that the claws hardly show," he passed me a jewellers glass so I could see the settings. "How much are you asking," He hesitated. "Am I right in thinking this might be for a certain young lady who used to teach you?" I'm sure I blushed, "yes it is," "I am going to talk to my father and see if we can make a special price for you. You've been a good customer this morning"

Ezekiel came back with his father and we all sat round the table. Monsieur Salomanson asked me if we were planning to leave France, I replied, "No" the gold is for a reserve against whatever currency might be imposed on us by the Germans when they occupy Vichy France." "It's a wise precaution," he said. "If you do have to sell, it may not be easy but I can give you a name and address in Aurillac where you will always get a fair price if you tell them you

123

bought from me" He wrote the name and address on a piece of paper, it was a quite typical French name, I was surprised

"That brooch," he said, "was made here in our own workshops, there is not a lot of gold in it and the precious stone chips have little value, all the value is in the gold-smiting and that is something I can give you. We may appear remote from the people of Saint Flour but we know who are the loyal French and a little gift to deserving people like yourself and your new partner is something I am proud to make"

I paid for the ingots plus only two percent commission. The brooch was put into a pleasing little box with a gold chain to use it as a pendant, for Yvette. I thanked them for their generosity, shook hands with Ezekiel and his father, who held on to my hand for some time, and said, "Do you have any idea when the Germans will come?" Ezekiel, hearing the question walked away. "Monsieur Salomanson," I said, "you have been most kind and generous, and I will tell you, in the strictest of confidence, that I know certain events will happen this year that will force the Germans to occupy Vichy France before the end of the year." "Thank you," he said, "I thought you would know"

On my way back to the Terminus I met Alexis by chance. 1 suggested a drink and we went into a bar opposite the Cathedral. "This has been on my mind for some time," I said, "but when you left the other night, a minute or so later Manuel came in and had seen you leaving. He must be wondering why you were so late in the Terminus and he could have come in while we had lists spread on the table. You know he's now living in and often goes out to various liaisons around the town and could come back at any time." Alexis recognised the potential problem," We need to have a serious talk with Manuel I think and see how he feels about the war"

Mid afternoon when I returned to the Terminus I managed to get Yvette on her own for a while. I gave her the gold Ingot parcel with the suggestion she think about where to hide the ingots, and then I gave her the little box saying it was a belated birthday present from me. She was thrilled and immediately pinned it on to her blouse. Then she thanked me as only Yvette could

We took Manuel on one side later in the week and asked the questions

Manuel's attitude was that he was a neutral, it was not his quarrel, and he was a Spanish national trapped in Saint Flour by the war. Yes he realised there was a resistance movement and that various people were involved, but he would never mention such matters to anyone, and in any case his Spanish nationality absolved him from answering any questions at all on that subject. We both formed the opinion Manuel was a man of his word and could be trusted

After Manuel had left us Alexis said that what Manuel was doing was quite understandable and that when the Germans moved in it would not be long before German soldiers would be sleeping with lonely Saint Flour women. I doubted this and said so. You've not been invaded for over nine hundred years, you've forgotten all about the 'spoils of war'

When we have a number of German soldiers in town separated from wives and families, it doesn't take long for the lone male to find the lone female and for natural needs to be satisfied"

I took leave to doubt this. Alexis went on," I will bet you that within two months of the German arrival some Saint Flour women will be sleeping with them." "Well then," I said, "Manuel will get a night off now and again"

Chapter 16

Dam Busters Again

The attack on the Montupet factory at Ussel took place on the night of 20th June. Although the explosives were taken into the factory and laid alongside the production lines and exploded completely and on time, there was little damage. Production was halted for only two days. This was a great disappointment and no immediate explanation was known. We had wasted a first class opportunity for want of attention to some detail and it was vital to find out what it was. As this was one of Pascal's operations I required him to find an answer

The summer of 1942 was not an easy one in which to convince the average Frenchman that the Allies were going to defeat the German-Italian-Japanese axis. Even though the USA had been forced to enter the war we had not yet seen much effect of this in Europe. The German conquest of the Balkan states was complete and they continued to advance in both Russia and North Africa. We began to hear of pinprick assaults against the Germans in occupied France and the inevitable retribution of the Germans against the French people. This was not the atmosphere in which the French were going to flock to the colours to make further attacks against the enemy. We were also hearing that the main activity against the Germans came from the Maquis and not the De Gaulle inspired resistance

The two attacks on the German war effort near to Saint Flour had been only quite minor events with little effect and thus were considered insignificant. So far, although the gendarmerie were investigating, no arrests had been made

During the longer days of summer I expanded my range of contacts considerably in Saint Flour and more especially among the hill farmers. People moved around more these long warm days and I was constantly meeting people who knew me and whom, In fact, I had never seen before. It would not have been possible without the intense support of all my family, Yvette and Alexis. Whenever possible I had someone with me. Late in June when I had arranged to meet Raymond who had just had his beard and moustache trimmed. What a difference in his appearance. A full beard plus a generous moustache on a bronzed complexion and dressed in his farm clothes he could pass as any of the local hill men or maquis. He had got to know many of the farms suggested by Alexis and had done some work for most of them. He had even extended his contacts by visiting some other farms recommended by his new friends simply to extend the range of people who now knew him

"I think its time you and I took some walks together down the valley and I'll point out the salient points of the dams and how they will have to be blown," he said. "The valley of the Truyere is not too much of a problem but after the confluence with the Lot the problems get more complex and probably more important

It will be easier for you to understand when you have seen the relative sizes and location of the dams in the valley of the Truyere. We should do it on foot otherwise we might be too conspicuous. The dams are all guarded by the gendarmerie but not all the time. You and I should be on a little walking holiday and look the part"

I agreed with him, he was now ready to start playing the special part for which he was there. "I am prepared to spend next Monday Tuesday and Wednesday with you, how far can we get in that time?" I said. He thought for some minutes. "If we make an early start on Monday we can do all the six dams on the Truyere, the dam on the Lot is much farther and the problem more serious, we'll have to have some form of transport for that part." In the end we agreed I should arrive at the Barrat farm in time for breakfast

For me that meant a departure immediately after we had seen the Monday breakfasts on to the bus to Clermont. The bike ride to the Chavent farm took me about half an hour. It was a beautiful Summer morning, bright sunshine on the hills but shade for the roads in the valleys. I was looking forward to an intense three days on a reconnaissance to plan an event potentially as destructive as the Dam Busters of the Ruhr

We intended to assess the first three dams on this trip entirely on foot using footpaths sheep tracks and country roads. We set off over the hills to by-pass Saint Flour and reach the lake formed by the dam at Grandval on its north shore. Once clear of habitations Raymond began to tell me about the river system

"The little river, the Ander, which flows through Saint Flour goes into a flooded gorge about two kilometres south of the town and that is the start of the lake we will get to about lunch time. The river Truyere rises in the hills of the three sisters near Saint Alban and joins with the Ander at Garabit. and we'll have

127

our lunch somewhere near there. The lake formed by the Grandval dam is the largest of all the lakes. It won't be full at this time of the year but there will be a lot of water there. We have to estimate how much"

We walked mainly on minor roads, there was no traffic. Raymond had used his time well to learn his way around. We arrived at one high point where he showed me the meeting point of the Ander and the Truyere. Both the rivers were at the foot of deep valleys so the confluence was in fact part of the lake. We could see that the water level was sometimes higher than today. Raymond said, "it's lower than last time I was here by over two metres." "When was that," I asked . "I came here two days after I arrived," he scribbled some figures in a small notebook. A few minutes breather and to take in the magnificent view and we were on our way again. We passed through a small village with a ruined chateau just above the lake. An hour later we arrived in the hamlet of Grandval. "If we climb to the top of that hill there is a perfect place for lunch and a perfect view of the dam"

I had never seen a major dam before. What I saw was a thick concrete wall rising several metres above the water level completely closing the valley and forming the lake. "It's much more impressive from the other side," said Raymond, You'll see that after lunch. While we were eating Raymond was making notes as he counted the numbers of layers of concrete visible above the water level through his binoculars. "That will be more accurate than a guess made at the side of the lake. "he said. I borrowed his binoculars and had a closer look at the dam. "There are armed Gendarmes at each side of the dam." I said. "Of course," said Raymond, "it's strategically very important. All dams are guarded"

We walked back to the hamlet and walked along the road to the bridge just below the dam. The dam was much more impressive on the downstream side. About 40 metres high and shaped to the size of the valley, but there was no water flowing

All of the water passes in the cliffs to the generating station just there, "Raymond said pointing to a large concrete building just below the dam and the water could be seen leaving and re-entering the river. "The dams on the Truyere generate about eight percent of Frances electricity," he added

Below the generating station the Truyere narrowed and entered a steep walled gorge. "We can't get any where close to the river until the next dam at Lanau." said Raymond, "and we'll stop for the night before we get there"

Raymond had arranged an overnight stop at one of the safe farms given to him by Alexis Lescaut. After about a kilometre we left the road and took to footpaths The going was rough with continuous climbs immediately followed by steep descents. Late afternoon we arrived at Chassagne and the farm of the Cappelle family. "How is the old tractor going," was Raymond's question after the usual greetings, "quite well," replied Louis Cappelle, "still burns some oil I think but it has not seized up again." French country cooking at its best with their own wine from their own small vineyard, a rarity in the Auvergne, a good night's rest and no payment asked or expected, repairs and service to a tractor are worth something too

We had only about one kilometre to go to the next much smaller dam at Lanau. "This dam is really here to provide sufficient head of water for a small generating station, "said Raymond. The narrow gorge was very noticeable on both sides of the dam. As soon as Raymond had completed his notes on water levels we hitched a lift on the main road to Chaudes Aigues and Lacalmi. From Lacalmi we were able to catch the local bus to a point only about half a kilometre from the next big dam at Sarrans. "If we had tried to walk from Lanau to Sarrans it would have taken a couple of days and perhaps cost us a sprained ankle or two," remarked Raymond

We approached this dam from downstream. The first thing we saw was the generating station and beyond it between cliffs on each side of the river a narrow but high dam. "How on earth did they manage to get all the equipment in here to build the dam and generating station?" I asked. "They built a special road on the other side of the river," replied Raymond. We climbed up the steep sides of the valley to a belvedere on the east side of the river. From there Raymond got his notes on water levels and I could see how they got the equipment in and out

From our viewpoint looking upstream we could see how the gorge of the Truyere had widened immediately upstream of the dam and formed a lake stretching as far as the eye could see, not as wide as Grandval but much deeper. The new road built as part of the dam project continued over the top of the dam and joined up with a narrow country road on the eastern side. We crossed over. Armed Gendarmes demanded our identity papers, the first time I had needed to produce them, a moment of some tension, but it was simply a routine check, we were not regulars on this bridge

Once over the dam we took a tiny road along the top of the cliff above the river. "It's only four kilometres to the next dam by river," said Raymond, "but over nine by road. We'll go across country and see if we can find the dam by instinct." It was very tough going but Raymond's instinct was good and in less then three hours we had found the dam at Barthe

If I had any queries about how they built the dam at Sarrans I was totally beaten to answer how they built the dam at Barthe. Although there was no generating station the dam itself was large and there was no trace of any road approach. "This is not a very important dam," said Raymond, "there's no generating station and it's function is simply flow control" "But how did they build it", I insisted. "I seem to remember that there was a road built but as there was no generating station and the local people objected to the cost of maintaining the road it simply faded away"

Our work was over for the day and we were lucky enough to get a lift to Saint Amans where we stayed in the Auberge as holiday makers

"Not far to go today," was Raymond's greeting at breakfast. Five kilometres and we arrived at the Couesque dam. It was large with a good size deep lake behind it. "This is the last dam with a generating station attached to it," said Raymond, "do you realise that every drop of water that passes here has generated electricity four times. How's that for economy"

I was impressed. We made our observations on water levels and noticed that this dam was not guarded. Our walk to the last Truyere dam at Cambeyrac was entirely along the bank of the river. The land was somewhat lower and less hilly, the river flowed more slowly, there were even a few boats to be seen. The dam was not as high as the others and it was solely for flow control. We found a quiet spot where we could talk.

"By the way you are English aren't you?" Raymond asked this right of the blue. "Yes of course I am," I replied. "Why do you ask?" "Because Jean Chavent said you were the son of the owners of the Terminus." I explained my cover story to him and swore him to absolute silence.   "There are only five persons who know and the number must always be kept as small as possible." Raymond said "All I was told about you in England was that you were established here and I was to keep you informed of all my needs and that you would handle all my communications"

For that matter I know very little about you until my last visit to England when I was asked how you were accepted, and then I got a few more details. You must have been quite a find if they had this project in mind." "They got the idea following the success of the dam busters raid and I believe there are similar plans in various parts of Europe to be activated if necessary when Europe is invaded. When my family returned to England I had to find a job and it was not easy so I joined the army. Much to my surprise they understood my French qualifications and I was commissioned into the Royal Engineers. Then there was the sudden order to attend a meeting in London, required to sign a more extensive version of the official secrets act, and this project was offered." "I wonder how many files they had to read before they found you," I said, "and had the common sense to recognise the value of their find"

"What is your first impression now that you've looked at your former workplaces with very different ideas in mind?" I asked. "I need to convert my observations on water levels into weights of water and work out how long the intervals between the blowing of the dams should be and make intelligent guesses at how much damage the water might do to the bridges over the Lot further downstream. How much water is available depends on the time of the year and how much water they have used for electricity generation, and nobody wanted to even guess when the invasion will take place. Do you know?" "No," I replied

"My understanding is that our job in the Auvergne is to prevent German forces in the North and South from linking up when the invasion takes place. The Rhone Saone valley is to be closed by groups operating out of the Alpes Maritime and the Grenoble area plus heavy air attacks on that route further north. Our job is to prevent any movement through the Auvergne and to do all we can to assist the groups to the west to cut the North-South road and rail links between the Auvergne and the coast"

"But the Germans don't have any troops in the South," said Raymond. "Once again in the strictest confidence, I have been told that the Germans will be forced to occupy Vichy France before the end of this year and that will change the rules of the game." "Now I understand." We both relapsed into silence

"The best way back to my place from here is via Aurillac and then the train to Talizat, then it's just a couple of kilometres over the hill to Barrat, and for you another bike ride, is that ok?" "Certainly," I replied, "This trip has been worthwhile, we've done what we set out to do and I feel we understand each other much better"

We went By bus to Aurillac and then as agreed. I finally got back to the Terminus in time for dinner, tired but feeling fitter than I had for some months. "Hill walking is good for you," said Mum

Raymond spent several weeks after that in exploring the Lot valley to complete his assessment of the damage that might be done by blowing the Truyere dams. His exploration of the Lot valley was followed by a considerable silence

Chapter 17

Summer Arrives

Now the weather was warm all the time and I noticed some other men were wearing shorts I decided it was time to show everyone I did in fact have one leg smaller than the other.

There were no actual comments but I did notice several persons looking hard at my legs, the one exception was Dr Bodanski. He stopped his pony and trap beside me one afternoon when I was returning from a meeting with Raymond, and after passing the time of day he said, "You're really walking very well. I think I would like to have a closer look at that leg and complete your medical notes with my conclusions

Yes, of course doctor," I had to reply, "next time you come into the Terminus, we can go through to the back and you can examine my leg as you will." I mentioned this to Alexis the same evening. He was surprised but said, "I am sure whatever conclusions he draws will be confidential but if another doctor takes over the practice there might be a potential problem. Listen very carefully to his remarks and we'll talk again after he examines you. He might even forget all about it

"But he didn't. About two weeks later he found me in the bar at the Terminus and reminded me. We went through into the back room. I sat down and took off my right shoe and sock. "Your calf muscle has built up quite well, I should think you've been standing quite a lot in that engineering factory?" "Yes quite a lot I said, and a lot of walking about." "Your foot is still as short as ever," he said, as he checked the movement of the ankle and toes, then as he ran his hand up my leg he found the join in my Achilles tendon

"That's very interesting," he said feeling all around it, "I didn't know Professor Elias was using that technique for, correction of a club foot as early as that. Joining the tendon in that position was developed by an English surgeon,

Alan Todd, I think was the name, at one of the London teaching hospitals. Does that join ever give you any problems?" "Nothing at all," I said," only the same old problem of a slightly weaker leg that gets tired more quickly than the other"

"I think what I am seeing is the best correction of a club foot it was possible to achieve at that time. Thank you for letting me see it again. You understand it will never get any better than it is now and it's far too late for any further surgical correction. At least it keeps you out of this wretched war." "Thank you doctor", was all I could think to reply

I left a message for Alexis to contact me urgently. He called in the same evening and we went through to the workshop as if he wanted a repair done

"Was he right in naming the English surgeon," was the first point Alexis rose. "Yes," I replied, "It was Alan Todd at King's College Hospital in London who corrected my club foot." "When did he complete the surgery," "Early 1932," I replied. "And when was Henri Dufour's surgery completed?" "1934" I replied. "So it was possible that Professor Elias could have known about the technique if Alan Todd published his work promptly." "How old do you think Professor Elias was when he operated on your leg?" I looked askant at Alexis. "Oh what a damn silly question," he said, and we both laughed

"I'm going to make some enquiries about Professor Elias especially about his current whereabouts, and I'll get our police surgeon in Aurillac to trace the published work of Alan Todd on club foot surgery and see if Professor Elias could have known about the new technique. But the implication is strongly that doctor Bodanski did not remember you having the joint in the tendon" "That's what I thought too", I replied

Felix had been searching all round the second hand shops looking for disused radio sets. He finally got sufficient parts to build a small transmitter with the idea of trying to tease these mlice detector vans that were still regularly operating round Saint Flour

Next time we could get close to one we tried it out and watched their manipulation of the detector aerial. We made a note of the frequency at which the first van appeared to respond to our transmission of simply a load of garbage Morse. Later the same day we got close enough to a second van and did the same thing and to our surprise the second van responded to the same frequency. "Perhaps we should listen to that frequency as well," said Raymond who was also present when this happened. Felix soon managed to find a receiver which could receive the frequency and we took turns to maintain a twenty-four hour listening watch. We didn't have to wait long. Within the first day we had received four Morse transmissions on that frequency each lasting about twenty minutes. We managed to get a transcript of the second message but it was all coded and we didn't have any chance of breaking the code. So who else in the region was transmitting something of interest to the mlice and the gendarmerie?

I advised Pascal of our findings in view of his regular transmissions. He replied that he never used the frequency we had detected. He also conducted a listening watch on the frequency using two receivers some one hundred kilometres apart and fitted with crude directional aerials. From his measurements he concluded the signals were coming from the town of Mauriac some fifty kilometres north of Aurillac and in the same department. I gave this one to Alexis to see what he could find out

The 12th July was my parents wedding anniversary. Fortunately this was one of the key dates I had committed to memory. I didn't think they were going to make anything of it so with Yvette's connivance we decided on a surprise party in the evening of the 12th which conveniently was a Sunday

In the days before the anniversary we made a point of talking to as many of their friends as came into the Terminus and invited them to he surprise party to start at 8.30 on the Sunday evening which was the time the Terminus usually closed. Manuel agreed to prepare a special cold supper, with the agreement of Madame Belmont, in the kitchens of the St. Jacques so that it could be brought over at the right moment

Manuel, Yvette and myself announced we would not be in for supper that night as we were going out and of course most of the Sunday evening regulars were not going to turn up early because they were all invited to the party. Yvette and I went over to the St. Jacques at about four o'clock to help Manuel having left Jean-Francois with the Pelletier's

When we looked out of the windows at the St. Jacques at about eight o'clock we could only see very few customers in the Terminus and we thought my parents would try to close early. They did and at eight-thirty the doors were shut and the lights were out

But not for long, friends were either hammering at the door for admission or helping with the carrying of trays from the St. Jacques across the Place de la Liberte. The surprise was complete and the subsequent party a great success

On Tuesday fourteenth of July, Bastille Day, the French holiday season began, At least for those who could take holidays. Not many people in Saint Flour or the surroundings went away. However the St. Jacques and the Hotel des Voyageurs reported being almost fully booked so there were some strangers in town

The usual celebrations took place in front of the town hail and afterwards the participants mostly moved on to restaurants and bars to enjoy the rest of the day. Some family gatherings at the larger residences remained apart but it was essentially a people's day. The Petanque pitches were constantly in use although the accuracy of the play decreased as the over indulgence increased

The Terminus was always popular on these occasions because of it's location. The Terrace, bar and restaurant area were packed with people although we served no meals that day. All of us and the extra staff were busy from midday onwards until well after two in the morning before the customers started to thin out

The fifteenth started much more gently. Saint Flour was recovering. The Terminus opened, eventually, just after noon but hardly worth while, not more than a dozen or so drinkers until the evening. Alexis came past in the afternoon to say he had his cells full last night but the Maire had issued a general amnesty just after two o'clock and no charges had been brought

The other news Alexis brought was that there was no sign of Doctor Bodanski. His home was all shuttered and he was not answering his phone. His car and his pony and trap had disappeared. Doctor Frankau, the only other doctor in Saint Flour was overwhelmed with requests for the various cures for overdoses of alcohol

That evening the BBC French service reported that General de Gaulle had decorated members of the Free French Forces on Bastille day in London. The name of the free French forces would now be 'La France Combattante'

Thursday brought more strange news from Alexis. The Salomanson family, all twenty-seven of them, had left the Saint Flour area. All of their premises were locked up and shuttered, their homes empty, and their vehicles all gone. Checks by telephone with their branches in the other towns told the same story. Alexis had of course to report these happenings to his departmental headquarters in Aurillac

He learned later that almost all the Jews in Aurillac and other towns had also gone. The conclusion was that they had taken advantage of the general increase in traffic on the roads to conceal their own movement and that by now they would all be in Spain. The sinister departure of these two families from Saint Flour disturbed the local people and rumours of an imminent German occupation were again rife

The immediate concern of everyone was the departure of Dr Bodanski. He was the family doctor to about two-thirds of the Saint Flour population, and Doctor Frankau could not cope with the sudden increase in demand for his services. In view of the urgency Alexis got the Maire's permission to forcefully enter Doctor Bodanski's home and surgery to get his patient's records. He reported that everything was in perfect order and the case notes were all written up even for the patients seen on the evening of the thirteenth.

Alexis had also taken the opportunity to look at my case notes following Doctor Bodanski's examination of my club foot leg some weeks earlier. All that was written said simply that he had examined the leg again out of interest and that the leg had strengthened significantly in the past three years and no complications could be anticipated. God bless Doctor Bodanski

The small hospital in Saint Flour dealt with emergency cases until an extra doctor was moved in from Aurillac as a temporary measure. The longer term solution did not take place until October. The two new doctors appointed from Clermont to take over Doctor Bodanski's practice had been specially selected by Pascal and were well established members of the resistance. We saw this as confirmation of Saint Flour's role because it provided for another essential function we may well need

I was especially pleased to get London's agreement to supply all of the items the hill men's requests although the drop could not be made until the nights became longer towards the end of August

While we had the extra staff at the Terminus for the holiday season Yvette and I were able to get some days free from work. I needed to spread the news about the confirmation of their supplies amongst the hill farmers so Yvette and I took to walking the hills with Jean-Francois in his push chair. It was hard going over the rough ground and for parts of the time Jean-Francois and his push chair had to be carried. Our visits were effective. While Yvette was showing him off to the wife I could quietly mention the confirmation to the man asking him to pass the message on to his neighbours

Before we took ourselves away from the Terminus I insisted we hid the gold ingots securely. They were still standing in a parcel on a bedside table. We went and talked to my parents about this, Dad admitted he had also converted some of his reserve cash into gold for the same reasons as we had, but at present it was in the bank vault. He had not thought about the possibility of all gold being seized by the Germans where ever it was stored

So under the pretence of clearing out the drains in the yard I did the necessary work on the two slabs selected for concealment of the gold ingots. Thus it would be safe even if the fabric of the Terminus was destroyed. We would each know where the others cache was in case either my parents or Yvette and I were killed. If my parents were killed their gold was to be divided between Mathilde and myself. If Yvette and I were killed then our gold would be held in trust for Jean-Francois

When we finally did start our holidays the weather had become very warm and it was a real pleasure to get away from the closeness of the lower town and up to the hills. On the high pastures there was always a little air moving even if it was more difficult to find shade. Jean-Francois loved being able to roam

136

about with nothing on except his shoes, and frequently kicking them off as well. Yvette was quite careful about his exposure to the sun, limiting it so that he did not burn. His protests at being dressed after his allotted free time were most loud

Yvette also sunbathed and now I know why she was the same colour all over. We found secluded hollows where we could see no habitation at all and we both revelled in the sun. The best time was when Jean-Francois had been fed at lunch time and put down for his after lunch rest. That's when I got my back sunburned!

On the days when the weather was not so kind I spent in encouraging others and in playing petanque. My main objective was to listen in on the conversations regarding the war, Vichy France, how soon the Germans might arrive and reactions to the disappearance of the Jewish families which was now made more of in peoples minds when they knew it was not only the Saint Flour Jews who had gone. My parents, Felix, Alexis and Raymond were also listening and we had arranged to meet at the end of the holiday season and pool our observations. Some time towards the end of July Stalin issued a statement to all European communist movements about participation in resistance to the Germans and Italians. In France he asked the communists to accept De Gaulle as their leader and work with other resistance movements. The coordinated communist groups in France accepted being renamed 'La France Combattante'. There was much reporting of this by the French service of the BBC but we could see no effect in our area and the news was almost ignored

Yvette had been moody for some days and asked me one morning if one of our days out could be for her alone to go to Murat on the 4th August. She wanted me to take her there and leave her alone at the Eglise Notre Dame for some hours, take Jean-Francois off somewhere to amuse him and then collect her and bring her home

Fortunately Mum had reminded me that Yvette's wedding anniversary was early in August and I guessed that was the day. Accordingly I agreed without question. When I returned to collect her at the Church, the priest, father Lucien was waiting outside the church to talk to me

"Do you know what day it is?" he asked, "yes it's Yvette's wedding anniversary," I replied. "You understand that she is still a married woman in the eyes of God and that her first responsibility is to Jean-Francois," "Oh yes I replied and I have been helping her in many ways to do that. Some years ago she was exceptionally kind and helpful to me and I see it as my Christian duty to help her when she is in need, as now." "I hope you are not taking advantage of her position and I would remind you of the Church's teaching regarding harm to children." I decided not to make further comment. Soon Yvette came out of the Church, she had clearly been crying, we both said goodbye to father Lucien and went to the bus stop. Fortunately the bus was on time and we did not have to endure the glares of father Lucien for very long. I had to try and comfort Yvette as well as Jean-Francois when he picked up his mother's distress

Chapter 18

Stephan

Over the past month extensive compulsory recruitment of Frenchmen for transfer to German war effort in France or else where in Europe where their talents were needed. Away from the larger conurbations many French men who had no defence against this compulsion left their homes and took to the hilly regions of France living as best they could by casual work in the community

Some joined the Maquis, but others who were opposed to the communist ideals had greater difficulties to manage

We had a number of these new faces appear in Saint Flour. They should of course have reported themselves to the police, but they did not. They did not cause any problem, and of course it was not in their interests to do so. Alexis was in a quandary as to what to do about it. If he knew officially about it he must do something. He asked me to let it be known among the hill farmers that if they had extra people working for them casually to advise those people not to come into the town on Mondays or Wednesdays because that would be when the police would be controlling any strangers and demanding to see their identity cards

Stephan was one of the men who had evaded involvement in the German war machine by abandoning his home and taking to the hills doing casual work for various farmers. He came into the Terminus very occasionally, always on his own. He appeared to wait until he saw me serving so he could engage me in conversation. He was a pleasant enough man of about thirty. Tall for Frenchman, blue eyed, suntanned complexion, dark brown hair receding slightly and tinged with a trace of grey. He appeared to be physically very strong. He made no secret of his evasion of recruitment into the German war machine and his hatred for the Germans. He said he came from Grenoble but never why he was in Saint Flour

At dusk one evening I was walking back into Saint Flour from a listening post and as I walked along the rue des Verdures Stephan fell in alongside me, wheeling his bicycle and we continued together. In a deserted part of the way he started speaking English to me quietly, saying, "I know exactly who you are and why you are here and now you know about it you can trust me completely." I was both astounded and scared

"I am sorry I can't understand you, could you speak French please," He went on speaking English saying how desperate the maquis were for supplies because armaments from Italy had to be smuggled across borders and through occupied France, losses were high and the arms were not such good quality. Again I asked him to speak French. He seemed less sure of himself now and did repeat in French. I reminded him of our recent meeting and agreement that they would have supplies for specific operations. This was clearly not what he wanted. When the maquis have found a target we don't want to have to wait and ask for the necessary supplies, we want to take the opportunity and attack immediately." "Is that what you did at the Dunlop Factory in Montlucon," I asked. "How did you know that was the maquis?" He demanded. I ignored the question, but asked "And where did you get the supplies for that?" "Personally I don't know," he said, "the maquis leader in Montlucon organised the attack." "But it was not very successful," I commented, "many of the charges did not explode." "We really don't know what went wrong," he said. "Perhaps it should have been better organised and carried out a little later," I commented

"Soon we will have an explosive expert and a detonator expert here in the Auvergne and their services could be made available to you so as to avoid failures like the Montlucon fiasco"

By now we were in a more congested area again and the discussion stopped.

"Come and have a drink or two," I suggested. We reached the Terminus and I took him to a quiet table at the end of the restaurant area, picking up a bottle of Chateauneuf du Pape on the way. "The explosives and detonators used at Montlucon are reported as being of British manufacture, and I have not yet had time to check our stocks." We couldn't take the matter further and the quality of the wine improved the quality of the conversation

We parted on friendly terms and Stephan had a long ride back to the Perrier farm.

Yvette and I continued our daily outings whenever the weather was fine and started going further afield by taking the bus for a few kilometres before starting to walk. Thus we extended out acquaintances with the hill farmers, continuing to spread the news of the August supply drop.

On one of our days out we arrived at the farm of Bernice Rodot. Bernice had been widowed in the last days of the 1914-18 war. She had struggled with hired help to run the farm until her two sons were old enough to take some of the burden. In spite of all the hardships they must have endured Bernice was a fine looking woman, Tall and upright, well fleshed, dark complexioned and dark hair and eyes

She had a serious attitude to life and was clearly strict with her two sons. They were both well built lads in their early twenties both well over six foot tall and well muscled from the work of the farm. We knew them slightly from their visits to the Terminus. The farm was clearly well run and prosperous. How her two sons had evaded the Germans remained a mystery for all the time we were involved with them. Bernice received us very hospitably and insisted we stay for lunch. She was taken with Jean-Francois who was drawn to a litter of kittens in the corner of the kitchen. After the mother cat had sniffed and inspected him thoroughly she allowed him near to her family and he was surprisingly gentle with them. When we all sat down for lunch we were joined by Stephan who was currently employed on the farm. It was a jolly lunch and there was much discussion of the state of the war

Stephan seemed to have some quite unusual ideas about the future strategy, of the war. He was convinced that Germany would lose the Russian war in the near future and that when the Allies opened a second front later this year then the Germans would have three fronts to fight on. I could not draw him any further on this occasion. We thanked Bernice for her kindness and hospitality and continued our day out. Yvette was also intrigued by the third front this year. We could not reach any logical conclusion

Family parties seemed to be the entire vogue this summer. Very few families from the Saint Flour area were going away. The substitute was often a family party and Yvette's parents in Murat were no exception. Monsieur Deville arrived at the Terminus one afternoon to see Yvette. Fortunately we had not gone walking that day. Yvette took him up to our rooms for a talk. He wanted her to come to Murat for a weekend family party mid August with Jean-Francois. Yvette said she also wanted me to come with her. This was a shock to her father who was unaware of the relationship between us. Her father left saying he was not sure what Yvette's mother would think. Yvette took the matter into her own hands and our next day out was a bus trip to Murat

Yvette intended to catch her mother alone so we arranged to arrive mid morning when her father was expected to be out. Madame Deville was surprised and delighted to see Yvette and Jean-Francois but she clearly did not know much about me. I sensed there was some estrangement between Monsieur Deville and his family

Yvette explained that I was Henri Dufour, son of Robert and Lisette of the Terminus and that she had now moved into the Terminus and planned to let her house so as to have enough income to support herself and Jean-Francois

She also said her father had not invited me to the party and she would not come if I was not invited. She then asked me to take Jean-Francois out into the garden, which I did and she obviously then told her mother that we were living together and why. Her mother was obviously shocked and when I returned into the house for lunch there was distinct hostility towards me. We left soon after lunch

We returned to Saint Flour on the next bus. Fortunately Jean-Francois was asleep after his lunch. Yvette was withdrawn and worried. Eventually she said, if her parents acted like that, what would Philippe's parents think and say. I explained that I had met her father in law on several occasions on resistance matters and that he was aware of her moving into the Terminus and that she was letting her house to contacts introduced by Alexis Lescaut. I also told him that Alexis had assured Charles Pelletier that they were reliable tenants because Charles and Marianne had made such a significant contribution to the cost of the house when she married Philippe

Yvette decided that she would have to tell her parents-in-law before anyone else did. She asked me to take Jean-Francois home as soon as we got off the bus so she could go up town to the Pelletier's. Waiting for Yvette to return was tedious. Late in the afternoon I gave Jean-Francois his supper and got him ready for bed. We made a game of it and he was good but as soon as I took him near his cot he was asking for maman repeatedly and almost tearfully

Eventually he fell asleep exhausted on my lap Yvette did not come back until well after eight and came straight up to us. She said quickly to me that everything was settled as far as Charles and Marianne were concerned. She took Jean-Francois to settle him in his cot and get him to sleep again, telling me that Charles was in the bar waiting to talk to me and I should go down at once

I joined Charles at a table in the far corner of the restaurant area. Needless to say I was somewhat apprehensive. Charles told me that both he and Marianne also believed that Philippe was dead and were reconciled to the fact that Yvette was likely to marry again although they had not expected quite so soon. Charles was a very pragmatic man, he knew we could not marry in the religious sense until Philippe had been declared dead by the authorities and that this would not happen for some years. He said Jean-Francois needed a father and that neither he nor Auguste Deville could fill that role. He was pleasantly surprised at how I had developed while I was away and how brilliantly I conducted myself in our resistance meetings

So he could think of nobody else he would rather see as a step-father to his grandson. He promised to meet Auguste Deville as soon as he could to make his position clear and to convince him that I was not the retarded cripple who left Saint Flour three years ago. Yvette lay very still and quiet in my arms that night

The next afternoon Yvette's mother came in to the Terminus and left an invitation for all three of us to attend the party on the following weekend. As luck would have it we were out on the hills and she had left by the time we returned. But this was a great help to Yvette and she was very happy. I was happy that Charles had dealt with Auguste so promptly

The party was a success. Now I knew where Yvette got all her cooking ideas from. Under Francine's direction her other two daughters who both lived in Murat had put together one of the tastiest meals I had ever enjoyed. The rift between Yvette and her parents seemed to have disappeared. When Auguste managed to find me alone he told me Charles Pelletier had been to see them and explained various matters that he did not know about and he was now willing to accept Yvette's choice of a new partner

On the following Friday Bernice Rodot came with her two sons to the market. Before they left she came in to the Terminus and spoke to Yvette inviting all three of us to stay for a few days at the farm saying a complete rest for those days would do us all good

Arrangements were made for Raymond to cover all the listening schedules and Alexis promised to let me know if any problems arose. Off we went by the early bus as far as Pierrefort where Stephan met us with horses

Yvette rode well with Jean Francois firmly strapped in front of her but I hadn't ridden for several years and I had rather a lively mount. We took about one and a half hours to reach the farm and I was very happy to dismount

The Rodot farm at Le Bousquet was lower down than most hill farms and consequently more versatile, the land was not so hostile to use of machines and several large areas could be worked with tractors to grow grain and harvest hay mechanically rather than manually

Bernice really set out to make us comfortable. We had a delightful large room with a smaller one adjoining for Jean-Francois. The views were magnificent. To the north the land rose quite steeply stretching up to the Puy de la Grousse. That land was all for grazing the wool bearing sheep. They had just been sheared and had not worked their way up the slopes very far at the present, and by the time the weather broke for the winter they would start coming down again. To the south the land fell away gently in a number of valleys radiating from the Puy and eventually more steeply into the valley of the Truyere

This was a busy farm. As well as the flocks of wool bearing sheep, Bernice kept a good sized flock of milking sheep for cheese making. They were larger than any sheep I had ever seen before and one sharp nudge from one of them could roll a man over so easily and they were not that docile with strangers. There was also a line of pigsties all occupied and piglets galore! A stable block had four heavy horses for moving fodder and anything else that needed moving and six riding horses. Jean-Francois was in a seventh heaven

He soon rediscovered the kittens which were now twice the size when he first saw them and their teeth were now sharp enough to hurt him. He soon learnt how to be gentle and not provoke them. He was not so successful with the piglets that were heavy enough to knock him off his feet. And of course the sheep and cows were big enough that he simply stood back and stared

Yvette and I both found plenty to interest us as well as looking after Jean-Francois. There was a barn with two stills in it and all the associated fermentation vessels for making liqueurs and cordials. A scrupulously clean dairy for the cheese-making and a large clean cave with a bricked up entrance for maturing the blue cheeses

Bernice welcomed Yvette in her kitchen and between them they produced superb meals. After several days of relaxing and amusing ourselves we began to wonder why we had been invited and treated so hospitably. The long chats we had after dinner each night with the two sons and Stephan usually became political and turned to the war situation especially when we had finished listening to the BBC French service news

One evening the two sons went off to a local village where there was a bar with a billiards table, Yvette was diverted into the kitchen on some pretext leaving myself and Stephan alone to talk. He quizzed me in depth about my early life and my handicap which I eventually showed him

Then we talked about my experience with Precision Metal especially about what they were doing for the German war effort. I could not answer all the questions and had to rely on describing the parts I had been involved in making and my guesses as to what they might be for. I believed they were all parts for automatic and semi-automatic weapons. I told him about the bomb and the cover story I had been given to explain why I was not killed by the same bomb and I thought he believed me. Because of the age difference between us I did not feel too comfortable about questioning him, but I had to do so

He came from a village some kilometres south of Grenoble. He had studied engineering at Grenoble University and graduated with high marks. After several short term jobs he was recruited by Fiat in Turin as a development engineer on motor car engines. He was recruited into the communist party during his time with Fiat. Late in May 1940 when it became clear that Italy was about to enter the war, he resigned and returned to France. Soon after that when France was partitioned, he decided to leave his home and family to avoid compulsive transfer to the German war effort and joined the maquis in the region of Vercors

He then slowly moved westwards until he reached the Auvergne where he felt more secure. He claimed there were many Maquis now in the Auvergne and that they would be the main force in any resistance movement. "I am nominated to lead this movement in this region and personally I am willing to work with any other resistance group but I am not going to accept De Gaulle's leadership or take orders from his officers. Your group led by Pascal I believe take orders from De Gaulle's office in London and can get supplies from them. We need supplies; I can exchange men to work with you for a share of your supplies"

Now I knew why we had been invited to the Rodot farm. "This is a matter I will have to discuss with Alexis Lescaut," I replied," there are many aspects to this, we are not satisfied with the situation either but I cannot tell you why without discussion with my colleagues, but I promise you I will have those discussions and meet you again"

That was the end of what Stephan had wanted to discuss and we went on to other matters of which when would the Germans occupy Vichy France was by far the most pressing. Much to my surprise Stephan claimed that the second front against the Germans would be opened in North Africa when the Americans invaded Morocco and Algeria. He claimed that the heavy reinforcements now arriving with the British eighth army in Egypt coupled with Rommel's shortage of fuel for his armoured vehicles would result in a strong push by the British eighth army next winter and the American invasion would coincide with this, thus giving Rommel two fronts to contend with. In Africa. When this American invasion was successful Germany would be forced to occupy Vichy France because when Rommel was driven out of Africa the Anglo-American forces would pose a threat to the South coast of France and if the Allies took the route through Sicily and the Italian mainland the threat increased

We listened to the Vichy French news.   Tonight's headline was the first raid by the United States heavy bombers on Rouen. High civilian casualties were reported because most of the bombs fell on residential areas and not on the industrial targets. Later the BBC French service also reported the raid as having only limited success. Stephan said, "So much for all their talk about the extreme precision of their daylight bombers"

We left the next morning. Jean-Francois was in tears he wanted to stay and play with the animals. He was pacified with the gift of a kitten of his very own complete with a carrying basket. The ride down to Pierrefort was uneventful. Stephan came with us to take the horses back. As we parted he said quietly "Don't forget." "I promise you I won't," I replied

We were lucky to find a Saint Flour taxi in Pierrefort and treated ourselves to a ride all the way back to Saint Flour. The second bus of the day would not have left until after four o'clock

There was a great welcome at the Terminus for all of us except the new kitten. Sambo simply swore at the newcomer and went out to sulk in the yard. I was anxious to contact Alexis and left messages for him to meet me urgently. He came the same evening and I related all the news

He agreed we should to involve Pascal and that he would set up a meeting as soon as possible. Like me was astounded at the report about the planned American invasion of North Africa, Raymond had also heard of our return and joined us later to report that the only message had been that the munitions drop for the hill farmers was planned for the twenty-sixth August with fallback dates of twenty-seventh and the twenty-eighth. He had also heard about the United States bombing of Rouen, "Lets hope they don't drop our supplies down the craters, we'd never live it down." he said

We agreed he could tell the hill farmers we now had drop dates confirmed at for end of August, but not to be specific for security reasons. Mum got very anxious about granddad in Lille. He had not been able to get a telephone installed in his new apartment because of the shortages of equipment, so our only contact with him was by letter. The post was not reliable and frequently censored, but we had not had a letter for almost four weeks. Lille was quoted as having been bombed several times each week now as the RAF increased its activity over northern France. Every day after the post had arrived and again no news, she was tearful. After all she had already lost her mother and two sisters in air raids

Anxious listening to the BBC in the evenings to hear where the day's attacks had taken place prompted more tears. I admired her extremely for her fortitude under these conditions. Then three letters arrived in three days, what a relief, they were heavily censored but at least he was alive and unharmed. When the letters were read we worked out that there were also missing letters probably destroyed by the censors because they said too much about the air raid damage

Raymond had been collecting comments from the people about the state of the war. He said there had been some swing in favour of resistance during the summer and Alexis agreed. We tuned into the BBC French News. This was exciting, British and Canadian commandoes had landed in Dieppe and had established a bridgehead

Further reports would be released as they came in from the Ministry of War. Those were the bare facts. Was this the second front? That was on everyone's lips. We hastily retuned to the Paris news stations which were not easy to receive in Saint Flour. They reported the landings by British troops in the locality of Dieppe and that the landings had been contained by our German allies

146

and the repulsion of this attempted invasion would be completed within the next few days

The arguments went on late into the night especially in the bar. There was some jubilation that something had happened at last, coupled with disbelief that the invasion could have been prepared so soon after the fiasco and losses of Dunkirk

We could not disclose of course that we had not received any advice from London, and we tried to play the matter in a low key as probably a probing attack to test the strength of the German defences. Many accepted this view because others supported us saying that if this was an all out invasion the outcome would not be settled so quickly as the Paris news was suggesting and there would have been bombing raids ahead of the invasion force which had not been reported by either side. One wag even said "Well that's what the raid on Rouen was all about, they thought it was Dieppe"

True or false, most of our customers went home that night with some boost to their morale

Chapter 19

Compromise

Over the past month there had been extensive compulsory recruitment of Frenchmen for transfer to the German war effort either in France or elsewhere in Europe where their talents were needed. Away from the larger conurbations many French men who had no defence against such compulsion left their homes and took to the hilly regions of France living as best they could by doing casual work in those communities

Some joined the maquis, but others who were opposed to the communist ideals of the maquis had greater difficulty to manage

We had a number of these new faces appear in Saint Flour. They should of course have reported themselves to the police but they did not. They did not cause any problem and of course it was not in their interest to do so. Alexis was in a quandary as to what to do about it. If he knew officially about it he must do something. He asked me to let it be known among the hill farmers that if they had extra people working for them, to casually advise those people not to come into Saint Flour on Mondays or Wednesdays because that is when he would be controlling any strangers in town by having police on duty checking identity cards

Yvette had some good news. The solicitors had completed their work on the lease of her house to the couple suggested by Alexis as tenants, so Monsieur and Madame Christian de Boni planned to move to Saint Flour on the first of August

Christian was a motor mechanic employed by the local bus operator and was related to one of Alexis' trusted policemen. Soon now Yvette would have a regular income from the rent. She was happy and said she would like to have some more time off during the holiday season

Pascal arrived the next day as a holidaymaker staying at the St. Jacques. Thus we were able to have frequent discussions over the next day or two. By far the most urgent matter was Stephan, his proposal for cooperation and his news regarding a North African second front. The first consideration was Stephan himself, was he what he said he was?, Could we trust him? His ideas over cooperation were not very different from our own

Everybody looked at me, "You've had more contact with him than anybody else," said Pascal. "Do you trust him "My instinctive answer is yes." I said. "Good," said Pascal, "then Alexis and I must meet him without you present and form our opinions, and that must be very soon." Alexis said, "Suppose I had you, Pascal and Stephan to dinner tomorrow night at my home, it's my wife's bridge night, so we can have the house to ourselves for three hours or so." Then, speaking to me Pascal said "Will you go and bring him into Saint Flour tomorrow, he can stay at the St. Jacques with me I know Madame Belmont has a room free. If he cannot come tomorrow, then as soon as possible"

Next morning I telephoned Bernice, thanking her kindly for her hospitality and asked her to get Stephan to call me as soon as possible. "Oh he's gone to work at the Pasquier farm at la Peyre for a week or so and they are not on the telephone," said Bernice. "You could call the Perrier farm at Courtines and ask them to get a message to him," and gave me the number. I had to look at the map, it was one area Yvette and I had not explored, but it was only about twelve kilometres from Saint Flour and it was a nice day for a bicycle ride I decided it was best to get there by lunchtime when Stephan would surely be at the farmhouse rather than somewhere on the farm

I left at once having told my parents where and why I was going and to tell Pascal if he came by the Terminus. It seemed it was up hill all the way. La Peyre was several hundred metres higher than Saint Flour and the sun was high and hot. I had not met the Perriers before and they were surprised to see me especially as I was asking for Stephan, "Yes he would be in the farmhouse for lunch and they hoped I would also join them." As lunchtime approached I made sure I was outside when Stephan came back. He was also surprised. I had to ask him if the Perrier's were trustworthy before I could talk at all. He didn't know and I very quickly explained he had to come to Saint Flour urgently this evening or the next day to meet Pascal and Alexis

Lunch was something of a strain. The Perrier's wanted to know why I had come all this way by bicycle to see Stephan but did not like to ask outright. Stephan and I talked about the days we had spent at the Rodot farm. I said I had come on behalf of Alexis Lescaut who wanted to see Stephan about registering him as a resident in the area and that the matter was urgent because he had been here so long and Alexis did not want to be forced to arrest him. The Perrier's seemed satisfied with this explanation and agreed they could spare him for the evening provided he was back ready for work tomorrow

We left after lunch Stephan riding a bicycle borrowed from Simon Perrier. The final approach to the Perrier farm had been difficult going up and I had to walk over half the distance from the road. Going down was definitely dangerous and again I walked some of the way. At least we could talk now. I explained that Stephan was to have dinner with Alexis and Pascal at the Lescaut home so that they could hear first hand the proposal and the news. I indicated that I expected the result to be positive. Stephan seemed satisfied with that. We stopped for a drink at Fraissinet just outside Saint Flour as we were quite early getting back and Stephan was also trying to find out more about me

I told him more about my time in Lille with Precision Metal and the German take over and what happened to my grandmother and aunts leading to the end of my apprenticeship. He knew of the company Precision Metal as a manufacturer of precision engineering parts and was surprised that I had got an apprenticeship until I explained about my father marrying into the Renaud family and my grandfather's position in the company. I questioned Stephan about his change of location.

He said he regarded the Rodot farm as his base but they did not have enough work for him all the time and he went to other farms as and when there was work to be done. I asked him who else he had worked for and he gave me three names, Bertrand Messenger, Jules Denier, and Jean Chavent. I went on with him to the Lescaut home and left him with Alexis somewhat early. I managed to intercept Pascal as he was leaving the St. Jacques Hotel and told him of my talks with Stephan and about the three other names he had given me. With Pascal in the St. Jacques for some days we were able to have meetings of the Monday club every night and we needed them.

So much was now happening and we had our policy towards our two masters in London to be agreed and put into effect. I first placed on record that I was not satisfied that SOE were telling us everything they knew and the reports from Pascal based on the information from De Gaulle's office were of little use to us. As an alternative I proposed we should regard that information apart from our own information obtained locally and based on facts and not politics. This point was provisionally agreed. After all other considerations, "you need to be friends with the other enemies of your enemies"

Alexis' main concern was how far we could trust Stephan and his offer to exchange men for munitions. I said, "I dislike the concept, there are tasks the Maquis can do better than us and vice versa. We should hold stocks of munitions for use by whoever is given the task but if this is to be our policy then we have to decide how far we are prepared to trust the Maquis as headed up by Stephan."

Pascal reported that both he and Alexis believed Stephan was to be trusted, which led us on to whether or not we should trust London with this policy decision. The argument went back and forth and slowly a new feeling towards our masters emerged. They haven't been completely open with us so let us be less open with them and we agreed on these points for future communications:

1. We report successes and failures without attribution, for security reasons
2. Allocate tasks without naming the participants, for security reasons
3. Never use the words maquis or resistance or La France Combattante or any name of a resistance group
4 Only describe targets as the enemy

Which means we are only telling London about half our information, and to regard the use of the word 'half' as a warning word in conversations or meetings where strangers may be present?

We finished up by drinking several half glasses to half winning our half of the war We very quickly reached a further unanimous agreement to use the maquis in any operations where we needed them and to supply the maquis with their needs for named targets that did not conflict with our purposes. Then the North African invasion was next for consideration. We all agreed that Stephan's idea of a second front in North Africa by means of an invasion across the Atlantic by the United States sounded wild

While we were all together I asked Raymond to explain the preliminary results of our survey of the Truyere dams. "The upper reaches of the Truyere collect the rain water from a remarkably large area of the Auvergne. That is the main reason why the dams were built as the water stored at high levels is an important source of electrical power from the generating stations located just below the dams By the time the water reaches the sea it has generated electrical power five or six times. The dams on the Truyere were built for that sole purpose. The cost of those dams will only be recovered over a period in excess of forty years." "As long as that?" remarked Pascal. Raymond went on; "I expected I was going to survey the Lot as well as the Truyere but now I have made the calculations from the water levels I observed last month I can already draw certain conclusions. They are as follows: If all the dams were all full and the generating stations were using their normal amounts of water for power generation there would be a period of the year from about mid-March to Mid-June when blowing all those dams plus two on the Lot at the right time would have some chance of severing most of the road and rail links between the Auvergne and the confluence of the Lot and the Garonne." "I can neither calculate what the cost of the damage would be nor the amount of the consequential losses"

There was a stunned silence lasting many minutes while we took in all of the implications. Pascal said, "I understand this idea was started by the success if the dam buster raid in the German Ruhr." "Yes," I said, "but there is an important difference, France is an ally and not the enemy, we have to think about the consequential damage and cost of doing something that is designed to prevent the movement of troops from North to South or vice-versa for a short period of time

My immediate reaction is that the cost would be far too high"

The long awaited reply to my request for our next drop came at last. The supplies would be dropped in two trips at different locations. The main munitions drop to include the extra radios and batteries, would be made at the same site as previous unless we suggested an alternative. It would comprise one hundred and twenty containers from two aircraft, each making two passes over the drop zone

We are required to find a suitable site for the hill farmers drop and advise location. The drop would comprise one hundred and eighty containers carrying the powder, shot, percussion caps and point twenty-two shells plus the Antilles rum

Both drops would have to wait until after the twenty-fourth of August when the nights would again be long enough for these operations

Considerable care would be necessary in selecting this drop zone. We would need about thirty men involved simply to move the necessary munitions to a place where the containers could opened and the contents distributed fairly between the hill farmers

We selected a site to the South of the characteristically shaped lake/reservoir behind the dam at Grandval. Planes picking out the lake could proceed due South and we could have a beacon alight on the high ground round St. Laurent de Veyre followed by the usual flares for the drop zone. The farms on the slopes of this high ground were very solidly in support of our resistance activities and there were numerous approach routes so that the extra movements of people and vehicles in the surroundings would not be too noticeable and the local farmers did not usually cut their hill hay until the end of August

The next matter to deal with was the imminent early arrival of our four new recruits. The message said they were now in France and expected to arrive with Mathilde during the next ten days. Matters continued to move fast. Only a day later Mathilde confirmed their arrival. Alexis made a sensible suggestion that we ought to know a little more about their capabilities before we decided who to place where. So I made a day trip to Millau on the train leaving at six-twenty in the morning and not getting back to Saint Flour until after midnight, a very long day but worth it

Chapter 20

News from Gibraltar

Our four new friends Victor, Sebastian, Simon and Patrice all in good form and with four new men to play up to, Mathilde was also in fine form. Alain was of course at work. We had a good introduction at a safe farmhouse arranged by Mathilde outside Millau on the road to Rodez. Mathilde had met me off the train and a trusted taxi driver took us to the farm. I judged all four of the new arrivals to be in their thirties and from their accents they had all spent some significant time in France

I did not want to let them talk too freely in front of Mathilde about personal matters so I constantly steered the conversation to their training prior to being sent to us in France. Simon and Patrice were weapon instructors and marksmen. Victor was an expert on explosive charges with especial reference to maximising the effect of a charge. Sebastian was a detonator expert. Madame Jordan had provided a most pleasing lunch for us all in a quiet secluded location and the conversation after lunch was most illuminating

It was no secret that the four had flown to Gibraltar and had to wait a considerable time before a suitable Spanish coaster could take them to Barcelona, whence another coaster had put them ashore at night to land in the shadow of Notre Dame des Anges on the beach at Collioure where they were immediately taken by the police to a safe house in the old quarter until two couriers could be arranged to bring them to Millau

It was their time in Gibraltar, where of course they were just other servicemen and could pick up all the gossip and Gibraltar had plenty of that. The real stunning piece of news was that the United States was planning to land troops in Morocco and invade Algeria by land, sea and air creating a second front against the Germans and Italians in North Africa. The invasion was to be mounted across the Atlantic in spite of the U-boat menace. Nobody had

153

mentioned any dates for this but the rumour was that an agreement had been reached between the President of the United States and the King of Morocco that United States forces would be allowed an unimpeded passage through Morocco. Another rumour was that Winston Churchill had been taking holidays in Marrakech and had also been meeting the King Muhammad of Morocco

As our four friends coming via Gibraltar had got the information in Gibraltar it appeared that leaks in Morocco were by far the most likely source of their information especially as it included statements about the agreement of the King of Morocco to the passage of United States troops through Morocco and Winston Churchill's holidays there. Thus it appeared to us that the German intelligence service must also have heard the same information. What was missing was the date and only I had any knowledge of that 'before the end of this year'

The mounting of a seaborne invasion across the Atlantic with so many U-boats operating did not make sense to us. Shipping losses in the Atlantic were ever mounting and our four friends could confirm this based on British news. The other news was all about the problems in trying to get supplies through to Malta and the losses of naval ships in doing so. We had not heard about this but the vital role of Gibraltar was self evident

The strategy of the first 'second front' being opened was so similar to the ideas put forward by Stephan. The similarity was astounding. But now we had similar predictions from two totally different sources. The only point that neither source indicated was the timing. However we also had a statement from a senior government official that it would be before the end of this year

I decided that I would locate Simon and Patrice at la Cham with the Mathis family as they would be nearer to our stocks of arms and could provide training to the hill farmers who needed it. They would travel back with me by train today arriving after dark and to sleep at the Terminus tonight and on to la Cham early in the morning. Mathilde sent a message to Alexis to advise Monsieur Mathis of their arrival and to arrange for a police van at dawn to move them

Victor and Sebastian were to stay on with the Jordan's until we could complete their moves. The Jordan's were to start their sheep shearing in a day or two and extra pairs of hands were always welcome at that time. I stressed to Victor and Sebastian, who had never sheared a sheep in their lives, to fit in with the farm arrangements

I got Mathilde to buy the tickets for Simon and Patrice to avoid alerting the railway that two strangers were travelling to Saint Flout on the same train as me. I made it clear that whenever we came into a station we must not be seen together. All went well and we arrived at the Terminus via the back door just after midnight

154

Alexis had alerted Mum who had a supper ready for us all and Yvette to serve it. An early start next morning, the police van arrived on time and the move to la Cham was completed It was not as easy to get two strangers into the farm of Fernand. Mounier at St. Laurent de Veyre

The only idea we had involved bringing Victor and Sebastian on the bus from Millau to St Chely D'Apcher and then for Mathilde to accompany them to Fuels where Fernand. could meet them. Mathilde could then travel on by the next bus to Saint Flour stay overnight and return to Millau the next day

Mathilde was not keen on the idea. There was the problem of how Luke and Jean might behave with Alain if they knew she was to be away, and Alain could not get a day off from his work without fear of losing the job because there were so many skilled unemployed older men in Millau. From this we could also deduce that Alain's employer was not pro-resistance

Alexis finally resolved this by using Max's good cooperation out of Rodez by taking them all the way by plain police van

Simon and Patrice were given the immediate task with help from Raymond of improving our Lysander strip situation. We needed a minimum of six strips so that even if it was known we were expecting a plane we would keep the location of the strip secret until a few hours before the operation. The Cathedral tower at Saint Flour had proved a satisfactory landmark for the pilots to find and if we retained this as such and gave the bearing and distance of our strips from that point we could bring in planes to a wide range of landing strips

We explained to Simon and Patrice the use of sheep to disguise the marks of the landings as a necessary condition for every strip. After they had started their search for extra strips Patrice came up with a sound idea. Our two present locations at Barrat and la Cham could be easily identified from the air as possible sites because of the large area of good grassland without any outcrops of rock or large boulders. We had already disguised the la Cham strip with Raymond's skid-boulders. Some of the possible sites they had already looked at were good but had large boulders on them that would make a landing hazardous, but if the boulders were dug out and dragged off the strip and replaced by Raymond's skid-boulders we got the same result

I liked this idea and especially complemented Patrice on the suggestion. It had all the simplicity and logic of a first class scheme. The only problem was that it might take longer to set up but we finally agreed we would wait a little time for the best approach to the problem. So Simon and Patrice became hikers enjoying the wide range of footpaths in the hills around Saint Flour, after all it was summer

They did such a good job in finding suitable sites that there was not too much digging out of boulders. Nearly all the 'boulders' we finished up using were made from light lava stone from the slopes of the craters stuck together with plaster and decorated with a special compound of old paint and animal dung which after a few showers of rain looked quite convincing from a few hundred metres away. Our 'boulders' weighed about a quarter as much as a real one of the same size

So we finished the summer with eight strips each of which could be made ready for a landing by three men in less than twenty minutes, and the 'boulders' repositioned afterwards in the same time. Then the sheep could do their part. Victor and Sebastian were given the responsibility to explore in detail and do all the preparatory work on the possible drop zone site at St. Laurent de Veyres

The main attraction of this zone was that some of the heavy moving could be done by tractor and trailer because the terrain was better than many sites. Only containers falling outside the main drop line might be a problem. There were enough caves to store the goods in the adjacent woods but they had to be cleared out. The seven farms surrounding the proposed zone had all expressed their enthusiasm to work with us and I was especially pleased with the efforts of Fernand. Mounier who coordinated their efforts

Nevertheless there was plenty of physical work to be done by Victor and Sebastian and it all had to be ready by the middle of August

I could now see matters moving better towards an operational structure. I decided to set up a meeting with Pascal. To do this I said I was going to see a friend in Vichy who had been in the same ward as me when I was in hospital. In fact I stayed with Pascal in Clermont

I really pushed Pascal to know what he thought about the way De Gaulle's office in London treated his reports about the situation in Clermont and the region with particular reference to the strength and involvement of the Maquis. He said all such matters were ignored and he was convinced that his reports were politically unacceptable to De Gaulle's office. We needed a further meeting to agree on common principles in dealing with our London masters

The location of such a meeting was a problem. We didn't have a safe house in Saint Flour, and the one in Brioude was rather too far for six people to visit from Saint Flour. Eventually we decided to meet at the Mathis family farm because Sabine Mathis had offered us such a facility knowing very well that their farm was remote and could not be approached without intruders being seen and she had the room for us to stay overnight if needed

Chapter 21

Happy Hill Farmers

During the fine summer days of August air activity over Northern France increased. Many different types of attacks were made on ports and transport by bombers and fighter aircraft. Of course in Saint Flour we were too far South to see anything of this at first hand but some of the visitors told of the vapour trails in the sky that were now a feature of the faster higher flying aircraft

The submarine bases the Germans had constructed at Brest, Saint Nazaire and Lorient were being bombed by day and night and Vichy was claiming that it was the civilians who were suffering from these attacks coupled with the Germans claiming that their submarine pens were bomb proof

As August moved on and the evenings shortened the hill farmers would ask quietly whether we had a date for the drop yet. I am sure there was some scepticism as to whether it would actually happen in spite of the preparations. I simply had to reply that we would only get information a day or two in advance and then finally confirmed a few hours before the drop by a message on the BBC French service. As soon as we had the proposed dates and the 'personal message' they would be told and should then listen to the personal messages every evening until it happened

Our plans were complete. There were to be two drops on the same night, one of all the munitions and the other described as Farmers Benefits. This posed a problem of manpower to handle the supplies. Felix was essential to the munitions drop as were Alexis, Simon, Patrice and myself. The first date when we received it, the 29th, was only 6 days ahead. Raymond, Alexis and I needed an urgent brainstorming session

It all seemed to fall into place quite neatly in the end. We would take the munitions drop at the same site as previously in the le Che valley with extra manpower from Simon and Patrice leading and six maquisades recommended by

Stephan. Their key objective was to clear the drop zone into the caves before daylight and to provide a 24 hour guard until the supplies were distributed

The second drop was the farmer's benefits. We decided to trust Stephan with the full responsibility for this if only as a sign of our trust in him. He accepted the task next day with obvious pleasure. He knew he would need many extra hands and immediately started a recruiting drive. I insisted Victor and Sebastian were involved to gain the experience

The 29th was a poor night and the operation didn't happen. The weather forecast for the next day was much better and it did all happen. We really felt the advantage of having the personal message broadcast by the BBC as everybody could listen and carry out their plans without any further warning

Because there would be much activity that night Alexis arranged for some' sheep rustling' to occur in an adjacent part of the Auvergne around Pont du Trembloux with some apprehensions by the police of suspects. He also arranged for local people to report planes flying low over le Maizieu and Mauriac just to confuse the opposition. Needless to say those arrested for sheep rustling were released next day without being charged because the examining magistrate considered there was no case to be brought for lack of evidence. The magistrate also let it be known that the vigilance of the police was commendable and he would deal severely with any real evidence of sheep rustling

Alexis was quite smug about the whole affair and told me that there was always some rustling at this time of the year, as the nights got shorter and the sheep were still on the hills well away from their home farms

That night must have been a 'France Special' for the RAF. Our drops were not the only ones that night because we were surprised the next day by an urgent message from London regarding a Whitley which had crash landed at St. Amand just North of Montlucon. The crew were reported as all safe with only slight injuries and were moving South to get out of France via Spain. "Please locate and assist" was the instruction

I sent Raymond and Felix at once to Clermont to contact Pascal for a linkage to the Montlucon group. We dared not use the telephone for this matter as the mlice were increasingly tapping the lines especially in situations like this. Raymond returned on the last train that night leaving Felix to meet the crew and tell of our plan to get them to the underground railway

The news was good. All the crew were safe and located in safe houses near Montlucon. Two needed medical attention and could not travel for some days. Pascal accepted responsibility with Felix to get them as far South as our safe house at Issoire when they were fit to travel

From there we were to get them to Mathilde in Millau who would arrange onward travel to Montpelier where they could pick up the regular 'underground railway' to Spain.

Next day the news was different. Reports on Vichy radio stated that the crew of the Whitley bomber that had crashed near St. Amand had all escaped uninjured and were travelling south in order to escape to Spain. Vichy radio said there were seven of them although Pascal only knew of five. The mlice and some gendarmerie were very active checking all buses and trains, and with random check points on many roads

The two spotter planes based at Clermont were constantly airborne, but seemed to be concentrating on cooperation with the road blocks. We got reports of local people overhearing radio contact between the planes and checkpoints. That evening Vichy radio claimed that two of the crew had been caught making their way Westwards on a train for Nantes

Felix returned next day with the news that the crew were still in their safe houses at Montlucon. He had actually seen them, and they would not be travelling for several days yet and that all five were completely safe, although two were injured. Pascal had arrangements in hand for them to travel to Issoire in two groups by roundabout routes when the interest had died down. By that time the two injured men should have sufficiently recovered. Felix was to accompany one group and Pascal the other. Coded telephone messages were agreed to advise us when to have the Issoire house ready

We made our plans to move them as quickly as possible to Millau, also in two groups, by routes sufficiently far apart that they would not fall into the same net if the mlice were lucky enough to intercept any of them

The drop in the le Che valley was exactly on time and most successful with the exception of one container caught by its parachute high up in a tree on the North side and extremely visible even in the moonlight. Two of the maquisades were able to detach the container but could not untangle the parachute from the tree

The container fell to the ground and burst open. We managed to collect all the contents some of which were damaged and went with the container down into the bog. The parachute was a problem until we got some paraffin from the nearby farm and were able to set it alight via the cords. Most of it was destroyed and it was barely recognisable as a parachute

All the remaining contents were safely hidden away before daylight, our ability to deal with the larger drop on this occasion worked really well. When we saw how well the bog absorbed the damaged container we decided we could use this as our dump for other containers as and when we unpacked them

Stephan did not report in until a couple of days later. I had become somewhat worried as the two spotter planes were quite active in the days after the drop away to the south. They made only one pass over our drop area

When Stephan arrived he was quite happy overall with the drop. So far one container was still missing, dogs had found five other containers that had fallen outside the drop zone and might yet find the missing one. Stephan was of the opinion that the parachute had not opened because he felt sure that if the spotter planes had seen a parachute the mllice would have arrived to investigate.

All the 'farmer's benefits' had been safely hidden until we could arrange for a share out. I made a point of specially thanking Stephan for his efforts. He was clearly impressed that the promises had been honoured and that all our reputations could only be enhanced when we had the share out. of the 'farmers benefits'

Alexis reported that the police had apprehended nine men on the night of the drops for sheep rustling and their cases were now being considered by the examining magistrates at St Chely and Mauriac. Also that reports of low flying aircraft had been received from many areas that night, even some that had not been 'arranged!' All, without exception, of the areas had been inspected by the spotter planes on the following days. Alexis said this confirmed his fears that there was still at least one informant in the police in contact with the mlice

We let it be known to the hill farmers that we would not be able to arrange the share out of the 'farmer's benefits' for some weeks. We had to give priority to passing the five airmen through our area safely and everybody would be involved either in escorting them or arranging diversions, but of course we could not tell the farmers this. I had one or two difficult conversations in the Terminus on market days with the farmers over this point

The news about the farmer's benefits reminded Dad that our wine stocks were getting low. The old wine cellar was now almost dried out and could soon be brought back into use. Mum and Dad started to plan a wine buying trip around their usual suppliers for October when the prices were at their most attractive

Eventually the number of road blocks and other controls were reduced and Pascal advised us that the five would be arriving in Issoire on a particular night. The house was prepared and the five were safely installed. The condition of the two injured had improved and we were able to move them on after only one days rest

Felix took a flight lieutenant and a flight sergeant via, I think, Murat, Aurillac and Rodez and I took a squadron leader and two pilot officers via Le Puy and Mende. We used local buses and stayed one night en route at farms nominated by Stephan as safe, all eventually arriving without incident at

Mathilde's safe house outside Millau. Felix and I stayed with them overnight before returning by bus to Saint Flour

I was intrigued by the fact that the crew of a Whitley was made up of four officers and a sergeant, but I dare not ask them why. Felix I discovered could speak a little English, just enough to escort the airmen. When Mathilde arrived in the morning and took over some of them visibly winced at her nonchalant attitude. The Squadron Leader complimented me on my good English as we parted. I dared not comment

Mathilde had arranged for all of them to travel together by lorry that day to Narbonne and promised them they would cross into Spain the next night. Later about the end of September we were thanked for our contribution to their rescue and told they had arrived back safely in England, so I guess it all worked out somehow. We wondered if they had picked up the same rumours in Gibraltar regarding the second front and if so had London believed them, because Winston Churchill would!

As soon as we had moved our escapees, we had to start and relocate our greatly enhanced stock of munitions. We simply had to repeat the former distribution arrangements about four times and it took us over three weeks. While this was going the local news was of a three day pilgrimage being arranged to Benedictine Monastery for parties of pilgrims from all over the Auvergne region. It emerged that tante Mathilde was among the organisers and was looking for strong support from Saint Flour

The very next day she arrived in Saint Flour. That evening she disclosed her plan If we could arrange a full bus load of pilgrims her local stock of armaments could travel on the same bus as various parcels and baggage of the pilgrims

This raised many problems, not the least was that we had already moved her stock to Tremouloux. "Oh well", she said, "we'll have to arrange bus loads from St. Chely and Aumont-Aubrac, as well to take care of that. In any event I need far more than you've allowed me anyway"

When she explained her plans in detail I could see the advantage of the move and as we were well stocked up, now agreed to the extra supplies. Alexis and I agreed that such a widely publicised event would be so well known in advance to the authorities that it would not be suspected

Raymond called a meeting at the end of September to present his final conclusions about the idea of blowing the dams on the Truyere and Lot rivers, asking that we use a safe house because there would be much time needed for discussion. I arranged to meet him at the Barrat farm one evening for a preliminary revue

161

I had not seen him since our walk to explore the dams on the Truyere. "Can you tell me in a few words what your conclusions are," I asked. "Not unless you can tell me to the nearest twenty centimetres what the monthly rainfall will be between now and the invasion," he replied

Raymond went on, "All of the factors I mentioned last time we discussed the matter still apply. "Taking all those factors into consideration plus the extra points I will raise now, there are only brief periods in any year when the plan has any chance of working and those periods are when the Truyere dams are over eighty-five per cent full

Then we have to consider how effectively we can judge the timing of blowing the Lot dams at Andressac and Camber. If we blow them too soon we lose the benefit of the water they retain, If we blow them too late we lose much of the water from the Truyere dams up the tributaries of the Lot and there area lot of them! No pun intended." "That's quite a dilemma," I commented. "I know you like figures on everything, the chances of the dams having enough water in them when the Allies invade in any summer period is about twenty percent and the chances of getting the timing right on the blowing of all eight dams is about thirty-five percent. Combine those two figures and I don't think the idea is viable and certainly not considering the cost to replace and repair the damage done"

We relapsed into silence for some minutes of thought. "I'm pleased with your quantification of the project's viability," I said, "You've justified my own feelings on the matter, it's too high a price to inflict on an Ally"

"But there is another way," said Raymond triumphantly, "We have many more men in the hills today avoiding recruitment into the Tricolour Brigade or transfer to German industry and I predict there will be more when the Germans occupy Vichy France. We should train them and be ready to move them west to reinforce the resistance groups based on Cahors, Brive and Tulle and blow the bridges by force and harass all German troop movements Northwards or Southwards. Then that just leaves the problem of the little railway lines through the Auvergne which they could also use , but they could all be easily blocked by induced rock falls or landslips at the critical moment at points that can be worked out in advance. If we have even two weeks notice of the invasion whether it be North or South the positions would be the same"

I liked his idea, "We would need to involve the Le Puy group in that planning as well," I said, "and just as a precaution we should destroy or block the N9 at some critical points even though the bridges are not strong enough to carry most army traffic. What I think we should do now is to report your conclusions and ideas to everybody and listen to their comments"

"The long term costs of your idea would be much less and the damage of very much shorter duration." "I think the chance of success is much greater and. I

162

will make sure you get full recognition for this proposal both in London and here. "I think your next task is to prepare a plan of the points where we should block the railways and roads." Raymond reached form his next bunch of papers, "It's already done," he said

Our meeting the following week at a safe house in Murat comprised Alexis Pascal, Pierre Dechaux (representing the Maire), Raymond Dad and myself. I asked Pascal to chair the meeting

As I introduced the subject of the meeting there was a stony silence. The reason for Raymond's presence in Saint Flour was known to all of these people and they were expecting bad news. I informed the meeting that Raymond had completed his strategic work and a plan had been prepared to be submitted to London with a recommendation that the final decision should be left to us when action was needed

Some relief was apparent. Raymond then presented his results and conclusions and little by little the tension eased. Pascal spoke next as chairman and thanked us for the care and consideration shown in the strategic planning recognising that we had paid due regard to France's status as an ally and not an enemy and he felt sure that common sense would prevail when the time came to take such an important decision Alexis, Pierre Dechaux and Raymond, left the meeting at this point. Pascal and I discussed getting the plan to London. This was clearly a case for a written plan to be hand carried to London. Pascal offered the services of his special courier who was departing next Wednesday, just five days ahead. Pascal assured me that this was a safe and secure procedure because in any event he would have to report our plans to De Gaulle's office. He did add that the plan would certainly be copied before it reached SOE headquarters

London agreed to my proposal to send this plan via Pascal's courier and I spent the next three days writing it up and getting Raymond to copy his map plans. When all was ready I found a reason to go to Clermont and hand it over to Pascal. We met at the same restaurant as our first meeting. Pascal had arranged a special meal for the occasion and he was most genial over the outcome. I told him I had asked London for a response within one month. "I don't think de Gaulle's office will respond as quickly as that," was his comment. "Fortunately I don't have to have De Gaulle's office permission to action the plan," I said

We were both wrong, it was the end of the year before London very reluctantly agreed to our proposal

With summer coming to an end with the evenings shortening I asked Alexis, Raymond and Felix to make independent assessments of how attitudes to resistance had changed over the summer period. I sensed there was a swing in favour of resistance and I had promised the 'senior government official' an update at this time, and I wanted to be able to say I had more than one opinion. I was

163

confident that these three would make a better assessment than I could. The results were in fact rather more favourable that my own assessment and quite similar. So I was able to report that an average of three assessments was that fifty-eight per cent of the local French were now in favour of resisting the Germans when they occupied Vichy France and that we could anticipate a further swing in favour of at least another ten per cent as and when the occupation actually took place

The report was duly transmitted and acknowledged

Shortly after, we received a request to prepare a further ten backgrounds for extra personnel to be put into the Auvergne. This was the beginning of London trying to match operatives to available cover stories. We took this as a sign of improving confidence in our operations

Alexis was the obvious person to take on this task and he did so

Stephan now started on the distribution of the 'farmer's benefits. London had been generous with the allocation of powder, shot, percussion caps and point twenty-two shells so that almost every farmer got over two years supply and they were more than happy with the result

The problems started when the rum was rationed out. Stephan lost most of the friends he had made over the shot and shell allocations. Those who had assisted in the drop zone felt they were entitled to more than others. Those who lived at the most exposed farms thought they were entitled to more than others. Those with the largest flocks thought they were entitled to more than others and so it went on. Everybody had an argument to get more. I washed my hands of the whole business and left it to Stephan but I stuck my neck out and said we could bring in some more for next winter

When the dust had settled down I asked Stephan if he could call a meeting of some representative farmers to review the success or otherwise of the dropped goods. With the cooperation of Bernice Rodot he did this and about thirty farmers and some of their wives were assembled at le Bosquet. Charles Pelletier joined us for this meeting thus for the first time demonstrating his involvement with us. Alexis had arranged a further anti sheep rustling operation that night so we could use some police vans for transport. Nobody from Saint Flour was keen to be found drunk in charge of a horse in the early hours of the morning

We managed to keep the group from deteriorating into a boozy party for long enough to learn that the hill men were most happy with the shot and shell Nobody was satisfied with their rum allocation, and demanded more next year. The French are no different from the English when it comes to free drinks

On the whole we came out of it well, we had kept our promises and would be treated seriously in future

164

The wives wanted to know about the parachute fabric, "could they have it for making underclothes?" I had to point out that there were risks attached. What would happen when the Germans had moved in and saw clothes made from parachute fabric; the conclusions were obvious. There was much banter at this point, Some of the farmers said if the Germans saw what their wives were wearing under their skirts, they deserved everything they got from the Germans, and afterwards from their husbands. I think they understood the risks and they reluctantly agreed to pack up the parachute fabric and hide it in the back of the cheese maturing caves until the end of the war. For hygiene reasons only the people who traditionally handled the cheeses were allowed into those caves

While this had been going on Bernice had prepared a huge supper which was now served with alcohol in all its forms and every one was checked to ensure it was up to standard. The inevitable question was "When are we going to do this again?" We had to point out that all the information we had indicated that German occupation was imminent and we had no idea what conditions might be like when they have moved in. The farmers left us in no doubt we had their support

Alexis took the opportunity at this point to ask for possible locations and cover stories for other personnel coming in. There were some new and interesting ideas for cover stories. "Why not", said Pierre Sentier, "have more than one man per identity. If they worked on different farms many kilometres apart it could be arranged that they were never seen together. Think about the alibi possibilities, Jacques Blanc who was seen blowing up a railway bridge could have an alibi supported by all those who had been drinking with him in the bar of the Terminus at the same time." We agreed to give this serious consideration

The party went on until about four in the morning. On the drive back we recognised that it might be difficult to maintain the exuberance of these men until the real enemy and targets could be nominated. During the drive back to Saint Flour Charles made the point that in talking to the hill men I had conveyed the impression that I was in contact with England and knew about and could arrange matters with England. He hoped that this point had not registered with the hill men. The following day the BBC reported that British troops had secured the main areas of Madagascar and that peace was restored in most of the island. Later Vichy radio admitted British force had made some gains but were being fiercely resisted by Vichy forces and local volunteers

Chapter 22

Increasing Unrest

Mum and Dad were now ready to start on their holiday come wine buying trip, and they set out on a Sunday leaving by train for Nimes. The intention was to get our cellar properly stocked before the Germans moved in. The bottles still in the cellar had all lost their labels during the flooding and although the contents were mostly still good we could only use them as house wine after opening and tasting

Manuel and I were in charge again with the holiday reliefs. Yvette became aware of the plans for a pilgrimage to the Benedictine Monastery and she asked me if we could take Jean-Francois with us. I had previously agreed with Alexis that I would not go because some of the men taking the stock were not aware of my involvement, and it would be better if I was known not to have been involved

I pleaded that with my parents away on the wine buying trip I could not leave the Terminus but I gave her adequate funds for her and Jean-Francois to travel and a few little treats for them

The date set for the pilgrimage was centred upon the feast day of Saint Gerard, one of the patron Saints of the Monastery Church, which this year fell on a Sunday. Many of the pilgrims were making a three day event of the celebration arriving on Friday and leaving on Monday. The buses from Saint Flour, St Chely and Aumont-Aubrac received special attention from our selves and Mathilde. The driver and several pilgrims were drawn from our lists of reliable men. The driver was to take the pilgrims to a stock point and fill the luggage bays with Mathilde's supplies

The other pilgrims had been asked to keep their baggage as light and as small as possible because the final hill up to the monastery was so steep. In all cases the bus arrived at the departure point with the supplies and our men already aboard. The buses were to remain near the monastery throughout the festivities so that the supplies for Mathilde could be unloaded and stowed away during the night. Buses from other points travelled at various times not all staying for the full three days

After Compline on Friday night when the superior of the order and the pilgrims had taken to their beds, the brethren and our pilgrims stowed away all of Mathilde's supplies in the special secret places made ready for them. Although she did not go on the pilgrimage, Mathilde was very much in charge of the Monastery end and made sure all was secure. Felix who went as one of the Saint Flour group said it was the slickest operation you could imagine

I was told that in all there were over 1,600 people travelling to the Monastery that weekend and I made that just over 70 busloads. Felix said the only police and gendarmes he saw were very busy sorting out the traffic congestion in the narrow lanes that were the only approach to the Monastery. A good idea well carried out. Now Mathilde's supplies were assured for some considerable time ahead

There had been two events in particular that pointed to the imminence of German occupation. The parades of Laval's Legions Tricolour through the streets of Vichy in the style of the German army, "ready willing and able to participate in the great German victories to come

When the Allied forces invaded Madagascar and were resisted by the Vichy controlled forces much bitterness crept into the Vichy radio bulletins, the reasoning behind the statements including that, "All true Frenchmen would rather salute Old Glory than the Union Jack" were most difficult to understand

The September raid on the German submarine base at Nantes resulting in heavy French civilian casualties was also presented as a further outrage against the French nation by the British. The BBC French service apparently did nothing to rebut the statements and French morale was again lowered

While Mum and Dad were away and when we were not busy with the pilgrimage arrangements Alexis, Charles and myself were busy with the rumour situation. Rumours were already rife about many subjects, some were contradictory, some were so ridiculous as to be ludicrous, and some were blatant propaganda. Charles Pelletier had long maintained that rumours as a weapon could be valuable if they were concerted and if the same rumour could be shown to come from many different sources. Thus the idea of the rumour machine was born

Unrest against the Germans was developing in many areas. Attacks on German forces and personnel were increasing in spite of the reprisals and hostage taking that followed every incident. The news about these events was usually delayed. In September some incidents in Paris led to the shooting of one hundred and fifteen communist terrorists for attacks on German servicemen. At the same time as the shooting the Germans imposed a curfew from three pm on Saturday until midnight on Sunday

News on the BBC also reported many arrests and executions of Norwegians in Trondheim for attacking Germans as well as Dutchmen being shot for attacking a German troop train. From the point of view of the people of Saint Flour the worst news was of the arrest of the Deputy Eduard Herriot by the Vichy government on unspecified charges. This man had regularly taken his holidays in the region and was popular with the people because he pleaded their problems in the French assembly with some success

Early in October there was a rumour we had to take very seriously. An English SOE officer was said to have escaped from a train taking him from Toulouse to Paris to be handed over to the Germans. I checked this report with London and got an immediate reply. 'Possibly David Turberville, if so must be assisted at all costs, held in safe location and returned to England'. Regular updates on situation imperative"

We put out an immediate request to all our contacts and the Maquis for information

Alexis started enquiries via the police and got confirmation that an English prisoner had escaped from a train for Paris at Albi. The local mlice and gendarmerie had closed a cordon round the area and the prisoner was assumed to be inside the cordon

Later a report told us that the prisoner had been arrested at the Maison la Rosa in Toulouse which was now identified as a resistance 'safe house'. London was informed. Again an immediate reply, "Last known location of David Turberville was Maison la Rosa. Assume escapee is DT and apply all resources to his safe return. He must not be allowed to fall into Germans hands alive

This became difficult, Albi was outside our area. If however David moved further away from Toulouse, he would soon come into our area and if he had been betrayed in Toulouse this seemed to be the most likely direction for him to move. Several days passed with no news except that the cordon was still in force around Albi

I decided to go South and told Mathilde I was coming regarding an urgent matter and to be ready to go on to Saint Sernin sur Renee. I knew one of her stronger groups was located there

She guessed of course why I was coming and met me at the station. She had a truck waiting and we went straight off to Saint Sernin with four of her group. All agreed that he would go East or North if he got through the cordon, and if he didn't then we couldn't help him anyway

We arrived in Saint Sernin in less than an hour. A group of eleven were waiting for us. While I had been travelling South that day five of them had been into Albi to find out first hand what was happening. The cordon was still in force and very rigidly operated. A search had been going on for some days of the area inside the cordon. Nobody had been found except two petty criminals wanted for other matters. The consensus opinion was that he was still inside the cordon

"If we could get him out, where would we hide him?" I asked," "On my brother's farm at Broquies, "said Bruno Marron. "There are so many caves we could hide an 'army there and nobody would know, and there are so many ways out you would need a regiment to seal them all." "OK," 1 said, "the questions are, How do we find him inside the cordon?, How do we get him through it and how do we get him to Brocquies"

Mathilde took over the answering,

"Getting him to Brocquies is simple he comes in our truck. If we do it on market day we will have plenty of tractors to close the road after we have passed through and if we leave about seven in the evening it will be too dark for any spotter planes to track our movements

On this poster you will see a picture of the David issued by the mlice and surprise, surprise don't you think Andre there looks a bit like him. If Andre attempts to pass the cordon without his papers and dressed like David, which we can arrange, don't you think he would be detained? And if some minutes later another man suitably disguised with perfect papers with a couple of friends with him would get through? Of course Andre, who is a little bit simple really, would eventually be released when his father the Maire of Millau hears about it and demands his release"

My only comment was "Brilliant", "But we haven't found him yet." Jean-Claude said, "I have spent four days in Albi talking to people and earlier today I found out who is hiding him, I have passed a message via my contact that plans are in hand to get him out very soon." "Is he in a safe place?" I asked. "The shop has already been searched and he was not found," said Jean-Claude." When?" I asked. "The day before yesterday", said Jean-Claude. "I didn't mean that when," I said. "When are we going to do it?" "Market day is Thursday" said Mathilde

We had been all of this time in a barn by the side of a lane. "Is there somewhere we can go and plan in safety?" I asked. "My farm is four hundred metres down this lane," said Jean-Claude, "quite safe." It didn't take long. Andre was the suspect and he was clear about his part. Jean-Claude was to make direct contact with David and find his size and get his disguise clothes for him. Bruno and his two friends Laurent and Frederic would be David's escort at the cordon control point

169

They would all be travelling in a truck that had been all day at the market and our truck with another group of six would be right behind them but not apparently associated with them. Several tractors would be available to move on to the road after we had passed to slow down and confuse any attempt to follow by the mlice

There was not much choice in which road we should use to leave Albi, it had to be the main road to Millau. Any other choice would be suspicious and it was the way most of the traffic would be leaving in the evening. The only problem would be the delay of the cordon control point itself. The control point was at the point where the railway crossed the road by an overhead bridge

I spent two days with Mathilde in Millau waiting for it all to happen. On the Thursday afternoon we travelled to Brocquies and waited patiently. At about eight-thirty we began to get anxious, nobody had arrived. By nine we were walking up and down and looking for lights heading our way. Finally at about nine-twenty they arrived, all very happy

Apparently arresting Andre had been quite protracted affair, he argued and fought the mlice so they were forced to call for extra assistance. All of this caused delay. When David and his friends passed the control point they asked what all the fuss was about and the mlice sergeant said "We've got him at last"

All arrived safely at the Maroon farm and he should conceal himself as requested by Bruno's brother Alain. When the gendarmes discover their mistake a wider search must be anticipated and we would not attempt to move him North until the situation had quietened down

On the following Saturday Andre's wife reported to the police in Millau that her husband was missing, he had not returned from his visit to the Albi market and he was not staying with any of his friends there, They had told her that he left them to travel home at about six-thirty on Thursday   The Millau police contacted the Albi police and slowly the story emerged. A man suspected of being the British SOE agent had been arrested at the cordon control point on the Millau road shortly after seven o'clock. By this time Andre's wife Angelique was calling her father-in-law the Maire of Millau to protest about the arrest of her husband. He contacted the Maire of Albi who immediately had Andre released into his custody and complained to the commander of the mlice about their conduct in arresting Andre

Mathilde was more than happy to have taken this revenge on the mlice. I left Mathilde with instructions to arrange to move David North when she judged it safe to do so with two of her group to the Mathis farm at la Cham. I then returned on the train to Saint Flour

My parents had returned in the meantime from the wine buying trip and we had plenty to talk about. I contacted London at my next schedule

170

reporting David safe and that he would shortly be in Saint Flour. I would advise them re pick up from the la Cham strip when known. Congratulations by return followed by a repeat of the ominous statement that he must not fall into German hands alive!

Then I could get down to tasting the sample bottles that my parents had brought back with them. As soon as the wines were delivered we would have enough stock to carry us through three years and by then the war should be over. The only unknown was whether they would all be delivered before the Germans moved in Most of the wine was for the bar and restaurant, all Vin du Pays. Dad had also found some good Gigondas and Crozes Hermitage 1934 for special occasions. He said all the good vintages of the late twenties had disappeared behind walls at the back of the caves as an investment for 'after the war'. The thirties had not been good wine years, poor yields and poor quality. The exception was 1934. Everything was promised for delivery to Saint Flour within the next two weeks

Mathilde kept me informed about the furore after the arrest of Andre. The Mlice insisted that they were within their rights to arrest him as he had no proper papers. The Maire's of Albi and Millau insisted unreasonable force was used and that this provoked Andre into acts of self defence against the violence of the Mlice

And so the contretemps went on. The local newspapers had a field day taking the side of the people against the Milice. When it emerged that the suspect SOE officer was being sent to Paris for interrogation by the Germans yet another furore was raised

'Wasn't the Vichy government capable of interrogating the suspect and taking whatever action was appropriate?' 'How did they know he was an SOE officer? After all he could have been an innocent Frenchman just like the one they arrested anyway, couldn't he?

The gendarmes ignored all the criticism and concentrated on the wider search for David. The local French people were quite incensed by the police actions and Mathilde's group felt they had taken some revenge for the last coup of the police in Millau

All of this meant that it was not possible to move David at all because the poice activity was now concentrated on people moving in the area by all possible means. They had recognised that David must be trying to leave Vichy France because his cover was blown. Every railway station had its barrier control supplemented by gendarmes, all bus stations were treated in the same way, anybody travelling more than locally was checked. Random road checks were in force, the major effort appeared to be in preventing David from moving South towards the well established underground railway to Spain

The gendarmes acting on Vichy instructions were now being treated as traitors by the French people of Tarn, Aveyron and the surrounding departments and there were many instances of deliberate non-cooperation and even some arrests as a result. That of course just made the situation worse. The communist groups in Toulouse became involved and the situation was not contained until the Germans moved in.

During this time London was getting worried about the safety and security of David. Our repeated assurances about his safety where he was hiding and the risks of moving him were not understood by London and the atmosphere became tense again. Finally London made me responsible for his security and safety. I accepted this responsibility provided local judgement of the safety and security of this man prevailed over views taken from a distance. Silence

Pascal came to see me. De Gaulle's office had been involved by London. At least he understood the position. I suggested he should visit Brocquies so that he could report to De Gaulle's office on the true situation as he saw it. "That will not be necessary," he said, "I will confirm to De Gaulle's office that I am completely satisfied that this matter is being dealt with in the best possible manner under all of the circumstances prevailing here in Vichy France. Also that I have every confidence that David will be returned to the UK as agreed at the earliest safe opportunity and in such a manner that his security will not be compromised"

Chapter 23

Laying Low

More news of atrocities following resistance to German domination came to light. A bomb attack in Warsaw killed a number of German officers and fifty-five hostages were executed. In Slovenia fifty hostages were shot following the killing of a German official

The war news got better, and with it the number of people listening to the BBC French service increased. So did the penalty for listening to the BBC but nobody took any notice and in Saint Flour there was nobody willing to enforce the penalties

Finally the German advance towards Cairo had been stopped at a place called El Alamein, which nobody had ever heard of. Eventually somebody found a map with enough detail to show the place and everybody was shocked to see how near to Cairo the Germans had reached. The advance towards the Caspian oilfields of Russia also ground to a halt in the mud around Stalingrad. At last the relentless advance of the German war machine had stopped on the two active fronts

The reports from North Africa placed great importance on the efforts of the British navy and air force in bombing the supply routes for fuel and munitions that were now very stretched. Malta continued to hold out against the air raids and continued to provide a base for reconnaissance flights which could direct attacks on Rommel's supply routes to North Africa

With the change in German fortunes Alexis decided it was a good time to start the rumour machine going. We decided to ignore the good news from Africa and Russia which was being talked about enough already. We decided to enhance the discomfiture of the Germans supporters by exaggerating the damage being done by the air attacks in the North on the railways and supporting this by the real lengthening delays in mail from occupied France

173

Then what had happened to Goering's wonderful Luftwaffe?, because they were powerless to stop these raids. It was less than a year ago when they had complete mastery of the air over all France

Air raids over the French mainland had now reached right up to the borders of Vichy France notably with the heavy raid on the Schneider factory at Le Creusot and a few days later the BBC announced that bombers had started attacking targets in northern Italy. Stephan was able to confirm this through his contacts in Turin This meant that now all of France was within the range of bombers from the Royal Air Force and the United States Army Air Force During October the news broadcasts of the BBC French service were being jammed more effectively by the Germans and it was increasingly difficult for the French listeners in Saint Flour to hear the news on the BBC. Vichy French news was incomplete and the content was being dictated by the Germans. I asked Felix to see what he could do about this "Nothing", was the reply, "unless I have unlimited access to radio components and other devices." "The best thing you can do is to pass the problem to Pascal in Clermont. The technical high school could probably do it if they could be trusted"

I did that but got no immediate response. We struggled on with many listeners trying to piece the BBC broadcasts together from part transcripts of the broadcasts. Probably we got the general idea in most cases but this was also an opportunity for the rumour machine and further daily rumours were started based on the gleanings from the BBC adapted to our interests and nobody could argue with our rumoured news

In spite of the difficulties in hearing the BBC French service we were able to understand that something momentous was happening in Egypt. The eighth army were not simply resisting the German advance but attacking the German lines and even pushing the Germans back, Not only with frontal attacks but also out-flanking movements through the treacherous sands of the Quatara depression to attack the extended German supply lines along the Mediterranean coast. For the first time there was news of the Fighting French forces from Chad also harassing the German Southern flanks

The rumour machine made good use of this greatly exaggerating the activity of the Fighting French with good effect on the morale of the general population. One bulletin that was received almost un-jammed dealt with the resistance to the Germans in other parts of Europe. A total of 93 French people in occupied France had been executed for attacking Germans. The unrest in Norway had increased especially around Trondheim which is now isolated from the rest of the country with many more executions taking place, News also of the unrest in the occupied countries of Eastern Europe, Yugoslav patriots controlling the mountainous areas of Croatia and other resistance groups active in

Herzegovinia. More problems for the Germans in Poland and Ukraine with much of the forest areas under the control of resistance forces

Early in November the BBC French news service announced a full scale retreat of German forces from the battlefield of El Alamein closely followed by news that an armistice was signed in Madagascar following complete occupation by allied forces including the Fighting French. Vichy radio made no report of these events

Pascal acted quite expeditiously over the subject of radio reception for the BBC French service. Other groups had the same problem. A group of trusted teachers at the technical high school came up with some portable receivers with very fine tuning possibilities and some method I didn't understand, for also receiving the jamming signal and subtracting it from the total signal received by the aerial so that you could then hear the BBC transmission even more clearly

The portability was valuable to us because, provided you had batteries available, and they were the heavy and difficult-to-move part, you could use them anywhere For us that meant up in the hills where reception was better anyway and some farms had batteries and charging facilities for them

So Felix became our chief listener and relayed news to Saint Flour each day from which the rumour machine concocted its latest propaganda. We insisted however that there must always be some element of truth in every piece of propaganda so that the credulity of the rumour was well founded. With the increasing amount of good news we could really see the change in the morale of the people

Now we had reliable news again we could keep up with the events on a daily basis. The news steadily got better. We heard that the RAF and USAAF were bombing northern Italy, and much to our surprise that the Russians were bombing some Eastern European cities. Every day now we heard of the battles the Eighth army were winning at El Alamein and the heavy losses the Germans were suffering at Stalingrad
People actually began to talk about the Germans actually losing the War!

All of this good news was arriving just in time for my birthday on the 27th. This was my first birthday back in Saint Flour and probably the last before the Germans moved in. My parents did their best to make it notable

Most of the wine my parents had bought arrived the day before the 27th as did Mathilde and her two sons. Yvette had her own way of making it special lasting for several days. Manuel unbeknown to everyone had arranged a special lunch menu and insisted I joined in all through the lunch period. Even Jean-Francois seemed to understand that it was a special day for me. The party really started with Manuel's lunch arrangements and continued right throughout the day and evening

I was embarrassed by the number of people who passed through the Terminus that afternoon and evening with the main object of wishing me well. Alexis of course was in the bar for part of the evening. After we closed up, quite late for a Wednesday, I asked him if he thought my identity was known to some of the townspeople. "No," he assured me, "they are simply pleased to see you making some success of your life in the community." I wasn't so sure that he was right

It wasn't all good news for everyone. Many people in Saint Flour had relatives in occupied France. Every day and every night there was also news of targets in occupied France being attacked and communications were more difficult especially after heavy attacks when the telephone system was overloaded and letters delayed by transport problems. After repeated bomber attacks on Lille and no letters Mum was again anxious about granddad Renaud

Chapter 24

Suddenly

After some weeks of laying very low at Brocquies Mathilde decided it was time to move David Turberville. Our rumour machine had also reached the Southern edge of the Auvergne and had a similar effect on the morale of the people. Mathilde now felt confident enough to move him North. I had already agreed a plan for the move with Pascal. He arranged with Francois Pelion in le Puy to use a safe house in Brioude. Mathilde brought him by truck to Millau and the next day went with him on the bus to Mende where he was passed to me at the terminus and I took him to Brioude. Mathilde pointed me out to him and told him to get on the same bus as me and to get off where I got off and to follow me to the safe house. When the bus came in to the bus terminus she gave him a typical Mathilde farewell, much to his embarrassment and he took his seat a couple of rows behind me

Just over three hours later he followed me off the bus at the Place de Gregorian de Tours, round a few corners into a quiet street and into our safe house

"So you must be Henri Dufour." he said as the door closed. "That's what they call me here" I said in English," and that's the only name you'll have for me, Now I must introduce you to Pascal and that's the only name you'll have for him." They shook hands. "Who was the rather large lady who brought me to Mende?" David said, "and didn't I see you when I arrived at that farm?" "Yes you did, and the large lady I saw hugging you in Mende is my Aunt." "I don't understand" said David. "Good", said Pascal, "and that's the way it will stay"

You can take it from me that we are all friends here to help you on your way. After that we don't exist any more for you Tomorrow night, weather permitting you will leave by Lysander for England. Henri here will take you to the plane."   "Now I will take you up to your room where you can freshen yourself up and relax until about seven-thirty when we will go out to dinner"

Pascal came down again at once. "I need to talk to you at once he said about this," handing me a decoded message. It read, Travel with DT in same Lysander. Expect to be absent two/three days. SGO demands meeting with you. This matter is top priority." I've arranged for you to be in Millau for a few days as a cover story" said Pascal. "De Gaulle's office has also required me to give you every assistance to cover your absence." he added. "So I guess you've got to go" "OK" I replied, I'll have to leave my small bag with you, I won't need it in England, and you'll have to arrange for it to be waiting for me when I get back I won't mention this to DT until I get into the plane with him, just in case"

We all met again at seven-thirty down in the salon. "I should explain," said Pascal," this town is completely safe for us, all the police and gendarmerie here are totally reliable. We can go to the best restaurant, where I am known, and we will get a good dinner. It is only about two hundred metres from here but please take note of the way, here is a key to the front door, check it on the way out. If, by any chance, we are interrupted at the restaurant Henri and I will deal with the interruption and you should immediately return here and wait for one of us to return."

"You seem very well organised," said David. "That's why we are still here, "I said. "From now we speak only French," said Pascal

Brioude is famous for its mushrooms and the season had started. We enjoyed a good, varied, very tasty dinner. David relaxed visibly as he became aware that everything Pascal had said was correct. The proprietor served us himself, the restaurant was not busy. We left at about ten suitably fortified with the local liqueurs and spent a restful night

The time dragged on the next day, we had nothing to do but to wait. Lunch at the same restaurant was drawn out to three o'clock. I advised David to sleep if he could in the afternoon as he would be up all night. We both slept and at about eight Alexis Lescaut arrived with the police van to take us to Barrat Farm strip

David was no longer surprised at anything, not even the use of a police van with a uniformed driver. Alexis did not consider it prudent to take the police van to the Barrat farm. We left it parked in its usual place and took to bicycles. Alexis took charge of my small bag. When we arrived at the farm Marguerite had a large tureen of good meaty soup ready for supper, "That'll help to keep the cold out for an hour or two." she said, "It will be really cold later and especially where you're going"

David remarked how much better the food was in the country, "In Toulouse," he said, "it was quite difficult for my hosts to feed an extra mouth and

178

the same in Albi, but here there is clearly plenty and it's good." Jean Chavent had been up to the strip and cleared the stones out of the way at dusk, so when the time came we wrapped up warmly in sheepskin jackets, took our torches and Aldis lamp and started the climb

I guessed it was our usual pilot, when we first heard the plane he was on exactly the same track as previously and as soon as he had turned round the Cathedral tower we could exchange signals and get the torches set out. He landed exactly on time

Not quite such a quick turn round as usual. There were two large heavy boxes to come off before the seats could be set up. "I understand you're coming along for the ride," the pilot said, as I climbed in after David, "Well you can't trust these runaways to find their way home."

David looked surprised, "Is this a personal escort?" he asked. "I was made responsible for your safe return," I jokingly remarked. I don't know whether he saw the joke or not. I was puzzled by those two heavy boxes

As the plane disappeared into the night, Alexis said to Jean Chavent, "Those two boxes are for Simon and Patrice, They contain some new type of sub-machine gun and we have to train everyone to use them, and then we cam call for further supplies"

Jean Chavent said, "It's too risky to take those down tonight, if we drag them down to the bottom of the gully I'll take them down at dawn when I come up to move the stones back"

The new guns were sten-guns and Simon and Patrice were quite excited about them, "They are as good as anything the Germans have and they're much lighter. They had seen prototypes during their training but did not know when they were to be issued. The training programme had gone well so far

Both Simon and Patrice commented on the difference between training men who already knew the basic rules about firearms, as distinct from the raw recruits they had to work with in England. One of the advantages of being in a country which had compulsory military service for all

There were no incidents on the flight to England. We landed in darkness and immediately two officers welcomed us and took charge of David and he was whisked away with barely time to say goodbye. I was allowed to sleep until after ten and then with an English breakfast inside me driven to SOE headquarters

There was quite a difference in attitudes from my last visit a bare five months ago. Certain urgency was in the air. "You have a meeting at 15 hours I was told as soon as I entered the building, there will be no home leave or home phone calls on this visit, and you have a second meeting late this evening. You will stay here tonight after the second meeting. Tomorrow is still being planned"

It was a small meeting in the afternoon, the formal business was over quickly mainly because so little had been prepared. I made a mental note to ensure all other meetings were at short notice. "You did a remarkable job getting David Turberville out of that mess, we are very grateful," remarked the chairman. "He spoke very highly of the efficiency of your planning and especially of the men who got him out of Albi." "I can't take much credit for that, the men who manipulated his escape from Albi were all 'Maquis', simply because it was their idea and I don't think any other locals would have been so enterprising.

The resistance contribution was his hide out and getting him far enough North for a Lysander pick-up." "Are you admitting that you actively cooperated with the communists in this matter, because if you are you have also disclosed David Turberville's mission to the communists" "I admit that I exercised my judgement of the available possibilities of getting David Turberville out of Albi bearing in mind that the city was ring fenced with control posts to try and intercept him. I could not disclose David Turberville's mission to the maquis because I am not aware of the nature of his mission. Furthermore the maquis are a valuable source of information to me because they are better informed than I am over many matters. For example I have been told of a plan for the USA to invade North Africa across the Atlantic landing in Morocco so as to create a second front situation in that theatre of war. I have also been told that the SGO I believe that I am to see this evening has been in Marrakesh on holiday and was visited by the King Muhammad of Morocco for confidential talks. It may also interest you to know that the identical story re a USA invasion of Morocco was also picked up by my four colleagues who arrived in the summer via Gibraltar in Gibraltar itself"

There were many seconds of pregnant silence. "Do you not think it likely that your own people may have talked to the local maquis?" "Of course I have interviewed all four of our men and they strenuously deny even mentioning the Gibraltar storys to any body other that myself and Alexis." "Do you believe them?" "Yes, and I would add that even the most lowly members of the maquis talk about matters in the bar concerning the grand strategy of the war and their prognoses sometimes happen. Please don't misunderstand me; I am not making out a case to have more information. I completely support the viewpoint that such matters should not be known by field officers for obvious reasons"

The meeting moved on to the vexed point of cooperation with the maquis. I had to come back on the Albi situation, "You should understand that the French resistance movements in Vichy France exist mainly in the smaller towns and country regions. In the cities the communists prevail because of the widespread support from trade unionists for the communist cause. When I checked the situation in Albi the answer was that there was an embryo French resistance group active in Albi and I considered it unwise to use such a group in the light of your statements regarding David Turberville. But I still had your direct order to use all means to get this man back to England alive and well and we have done it. So far I have not heard anything about his mission, and I must add not even from the maquis"

You speak as though you are in daily contact with the maquis." "Yes I suppose I am, I doubt if there is ever a day goes by when one or more known maquis members come into the Terminus, I don't start the subjects of conversation and much of what I hear is what is said between people at the bar. If I want to contact them in any sort of official capacity I do it via Stephan who claims he is the local coordinator and he is clearly regarded as having some authority by all the men of the maquis

However I cannot rule out that there might be someone else who has yet to make an appearance. You must understand it is quite easy for any one who wants to be unseen to remain so up in those hills. I should also add that Stephan says he knows exactly who I am and why I am in Saint Flour. So how good is our security?"

"Are you concerned about your cover being blown?" "I think 'blown' is too strong a word. I trust Stephan completely, and I do not think my identity is known to anyone other than the men under my command, and the few senior members of the Saint Flour resistance group about whom you know

The only other person who I think might have worked it out for himself is Doctor Bodanski," and I related the conversation that took place when he examined my leg and his notes thereafter adding that Doctor Bodanski had now disappeared when the Jewish families moved out." I remember your report about the Jewish families leaving," said the Chairman," "that was in the summer I believe?" "Yes immediately after Bastille Day," I replied." "Does anyone have any news of where they went?" "Rumour says they, with all the Jewish families from neighbouring towns crossed into Spain a few days after they left here. I think that is almost certainly true." "Why do you think they went at that time?" "Because is the busiest time of the year on the roads in France and when families travelling together would not be conspicuous Once again so little understanding of France

With a few other routine matters the meeting drifted to a conclusion with one last question from the chairman, "Do you think we understand the real situation in France well enough?" "I can only answer No," I said, "but I understand your problem, you are inundated with reports from the Free French in London. What they say may be partly true in Paris and other large cities but it is not true in the rural areas or in the smaller cities where industry is the main commercial activity, and that is where the communists have their strength in the trade union movement and consequently most of the resistance activity is carried out by organisations like the maquis"

"Fortunately the people like yourself are all telling us similar storys otherwise you would be in trouble, you are rather blunt with some of your comments. We are not too keen on disclosing how many reports we have that contradict the free French statements. They want the whole liberation of France to be carried out by Frenchmen"

After an early dinner I was standing by to be summoned by the SGO. Very late in the evening it came and the car took me to the same doorway for the same security checks. The SGO did not keep me waiting long this time. He rose to greet me hand extended, "I want to congratulate you on the way you handled the David Turberville matter," was his greeting. "Getting him out of Albi was most ingenious, was it your idea?" "No, I can claim no credit for that part of the operation it was the Albi group who came up with that plan which depended entirely on local information which I could not have known. I have already expressed our thanks to that group." "Good, I don't intend to take much of your time tonight. The report from this afternoon's meeting is most encouraging; they are beginning to believe you at last, as I do. You should have an easier time from now on. I am pleased that we no longer hear of our supplies being used by the maquis and I want you to keep up the success rate and improve on it when possible. It won't be long now before the Germans move in; so prepare yourselves

You seem to be as well informed as we are! and before you ask I did enjoy Marrakesh. You should go there at the first opportunity." With that said I found the inevitable body at my elbow to usher me out

Again I was offered a very fine brandy while waiting for my car. Then back to headquarters and a good night's sleep. Instructions to relax in the morning, take lunch with the chairman of yesterday's meeting, and be ready to leave at 1530 to return to Saint Flour

Lunch at the Ritz with the chairman was delicate to say the least. I suspect that he had been told to take a revised approach to the Free French and he was quite affable over the support I could expect in the future. Almost as an aside, at the end of the meal he said, "Your promotion to Major will be gazetted sometime in the next month so you can inform your colleagues as soon as you wish. Your pay will be adjusted as from today, and is in line with our intention to promote all SOE French section personnel. Therefore all of your men can expect a step up, so please tell them this from me at the first opportunity. In all cases the pay increase will date from today." I thanked him for myself and for my men. I took the opportunity to raise the idea of dual use of duplicate identities as proposed by Pierre Sentier. "I think it has some merit," was the chairman's first comment, and used sparingly could confuse the authorities, but repetitive use might alert the authorities to the scheme with perhaps some retribution on your people as they would be identified as resistance members." His point was valid and we agreed that use of the twins should be left to my judgement in the field

My car arrived on time and I enjoyed a comfortable ride to the country on a warm autumn afternoon. I knew exactly where I was as far as Pulborough. but then we turned into lanes with no signposts. Apart from knowing that I was somewhere in the triangle between Pulborough, Arundel and Petworth and on the North side of the downs, I was lost. We arrived at a smallish country house where we were clearly expected by the inevitable ATS ladies to search us for concealed evidence of having been in England

Two more SOE men were also undergoing the same treatment and soon it was clear they were on the same flight. "Pascal will be meeting these two gentlemen when you land and taking them on to their destination." said the dispatcher. "And no exchange of information between you is permitted for all the usual reasons." Although we were not supposed to talk it rapidly became clear that there was a panic on to get men into France. Over our final dinner we learnt that several were going out every day

Our Pilot confirmed this later, "It's just like a bus service nowadays except that the route is never the same."The flight was without incident and we landed on time. Pascal and Councillor Fernand Leman were both waiting. We warmed up at the Barrat farm before Pascal left with his new recruits. It had been a really cold flight, so Fernand and I took a little longer at the Barrat farm to warm up

We thanked Marguerite and Jean apologising for keeping them up late again before taking to our bikes for the short ride into Saint Flour. In spite of all the excitement of the sudden trip to England I was relieved to be back among my family, I seemed to belong there. Yvette was surprised as I slid into bed beside her. She had been told I would be back tomorrow from Millau. She could not understand how I arrived in the middle of the night. I concocted a story about hitching a lift in a truck so as to get back to her sooner

Every day now we had news of the raids by both the RAF and the USAAF all over Europe including also including raids by Russian bombers coming in from the other side of Europe. Probably there were no parts of German occupied Europe that could not now be attacked from the air. There was again no news from granddad Renaud and so often Lille was included in the targets being raided. Then one morning we got a whole bunch of letters covering a time span of eight weeks. The date is well remembered. Later that day the BBC French service announced the start of Operation Torch

Chapter 25

Torched

Although the reports we had from our four men who arrived via Gibraltar and the news from the maquis via Stephan had predicted this operation there is nothing quite like the fact of it actually happening to stimulate feelings of elation that at last a very large initiative had been started

A second front in North Africa could achieve so much, the liberation of Algeria and Tunisia from the axis powers and now a three-way pressure on the axis forces from the East, West and the South

We turned the rumour machine on to the subject that this second front in North Africa would inevitably mean the occupation of Vichy France by the Germans As a result most people believed the rumour and everyone was preparing for the worst situation they could imagine. However in spite of the foreboding there was now good news every day now on the French service. More details of operation Torch almost every hour. Troops had landed in Casablanca, Oran and Algiers. Algiers surrendered within a few hours of the landings

The announcement that General Giraud was cooperating with the Allied forces in Algeria was a surprise and was welcomed by all. He had been captured by the Germans and imprisoned in Saxony. He escaped in May 1942 and reached safety via Switzerland and eventually England

Just two days into Operation Torch and Oran was captured. The Vichy government immediately broke off diplomatic relations with the United States of America German paratroops occupied all major airfields in Tunisia

After only four days of Operation Torch Admiral Darlan ordered all French commanders in Algeria and Morocco to cease hostilities. So in such a short space of time the Allied forces had secured firm bridgeheads along a vast stretch of the North West coast of Africa

Later that same day German and Italian troops start to occupy Vichy France

The euphoria arising from the successes in North Africa was tempered by anxiety about what the occupation of all of Vichy France might mean to the people of Saint Flour

Vichy radio was working overtime trying to pacify the situation blaming the "unlawful occupation" of Algeria and Morocco by Allied forces for the German and Italian occupation of all France so as to 'protect, the French people from any onslaught from the South. The boldness and the success of operation Torch convinced many Frenchmen that the liberation of France could come from either North or South or possibly both at the same time, and we listened to endless debates in the bar on the merits of all the alternatives

There was some resistance to the Germans especially in the area around Tulle and in Clermont but it was rapidly suppressed and some members of the resistance groups were taken prisoner. The prisoners were tried by Court Martial after a few days and executed

The first news in Saint Flour was an announcement by the Maire. He said he was "Speaking for the Gauleiter of the department of Cantal based in Aurillac. In future the people of Saint Flour were to be governed from Aurillac and all administration would be from there. German troops would shortly arrive in Saint Flour and the people were advised to welcome them and cooperate with them so as to avoid any repetition of the unfortunate events elsewhere"

This announcement was made in the Place d'Armes and in the Place de la Liberte. It was greeted with stony silence. Some of the more left wing young men who had so far escaped the transfer to the German war machine left town life and joined the maquis. A few others left their families in the town and became itinerant workers with the hill farmers constantly changing their location and sometimes creeping back into town to help their families

My own position was now questionable. Although I was 'unfit for military service' in an operational sense many young Frenchmen had been compulsorily enlisted into other parts of the German war machine, so why should I not be so enlisted? Alexis took me into the Mairie and got my file. He showed me the original entries made when my 'alter ego' had been inscribed in the town register relating to my mental condition and the need for me to be educated in special schools. He pointed to the extra entry that had been added when I returned from Lille which had elaborated on the point that although I had received part of the training as an apprentice at Precision Metal the German management had found me unsuitable and returned me to Saint Flour. "All the people who handle these files understand the need to keep you here," said Alexis. "But what if it does not satisfy the Germans?" I questioned. "Then you'll have to take to the hills like some others." "Suppose they simply have the gendarmes grab me as they have some others," I asked. "In that case we'll arrange another David Turberville operation for you. Remember we're much better placed to do that here than in Albi." In spite of such reassurances I felt apprehensive about the Germans moving in. Four days later two columns of vehicles from the German army arrived in Saint Flour, one via the road from Aurillac and one via the road from Issoire

The officers commandeered the Hotel des Voyageurs in the rue du College in the upper town and the men and non commissioned officers were garrisoned in the old Gendarmerie barracks along the avenue du Commandant Delorme quite near to the Terminus. The first troops arriving in Saint Flour were made up mostly of men in their fifties, many of whom were first-world-war veterans. There were a few younger men who were unfit for combat duty for various reasons. The locals immediately christened the elderly ones as 'Les cheers vieux grand Peres'.Later for our communication purposes we anglicised this to the dear old granddads (DOGS.) The German administrators who arrived later were called Les Sales which we kept as (SALES) for communication purposes

Their behaviour was faultless in the first few days. After that there was a sweep made through the town and all men under the age of 65 were interviewed by the officers for potential service in the German army or war machine. Some further men evaded the sweep and disappeared into the hills

The Germans had the list of inscribed inhabitants for Saint Flour from the Maire's office and attempted to reconcile the men they interviewed with the list. There was a huge discrepancy. Their problem was greater because they had not understood that many of the people in the sub-prefecture of Saint Flour who lived outside the town rather than within the town itself

They had clearly spent time in the Mairie. When they came into the Terminus to interview us, they were in fact quite polite. Dad's position was clear. He was exempted because of his poor health resulting from his gassing in the first world war. They paid little attention to me presumably because Alexis and the Maire had made it clear I was not of much consequence and made it clear that they wanted the proper running of a bar to continue because that was important to maintaining the morale of the German troops and provided we continued to give good service we were 'doing our duty to the Third Reich'

Manuel however was a very different matter, even though he produced his Spanish passport and other papers they tried very hard to recruit him into the Tricolour Battalion or to go and work in Germany for their war effort. They stressed the support General Franco had for the national socialist policies

Manuel rejected all their arguments and simply said that if they persisted he would return to Spain and then both the Terminus and the St. Jacques hotel would be short of a chef. They finally had to agree that they had no claim on his services because Spain was officially neutral.

After they had finished their recruitment attempts, we made them quite welcome in the Terminus and even gave them a lunch 'on the house'. As Dad said, after they'd gone, "It was a little investment in the future but God alone knows what it will be." The next attempt, which everyone had foreseen, was to try and repeat the same operation in the small outlying communes that made up the whole of the Saint Flour sub-prefecture. As soon as they made any attempt to move out of Saint Flour the bush telegraph warned all the communes along whichever road they took in advance. Thus only the men who chose to be found were actually interviewed. They were the very elderly, the infirm and disabled, and boys who had left school to work on the farms in place of fathers engaged elsewhere

The Germans next tried to visit some of the even more outlying hamlets along 'roads' that were little better that wide footpaths arriving at a hamlet comprising a farm and a few outlying cottages. Any men who lived there made sure they were working as far away as possible and could not be found. Any women and children who were about at the time of the visit would generally resort to their local language of Auvergnat and did not understand the Germanic French spoken by the interviewers. There were some fourteen hundred names of men liable for service in the German war machine inscribed in the Saint Flour Maire's list. Of these some had already 'volunteered' for service, some had taken to the hills, some had gone elsewhere and because they were still on the Saint Flour list they had clearly not been inscribed in any other list. Some men were in protected jobs for companies already heavily engaged in work for the German war machine. Even after they had reviewed the men in protected jobs and taken those they wanted, the total actually recruited was only 194

Unfortunately Auguste Deville, Yvette's father, was amongst them and was compulsorily enlisted into one of the Tricolour battalions. This caused great distress to Yvette especially as she had already lost Philippe

The maquis had arranged a series of lookouts on all the roads leaving Saint Flour. There were only seven of them, and as soon as a move was made alerted all likely communes and hamlets by phone, by waved signals, with shouted messages from hilltops and even sheepdogs sent home with a message tucked into their collars. I do not believe the Germans ever recognised how efficiently they were being watched

Nor did they even guess at how many able bodied men were living in the hills constantly changing their locations and being accommodated by the outlying farmers

This message system of the maquis endeared them to all, even to those who found their politics undesirable The Cantonal Gauleiter in Aurillac was clearly not satisfied with the result

"The unsatisfactory result of our recruitment in Saint Flour is the worst in the whole department must be improved," was the ominous announcement. The Gauleiter himself plus his entourage, supported by SS officers arrived in Saint Flour. A whole day was spent with the local wehrmacht officers and when the Gauleiter left later we got the full force of his wrath

A curfew was imposed from twenty-one hours to five hours. Late bus services were retimed to finish before the curfew hour. Any non-German found on the street after this time would be arrested unless he had a permit from the German commandant in Saint Flour. The permit system was administered by the SS officers who remained behind in Saint Flour. The attitude of the people to the occupiers hardened

The loss of a 194 men from the town was immediately noticeable. Many of them had been regulars at the Terminus. The curfew at nine also meant loss of valuable evening drinking time, although the few remaining locals did their best to be drunk by curfew time. Dad made an offer to the occupying troops that we could remain open after curfew to serve drinks and a small evening menu to the off duty men if they would like that, without breaking the curfew rule ourselves

This was taken up with alacrity and we guessed that German field rations were not too tasty. So at nine o'clock in the evening it was a total change over. After the locals had gone we had to prepare for our new clientele. The locals didn't like it but Dad said, "We couldn't afford to open at all unless we had the German evening trade and we had to survive"

Initially nobody went out after curfew. Patrol groups of troops supervised by the SS officers were constantly moved about the town. This created all sorts of problems. Not the least of which was getting news. In the town itself nobody dare listen in to the BBC. The jamming had now stopped but with German troops moving about the town, and they had been seen listening at windows, having your radio tuned to the BBC was a risk you did not take. In his location Felix had no problems of that sort. We let it be known to the Germans that Manuel and myself would have to go foraging in the countryside if we were going to provide them with tasty snacks in the evenings. This gave us the opportunity to meet with Felix and get the latest news on the days when we went foraging

Chapter 26

Restrictions and Curfews

The presence of the Germans necessitated much rethinking of our plans. Quite suddenly everything we wished to do have become more difficult. Fortunately our stocks of weapons and other hardware was all well dispersed and hidden. However the enemy knew there were more men up in the hills who could carry out sabotage operations against them and regular checks of people movements went all the time

As well as the curfew restricting night time movements any journey over about twenty kilometres needed a permit Permits were issued at the place where the traveller lived and had to be surrendered at your destination so that a return permit could be issued for the return journey

Daytime life was little affected within the town itself. No attempts were made to follow people who left on bicycles but the buses would not take passengers beyond the defined limits unless they had the proper permit. Occasionally people returning late in the day and were searched as they re-entered the town. The searchers were well mannered and polite unless there were SS personnel in evidence nearby, when shouting replaced the politeness and sometimes something quite trivial was confiscated

All the police and gendarmes had permits to be out after the curfew hour, as did hospital staff and some of the Marie staff. For the rest of the inhabitants evening socialising simply stopped at about eight forty-five. With the presence of German troops in the Terminus our evening meetings had to stop resulting in serious loss of communication and almost brought our planning to a standstill

Even Manuel was given a permit so that he could move from the St. Jacques to the Terminus after curfew, but granting that permit was in the interest of the German soldiers!

The local police were supposed to assist the Germans in enforcing the curfew so we had good information about how they patrolled and their numbers. They were certainly efficient and very few people who went out after curfew evaded them. Penalties were quite stiff fines levied in the Court on the following day after their arrest. Being caught a second time usually involved an unpleasant interview with the SS Captain on temporary attachment to Saint Flour plus an even larger fine levied by the Court. Repeat offences were few, people could not afford it

Resistance activity in Saint Flour itself came to an abrupt halt. Organisation of any activity was very difficult and the brutal reaction of the Germans at Tulle and Clermont had left the townspeople fearful for their lives. Morale needed rebuilding

On the other front the men in the hills were already sniping at German vehicles on the more deserted stretches of the roads. Reaction was immediate from the Germans. Vehicles stopped and fire was returned, but the maquis, the smell on the hillside, had evaporated. Only minor German casualties but the annoyance and delays thus caused wounded the German pride. Heavily armed patrols went into the hills

The maquis warning system worked well, and when the Germans arrived at any farm or hamlet they found only women and children and never of course the least sign of any weapons. Nevertheless casualties occurred. Heavily armed men not used to the terrain inevitably tripped, slipped and felt. The injuries were essentially trivial but the men were out of service for some days. German pride was again dented. More lightly armed night patrols found their way blocked by sheep with the tracks made more treacherous after dark by sheep dung. When they did eventually arrive at a farm they might find a very elderly grandfather at the fireside as well as the women. The Auvergnat language presented its usual problems. Some patrols took revenge by stealing sheep on their return journey to improve their rations

The Maire received many complaints of these thefts, and they numbered far more than the actual number of sheep stolen. The complaints were passed to the German commandant who rejected them. The Commandant issued warnings that the curfew applied equally to the open country as well as the town, and that his men were ordered to fire after a single warning on any person moving around during the curfew hours. There were concessions for farmers with milking sheep or cattle when the surroundings of the farms were considered as home territory. It was now the end of November and the curfew restrictions were a real burden on the local people

The war had finally come to Saint Flour

The Commandant was ordered by his superior in Auriliac to take the local force of Gendarmes under his command and to use their local knowledge to enforce the German edicts. Further statements said that the resistance forces operating in the hills would be ruthlessly eliminated for the benefit of the French patriots of Saint Flour

This caused an immediate problem. The local police sergeant, Alexis Lescaut, had the prime responsibility to the Maire for maintaining Law and Order in the town and commune of Saint Flour. This responsibility was shared with the Gendarmerie who had greater powers and could operate anywhere in the department of Cantal, they reported via their own chain of command to the departmental government in Aurillac. In view of Alexis Lescaut's involvement in the resistance movement this was a crisis because he had to maintain some semblance of cooperation at a local level with the gendarmerie

News filtered through that similar activity was taking place around Aurillac and getting the same reaction from the Germans. Retaliation in this area included the search of the buildings of a religious group near Badhilac quite close to Aurillac

Our immediate concern was had the Germans got some hint of resistance supplies being stockpiled in a monastery. Alexis immediately got a message off to Mathilde informing her of that event

The Maire stepped in by telling the commandant that it was not reasonable for the police, who were part of the local community to have to cooperate with the gendarmerie who now were part of the occupying forces and that consequently he had ordered Sergeant Alexis Lescaut not to cooperate in any way with the gendarmerie. The tension was rising

The weather on some days was crystal clear, not a cloud in the sky. On these days the Storch planes were up from Clermont presumably searching for clues to resistance activity. Our local commandant now added patrols of vehicles and men on foot operating in some conjunction with the planes by signal lamps. This made life and work more difficult for the resistance men who had to work in order to survive

Very few of them had identity papers of any sort and could not pass any examination by the Germans. More ingenuity was required. Those with genuine identity papers became very prominent, some being checked several times in the course of a day, and of course they were never carrying a weapon

The others simply disappeared into caves, or thickets or farm outbuildings out of sight of the patrols. When the Storch planes came down low for a closer look they were likely to be fired upon but we did not hear of any damage to the planes. The maquis were very good marksmen and if it was farmers using shotguns they probably would not reach the planes with their shot so we concluded that the firing was only a deterrent

On one such day the commandant gave orders for all the men his patrols found, to be brought in for questioning. He finished up with over thirty very cross individuals who had been taken away from their work and whose papers were all in order. From the talk in the bar after event it was evident that these men gave the Germans a hard time. Jean Chavent was among those brought in. Jean said, "They asked me why I was not carrying a gun, and I told them I only carried a gun when I wanted to shoot something, Then they asked me if I had heard any shooting that morning. Yes I said, over towards Coltines several times when the planes came down low. "Who was shooting" asked the Commandant. "No idea," said Jean," I can see a plane at five kilometres but not a man." "What sort of guns were they firing," asked the commandant. "The ordinary sort," said Jean, Where you put the shells in at the back and it all fires out of the end of the barrel." And over the next few days we heard similar tales from others questioned

Supplies of local produce for the evening menu became difficult. The local farmers who had been supplying to us for a better price and to keep the Germans off the streets after curfew said that with the problems of the curfew and the friction developing between the locals and Germans over the many restrictions on travel they would no longer supply us at any price. The smallholders around the town joined with the farmers. Dad had to go to the commandant and say that we had to withdraw the evening opening unless the Germans could supply us with provisions for the evening menu and if we could not serve food we could not afford to open in the evenings after curfew

The evenings were rapidly getting shorter and the effects of the curfew were greatly resented by the town dwellers. Evening socialising had almost ceased. Breaches of the curfew increased with more cunning being used. Diversions would be created to attract the German patrols away from certain areas by arrangement. Stone throwing at the patrols started. The Germans retaliated as best they could but very few arrests were made and unless they had caught the stone throwers red-handed, the accused all had quite remarkably well supported alibis

The Maire applied for a travel permit to go to Aurillac to raise matters with the cantonal authorities, it was refused. The Maire wrote to the cantonal authorities but his letters were intercepted. The Maire sent the same letters, with an explanation of why he was doing so, via a series of couriers across the open country and it was hand delivered to the cantonal Prefect as he arrived at the Maison de Cantal one morning by somebody who was not known and disappeared immediately into an arranged crowd

192

On the following Friday when Michelle Mathis came into Saint Flour for the Market she brought me a message from Stephan asking me to meet him at la Cham. The meeting was set up for Monday when I usually went foraging for supplies

I left early on my bicycle as usual. I was looking forward to this visit as I had not been in touch with Simon and Patrice since the Germans had moved in. Stephan had gathered together about thirty maquis as well as Simon and Patrice. Lookouts were in place on all approaches. The first thing I learnt was that it was Stephan who had arranged for the delivery of the Maire's letters. Patrice added that one of his trainees, Pierre Courier, had a close friend employed in the Maison de Cantal in Aurillac with direct access to the Prefect

Patrice's contact could get full information about the Prefect's intentions almost as soon as a decision was taken. The problem was getting the news to Patrice

La Cham was about 60 kilometres from Aurillac and the only means of contact was via a cooperative bus driver who was not always on that route, and written communications were dangerous for all concerned. Telephones were frequently tapped and couriers took too long. Both Simon and Patrice were trained as radio operators and the spare sets I had in store were now needed. We agreed to place a set with Pierre Courier in Aurillac, and another at la Cham. Patrice would have a signal schedule set up with Pierre who would use to one of our safe houses in the outskirts of Aurillac. Pierre's friend was given the code name Orion. Orion was very cautious, he would only pass information via Pierre Courier and would not agree to have any other contact. Pierre Courier lived quite near to our safe house and could go there via back gardens even after curfew without being seen. When la Cham received a message they would telephone the Terminus offering something special for our restaurant and arranging a time for a radio contact. My listening schedules for London would not allow for a regular schedule with la Cham or Aurillac. Patrice agreed to collect the sets and accessories from Orphanges the next day

Orion had already passed out much information from the prefecture. The Germans did not regard Cantal as important strategically. Their main concern was to make the farmers meet their quotas for shipment to Germany. So far Cantal had never met their quota and the worst offender was the sub-prefecture of Saint Flour. Hence the rather large German establishment in Saint Flour, more personnel than in Aurillac. I had to question the trustworthiness of Orion. Who had vetted him?, where had he come from? Did we find him or had he found us, if so how? Could I be told his real name? Stephan answered. Orion was an established French civil servant in the local government of Cantal. Exceptionally he was also a member of the French communist party and had made an approach to a maquis member whom he had known for many years. Stephan was satisfied with Orion because he had checked him out via his communist party membership. I asked that his information be cross checked as much as possible and that I would also cross check via my channels. Orion was also well informed. He knew about Pascal and the connection to De Gaulle's office in London and said it was a condition of his cooperation that his information should not be passed to De Gaulle's office as the nature of some of the information might pin point his identity

Now was the time to start asking Orion questions and compare his answers with other sources

I finally filled the bicycle baskets with enough produce to justify my absence for the day and set off back to Saint Flour. I could not wait to meet up with Alexis Lescaut to tell him all the news. I had a very good impression of Stephan and the care he had taken in setting up this meeting. His relations and cooperation with Simon and Patrice were clearly excellent. Also clearly Simon and Patrice had done an excellent job in training the locals. There was a feeling of anticipation and readiness for anything

Chapter 27

Dodging the Germans

I was fortunate enough to meet councillor Leman as I entered Saint Flour and told him of the urgent need for a meeting. He agreed to arrange it tomorrow with Alexis Lescaut. Mum and Dad were told as soon as we had closed in the evening. Dad had some regular dealings with the Maison du Department in Aurillac and was racking his brains to guess Orion's real identity. I simply told him I did not want to know. Orion would be judged on the quality and reliability of his information

Alexis Lescaut came into the Terminus early next day with some 'official enquiry' forms that my parents must complete. We left Manuel and Yvette in charge of the bar and retired to the back room. "Tomorrow I have to go to the Derbies farm at Voltaic because they have notified the Maire that some of their cows have failed the tuberculosis test," he said with a smile on his face," I also happen to know that councillor Leman might also be there," he continued. "Don't you get your milk from that farm?" "Why yes of course we do" Dad replied, and turning to me said, "You must go too and make sure the samples are properly taken." What time," I asked, "We'd better be there at eight o'clock as soon as they have finished the morning milking" said Alexis. While we had been talking two of the German officers had come into the bar so we repeated part of the conversation in the bar as Alexis was leaving. We didn't know how much of the conversation had been fully understood by the Germans but it couldn't do any harm if they did understand

"I suppose this will have to be the pattern of our meetings from now on," Dad remarked later in the day. As I left on my bicycle next morning in a thick mist I was thinking over the BBC French news service reports of yesterday. There had been some jamming of the service ever since the Germans had arrived but last night reception had been quite good. Regular air attacks were taking place all over France especially on the German submarine bases in Western France. The Russians had taken the offensive in the battles around Stalingrad

Alexis had chosen the infection site with his usual care. There was only one approach via a very narrow lane so only one lookout was needed and in the ten minutes warning we would have of any approach by suspicious people we could put on a very convincing demonstration of samples being taken. We were not disturbed

We had already suspended all resistance activity as soon as the Germans arrived because we had no details of their strength or location. So the first task set for Orion would be complete information on the distribution of German personnel for as far around the area as he could get information, not simply in Cantal. We would ask for details of strength, arms and vehicles, names of senior officers and especially details of the SS units deployed with the Wehrmacht. Next priority, details of their supply arrangements

We had already seen regular vehicle movements between Aurillac, the sub-prefectures and other points where the Germans had established themselves. What were these vehicles carrying? Did similar movements occur with other departmental prefectures? To whom did the Gauleiter of Aurillac report? What were the strengths of the German forces in all the neighbouring departments? Were the occupation troops under the command of the main German fighting army group and was army group G the only group covering our area?

The final question concerned the state of the relations between the SS and the Wehrmacht, and how we might widen the differences between them. It had been immediately apparent when the SS personnel were in Saint Flour that the senior officers resented their presence and the lower ranks were afraid of the SS

Rumours had been circulating that SS ranked officers could countermand the orders of higher ranked Wehrmacht officers, is this true?

After we had put all of these questions into a succinct form it would clearly be a large task for Orion, but also a good test. If he could answer even half our questions we would be much better equipped to deal with the occupiers

Although it was clear that all information we got would have to be transmitted to London, we would also have to retain it and keep it updated for our own use. Where? It was not the sort of information you would want to have in your back pocket when you were stopped by a German patrol

Councillor Leman, who was intensely patriotic, had long forecast the need for a headquarters for the local resistance. He now came back to this point since we were going to have a supply of information to which all active groups of the resistance, maquis and any other groups might need access. He was sufficiently single minded to recognise that all the resistance groups, regardless of their political attachments, must work together for the common purpose of harassing the Germans He also recognised that if the Germans ever got any idea of the existence of such a headquarters they would use every means to destroy it and arrest all persons involved

"How many radio sets have you got available?" he asked, "Only four not allocated", I replied. "How many more could you get?" "In time as many as we need, they are in free supply," I said. "If we had a secret remote location for our headquarters up in the hills with two or three people only handling all the information and keeping it up to date with the only contact in or out by radio the active groups could get the latest information, they do not have to know the location

Similarly any information they collect can be passed to the headquarters by radio for the benefit of all concerned." We soon agreed that this was an aim had to we achieve. The first matter to be addressed was where. We agreed to meet again within ten days and compare ideas

I immediately put in an urgent request for a further twenty-four radio sets expecting to get about six. The next thing was a meeting with Felix to tap his better knowledge of the problems that might arise. Fortunately he was able to come to Saint Flour the next day. After the lunch time business we went round to the back yard workshop and talked the whole matter through

The final picture began to emerge. Felix was excited over the plan and of course wanted to know where the headquarters was to be located. "Your best location in this terrain is always as high as possible. Limit your transmission strength to a range of about a hundred kilometres, that's quite a low strength signal and any detectors are not going to be very excited about your signals because they are not really going anywhere. The same applies to your inward traffic and always remember the ten minute rule, in any event your messages inwards will always be the short ones, and It is the outgoing ones that could be long. You should have some sort of shorthand code agreed to keep your air time as short as possible." "Thank you," I replied, "In those few sentences you have really answered all my questions"

"When do you think you'll get your sets?" he asked. "No reply as yet," I answered, "but I'll keep you informed because we'll need some help from you with the training programme. "This will be our first drop since the occupation," I said "and I wonder if we will get such a small drop agreed by London because I don't think they will understand the urgency." "You could start some training immediately with your spare sets," said Felix. "But this is so new I don't even know who the trainees will be," I said. "Just let me know when you're ready." Felix left on the afternoon bus. They had much less trouble in Clermont with travel permits than we had in Saint Flour. London replied next day, 'Your sets can be dropped on the twenty-first of December weather permitting. You should also take twenty-four containers to make the operation viable. Please advise packs you need and drop zone to use"

As soon as Felix had left on the bus I hurried off to the upper town to find Alexis. "You haven't wasted any time," he said when I explained how far I had progressed

"We must have a further discussion as soon as possible, can you and Councillor Leman join us this evening. Alexis immediately called Leman and talked about an urgent road problem in the Place de la Liberte that had to be settled this evening. Using their curfew passes Alexis and Leman arrived at the Terminus when the evening was in full swing for the Germans in the bar and restaurant. They lingered for a while in the bar before excusing themselves to discuss some town business in the back room, leaving Mum Yvette and Manuel to entertain the troops

Both Alexis and I had been thinking since our afternoon meeting and we rapidly brought Fernand up to date." I think I know exactly the place you need but the people might be a problem." said Fernand. and went on talking mainly to Alexis. "You remember that place near the Col de la Cere where the children are never sent to school and you never know who is married to whom and there are more wives than husbands" "Oh yes," replied Alexis. "Do you know who owns that farm?" said Fernand, "Tell me," I said. Sensing some surprise in store. "Bernice Rodot" answered Fernand in triumph. "I never knew that, "said Alexis, "She will certainly cooperate and she can be completely trusted but if I remember correctly the three brothers only speak Auvergnat, "I replied

"One of them does speak French, said Alexis I can't remember which but if we put, say, three of our resistance men in there to do the work permanently then it does not matter if they only speak Auvergnat." "They also have their own generator so batteries will not be a problem, and they are in some way related to the Rodot family, but I can't remember the details." Dad entered the conversation, "I remember Pierre Gibory, huge man, when he used to come in to town for the market. He is the one who speaks French. Turning to me, Dad said, "You must remember him he was always hitting his head on the door frame." Well, he told me they already have four extra hands on the farm and feeding them is difficult, I am sure you would have to provide for them" "If we can agree that this is the best place we can use for our headquarters, I feel sure Bernice Rodot will cooperate to the full," said Alexis"

I propose that you Fernand, should make an immediate visit to Les Bouquets and try to find an arrangement. Then we must meet again on your return"

Fernand left early the next day. He did not return until late the following day after being delayed by a German patrol when he came back to Saint Flour. He telephoned the Terminus asking Dad if we could continue our discussion on town business tomorrow night. Dad said "From the sound of his voice it was obvious he has been successful." In the morning I went to see Alexis to complete the arrangements

Just before the midday rush I got Dad alone with a large scale local map. Ever since Fernand Leman's remark about Bernice Rodot being the owner of the farm at the Col de Cere I had been puzzled about the connection. To get to le Bosquet you left Saint Flour going South and to get to the Col de Care you left Saint Flour going North West. The map showed me just how ignorant I still was of the geography of my patch

In actual fact the map showed that the farms at le Bosquet and near Saint Jacques des Blast adjoined each other although the farmhouses on each farm were over ten kilometres apart. Of much greater interest to me was that it was all open country in between, no roads to cross and some quite significant hills to climb or go round. To get from our drop zone at le Che to our prospective headquarters was about six kilometres and only one minor road to cross

It was now Tuesday 1st December and our drop was proposed for Monday 21st.

Fernand. and Alexis both arrived and spent some time socialising with the officers in the bar before passing on to town business. Some improvement in relations between the two sides was apparent. I could scarcely contain my impatience to get on with our business. At last Mum, Yvette and Manuel were left in charge

Fernand. was like magician pulling things out of a hat each one more spectacular than the last. Bernice would give us every cooperation, She knew that the Gibory brothers were willing to give us every facility we needed; and if they didn't she would make them. She recognised that there would be a feeding problem and promised to solve that by getting the neighbouring farmers to contribute

Bernice had very considerable stocks of oil she had accumulated for her tractors and generator she said enough for about fifteen months and she bought at every opportunity. The brothers also had some stock but she said she was willing to provide what was necessary. In fact the best way to get oil to the brothers was via le Bosquet because of the very poor tracks to the brother's farm. She could get a tractor and trailer to within three kilometres of the brothers but the last part would have to be with twenty-five litre panniers on horses. Bernice said the best way would be for her to stock pile twenty-five litre containers in a cave in the hills known only to the brothers and for the brothers to draw from the cave as they needed because it would have to be done at night otherwise the horses would be seen crossing the ridge from the main road or from the air. Her tractor movements up the valley were always going on with fodder going up and animals coming down and would not excite any comment

Having solved the fuel problem Bernice considered the food supplies a minor matter. The brothers had plenty of refrigerator and natural cold storage space and were quite used to keeping large stocks of food for the times when they were cut off completely

Bernice was also quite prepared to keep reserve stocks at le Bosquet and would move one of her refrigerators into a cave so that her food stock levels would not be seen to be too high. Bernice felt sure she could rely on other farmers to support her efforts. She assured Fernand that our farmers supply drop had created much goodwill towards the resistance in all its forms. Bernice went on to suggest that Yvette, Jean-Francois and myself should go and stay for a few days so that I could satisfy myself about all the aspects. She had even given Fernand a letter to me so that I could show the Germans that I really did have an invitation to bring Jean-Francois to her Saint Nicholas day party. We all paused for breath at this point. The support exceeded our wildest dreams and it made the establishment of our headquarters a certainty unless I could find some real objection. I was quite elated firstly at the result and secondly at the prospect of a few days away with Yvette all to myself. Some of the attention she had been getting from the German officers annoyed me. After we had talked the whole matter through we agreed that I had to accept the invitation

Next morning I was early at the bus office and first in the queue for travel permits. Permission was granted without any demur. I went back to the Terminus in high spirits to tell Yvette that we were going off for a few days holiday. She was delighted

At my next schedule I confirmed the drop date of the twenty-first at the le Che site and that we needed twenty-four type B containers. Immediately afterwards I asked Alexis to contact Stephan to organise the reception party to shift the entire drop into the caves for a few days and to arrange some diversionary activity to confuse any reports the Germans might receive about air activity. I did not want the Germans to see extra activity immediately after the drop which I anticipated might be known to them almost as soon as it happened. We had also to hope for good weather on the twenty-first or the next two nights, otherwise it would be a busy Christmas

Unbeknown to us at the time the Maire had made a request to the German authorities in Aurillac for a suspension of the curfew over the Christmas and New Year period so that more normal social activity could take place. He embellished the request by saying he would use his good offices to promote better

200

relations between the occupying forces and the townspeople over the holiday period

We left on the first bus on Friday morning to go to the Rodot farm. It was a cold dull December day. Yvette and Jean-Francois were well wrapped up. Yvette made a special effort and looked ravishing. She responded to attention as only Yvette could. Jean-Francois was excited and said he wanted bring all the kittens back that he hadn't got last time!

The journey was uneventful and Stephan met us at the bus stop with the horses. It took us almost an hour and a half to reach le Bosquet. The roads were in a very slippery muddy condition and I don't think even a tractor would have coped with such conditions, after all it was almost midwinter. When we did arrive the welcome was almost overwhelming. Lunch had been held back for us. We had the same rooms as last time and soon Jean-Francois was having his afternoon nap. I left Yvette with Bernice and went out to the stables with Stephan

I had been thinking very seriously about Stephan during the ride up to le Bosquet. Now I took the plunge. "Stephan," I said, "You and I are on different sides of the political spectrum, but that doesn't mean we cannot trust each other, can you agree with that?" "Yes, I feel quite confident about trusting you," he replied. "Good and I feel confident in you. In the course of the next few days you will become aware of the location and function of a headquarters for the resistance

I believe it is necessary that you should know about this and I expect you to contribute to its functions and to benefit from it's functions. This information is personal to you and you must promise me that you will not disclose the information to anyone else whomsoever they might be." "That's quite a serious matter for me too." Stephan replied, "What if I am injured and incapacitated, what can happen then?" "I've also thought about that," I replied, "and at some time I quite understand somebody else in the maquis will have to know. When you have decided who that is to be, tell me, and I will want to meet him before I will agree to his knowing. I will not promise to accept your choice and as I get to know your friends more closely I might have some ideas myself, but until then the information is for your eyes and ears only. Will you promise me?" "Yes I will," Stephan replied," That must have been a hell of a decision for you to make and I thank you most sincerely for the confidence you have in me, I won't let you down." "When we get back inside I will tell Bernice about your promise so that there is no misunderstanding."Stephan asked, "How is Bernice involved?" "Please let the situation reveal itself over the next few days, I am not yet sure how it is going to work out, but it will work out and then you will be among the first to know"

201

After dinner that evening, Laurent and Michel went off for their usual Friday night billiards evening. Jean-Francois had been playing with the cats in front of the fire and finally became tired so Yvette took him up to bed and stayed to get him off to sleep. "Bernice," I said," I have taken a promise from Stephan to keep our secret about the use of the brothers farm as a headquarters, so he is privy to all our plans and conclusions". "Well I am surprised, "she said, "but I believe you have made a very wise decision. It could not have been easy for you"

"Now I have some questions for you about these brothers. I have been told they are related to you in some way. Can you explain the exact situation?" "They are the sons of my Aunt's first husband and she almost disowned them when she married again, I don't know why. They never went to school but they are not stupid as some people say. They are very good with animals and fiercely independent. When I let that farm to them it was entirely out of charity. Although I own the land it is remote and was not economical for me to farm. They only pay a minimal rent but they now make a profit from the farm and I really don't know how they do it." "What do you think they will say about the plans we have for that farm?" I asked, "They are extremely patriotic and already they have many maquis staying around there and they are feeding them somehow." "That's right," Stephan cut in, my people speak highly of them. I've been up there twice and been most well received. They are far more knowledgeable than they are given credit for. You know they are teaching themselves English so that they can listen to the BBC news bulletins"

"Bernice," I asked, "Could you come up there with me tomorrow, I simply have to see this situation for myself." "Certainly", she replied, "We can leave Stephan in charge here. He can cook dinner for us. I'll just talk to them on the phone, you know we have a private line to them?" She returned in a minute or two, "Everything is arranged but there will be very much to see and discuss, I think we should leave as soon as it is light"

As always Bernice was as good as her word. After a substantial breakfast we set off as dawn showed its first light. We ascended the slopes of the Puy de la Grousse and made a left turn skirting the hamlet of Malabo to the north, crossed a stream and took to a series of forest paths turning steadily North. It was misty and bitterly cold as we went steadily higher. We crossed another larger stream, the Brome, I was told, and continued on the west side of a ridge crossing numerous small streams as we climbed and descended all the time in the forest

"Do you think you can remember your way again?" asked Bernice. "Not after just one journey," I replied, there are too many chances to go wrong," I added. "There is a more direct route you can use in the summer," said Bernice," but its too dangerous in Winter and it is exposed, you can be seen from many kilometres away on the hillsides, this is the secret way

The other way is a good way to go by moonlight on a summer's night." After almost three hours we left the forest and come on to open hillside, grazing land. Rising above us on the right was the local high spot, the Plomb du Cantal. We stopped to give the horses a breather. Bernice pointed to a distant cluster of rocks and some buildings among the rocks. "This is the only place where you can get a good view of the Gardes farm and appreciate its isolation and how difficult it would be for anybody to surprise the location." I had to agree. Looking all round now the mist had gone I could see over ten peaks, all with the characteristic shape of extinct volcanoes and through the gaps the same sort of peaks but more distant. "Down in that valley," said Bernice pointing left, "is the main road to Aurillac from Murat, but the sides are so steep they cannot see up here." It really was a strange but very useful location

We continued along a track winding in and out of rocky outcrops. Soon we saw a rider coming towards us. "That's Pierre coming to meet us. He was probably watching us as we rested the horses and would have known almost to the minute when we would arrive here"

Ten minutes later we met. Pierre could only be described as huge, vertically and horizontally, Poor horse I thought. I guessed his weight as one hundred and fifty kilos, "Well," I said after the introductions, "you're a big man." "Oh we're all like me up here you know, gravity's lower so we grow faster, bigger and better." "He's right" said Bernice, "You wait until you meet his brothers." Bernice and Pierre talked in Auvergnat all the way to the farm. I could only make out the odd word or two

Brothers Henri and Jean were just as big. No midget myself, they all over topped me by at least twenty centimetres. After the introductions and getting out of our heavy coats we settled down in the farm kitchen and hot toddies appeared as if by magic. Bernice said, "It might be a slow conversation if we have to wait for Pierre to translate. How far have you got with your English?" Henri answered in English, "We now take the BBC English news and we can understand that, Does little Henri speak English then?" "Oh, I'm sure he does." replied Bernice. How did she know that? So we continued in English

I explained the reason for my visit. "So this is something you, Leman and Lescaut have cooked up between you," said Jean when I had finished. "Well you had better come and see round our place and see if you are still interested before we have our meal or it will be too dark"

Chapter 28

Communication Centre

Well warmed internally and heavily coated again the farmyard was quite pleasant. Huge by any assessment roughly triangular in shape it had been cleared of all stone outcrops. Two sides of the triangle were each about one hundred and fifty metres and the third side on the south about a hundred metres. The farmhouse where we had been welcomed was at the south east corner. "I expect you've been told," said Jean, "that we've got some caves as well, "Yes, and I'm especially interested in those." "Do you know how many?" asked Pierre, "I believe it's six isn't it," I replied. "So you know more than we do then," said Henri. "Stop teasing," said Bernice, "you know its more than that." Henri spoke again, "If you put a nought after the six you will be nearer the truth, and the truth is that we don't really know except that we have far more space underground that we do above ground and it's almost all perfectly dry and some of it is quite warm

So how much space do you want?" "We don't need that much," I replied," One large single area of about 20 metres square for a plotting room, another room of about eighteen square metres for a coding room close to the plotting room, and another room for the radios about the same

The radio room should be as close to the aerials as possible. Then there would be living accommodation for probably, six men, and occasional accommodation for another two" "If you look around you," said Pierre, "you will see the farmhouse there where we will eat soon, and each of us has a small stone house there, there and there, he said pointing out three stone cottages, then there is a school room there for the children, a cattle shed, stables, those indoor pens for the sheep, some pigsties, and lots of barns but much of our fodder is stored in caves. Another cave is used for our generator fed by the oil tank over there

That new building there is a dairy, mainly for cheese making and another cave is used for maturing cheese." How many people are there living here? I asked. He turned to his brothers, "how many is it now?" he asked. They went into a huddle, "About thirty-six regulars including fourteen children," said Pierre," plus anything up to six or eight passing workers when they are passing, but please don't tell Lescaut those figures, because if he knows he will have to do something about it, and that will just mean a lot of visits and forms, we're farmers, not clerks." "I promise." I replied smiling. "Let's go and eat said Jean and we can continue to talk

We returned to the farmhouse kitchen and more hot toddies. "This is the best thing about winter," said Henri, finishing his at one gulp. As soon as my glass was empty another full one replaced it. We all sat at one table and all the others at another very large table but the women served us first. I asked if I could assume that they would agree to our using their farm for our communication centre. "Of course" replied Jean," you wouldn't be here if we were not going to give you every possible assistance

I had to ask about security. "Nobody here will talk," all agreed. "We don't even talk to our own town hall so we're certainly not going to talk to the Germans"

"When will this start" asked Henri. I'm expecting most of the equipment to arrive with Father Christmas," I replied. "As distinct from Saint Nicholas?" questioned Pierre, "Yes I smiled, but it is unlikely we will get the equipment up here before Christmas." "Don't forget, if we get snow any time now, it is unlikely to clear again until early February, or even later," said big Henri

The meal dragged on. "Before I go, I said, "I would like to have a look at your generator facilities." " Of course" said Pierre, "But you're not going tonight, It's already too late to get to le Bosquet in daylight and too dangerous after dark," He turned to Bernice," you'd better call and tell them so they don't worry." He turned to the women at the other table saying, "In another few weeks you'll have some soldiers here, OK?" Smiles all round

After the meal I went with Pierre to the generator cave. As we passed the fuel tank I asked, "How did you get that huge tank up here?" It was much bigger than I expected to see. "It's an old petrol tank", said Pierre, "when the garage in Murat went bankrupt, we went down there and dug the tank out, built a sled under it and used all our horses to drag it up here, including the two-legged ones"

The generator was a good modern unit with over twice the capacity needed for all the farm which was very satisfactory. There was also their original generator as a standby. "Fuel is a problem," Pierre admitted, we do have to take every opportunity of getting fuel up here but at a hundred litres a time we can manage it. How much power are you going to need?" "Very little for the radio operation," I said, "our larger need will be for lighting and I can't guess how much at this moment," I replied. "Could you use oil lamps? Pierre asked "Possibly," I said. "Be sure we will find a way. We always have plenty of firewood as you have seen, and somewhere we do have an old steam generator which was in use up to seven or eight years ago. I wonder where it is now, we never sell anything that we might need again"

We went back to the farmhouse. Bernice had telephoned le Bosquet about our staying overnight. Talk turned to the course of the war. It seemed so strange to be sitting in a remote farmhouse in the middle of France with a community of farmers discussing the war in English. "What would you do if the Germans did make an all out attack on you," asked Bernice. "I think we would give a good account of ourselves," said Jean. We would always have plenty of warning of their attack unless it was from the air." "Do you think you need a cache of arms here," I asked. "I would like that," said Jean," and we could always use them against the Gendarmerie if they come calling after the war." I promised to provide arms and offered the services of Simon and Patrice to train their people

After supper which was now taken by all including the children, at the one large table there was wide ranging talk about the farming tasks in hand as well as their local problems. Provided they could get fuel for their generator they could be entirely self sufficient with some bartered help from their neighbours

The extra dozen or so mouths to feed were going to be a problem. Bernice offered to enlist further help from her contacts and as she said, "if you have the food the Germans can't have it. We've never met our quota yet, so what changes"

As soon as supper was finished it was play time for the children. They ranged in age from babes in arms to teenagers. The little ones got the first attention from all the adults until they were so sleepy they disappeared with their respective parents to bed. I was surprised by the older children. They were proudly showing off their schoolroom work and I deduced that two of the extra women were providing the education, and that the children were a real credit to them. "It's better to do it up here." said big Henri, "it would take the children over an hour and a half to get to the school when the paths are passable, and there are many days each year when they are not, and some days when they are really dangerous"

The children talked Auvergnat between themselves and their parents, but readily switched to French when they found out that I did not understand them. "Some of them are getting good at English as well," said Pierre, calling the twins Michel and Maurice over, "Little Henri here speaks quite good English so you can practice with him." I was pleasantly surprised at their competence. "Some of the extra people will be French-speaking Englishmen," I said quietly to Pierre. "That will be an excellent chance for the children was the reply"

Bedtime was early for all. This was a farming community and the day started at five o'clock. Breakfast was at seven, just before daylight showed. As soon as it was full daylight Bernice and I saddled up and set off. Jean accompanied as far as the view point where we had stopped on the upward journey. His parting words were "If you honour your promises to us we will never let you down"

We rode on in silence for a long time. The descent was slippery and the horses were having more difficulty than on the way up. They didn't need a rein, they were on their way home and they knew it. I broke the silence, "Is that telephone line direct or does it go via an exchange?" "It's direct", replied Bernice

"We laid it ourselves about eight years ago. It's powered from le Bosquet. It has broken down twice during it's life each time because some animal dug up part of it and gnawed it. It's laid in one kilometre sections and we have a plan showing where each junction is. We should have buried it deeper but it was a huge task. When we have identified which section has failed we simply replace it and bury it a bit deeper but digging a trench a kilometre long in this terrain is no mean task. They do it from Gardes because the power supply is from le Bosquet and it's mainly in their interest to have the line. They have plenty of spare cable up at Gardes." We relaxed into silence again and let the horses pick their way

As we descended it got somewhat warmer, the mist thinned and watery winter sunshine appeared. It was a little more conducive to conversation. Bernice broke in to our thinking. "I did not really know what they would say but you made a very good impression and they liked you and I am sure they will do everything they said. Jean took me on one side last night after you'd gone off to bed and asked me if you really were the son of Robert and Lisette. Of course I said you were and told them about your liaison with Yvette. I think they were satisfied. I hope you didn't mind the 'little Henri' it was a simple way of making the difference"

"I feel very comfortable about the whole situation up at Gardes except for one problem. The children, What would happen to them if the place was stormed by the Germans? That place could be a considerable fortress and I don't think the Giborys would surrender, do you?" "No they wouldn't," replied Bemire. "There is only one way I can consider doing this and that is if they are attacked they should immediately put all the children in one of the deep caves with the entrance clearly marked, in German, that only children are therein and hope that the Germans respect the notice. Can we put that point to the brothers on the phone tonight and apologise for not thinking about it sooner." "I am sure they will understand," Bernice replied

Yvette had a good hot soup ready for as we arrived at le Bosquet. It had taken us longer time to come down than go up. I remarked on this to Bernice and she was not surprised, "It usually does in the winter," replied Bernice, "The only safe way is to let the horses do it at their pace. In the summer a steady canter can get you down here via the other way in just over the hour"

I spent the afternoon with Yvette and Jean-Francois but my mind was not really with them. Yvette had a lot of questions but I asked her to wait until the evening when we could have a round table talk after supper

Stephan joined us for supper. We talked after the meal while Yvette was settling Jean-Francois down for the night, no problem, he had had an exciting day and was tired. Bernice came back after telephoning Gardes and said that they agreed and thanked us for our consideration over the matter of saving the children

Bernice knew we wanted a serious discussion and told her two sons to clear and wash up, then led the way into her parlour, a rarely used room. As we moved I took Stephan to one side, "You have guessed about my identity, but Yvette does not know and must not know." His response was a sharp intake of breath as he nodded. We settled down to a recapitulation of all the points agreed with Gardes in a less random way. Stephan was clearly impressed and pleased. Yvette was worried because she thought that I might be spending time up at Gardes and was worried about the curfew. I assured her that I would be spending very little time at Gardes because I could trust them and talk to them as required on a secure line from le Bosque

On Tuesday we returned to Saint Flour. Our return was duly noted and Alexis Lescaut and Councillor Leman turned up as usual to discuss town business. I had given Mum and Dad a brief idea of what we could do with the Grardes farm but after we were all settled down in the backroom I filled in all the details including Bernice Root's comments. Everybody was favourably impressed with the final result. Even Alexis Lescaut said he would be more lenient in his approaches to the Giborys now he knew they were helping in such a positive way

Finally I said, "It seems to me that headquarters is not quite the right term for what we will do at the Gardes farm, it is more of a communication centre, headquarters will continue to be wherever we meet"

So it was agreed we would confirm the drop on the twenty-first and ask for four more operators for an initial operation at Grades farm to arrive as soon as possible. Councillor Leman added that while we had been away the German Commandant had agreed to a relaxation of the curfew from Saturday the nineteenth of December until Sunday third of January and that the Maire and the German commandant would make simultaneous announcements next market day

The immediate question was, what would happen to the relaxation if the Germans became aware of a drop right at the beginning of the curfew concession? The adverse reaction of the Saint Flour townsfolk would not help the resistance cause. We knew from our previous drop in the le Che valley that our main guiding beacon fire on the slopes of the Puy de Cantal could be seen from the upper town in Saint Flour but the Germans were not present then. Such a beacon fire and the noise of the planes now the Germans were on our doorsteps would not be tactful at the start of a curfew concession. Alexis Lescaut promised to deal with this problem by the creation of diversions and false reports of air activity. He promised to complete his plans by next Tuesday fifteenth of December only six days before the first date of the drop. We agreed that he could call on Stephan for help in his planning as he had access to out-of-town men who were not restricted by a curfew

Next day I received a message questioning the need for four trained operators and had to send a long series of replies detailing our plans for a communication centre operation with low power radio contacts to outposts. I forgot to give the map reference of our proposed communication centre

I had also forgotten that Christmas starts with Saint Nicholas day in this part of France which was last Sunday and the next morning was started with Jean-Francois opening his presents, this was a pointed reminder that I had better prepare for Christmas. There was nothing to buy in the shops suitable for presents. Most of Jean-Francois' presents were small cuddly toys, home made, bricks or toys made from scrap wood and painted in bright colours. It was not going to be a real Christmas for children.

The only chance I could think of was Friday's market in the hope that the stallholders might have found something to sell. I decided to be out early on Friday morning to get the best choice. Councillor Leman came by mid-morning and signalled that he wanted to talk. We went into the workshop, Alexis had gone missing, leaving his deputy in charge, but the Maire was asking for him and councillor Leman did not know how to reply. The Maire's position was anomalous. He had to be seen to be cooperating with the German authorities in the interests of the townsfolk and at the same time covering up certain other activities

Fortunately Alexis had anticipated the situation and later in the day there was a message from him to say he would be absent for some days on departmental business and could be contacted via Orion, but using his real name, in Aurillac. Alexis was on the job!

I was lucky on Friday morning, almost immediately I found a brooch for Mum and a silver cigarette case for Dad. Yvette was a problem until I found one of the stalls with some under-the-counter perfumes. It was real French but the price was horrendous. Jean-Francois would have to be content with the windmill I had made for him in odd moments. Definitely it was not going to be a children's Christmas

The announcement of the curfew concession came mid-morning with both the Maire and the commandant standing on the Terminus' steps. There was muted applause. The commandant also announced that his men had asked permission to hold a party for the town's children on Christmas Eve. This got no response at all

The market was busier than it had been for many weeks although not much money actually changed hands. From what I overheard of the deals made it was all about the meat for the Christmas meal to be had via black market slaughtering on the farms and held there until the lifting of the curfew would enable it to be delivered after dark.

Alexis Lescaut returned late on Sunday. Early on Monday morning he made his peace with the Maire. In the evening both Alexis and councillor Leman turned up for a discussion on town matters. They spent some time in the bar with the commandant who was anxious to discuss the arrangements for the children's Christmas party. Invitations had been given to all the children at the town's schools and the commandant was anxious to get invitations to the under sixes and wanted the town police to deliver them. In the end Alexis had to agree to do it simply to get away

By careful measuring he had proved that it was possible to move the site of the beacon fire on the Plomb de Cantal and bring the planes in on a different bearing starting from Brioude which was their first turn before picking up the Saint Flour Cathedral tower. Thus the planes would not over-fly Saint Flour and would approach le Che more directly. Then if the fire was screened from Saint Flour by a wooden construction only a faint glow would be visible from the ramparts of the upper town. Without any loss due to mist or other weather effects, We would have to have a different line of lights in the le Che valley to indicate the actual drop zone but being in a valley those lights could not be seen except from the air.

Alexis had also been into the neighbouring departments of Haute-Loire, Maryanne and Lozier and arranged for many reports of aircraft over-flying starting at Brioude and following a long sweep about fifty kilometres to the east of Saint Flour. He was now going to visit his regular reporters of air movements along the real flight path and ask them to be especially deaf on the night of the twenty-first and any other nights up to Christmas because i would only be Santa

Claus. Next he would arrange for parachutes to be reported as falling between Le Puy and Langhorne in very remote country just right for Maquis activity. Any stray reports that did come in about air activity would be discounted because none of the regular reliable reporters had heard anything

Additionally he had arranged for some sheep stealing to be reported well to the south of Saint Flour that would take the local Gendarmerie away from the town

We were not entirely happy with the plans and insisted that a test fire should be lit when the screen had been set up just to confirm the reliability of the measurements. Councillor Leman and his friends were to arrange parties for that night to keep people moving about from house to house and thus distract the German patrols. As Mum remarked it was also likely that by now some of the lonely women in the town might be tempted to invite some soldiers in for a drink!

I wrote off my bet with Alexis!

With all this going on during the night of the drop, at least it would be easy to have the right people in the right place, and to move the supplies into safe hiding. We agreed that once the supplies were stowed we would not try to move them to Gardes until the last two nights of the curfew concession unless the Germans were not deceived by our diversions and retaliated by cancelling the concession, in which case we would have to rethink the whole matter

Councillor Leman said, "now we've completed our plans to deceive the enemy wouldn't it be nice if when we left by the bar he could say to the Germans that we had in some way decided to help with invitations for the children's party." Mum said, "if I had a supply of the invitations I could give them to all our clients who had children at home under six," Unanimous agreement. "What about asking Father Albert to distribute to his congregation and father Peter to do the same in the Cathedral and the other priests at Saint Vincent's and Notre Dame", I asked; again agreed. I volunteered to talk to fathers Albert and Peter and Councillor Leman said he would do the same for the other Churches

So as Alexis Lescaut and councillor Leman left the bar that evening they spoke to a sergeant who understood some French, "Please convey our compliments to your commandant and if he would be so kind as to let us have a supply of invitations we would get them to the under six year old children via the bar and the Churches." This also left all the Germans in the bar convinced that we really had been dealing with town business

Chapter 29

Christmas Party Time

With all our plans made we could prepare for the holiday and hope that the drop on the twenty-first was on schedule. We had only two days in reserve if the weather or other operational factors caused postponement

Any sort of Christmas decoration could only come from previous year's carefully hoarded, items; there was nothing in the shops. Some market traders had promised to bring Christmas greenery to the market of the eighteenth and even a few Christmas trees but these were not highly sought after because of the German connection

Food was less of a problem, most people already had private arrangements made and welcomed the relaxation of the curfew because it would make the after dark deliveries so much easier

Much time was spent on discussing the German Christmas party and whether or not to let the children attend. Most eligible children between three and fourteen now had invitations and most wanted to go just out of curiosity and in the hope of an extra present. In the end the willingness of the Mums to have children out of the way for a few hours in the run-up to Christmas was the usual determining factor

Stephan had already made arrangements for the drop to be received with Simon and Patrice to take care that my instructions would be carried out to the letter. Thus all the personnel in Saint Flour who might have been involved could be very visibly present in Saint Flour on the night and all said they would make a point of talking to a few Germans that evening

Friday's last market before Christmas was quite a jolly affair. Plenty of greenery and some Christmas trees for sale with records of carols by school children played over loudspeakers adding to the gaiety. While wandering round with Manuel, who was trying to get something a little different for his menus, I saw money changing hands for no goods and a conversation such as, "Good, after dark about seven on Monday then." Reply "OK, we'll see you them." People were taking advantage of the curfew concession, and Monday was going to be a busy night

The weather had settled down to a pattern of misty mornings clearing by about ten followed by wintry sunshine for a few hours and then a frosty clear moonlit night. The locals were saying this could well continue throughout the Christmas period

The Germans had got a large Christmas tree from somewhere and put it up outside their barracks and dressed it with some electric lights. Nobody would admit to supplying the tree. Rumour was going round that the men had given up a proportion of their rations to feed the children. Manuel had been talking to their chefs and had given them some of his special cake flour so that they could prepare some sweet delicacies for the children. Dad was becoming quite touched by the efforts being made for the children and sent round three dozen bottles of southern Rhone-Valley wine for the men organising the party. The Maire managed to get hold of a good supply of sweets for distribution to the children, and nobody asked any questions where they came from A feeling of euphoria was prevalent with such comments as 'why can't we cooperate over other matters too'

Monday came and the weather was still fair. The coded message came through from London quite early in the day and was passed round. The previous day, Sunday, had seen the town distinctly 'en fete'. There were large congregations at all the Churches and in the cafes and bars afterwards. The partying went on well into the evening, and some doubt was expressed as to whether they could keep it up the next night and wondering if the alcohol supplies and the will to consume it, would continue

Although Monday was a normal working day I had underestimated the capacity of the Saint Flour people to make up for the six weeks of social deprivation they had just endured. The bars filled up as people finished work and there was no need to rush off home before the curfew hour

Impromptu house parties started, around nine and for the first time I saw Germans being invited home to a few of these parties. The Terminus was very busy with both sides mixing socially in the bar for the first time. There were several anxious moments when arguments started. Fortunately the real antagonists on the French side were all keeping a low profile or were 'otherwise engaged' at or around le Che

Councillor Leman was in a bar opposite the park from where he would see if the beacon fire on the Plomb de Cantal was visible and was in a good place to hear any aircraft noise. Alexis was 'working late' at the Town hall in the Place

213

d'Armes, another good vantage point for seeing and hearing anything going on to the North-West. Yvette and I had secured invitations to several homes and were out and about very visibly. Quite a number of farmers from the hills were in town no doubt delivering some of the promises from last Friday's market and in general the town was busy

A few of the shopkeepers had taken up our suggestions that they stayed open late that night and publicised their intentions. Father Peter who had become quite a significant behind-the-scenes supporter of the resistance had his bell ringers standing by for a practice on the Cathedral bells as soon as one of his assistant priests who lived near to the flight path reported by phone that planes were in the area

He had widely spread the story that he would now be able to ring the bells at Christmas provided his ringers could find the time to practice. He had also written to the German commandant thanking him for the curfew concession thus enabling the Cathedral bells to be rung as usual at Christmas

One exciting event in the evening was the sudden departure of the Gendarmes in great haste leaving on the road for Ternes. A rumour started that there had been an attempt to steal some pigs from a farm. We encouraged the rumour by adding that it was," just the sort of thing black marketers would be doing at this time of the year"

The following day we had a visit from Laurent Mathis. Manuel was very pleased to see him especially as he was bringing some badly needed supplies for the kitchen. While he was unloading he casually mentioned that the drop started exactly on time, "just as the Cathedral bells started to ring. Wasn't that rather late for a practice," he asked. "I understand that some of the ringers had been partying and didn't turn up until late," I replied. Laurent added quietly," We got every single container, all safely stowed away; the whole thing went like clockwork. Stephan and his crew handled the matter perfectly"

"What were you doing last night then?" I asked, because a German had just entered the yard. "We were going to come in to Saint Flour to see the wife's sister, they were having a party, but Evelyn was not well and the wife wanted to stay with her." The German reached us. I forestalled any question of his by asking," Do you know why all the Gendarmes left in such a hurry last night?"

"There was a lot of trouble at some farms near Seriere. Some armed men with two vans tried to take pigs and calves from their winter quarters. Some dogs raised the alarm, the farmers went out to see what the trouble was and were held up at gun point. One of the women saw this and called the Gendarmerie. They responded quite quickly but it was a still night and the robbers heard the sirens coming and they ran off. The farmers got the numbers of the vehicles. We've thrown a cordon round the whole area and we might get them." Do you work with the Gendarmerie then?" I asked. "We like to help when we can." He answered. "I really wanted to speak to Manuel, he said, and turning to Manuel asked, "Have you any more sugar you could let us have for the children's party?" Manuel gave him another four kilos. He was grateful and left

Manuel asked, "Was something going on last night?" "You don't want to know anything about it," I said. "We simply didn't want the Gendarmes in town last night." "I'm sorry I asked but I'm neutral and dumb," he replied

Early that evening councillor Leman, Alexis and I all met up at the Leman home, for a party of course. Well we did, it was the relief all felt. Councillor Leman thought he could see some red glow reflected off the slopes of the Plomb de Cantal because he was looking for it. Nobody else near him remarked. Alexis said he could hear some aircraft noise but it was well drowned by the bells. He had received several complaints about the late ringing of the bells and one or two reports of aircraft noise but nothing from his reliable reporters

More importantly he had one report of parachutes being seen by a bus driver in Murat. He had sent a police agent to investigate. I complimented him on his diversionary tactics, and told both about the complete success of the drop. Both councillor Leman and Alexis were cautiously optimistic so I agreed that we would be very cautious for the moment and review the timing of the move from the caves to the Grades farm in the light of any developments

Next day the SS arrived. They immediately divided, one group going into a conclave with the German commandant and the other with the Maire and Alexis Lescaut. They left the same evening. Storch spotter planes had been seen several times during the day

We didn't immediately hear anything about the meeting with the commandant, but Alexis told me that they were investigating reports of enemy air activity over a wide region. No bombs had been dropped and they were concerned that the activity was the dropping of supplies to illegal groups operating in the region. Only a few reports had been received about activity in the Saint Flour area, most of the reports came from the Haut Loire, Mayenne and Lozier where extensive searches and investigations were in hand. They were here especially because of the report by the Murat bus driver of seeing parachutes. Alexis showed them the report of his police agent

The report stated, "As I was leaving a party at Lavaisenet about ten o'clock I saw a number of white parachutes in the sky to the west. I stopped the car and got out. I could hear a faint noise of aircraft all round. When I looked again for the parachutes I could only see one and the noise of the planes had faded away, then I heard the faint noise of church bells ringing and I wondered if an invasion had started so I stopped at the next village and telephoned the police." Observations by the police agent were added. It was a clear bright and well moonlit night. The bells of the Cathedral in Saint Flour were rung between ten and eleven last night. On a moonlit night it is possible it imagine all sorts of things in the sky especially if you have been drinking substantial amounts of alcohol. I recommend no further action

"What do you think about it?" asked the SS Captain. "I would agree with the 'no further action' but now I have also this report, by a farmer at la Stagnate, "I was just checking that all my barns were secure when I saw a flashing light in the sky sending dot-dash Morse code signals The light was to the North-east, the signals only lasted a few seconds. It was a clear moonlit night and very still. I could hear the bells of Saint Flour Cathedral quite clearly." Alexis added, "My agent is trying to see this man today "Please let us have your agents report as soon as it comes to you," asked the SS Captain. "Where were you while all this was happening," interjected the SS Lieutenant. "Earlier in the evening I was with the Maire in the Town Hall. When I left I called in at the Paradise bar in the Place d'Armes on police business. As I left, the Cathedral bells started ringing in a practice for the Christmas services. I thought it was really too late for such a practice and went into the Cathedral. Father Peter told me that they had only just got enough ringers together because they had all been partying through the earlier evening." "Thank you, please keep us informed of any further developments," said the SS Lieutenant. "You may now return to your normal duties"

At our next meeting Alexis was clearly worried. Speaking slowly and precisely he said, "Someone in my office or the Town Hall is passing information to the SS. The only people who knew about the report from the Murat bus driver were the Maire, myself and agent Fourier." A stunning silence ensued. "Any thoughts," I interjected. "Agent Fourier I have known ever since he joined the police, about 8 years ago, he is not very bright but he does his job well, but I do not think he will ever be more than an agent de police, I can't really suspect him." "The Maire!" asked councillor Leman, I have known him since we were at school together, and I could not believe it of him." "Who else possibly could have seen the report from agent Fourier," I asked. "I think we must ask Orion if he knows how the information arrived at Aurillac," said councillor Leman. "I'll put that in hand immediately via Stephan," said Alexis, I said, "No that's too risky we don't want him to know about our problem. It must have been a telephone call to Aurillac. I can check the call records at my office and the Town Hall"

Alexis did that and came to see me on the morning of Christmas eve. "It must have been during the call to the Departmental Mairie by Mlle Hugo, the secretary to the Maire. That was the only call to Aurillac after the time I passed the report to the Maire." We decided that there must be no more involvement of the Town Hall in our business however difficult until we knew more about Mlle

216

Hugo, Alexis was going to meet councillor Leman to advise him and then to Charles Pelletier who he believed knew Hugo family socially

Fortunately Christmas was upon us and we had some respite from all these concerns. Yvette and I were invited to the Pelletier's party held on the twenty-seventh. I was quite surprised to find such a large gathering which included the Maire's family and Mlle Hugo. I only knew her by sight up until that time. In the course of the evening we were introduced. "Oh yes," she exclaimed when the introduction was made, "of course I read all about you when you were re-inscribed in the residents register "Now I was worried, but she continued in a friendly manner," I think you and Yvette are so well suited, it sounded such a romantic story when I heard that you were helping her so much after the way she helped you, and when I heard from Charles that he approved of your relationship, I couldn't have been more pleased for you both." I kept the conversation going and Yvette joined us. She was easy to talk to and I led the subject round to my time in Lille working under the German management of Precision Metal

"I expect it was a big improvement under German management, they're such good organisers." "Yes," I replied, "what we had to make had to be finished with much greater accuracy and our machines were not capable of such accuracy unless the operators were very highly skilled, but I was not fully trained and I couldn't do it, so they discharged me on the day after the air raid that killed all my aunts." "That must have been very hard for you." she sympathised. "My grandfather couldn't look after me so I had no alternative but to come back to Saint Flour. I would have liked to stay on and have been trained to the German way of working, I think it was better." I said temptingly. "I am certain it would be," she said, "and now that the Germans have occupied all of France I am sure that will also be better for all of us. The English were never really our friends"

The conversation continued on many topics and I slowly edged out of that particular group and looked for Alexis

He was deep in a discussion with several families who had experienced difficulty making their children observe the curfew, and what was likely to happen if they were ever caught. Eventually I distracted him and we went into the hallway where I rapidly relayed the conversation with Mlle Hugo and the conclusion that she was a German sympathiser. "Leave this matter with me." was the sinister reply

When we got back to the Terminus there was another inevitable party in progress in the bar. Yvette pleaded the need to see to Jean-Francois and I was able to escape after only a few more glasses. And so to bed

"You're suspicious of Mlle. Hugo aren't you?" questioned Yvette, "and you were leading her on." "Well she certainly is a German sympathiser," I said.

"Yes," said Yvette, "and quite unsuitable as the Maire's secretary. I shall certainly have to talk to Alexis about this and he will have to talk to the Maire, She could cause us an awful lot of trouble and probable danger." I replied

The party in the bar went on and on. Yvette slept but I could not, I was really worried about the Hugo woman. This was one thing we had never considered, that there might actually be German sympathisers in Saint Flour

We were well aware of the original apathy but this had moderated quite a lot as news of German atrocities became general knowledge. Bleary eyed on the following morning I was the last one up. Stephan was already waiting to see me. The bar was otherwise empty of people but many bottles and glasses remained. We cleared a table and I brought some coffee

"I can guess what you did last night." teased Stephan. "It wasn't really the alcohol, I said, and told him about Valerie Hugo. He listened in silence. "You must keep this to yourself but never lose sight of the fact that she is a German sympathiser." "Do you know what I heard yesterday," Stephan continued, "that major Kempf (the German Commandant) is seeking a French secretary to help him with his necessary French correspondence. Perhaps the Maire should lend her to him," he joked. "I don't think that's so funny," I said, "I think it's a bloody good idea!"

We talked to Alexis, Alexis talked to the Maire with support from Councillor Dechaux and they agreed that in the spirit of a New Year the Maire should insist that his secretary should provide her local knowledge and talents to the assistance of our German colleagues with the intention of improving the smooth running of the town

In her place the Maire would call back Madame Person from retirement which in any case was a charitable matter as she really needed the salary. After a meeting between Major Kempf and the Maire it happened

A very fortunate and tidy solution, made more so early in the New Year when Orion reported via his channels from Aurillac that he was aware of many friendly style telephone conversations between SS Captain Fig and Valerie Hugo

There was also a tidy solution over the contents of drop on the twenty-first which were all moved to the Gardes farm with out incident. So we entered the New Year with a sizeable stock of munitions well located and an immediate need to activate our communication centre ready for the operators as soon as they arrived

First job for the New Year was to get Felix up to Gardes farm. Communications with Pascal were now difficult; telephone too risky, mail the same. The only way I could think of was using one of the weekly commuters to Clermont as a courier. I asked Alexis if he knew any of the weekly commuters who could be trusted for this task. After much thinking and checking of files the answer was, "not really. "The only safe way I can think of, is to send a message to him via London to be handled on an urgent basis. I did this and it took five days before Felix and Cesaire arrived at Le Che where I could go and talk to them in safety

They were first astounded at the idea but quickly understood the sense of the location and facilities offered The weather being kind we were able to take them to the short approach to the Grades farm from the Prat de Bouc.

Without any baggage this steep path was only one and a half kilometres but you climbed eight hundred metres. By starting at the crack of dawn they made it there and back before curfew. Both were now far more enthusiastic about the project and had worked out exactly it could be done. They were also intrigued by the three brothers and their unusual establishment especially the children. In order to make the set up more attractive to the Giborys, Cezaire had offered to use the same aerial assembly as we needed to improve the quality of reception of the BBC French service. A good deal for all

Chapter 30

SS Intervention

As soon as the New Year festivities were over, SS Captain Fieg with a platoon of SS other ranks arrived unannounced in Saint Flour. Major Kemp was clearly embarrassed

Over the holiday period relations between the townsfolk and the Germans had improved. The children's party was a great success, almost all the Saint Flour children attended. Many of the wehrmacht personnel were homesick and the gaiety of the party was some consolation for missing families

Some entertainment of the German troops was evident but so far none of the threats made to tar and feather any French people fraternising with the Germans had occurred

SS Captain Fieg announced that he believed there was significant resistance activity in the area, and that because the sub-prefecture of Saint Flour had never met its quota of food to be sent to Germany, he would personally ensure that in future the full quota would be assembled in the Saint Flour barracks and shipped to Germany on a weekly basis

He started by commandeering from the shops the full quota of dry goods for the month of January. In effect this meant that flour and bread would be in short supply; sugar had disappeared altogether, about half of the shop's stocks of pulses, rice and pasta had been seized. We stopped serving our evening menu to the Germans immediately. Within a day or two of the first seizures of food reports came in from many smaller towns in Cantal, that the local gendarmerie had been reinforced by either wehrmacht or SS or both. This move resulted in many more movements being made by the Germans. These detached units such as the troops we had in Saint Flour had to get their rations, pay, beer and medical supplies to mention only a few of the items. All of that had to be delivered on a weekly basis and on their return journeys these vehicles carried any of the quota foodstuffs that the reinforced gendarmerie managed to extort from the local shops or farmers

Now that the curfew was restored movement around the town after dark should have ceased. It didn't. For a few days the German patrols were content to only warn the offenders. This soon came to the attention of SS Captain Fieg. He sent out his men one night who instantly arrested all the offenders that they could find, eighteen of them

Next day Fig was in Court when the offenders appeared. Three men in their sixties were first before the magistrate, Fieg demanded compulsory transfer to Germany for war work for all three. The magistrate refused and simply applied the maximum fine. A number of the offenders were under the age of 16 and accompanied by one or more parents. The magistrate applied a maximum fine to the parents and a warning to the youngsters. The remainder were women of various ages. The excuses they offered ranged from simply returning from a friends house after some sort of social meeting to outright claims that they were on the lookout for their German friends who might be on duty. The fines varied on the whim of the magistrate Fieg left the Court furious and complained to Major Kempf that law and order in the town was too lax and that Kempf should bring charges against the magistrate and the Maire for not enforcing the Law in a proper manner

In the meantime the three men involved and several of the women had disappeared putting themselves beyond the reach of the authorities

A meeting occurred between Major Kempf, SS Captain Fieg, the Maire and several town councillors including councillor Leman. Fieg, reluctantly supported by Major Kemp demanded stricter enforcement of the Law. The Maire replied that the curfew was a German regulation and it was his responsibility to enforce the Law notified to him by the government of Vichy France or the Cantonal Prefect which included a scale of penalties in which there was little latitude. He did not have any authority to enforce German regulations essentially a stalemate

SS Captain Fig next used his own men to visit farms in the hills with the declared intention of enforcing the quotas. It was not the best time of the year for venturing into the hills and Fieg could get no guides from the wehrmacht or the local townsfolk. He had maps but they didn't tell him which roads tracks and paths were passable and he had no horses

The farmers soon heard of his plans and the watchers were out. The storys came back to us. Wherever he arrived he found only Auvergnat was understood. His searches yielded very little except screaming abuse from the few women left around. At one farm his patrol was met by two ferocious dogs, so ferocious that one of his men raised a rifle to shoot the animals. Before the trigger was pulled the man's trigger hand was shot

The patrol immediately went to ground. No further shots were fired and nobody was visible   They accepted the warning and withdrew

We never knew whether Fieg told Major Kempf of his experience; but we later observed a certain smugness on the part of the wehrmacht at the failure of the SS initiative. A few days later Fieg and his men returned to Aurillac

Jean-Francois' second birthday was imminent. What could be found for a two year old boy under Saint Flour circumstances? There were some second hand toys about but the condition was not always good. Then I heard about a woman in one of the villages who made teddy bears to order. I went to see her. She had been busy in the pre-Christian period but was pleased to take an order for quick delivery, in fact only four days. I paid the deposit and she promised it for delivery at next Friday's market. Jean-Francois' birthday was on Saturday

Yvette had found two push along cars for him just before Christmas and saved them for his birthday. We held a little party for him with four other little boys in the restaurant area during the afternoon. Some games were managed and he went to bed happy with his new sleeping companion held very tightly. Yvette was thrilled by the fact that I had taken the trouble to find him such a bear and showed it later that evening

The anticipated increases in German traffic between the extra outposts started. Stephan asked for a meeting to decide what should be done about this. I arranged to meet him during one of my foraging trips into the hills. Stephan was as well informed as ever. There were so many options to be considered." We are well enough prepared and armed now to stop the movements completely with your help." I said. Stephan agreed," but is that what we really want to do?" he questioned." That could lead to an all out fire-fight and eventually we would lose when the Germans brought in enough troops." "OK", I said, "but if we look at the situation strictly from our point of view, what might we do? The Germans have to feed themselves, pay themselves, get their medical supplies wherever they are located, so why don't we let them make their outward journeys and raid their return journeys when they will be carrying the quotas they have commandeered back to Aurillac. At least we can argue that we are only recovering what they have stolen." "I like the idea," said Stephan, "but we will have to get quite a lot of information about their intentions and you are in the best place to do that"

The urgent need to establish our communication centre at the Gardes farm now demanded top priority. I asked Pascal for the help of Cezaire and Felix. Their accommodation at the Gardes farm was simple, how to explain their absence from Clermont was the problem. Felix was a senior lecturer at Clermont's technical high school and would be missed by many people. Cezaire could fulfil his job from the Gardes farm with couriers moving between the farm and Clermont for a short period. He was not expecting heavy radio traffic during the period of his absence. Felix had to be 'taken ill' while visiting his sister at Moissac and Pascal arranged for the necessary medical certificates to be received by the very cooperative professor at the high school

The extra men at the Gardes farm were made very welcome. The need for the four extra radio operators became urgent and the urgency was emphasised to London. Arrival was promised for second week February

The news of the final capitulation of German forces around Stalingrad was suppressed by the French news services. It was only after the listeners to the foreign news services that some people started to talk about this defeat. In the bar one evening a lively discussion on the Russian front was interrupted by some Germans entering the bar but not before they had heard enough to ask what was happening and how the locals knew about it

It was then clear that our German occupiers knew nothing of the situation in Russia. Two of the non-commissioned officers tried to get the identities of the listeners to the foreign news services. Everybody had heard it from somebody else they did not know in another bar or a shop often in another village. The Germans left without any hard information

Next day the SS returned to Saint Flour in some strength. They came immediately to the Terminus bringing the same two non-commissioned officers from the previous evening with them. They demanded the names of all the persons who were present in the bar last evening. And while we were being as slow as possible to remember they searched the whole of the Terminus for radio receivers. They discovered the aerial I had been using up to a few weeks ago still with a plug on the end. Their renewed search for a receiver was ruthless. They emptied every cupboard and searched every room including the lofts. The only hidden receiver found was in the loft, an old crystal set that Dad said he remembered his father using before the electricity was connected and that was the aerial he used. Fortunately the weather had aged the aerial and it did not look new The SS officers seemed to accept this statement and we all realised we had a narrow escape

Notices appeared all over the town warning that anyone found listening to foreign radio stations would be dealt with severely. A further warning about circulating the false reports from foreign news programmes included imprisonment for up to ten years

These notices frightened many people and it certainly put a stop to all conversation regarding the war in public places. I was pleased to note that the small hard core of resistance supporters reacted by pointing out that the Germans had not even told their own troops about the losses around Stalingrad

The continuing good news from North Africa was being linked with the Russian front leading to the conclusion that perhaps the tide had turned in favour of the Allies at last

There were two other aerials in Saint Flour that needed to be removed in case the Germans recognised them and took revenge on the people living nearby. At some risk Alexis took care of their removal late at night and passed them to Raymond for use elsewhere. I moved Raymond from the Chavent farm and Simon and Patrice from the Mathis farm to Gardes to look after our interests there. Raymond was pleased to have something constructive to do again and the direct control of Simon and Patrice would test his skills to the full. I sensed had been getting bored with the lack of his direct involvement in our work

He set to with great enthusiasm. In two weeks the whole set up was ready to operate, Raymond now understood how everything worked and said he was ready to settle the new operators in as soon as they arrived I expressed my delight at the rapid result and remembered to tell him the news of his promotion to Captain which had now been gazetted

Victor and Sebastian after their arrival had investigated why the explosives used at Montlucon tyre factory had failed to stop the production for more than a few days.

Their conclusions were quite different from those of the resistance groups who made the attacks and who subsequently blamed the both the detonators and the explosives

When they got to know some of the resistance men with the help of Stephan they organised some demonstrations of how to use the explosives correctly and how to accurately set the detonators. Pascal arranged for men from the Montlucon and Clermont groups to attend these demonstrations so their mistakes would not be repeated. The German occupiers with their SS overlords might make it more difficult to carry out sabotage so when we did so it must be effective

In view of Raymond's greater responsibilities at our new communication centre I transferred the responsibility for severing the rail and road links through the Auvergne to Victor and Sebastian They set to with alacrity and after looking at the points worked out by Raymond arranged sites for caches of explosives near to each point which could be covertly stocked up well in advance thus minimising the risk of anybody being caught with such items

When they had completed their plans we placed our orders on London. Four drops were needed to get the necessary amount required and London promised they would get the explosives and detonators to us at least three months ahead of the time when they would be needed. This freed up our current stock and Victor and Sebastian were designated to provide expert aid to any resistance groups who in the region who had targets to attack

I also made a point of talking to all the four men who came via Gibraltar about their increase in pay. They were duly grateful and thanked me for the promotion. I denied any involvement in the decision telling them they deserved it

Chapter 31

Spreading our Wings

I met Pascal at the safe house in Issoire. When I explained what I wanted done he agreed at once to start the planning needed. He said there were about thirty factories in his area to the North of the Auvergne known to be working for the German war effort. We agreed that we would establish secondary caches of arms, explosives and detonators for his use nearer to his targets. I explained about the role of Simon and Patrice and that when he had a target ready they could provide expert advice to the saboteurs to avoid a repetition of the previous failures

Pascal gave me the names and contact details of his opposite numbers in Le Puy, Tulle and Brive and promised to advise them that I would be in contact. I told him that Mathilde would be doing the same thing to the South of the Auvergne and that she already had contacts in Albi and Montpellier

"What are you planning for Stephan?" was the next matter. "I see the main problem as one of co-ordination," I replied, "he and his group are very keen to become active but I do not want to have a situation develop where we force the Germans to take reprisals against the general population because of the enthusiasm of the wild hill men. I am proposing to make supplies and special advice available to them on a target by target basis." "They could be very strong in factories where union representation is established," said Pascal. "I will not let the strength of union representation be a factor in deciding on whether or not to sabotage a particular factory," I said, "The decision has to be based on what they are producing and how well we rate the chance of success"

"I am relieved to hear you say that." replied Pascal. "I always have to remember," I said, "That I am forbidden to supply any British equipment to the maquis." "And I have to remember," said Pascal; "that reports from occupied France indicate that Maquis operations are more effective than Resistance led operations"

I talked to Alexis as soon as I was back in Saint Flour. "I have to go and meet a number of resistance leaders in the next few weeks and it means a lot of bus travel," I said, "It is sure to attract the attention of the Germans, what ideas do you have about it?" "You've obviously forgotten about Christian and Valerie." said Alexis. "Of course, the de Bonis, I'd forgotten all about them, they are so reserved and keep so much to themselves, we hardly ever see them except when they come in to pay the rent. He can get you travel permits whenever you need them. All you have to do is to get on the bus at the first stop after it leaves the Terminus with a your permit, the driver will cancel it in his machine, you keep it until you are ready to come back and go to the nearest main bus stop and they automatically issue you with a return travel permit, you get off the bus one stop before the Terminus and walk home. Christian will tell the driver of your bus not to ask any questions and all the other passengers will see you with a permit and assume it is just like their's"

"I will only be away for a day at a time and I'm sure to find some excuse for that." I replied

Two Mondays later when I went to meet the local leaders from Brive and Tulle, I left on the first bus for Tulle with a large parcel. Regis and Alain were waiting for me at our rendezvous by a massively constructed safe house in Tulle. The house must have been a large family residence at one time, large rooms, thick walls, and apparently disused. We went down into a basement room with no windows.

Both men were in their fifties and were not inclined to take my proposals very seriously. "You are saying you have men to help us with sabotage and the necessary explosives and detonators all ready to hand?" was Alain's first response to my proposals

"We are prepared to move stocks from our present locations nearer to you in convenient places." "That will mean you knowing where our stock points are, we have already disclosed this safe house to you, against our better judgement." "We have to learn to trust each other, I will not disclose the location of this house to any of my group without your agreement in advance, you can check with Pascal about our use of the need to know principle." "Is Pascal aware of this meeting, said Regis speaking for the first time. "Yes, I replied, "he suggested it"

The tension eased. "I will be making the same offers of help to other groups adjacent to Saint Flour and Mathilde my aunt, who already has good stocks in place, will be making the same sort of offer to groups such as yours to the South of the Auvergne." "Where are her supplies located?" asked Alain. "You don't need to know that," I replied smiling, and the tension eased further

"It's about a hundred and fifty kilometres from Saint Flour to Tulle," said Regis. "What are you going to use to move the stuff." "We normally use pack animals or travois" I replied. "You can't move all that way in one night even if we could meet you half way." "You shouldn't assume we are starting from Saint Flour, our stock point is only about sixty kilometres from Tulle in a straight line, say seventy by track and minor roads so a true half way point changeover could be done in one night up to about mid-April." "You stock your supplies well out of towns I suppose," said Alain. "Yes, and I hope you will do the same, there is no point in making anything easy for the Germans, I'm afraid the ordnance is very obviously British" "How are we going to make the detailed arrangements for the rendezvous?" asked Regis. "Before we talk about that matter I need to have your commitment to work with us. Pascal has told me you are both men of your word so your word is good enough for me." I said

"We will leave you alone here for about fifteen minutes," said Regis, "We need to talk together, please don't leave this room, you are quite safe here." They left. The old house was completely silent. I couldn't help but wonder what this house was used for, it was not cold but there was no apparent heating. What I had seen was obviously well cared for and clean and even had a feel of luxury about it

They returned after about half an hour. Both were smiling and I knew we would work together. "Let's go and have a little lunch together," said Regis, "at my home where we will be quite safe." "Before we go," I interjected, "I have a present for you and picked up the large parcel I had brought with me from Saint Flour

This is a radio set with which you can communicate with our centre and arrange all the details with Raymond. Code books are included and I have been told that you are both competent operators. If you do need any help with the operation of the radio, Pascal can provide it. I will arrange for Raymond to open contact at an agreed time on Thursday at say, twenty-two hours or Friday or Saturday at the same time to agree a call schedule and a listening watch arrangement." "You took a risk bringing that all the way from Saint Flour on the bus," said Alain. "We all have to take some risks when necessary." I replied. "You were sure you were going to get our agreement?" questioned Regis, "I was not going to leave without it." "Let's lunch," said Regis"

Lunch was unremarkable and somewhat strained. I was introduced to Madame Armengaud as a friend from Aurillac but no mention of any resistance activity was made. I left immediately after the meal. I took advantage of being in a larger town to go shopping for a birthday present for Yvette. I was lucky enough to find a perfumer who still had some pre-war stock. Even then I still caught an earlier bus than expected. It had been a good day. The return travel permit arrangement worked perfectly

I felt sufficiently encouraged to plan the trip to Le Puy for the following Monday. Yvette's birthday was on Sunday. The perfume was a great success. I was pleased that both her parents and Philippe's came to our dinner party that evening

Raymond opened radio contact with Tulle at his first attempt on Thursday and completed all the arrangements. Alain and Regis nominated four targets to be attacked on an urgent basis so a rendezvous with Simon and Patrice was arranged for the following week

Francois Peillon agreed to meet me at Loudes which shortened my journey by some twenty kilometres. I left on the first bus with a travel permit for Le Puy and another well disguised radio. Francois met me at the main bus stop in Loudes. Outwardly he was an insignificant little man with a limp from the last war and an intense, almost dangerous, hatred of all things German. "How on earth have you managed to stay out of the war," was his greeting over a long handshake. "I don't want to talk about that here," I replied. "Let's go then," he said leading me to his car. "We have a safe location at a disused airstrip just out of town where we can settle down to talk

Le Puy is swarming with Germans at present on resting leave from the Eastern front and all very hostile to the locals let alone strangers." We drove a few kilometres South and turned off the main road to a large grass field which still flew an air sock. There was a small building at the roadside apparently used for some small manufacturing work

"We are quite safe here, everyone here is a resistance member, and this is where we keep most of our munitions." "I understand you've made several attacks on the generating stations on the Rhone," "Yes," he replied, "They are an easy target because we have plenty of resistance supporters working there but the effect is not very specific, everybody loses when the power is disrupted and there is no longer any support for further attacks on the generators."We have got to attack those manufacturers who are known to be working for the Germans." "That's understandable I replied

By this time we had reached a small meeting room, coffee was served and we got down to business. "Between Montelimar and Lyon there are about thirty-five factories and most of them are doing some work for the Germans. Some eight are clearly important because they have German guards on the gates. In Lyon itself there are many more factories and there is an active resistance movement but only with limited munitions. Most of the supply drops intended for them were intercepted and many of the resistance men were killed or captured, morale is somewhat low. We have tried to supply them but getting supplies into Lyon is not easy, road blocks are frequent with all vehicles being searched, especially immediately after any supply drops have been made"

"Thank you for summing up a situation with plenty of potential and plenty of problems," I replied" Do you have any problems with your supply drops?" I asked "Not really, our situation is quite like yours, Pascal has told me about your diversionary tactics and false reporting of aircraft noise. We have tried it and it certainly does divert the attention of everybody from what is really happening." I don't want you to tell me where your stock points are," I said, "but I hope they are not in Le Puy. Do you have any difficulty in moving them into the Rhone valley?"

Oh no," Francois replied, "You are sitting on our main supplies at this moment, we take our drops on the field over there, they are stored in the old fuel dump for the airstrip, we repack them in the factory here and deliver them by normal transport. The local police and the local Gendarmerie are quite cooperative, we tell them when we are making special deliveries and they always have activities elsewhere on those days, but nothing ever goes through Le Puy." "You are well organised," I commented"

"What about the effectiveness of the sabotage operations you have carried out," I asked, "Have you got the results you expected from the charges you used? I have to ask this question because of several failures in our attempts even when the charges were correct." "We have many members with experience from the last war and they know exactly what is necessary but they are reluctant to use plastic explosive because it is unknown to them." "I understand why," replied Francois, "Pascal has told me about his problems, but personally I don't understand it

I have two experts, Victor and Sebastian, who are up-to-date on all the current materials and techniques who are currently trying to find out what went wrong with Pascal's sabotage attempts. They could be available to you to assist your men in understanding plastic explosive I understand that this will be the only explosive to be available to us in the near future"

"How soon can you arrange for Victor and Sebastian to meet with some of my men and where would be safest?"

"Before we talk about that I have a little present for you, I said; and picked up the parcel I had brought with me. "Here is another of the radios you are familiar with and it can only be used for contact with our communication centre using the codes enclosed. If you advise me of the best times for you to make contact I will have the main frequency listening in daily at those times and the arrangements can be made directly with Raymond, who is my second in command." Francois was amazed, "You have a communication centre in Saint Flour?, Isn't that terribly risky with two hundred or so Germans about?" "The centre is not in Saint Flour and you don't need to know where it is, and I'm sure you understand why." I replied. "Of course of course," replied Francois reassuringly, "I had no idea you were such a big group." "Big or small is not important," I replied, "I haven't asked you how big your group is and I don't intend to. By the way," I added," "the emergency frequency on your radio is listened to all the time and is only for true emergencies"

We talked about the timing and location of the training sessions for his saboteurs but could not agree on times at this stage so it was agreed that the first emergency transmission would be to set up the listening schedule. Le Puy was many times the size of Saint Flour and consequently got much more attention the occupying troops. We talked about the behaviour of the Germans and I told Francois I had lost my bet with Alexis over how long it would be before some ladies would be entertaining the troops. He laughed, "You are not old enough to remember last time the Germans were here, and this time is no different. I reckon there are at least a hundred ladies in Le Puy regularly receiving members of the wehrmacht at home, although, so far, the commandant has not issued any sleeping-out passes"

"We do have a dozen or so ladies collecting pillow-talk information, but so far no real gems have come our way." "What is the general view about the total occupation?" I asked, "Yes," said Francois, "We've been asked repeatedly about this by De Gaulle

The answers you get are so often what the person you ask thinks you want to hear. I have reported about sixty percent totally apathetic but I have not reported that I expect that figure could be high or low by twenty percent." "That's somewhat more than Saint Flour and we have noticed a decrease in apathy since the total occupation to around thirty-five percent. That was mainly because of incidents over the Christmas and New Year. Nothing particularly nasty but the SS was involved and was heavy handed over minor matters.

We had to totally suspend any activity for a few weeks." Comparing notes like this was of interest to both of us As the morning drew to a close, Francois invited me for a lunch in a little safe restaurant in the village. Afterwards I begged a lift into Le Puy so that I could return from the place my travel permit said I could visit

Now there was the problem of getting a radio to Mathilde in Millau. I had used up all the reasonable excuses for getting a permit to visit Millau. I spent several sleepless nights over this in spite of Yvette's ministrations. I did not want to involve Mum or Dad in such a venture

The main problem was the fact that the trip almost certainly meant a night away and this demanded a different type of permit with many questions to answer. Amongst others I mentioned the problem to Christian de Boni, one of Yvette's tenants, because of his close connection with the bus services.

Some days later he came back to me with a sound scheme. "If Mathilde takes a bus from Millau to Aurillac with a day return permit and you take a day return permit for a trip to Rodez the two buses meet at Espalion, and it is a guaranteed connection. Two identical parcels could be exchanged in the melee of people changing buses and both continue on their way.   "That could work," I responded, "even though you don't know Mathilde you could not possibly miss her"

"We could also reduce the chance of mistakes if we agreed in advance on the size and colour of the parcels," added Christian. "Do you have a code agreed with Mathilde?" asked Alexis, who had joined the discussion, "Yes," I replied, "Then you could give me written instructions which I can get to her via our police contacts in Rodez. There is almost a daily movement of agents de police between Rodez and Millau"

I drafted a long coded letter to Mathilde detailing how carefully she should pack the birthday present she was sending to Dad in view of its size and weight. On the day of the exchange I received a telephone call from Mathilde while she was killing time in Aurillac telling me to be sure and help Dad unpack his parcel as the contents were valuable

Christian arrived back on time and the parcel was put on one side until we had closed for the evening. Mathilde had clearly guessed what was to be in the parcel for her and had adjusted the weight with pieces of stone. She also enclosed, an unencoded list of her sabotage targets plus a demand for further supplies by containers to be dropped at the site we had agreed to use on the Levezou plateau near the Benedictine Monastery

I showed the unencoded lists to Christian and Alexis and we agreed she had exposed Christian to unnecessary risks but a Christian said "You can't put her over your knee and spank her." I severely reprimanded Mathilde when I saw her next. She simply said she hadn't time to code all that

Chapter 32

What Quotas

With communications now established between the neighbouring resistance groups a better understanding of each others problems and needs emerged. Requests for help from Simon and Patrice were frequent. And the benefit of having our stocks of munitions near to the local groups paid off

We put together a total list of the potential targets for sabotage and advised this to London. There were over one hundred and twenty targets on the list and over two thirds of there were in the area of the Le Puy group with already several successes achieved. We asked all of the neighbouring groups to advise us immediately after an attack had taken place whether successful or not because the Germans would be specially alerted and active which might endanger any attacks planned in the following few days. We promised to pass such advice on to all the other groups

French radio made only rare statements about sabotage attacks and always long after the event. Jamming of BBC broadcasts had increased in intensity and duration. Reception was so erratic that it was only reliable as a news source of events outside of France; the BBC did not know about all sabotage events

In the spring period we brought in three substantial drops one for Mathilde's group and the other two to boost our own stocks of the munitions supplied to Clermont, Brive and Tulle. Our diversionary tactics were as effective as usual

For good measure we also arranged diversionary tactics for the four following nights in areas well removed from the actual drop sites this seemed especially effective when we saw how many Germans who might have been active in the immediate areas of our drops were diverted elsewhere for the period when we wanted to be moving supplies on to the users

Sabotage attacks on previously identified targets fell generally into two categories. Some were carefully planned and timed to cause maximum damage and loss of production. Others were opportunistic recognised planned and carried out in hours rather than days or weeks. Some targets were attacked several times. The record was achieved by the Clermont group with their five attacks on a steel plant, each time stopping production for some weeks

Next in line was the factory making cylinder heads for aero-engines attacked four times, the last in March 1944 stopping production completely until after the liberation. The effect of these attacks on the attitude of the people was minimal. Ceased production meant loss of wages for those temporally unemployed. Occasionally some workers were injured and regretfully a few died. In most cases the unions cooperated and actively helped in getting workers out of danger in the last minutes before the attack. In a few cases the unions organised the sabotage. I do not believe that the sabotage changed the attitude of the civilian population; those who supported it accepted the extra hardship as part of the price of liberation, those against it were unable to do very much against sabotage other than to report anything they knew to the authorities. In doing so they risked reprisals and even their lives if it became known

The Le Puy group were by far the busiest with their efforts Hardly a week went by without some successes being reported. They were even bold enough to arrange simultaneous attacks on different targets at the same time. Francois told me that this tactic neatly diluted the efforts of the Germans after the event and led to complaints from the manufacturers attacked to the Germans that they were not being properly protected for working for the German war effort. Success has its price, his group suffered more losses than our four other groups combined

As the weather improved Simon and Patrice took the theory they had taught the hillmen and the Maquis into the hills. Results were promising but controversial. The hillmen amazed both the instructors with the accuracy they achieved with their ancient weaponry, simply because they had grown up with those guns, but their firing rate was poor. Hillmen shooting for the pot wanted to make every shot count whereas the instructors wanted a high firing rate to keep the enemy occupied. Most of the Maquis had little experience of guns and were more easily convinced to do it the instructor's way, except for Pietro. Petro was in Greece when the Germans invaded the Greek part of Macedonia and fought with the partisans. They were desperately short of ammunition and needed to make every shot count

At one of the evening inquests of a gunnery-day's training; Petro explained about the Greek single shot ambush. The terrain in Greek Macedonia was not unlike the Auvergne but with less cover from vegetation and more cover from the terrain itself. A German unit moving through a valley where the Greeks had set up an ambush would be fired on by one partisan using one shot which either took out a man or a windscreen. All the Greeks were under cover the Germans fired heavily wherever they thought there was a movement. No fire was returned from the partisans. After some time the Germans decided to move on

Another single shot took out one of the Germans or his windscreen and all the others took cover again. Perhaps a small rock rolled down the hillside and attracted a hail of fire from the Germans. By this time the Germans had probably called up support by radio but as soon as any support was sighted the partisans quietly withdrew and the valley was as silent as the grave. According to Petro the only time his group took any casualties was when the Germans had air support and the withdrawing partisans were machine gunned from the air

The hillmen were quite impressed by Petro's description and almost all of them recognised the potential of this sort of attack for use on the foraging patrols that the Germans were increasingly using to try and get the quota out of the region. Almost every week patrols of up to eight Germans with dogs would leave Saint Flour in a truck and visit a particular group of farms where they would search for food supplies they could commandeer for the quota. They were normally accompanied by one or more Gendarmes. The hillmen's system of warning of the approach of Germans towards particular areas or hamlets was established and worked well

The Montagne de la Margeride lies to the East of Saint Flour. The higher ground is well forested but the South-West facing slopes are dotted with many prosperous farms between the mountain and the river Truyere. An area regularly visited by foraging German patrols and all agreed overdue for another visitation

No German personnel would be fired upon. Depending on the location of the ambush either the dogs would be shot or the windscreen of the vehicle. When the Germans decided to move forward again shots would hit the ground just ahead of them. "If any of them are smoking," said Jean Chavent, "I'll shoot the fags right of their mouths." We urged him not to try because of the reprisals that might follow if he missed and hit a German soldier. From what I had seen of his shooting he probably could have done it but the risk was too great. When a German soldier had been shot dead last month in Aurillac ten local men were hanged

The group for the attack on the forage patrol was made up of Maquis plus Victor plus Jean Chavent. The hillmen would keep watch on the movements of all German patrols that day. The resistance group in Saint Flour that day would be conspicuous by their presence

Our watcher at the barracks reported the usual vehicle being prepared on the following Thursday. It left at about seven-thirty on national nine and it looked like this was the day. By eight it had turned towards Ruynes so the foraging area was confirmed. A farm near the hamlet of Gizerac approached by a track that was too narrow for the vehicle was chosen because the Germans habitually got some coffee and food there. The track was deeply rutted and quite slippery after the winter rains. The vehicle was left with two of the patrol at the junction with the road. The remainder of the patrol had two dogs with them and were in single file carrying sacks for the produce they would seize

The first shot killed one dog. The patrol took cover as best they could. After some seconds the second dog was released and told to seek out the enemy. Immediately a second shot from the other side of then track killed the second dog.   The Germans sprayed both sides of the track with automatic fire, but no shots were returned.   The sergeant in charge ordered his men to proceed leading the way himself. Immediately two shots hit a small boulder barely half a metre in front of him

The patrol stopped again and sprayed the sides of the track with a hail of fire, and then moved forward again

The two Germans left with the vehicle heard the shooting and were somewhat alarmed. Then a single shot smashed the windscreen of the vehicle and they took refuge behind the truck. Single shots at intervals flattened all the tyres and the Germans moved away from the vehicle behind a low stone wall. They did not return any fire. They probably never saw a target

The Maquis plus Victor and Jean Chavent quietly withdrew and made their way back over the Truyere to where they had hidden their horses and bicycles and then home via minor roads and footpaths, seeing only very few people

The following day Major Kempf issued a statement that he wanted all information on all persons missing from their normal locations on the previous day. Nobody volunteered any information.

German personnel made door to door calls throughout the town centre in the late afternoon and evening. Very few names were forthcoming and those few were taken in the next day for questioning. All were eventually released as no involvement in the ambush could be established

Major Kempf interviewed the Maire and required him to put up notices throughout the whole sub-prefecture of Saint Flour stating that attacks on German personnel would not be tolerated and all persons involved in such attacks would be tried by a military tribunal and if found guilty, publicly executed

As the days lengthened German patrol activity increased. In the hills they were regularly fired upon unless the weather was fine enough for Storch spotter planes to operate and locate the source of the attacks. The training of the Maquis by Simon and Patrice, coupled with their own instinctive approach made these patrols very nerve wracking for the Germans who were not front line calibre troops

The Germans soon lost all their dogs to accurate sniping. When a German took aim to fire at farm dogs he was likely to have his rifle shot out of his hands or to be shot in the leg. Farm dogs were valuable to their owners. It is unlikely that the Germans ever arrived at a farm without the locals being warned in advance. The men were always out working somewhere else and the women and children only spoke Auvergnat. The amount of quota to be had at the farms steadily decreased, as did the morale of the German troops

The news of the war from North Africa was not good for the Germans. Regular listeners to the BBC French service kept the locals well informed and in quiet conversation with the Germans they might say, "Is it true that the British Eighth Army have broken through the Mareth line?" or "Have the Germans in Tunisia really surrendered?" and later when all German and Italian resistance in North Africa had ceased, "How many of your troops were taken prisoner?"

Discussion in the Terminus bar even in the presence of German troops and officers could be the relative virtues of the second front being opened in the South or the North of France or perhaps both simultaneously. Pressure from Stalin for a second front to open in Europe was increasing as were the Russian successes against the German invaders. German morale declined steadily in spite of the talk of the secret weapons being prepared

Chapter 33

Diversions

With improved communications the real resistance activities were consuming our supplies. New drops must be planned before the nights became too short. Mathilde was also repeatedly demanding replenishment of her stocks, During April we took in four large drops using all our possible sites once only

The explosives and detonators dropped at le Che needed to be widely distributed throughout the whole of the Auvergne region

All of the surrounding resistance groups had accepted Raymond's planned closure of the railway system and certain key roads. In all there were twenty-eight sites and that meant twenty-eight caches of explosives. The detonators were concealed separately by the members responsible for the actual blasting. Victor and Sebastian managed to make all the moves without once being noticed by the Germans, but it took all their time for over two months

With these supplies in position talk turned to the timing of the second front invasion. Would it be in June and July when the days were longest or at the traditional time for such military movements in September? Would it be in the Pas de Calais or on the southern French beaches or both together? All of the options were argued endlessly by the local experts, none of whom were members of the resistance, and whether the German troops were around or not

The dropping of supplies to resistance group throughout all of France built up steadily through the spring of 1943. Inevitably some of the drops were intercepted and the captured resistance members subjected to torture if they were handed over to the SS

This became the new threat of Major Kempf. His latest dictate, "Any person suspected of being a resistance member will be arrested and handed over to SS Captain Fieg in Aurillac for interrogation." This had the immediate effect of stopping all such discussions in the presence of German personnel

By now my long-lost bet with Alexis over the 'entertainment' of German troops by some lonely ladies in the town was also producing some results. A small number of very brave lonely ladies were actively encouraging pillow talk with their guests and reporting the interesting information to their local agent de police

Thus we learnt that Major Kempf was worried about what he should do if he did actually have to arrest anyone for resistance activity. This announcement was made to put on record that he would not be involved in any of the sort of interrogation that was carried out by the SS notably in Lyon and by implication in other large cities where there was a large SS presence. Although Kempf was not liked it was generally thought that his attitude to the people of Saint Flour was correct

We knew from past events that the SS regarded the price was; ten local men for one German killed by the resistance. What would be the price of an SS man killed by the resistance? We needed a clear understanding that we should not kill Germans unless absolutely necessary, and we needed to get the agreement of all neighbouring resistance groups to this principle and to understand the reason for it

People still died in Saint Flour. Thus there were regular funerals and this was an excellent opportunity for people to get together. The Germans did not know who was related to, or close friends of, or how highly respected, the corpse.

Some families were thus surprised at the large attendances at a funeral. A local funeral was an ideal opportunity for all sorts of people to get together on an occasion that even the Germans respected. There were never any identity checks made at a Saint Flour funeral

In general travel permits to attend a funeral were issued without demur Madame Persan volunteered her father as a corpse. He had been extremely ill for a year or so and she had just arranged for him to go to a convent rest home near Sarlat where he would be cared for until his end

He no longer knew any one of his family and Madame Persan could not cope with his care needs. She quietly arranged for his removal to Sarlat with a closed car arranged by Alexis. A few days later his death was announced. Pressure was put on father Pierre at the Cathedral to perform a requiem Mass in honour of an empty coffin. People came from all over the department of Cantal and even further afield to attend the requiem Mass and the reception afterwards held at the Saint Jacques Hotel During the reception we managed to get the agreement of all the neighbouring resistance groups to the policy of only killing German personnel when unavoidably necessary. However we had to concede that when the invasion of France started, such a war-situation, would demand the killing of any German troops as a duty

Mathilde's first supply drop on the Levezou plateau just above the monastery went off without a hitch. She said she would arrange her own diversions which directed the authority's attention to the Causse Noir a high area to the East of Millau. She acknowledged the drop but added that she would need the "same again" next month and the month after that. She had to be told to make every bullet count as the nights would be too short for any repeats until late September. "But that will be after the invasion," she said. I could not comment. But I did wonder if she knew something I didn't

Fernand Mounier also said he would arrange his own diversion and I knew he could be trusted. He had been a key player in an earlier sheep rustling diversion

This time he came up with even more effective idea. Saint Laurent de Veyres was actually in the next department of Aveyron and strictly speaking was Mathilde's responsibility because Millau is in Aveyron

Fernand had many times proposed using the Causse Mejean as a drop zone. It was bleak upland area with very few roads and a sparse farm population, some of whom were related to Fernand and trustworthy. The area was too far from Saint Flour for us to consider using with Saint Flour personnel but was, as Fernand was always pointing out, closer to the Monastery

Fernand's plan was simple and effective. He asked for some parachutes rescued from our previous drops. On the night before the drop when we had confirmation he arranged for the parachutes to be poorly hidden on the Plaine de Charnet in the middle of the Causse Mejean. On the night of the drop at Saint Laurent de Veyres and before the drop was even scheduled, telephone calls to the Gendarmerie in Mende were reporting American and British aircraft activity over the Causse Mejean. Later in the night one informant specifically said he had seen parachutes falling on the Plaine de Charnet

Before dawn the next morning the whole area of the Causse Mejean had been cordoned off. Every road, track and footpath closed by German troops supported by the local Gendarmerie. Later in the day parachutes were found on the Plaine de Charnet and identified as British. The cordon remained in position and Parties of German troops started searching farms on the fringe of the Plaine de Charnet and all the caves they could find

Colonel Weber announced that supplies had been dropped to the resistance on the Causse Mejean the previous night and that the area was out of bounds to all persons except the German troops and the Gendarmerie assisting them. Any person found in possession of supplies would be arrested, interrogated and executed

All persons suspected of being involved with the resistance were arrested at daybreak. Those with indisputable alibis were released after being cautioned about the penalties for resistance involvement. The remainder were interrogated by SS Captain Metzner and imprisoned on suspicion of resistance involvement

During the night before the supposed drop plenty of tracks were left for the Germans to see and they interpreted these tracks as signs of supplies being moved after the drop. All they actually found were some more of the better concealed parachutes

Colonel Weber was clearly convinced that a supply drop had taken place

He imposed a stricter curfew and vigorously enforced it throughout the whole department. Life became more difficult for the people and resentment grew because not a shred of hard evidence of a supply drop had been found. Many of the informants regarding the aircraft activity were called in again for questioning. Most of them stuck to their earlier statements and there were confirmations of parachutes being seen. Parachutes had also been found and Colonel Weber's conviction was undiminished

Colonel Weber called in additional support from Cantal and Aveyron and Haute Loire. While all of this was going on the supplies dropped at Saint Laurent de Veyres were quietly moved to Mathilde's stock points

With the supply position improved the resistance activity increased with specific attacks on factories working for the Germans. Success rates improved with the better preparation of the attacks due to the training from Victor and Sebastian

The minor disruptions of the 1942 sabotage became total loss of production for some weeks. Almost every week there was a success to report to London. One night after the bar was closed and we were musing over that night's report, of a further success at an Ancies factory, Dad said, "It seems to be happening everywhere but in Saint Flour, I don't think that is right, If I can see this as an oddity, so can the Germans." Alexis agreed, "Some time some German will ask, why not in Saint Flour? After all there are over two hundred Germans here." "But as far as I can see there are no factories in Saint Flour who work for the German war effort," I said, "and how can you justify simply damaging the local economy?, it's difficult enough for the people to manage at the moment." "I wasn't thinking about the local factories so much as disrupting the Germans life," said Dad, "For example that truckload of the quota that they collect each week and send off to Germany, why don't we hijack it and give it back to the farmers on the condition that they sell it at special prices to the locals at the next Friday market." "There's some food for thought!" said Alexis

I knew that Stephan was currently working on a farm at la Chaumette. Next morning I set off by bicycle to meet him at lunch time. There was no telephone at la Chaumette and I had to take a chance on meeting him. I was lucky, he arrived back for lunch about twenty minutes after I arrived. Madame

Gourrier insisted I joined them for lunch. "I'm haymaking on the top meadows all today," said Stephan, "Then I'll come and help you," I replied. I did not know the other two men who were at lunch so we talked about the war in general

Expectations were higher than I imagined possible. Stephan was insistent that the Americans would invade Sicily in the next week or two and then there was also the possibility of a landing in the South of France before the summer was over. He was teasing me for information and he knew I dare not respond in the presence of strangers. There was complete agreement that the Germans had lost the war and it was only a question of time before the invasion of mainland Europe would cause German capitulation. Again I dared not comment. Apart from saying I hoped German greed would not starve the people of the occupied countries

We let the two others get well ahead of us on the walk up to the hayfield

"You didn't enjoy your lunch as much as usual?" questioned Stephan, "but you did I'm sure," I replied and we both laughed. What a pleasure it was to be able to mentally relax with someone I was not supposed to deal with, and knowing full well that he was probably going to solve the stalemate that we had created

He knew about the policy regarding not killing German personnel and gave the SS the opportunity to kill ten for one in revenge. "I'm only going to agree to the no killing policy until the invasion," said Stephan, "then as far as the Maquis is concerned it's an all-out war situation, and they are the enemy to be destroyed"

"And I suppose you know when and where the invasion will be?" I taunted him. "How can I know when the decision has not yet been made," said Stephan

How amazing it was that I had to tease any information we needed out of someone with whom I was forbidden to cooperate. "The Allies will invade Sicily very soon and that will be a hard bloody battle," said Stephan, "and then mainland Italy probably by leapfrogging landings further North up both the East and West coasts, at that stage I expect Italy to surrender, but the Germans will not withdraw. And then nobody can guess what is going to take place." he continued "and that is why no decision has been taken regarding the invasion of France"

I was flabbergasted. Here in the middle of France on a glorious summer's day I was being told about the events to happen over the next year or so with the confidence of someone who really knew the future course of the war. "I suppose you have a direct line to the allied high command?" "Not exactly," he replied, "but my sources are quite reliable. What I have told you is for your ears only, you need to know and I trust you not to report this back to London, such

242

an action would completely compromise you.   The trust that we have in each other is good enough for me and it must be good enough for you also"

"Now why did you come to see me today?" questioned Stephan, "Haven't your sources told you," I replied, and we both laughed again and relaxed. "I've heard about your ambush of the quota collectors", said Stephan, "it was well arranged, do you want me to do something similar?" "No I think we can do all that is reasonably possible, if we do too much the Germans will react and someone will get killed and cause the inevitable consequences. What I want to do this time is more ambitious. I want to stop the weekly truck that goes from Saint Flour to Aurillac on Friday evenings with that week's quota collection and return it to farmers who will sell it in the following Friday market at a discounted price to local people." "I like the idea," replied Stephan

"Could we work out a way to do it between us and then make it a combined operation of Maquis and resistance because many hands will be needed"

"The truck always goes by the same route via Murat I believe," said Stephan, "Yes," I replied, "and there is one ideal spot for the hijacking, the Col de Cere." "I know it," said Stephan. "Let me think about it. Come and see me again in later in the week when we've finished the hay, say on Friday when we can have the place to ourselves while Madame Gourrier is at the market." "Agreed", I said, "and could you get Pietro to come along as well"

During the afternoon I was introduced to the art of haymaking. It should have been a pleasure but within an hour my nose was streaming, my eyes were sore and I was dizzy with hay fever and I retired hurt. My return to Saint Flour on a bicycle was erratic and not made any easier when I reached the Terminus by Yvette's remark that I should have known better, "You always suffered from hay fever." But I didn't know that

The same evening after the last Germans had left we had one of our late discussions, between Alexis and Councillors Leman and Dechaux using their curfew exemptions plus Dad, Manuel and myself. Manuel had recently been admitted to our inner circle because he had demonstrated his active support for the resistance. Being a Spanish national and always reminding the Germans of this point he often picked up bits of information from the Germans that they would not have said to a Frenchman. Some of the German officers even questioned him about what was said to him by the French so we kept him well supplied with titbits of information we wanted the Germans to know

There was reluctance on the part of the councillors because they could not conceive of a high jacking without German casualties and the consequences that might follow. "Who is going to command the operation? asked Councillor Dechaux. "Not yet discussed," I replied. "If it's Stephan," said Councillor

Leman, "I don't think he will accede to our ruling about no German casualties." "In a recent conversation with him he agreed to do so until the Allies land in France but then he said he would treat the Germans as enemies to be destroyed"

I then put everyone on their honour not to repeat what Stephan had told me "Well he was right about Morocco," said Alexis, "and I didn't think that would happen." "What he says about the invasion of the Italian mainland makes sense to me," said Councillor Dechaux, "and I for one believe him. Remember those radio signals from Mauriac are strong enough to reach Russia, I believe he has a direct contact to the Russian high command." There was silence while all considered the proposition

Manuel tried to break the deadlock, "We could always use the quota we confiscated and feed it back to the Germans again and make a profit." the laugh that ensued did break the deadlock. We rapidly focused on the essential elements of the plan. We must not kill any Germans, we must let the local French derive some benefit from the hijacking and we must escape unscathed ourselves or we could be captured. "I assume that Stephan will be the leader as far as the maquis are concerned," said Alexis. "I'm sure you're right," I replied, "and I intend to witness the operation simply to see how the maquis and the resistance work together"

"When you stop the truck, how do you get the Germans to leave the truck?" questioned Dad. "That's a detail we have yet to work out. What I want to come out of this discussion is agreement to continue planning such an operation until we have a workable plan and then we can tell you all about it. I have an arrangement to meet Stephan on Friday to do exactly that. I am planning to take Sebastian with me because he knows about weaponry capability and I asked Stephan to bring Pietro with him because of his experience of ambushing German patrols in Greece"

Chapter 34

Highjacked

It was going to be a busy week, back to la Chaumette the next morning and straight up to the haymaking field. I took Stephan aside from the others for a quick decision from him as to whom we should have at the planning meeting. I told him of the feelings I had from the previous evening's discussion and he was not surprised. I said I wanted Sebastian for his weapons knowledge and Raymond because there was going to have to be a rockfall or two and we would need his help for that He agreed and also wanted Sebastian for the same reason. Stephan also proposed Pierre Gibory because of his close local knowledge of the location

We next agreed that the best place for the meeting was at the Gibory's farm because of the remoteness and the ease of an early warning programme should any strangers approach the farm. This meant I would have to arrange for my absence on Friday night but all the others were outside the effective curfew area. All agreed readily and I escaped from the haymaking dust before it affected me as seriously as yesterday. Stephan said he would contact all of the others with my authority in the case if Sebastian and Raymond agreed

Friday was a difficult night to be missing from the Terminus. I thought about it during the ride back from la Chaumette with no good ideas. "Couldn't you go with Yvette and Jean-Francois and stay with Madame Rodot for the weekend?" asked Mum, "At this time of the year it is only about two hours on horseback up to the Gibory's. I could talk to her on the phone later today about collecting those 'special cheeses' and she will guess it is important and agree. Getting a travel permit for your family to visit friends at this time of the year should not be any problem

"So I went out with Yvette straight away to the bus depot to get the travel permits. When we returned Mum said to us, "Bernice Rodot just telephoned to say those cheeses are ready and suggested you should take Jean-

Francois with you to see the new piglets this weekend." There were plenty of witnesses in the bar to hear this just in case any questions were asked. Yvette was pleased with the idea of a break and Jean-Francois could not stop talking about what he was going to do with the piglets, lambs and kittens

Alexis and Councillor Dechaux came in again that evening and we got down to a serious discussion about how we could separate the Germans from their truck without a shoot out. We easily got as far as agreeing that there should be one minor rockfall on the Aurillac side of the Col de Cere just enough to make the road impassable Then no witnesses could approach from that side. A second rockfall about five hundred metres higher up the pass would stop the German truck at the point we wanted it to stop. And a third rockfall on the Murat side of the pass would prevent any approach from that side. The timing of the rock falls would have to be carefully planned

So much for the stopping and isolating of the truck on the road. "What about the footpaths that cross the Col de Cere," said Alexis, "if the weather is fine there are likely to be some hikers up there at this time of the year." "I can confirm that." said Councillor Dechaux, "I know those hills well, there are two long distance footpaths cross the Col de Cere as well as several less important ones and people like to stop there because of the fine views." "I think the answer to that is simple," said Dad, "just get plenty of the resistance people to close off all the footpaths saying there has been an earth tremor in the area and the road has been closed by rock falls as well as the footpaths and that the area is currently unsafe." "That will also keep any witnesses out of the area," I said and agreed with the idea

But how to get the Germans away from their truck remained as a difficulty. "We have to find a way of making them see a real danger approaching them and their truck. Suppose we arrange a further minor rockfall around the truck just after they have stopped so that there is no possibility to turn around, then they could only leave on foot." said Alexis. We all pondered. Somebody piped up "Cattle stampede?"
"Not at that height." said Dad

The summer weather was settled in. Friday morning's bus ride to Pierrefort was hot and sticky. The bus was almost full as we left Saint Flour and picked up more holiday travellers the standing passengers made it much worse. At each stop passengers had to get off in order for others to leave the bus but there always seemed to be more to get on. At Pierrefort Bernice had arranged for a neighbour with a small van to take us up to le Bosquet. We arrived just in time for the midday meal

Sebastian was already there and Pierre Gibory had just arrived with horses for all. Since we had set up our communications centre at the Gibory farm the Giborys had increased their riding horses so that they could always have a mount available when needed. I thanked Pierre for his foresight. "It is necessary so it is done," he replied

I really enjoyed the afternoon ride up to farm We were the last to arrive. It was some months since my last visit so I filled the time up to dinner with a tour of inspection. I was well satisfied with Raymond's achievements. He also commented on the Gibory attitude to resistance. "Whenever I had a problem or needed any help or wanted to rearrange equipment, as soon as I mentioned it things were done, no suggestion of any payment for what they provided or their time involved." "Do you think I should pay them? I took the precaution of bringing funds with me in case the matter came up," I said when we were alone. "There is always the risk you might offend them," said Raymond, "and if they are not your friends then we might be in some danger"

After dinner when all the 'wives' and children departed we got down to the business. Agreement was soon reached on how we could stop the German truck where we wanted it and how we could discourage any intruders from the scene. The Giborys had a number of ideas, they had foreseen the problem and we simply had to decide which idea was most likely to succeed. The other matter was to decide how we were going to get the contents of the truck back to Saint Flour for the next Friday's market

"The quota will have to be removed after dark," said Pierre. "We should choose a night with a good moon and then we can use travois to move the goods down to the railway line at le Lioran, that's less than a kilometre. We have a trusted friend there and he will have an empty van waiting ready. He can then have the van shunted to either Talizat or Saint Flour itself ready for you to unload. We thought Talizat might be better for you because the curfew cannot be enforced there. The superintendent at Talizat is also a friend and can be trusted completely." We had all listened in a stunned silence

The simplicity and audacity of the plan. "Have you used these two friends before?" asked Raymond. "You have trusted us with your radio systems and we will not let you down. We now trust you with some of our secrets. We sell our fleeces to the factory in Saint Flour for cleaning and grading. They are always delivered that way and we do not pay for transport. And you will not let us down will you." There was a distinct element of menace in his tone. I looked around the room, "I take it you will all forget you ever heard about this." Complete assent was agreed. "Good," said Pierre, "Now let's talk about how we are going to get the Germans out of their bloody truck"

"We've agreed that immediately after the truck has stopped moving there should be another small rockfall, just enough to make it impossible to turn the truck round and drive back the way they've just come. That should at least start some alarm in their minds." I said. "Suppose there was a uniformed

Gendarme at the scene who could point out some rocks that were about to fall and that might crash into the truck." said Raymond. Jean Gibory understood something of what was being said and spoke in Auvergnat which Pierre translated "Jean reminded me that we did do something like that when the government inspectors were about to call on us and they turned round immediately

We had chosen a rock above the path up from Saint Jacques des Blats which was the way they always came. We loosened the rock so that all we had to do was to lever it off its perch at the critical moment." "So we must choose a stopping place where there are loose rocks high up on the sides of the gorge." I said. "There are loose rocks all along the gorge which is why the road is so often closed by rock falls." said Pierre, "The best place is right on the second bend where the gap in the cliff on the opposite side gives that magnificent view and if the rock was big enough it could sweep the truck over and down into the valley." "Then that is the best place so that we can arrange for the truck to go over the cliff after we have emptied it." I said. "Not immediately please," said Sebastian, "We must let our friends here empty the fuel tank and take the tyres off and any other spares they need." "My friend indeed," said Pierre putting his arm round Sebastian's shoulders

The next day was spent looking at the site. Councillor Dechaux was right, there were hikers on the footpaths and the footpaths were very close to where we were going stage the ambush. We worked out the timing of the various rock falls planned the route for the travois to take the contents of the truck to le Lioran. On the way back Raymond said "Can we get some local people to report feeling earth tremors at the time we close the road." "Hardly necessary," said Pierre, "There are tremors almost every month and we live with them." "But with all the rocks we are going to bring down it would have to be a strong tremor," argued Raymond. The consensus view was agreed and we would have some severe earth tremors reported

Stephan had hardly spoken a word all through the planning discussion. "You've been very quiet today," I said during the walk back to the Gibory farm. He put out a restraining hand and held me back a little until the others were out of earshot

"I was waiting to see if the resistance could come up with a workable plan without our input." "Have we done that?" I asked. "I think the plan is good and will work. You will need more people than are here today, I can reliably promise you sixteen trusted and competent men, possibly more if needed." "Thank you," I said. "There is just one loophole that Pietro pointed out to me, suppose the Germans are carrying a radio and can contact either Aurillac or Saint Flour when they are stopped and suppose they are ordered back to the truck despite the risk." "After dinner tonight we should discuss this matter," I said. "Good let's leave it at that for now." I said

We slowly started to catch up with the others. Then day was hot and the going was rough. When we reached the farm Pierre called for drinks. They had a very locally brewed type of beer and it certainly quenched the thirst. Pierre took me to one side. "I saw you deep in conversation with Stephan, are we going to get their support?" "I'm sure we are, he likes the plan, he has promised at least sixteen men but he thinks there is a gap in our plan and it needs to be talked through this evening." I replied. "But we must draw him more in to the planning later this evening"

Dinner was much more relaxed that evening. The fact that we had agreed a plan seemed to be known to all. The ladies lingered after the children had gone off to bed and there was more than a little fraternising. Clearly the ladies were enjoying the presence of the extra men. I doubt if they all slept alone that night!

We talked late into the night. Stephan promised enough of the maquis to close all the footpaths and if the hikers did not accept the advice about the danger that some force might be used. The hikers would not be able to report it until long after we were finished

We considered what the Germans might do if the rockfall was reported back to Saint Flour or to Aurillac by radio. It would be at least an hour before they could get a truck to the site from either direction. Stephan said his men would enjoy deterring any interference from either direction with some well aimed sniping. We agreed to this but stressed that there was to be no killing of Germans."Do you have any idea of how much food they normally send off to Germany each week?" asked Pierre. "The truck is never full," said Jean Chavent, "but they often send other goods as far as Aurillac." "What are the other goods?" asked Raymond. "We don't know and it probably varies." replied Jean. "We'll simply decide on the day what to do with them. If they are of any use to any of us we'll either bring them here on a temporary basis or they go over the cliff with the truck." All agreed

I said, "The truck usually leaves the barracks about two o o'clock which means it will be at the Col de Cere about forty-five minutes later so we need to time our first rock falls for about thirty minutes after they have left the barracks. That way they will not be able to cancel the trip. We can get a simple agreed message to you here within a few minutes of them leaving, no need for coding delays, just truck left at fourteen fifteen or when ever" "Good", said Pierre, "Then we will fire a big rocket so that everyone will know the job is on." As simple as that, I had been worried about how we could get the message to all the groups who were involved

"So all we have decided now is which Friday," said Raymond. "Before we do that," I said, "I want a solemn promise from all of you here that this date is kept secret until the morning of the day when you should start deploying your men. Can you all do that?" "I think I need about two weeks from now to organise my men," said Stephan. Raymond and Pierre went into a corner and talked for some minutes. "Yes we can do it in two weeks," said Raymond. Everyone was counting on their fingers. "I make that the ninth of July," I said. "Agreed," said Stephan

The following morning I rode back to le Bosquet with Pierre and Jean plus some other pack horses. They were taking advantage of the trip to replenish their fuel oil supplies. "I'll be back here on the seventh of July so that I am on site for any last minute problems." I said to Pierre as soon as we were clear of the farm. "I need to see for myself that the resistance and the maquis can work together and this job could reinforce the confidence we have each in the other"

Yvette and Jean-Francois were waiting for me. Jean- Francois proudly showed me the basket of eggs he had collected without breaking even one. Bernice said was as good as gold with the animals. Jean-Francois just wanted to know how many kittens he could take back this time! He was pacified with a baby rabbit. Stephan stayed on at le Bosquet. The same van took us to Pierrefort for the bus. As we parted from Stephan he said quietly "We are going to make this work"

We were back in Saint Flour in time for me to go to the evening service. A good chance to speak to all the people we would need for the usual Monday night after hours talk. The night was quite disturbed. Jean-Francois had taken his new pet to bed with him. The following morning we discovered the flea bites. Dad's first job Monday morning was to make a hutch for the new pet

I went through the plan in detail to a very quiet audience. At the end I added, "We have to provide as many people as we can or be dominated by the maquis. Our essential functions are the radio message to the communications centre to alert everybody to start their jobs. Before that those who are involved will have to have arrived at their places by noon at the latest so that the final arrangements can be completed. Victor and Sebastian will select the best marksmen from among the farmers to provide deterrent fire if the Germans do not move as we intend them to do, so. I will also be amongst that group.

Arrangements have been made for the quota goods to be delivered to Talizat and to await our collection for the market on the following Friday. This will have to be done discretely using the stallholders who will sell the goods as far as possible We have to decide who are the best stallholders for this task. With the exception of myself all of you should be well and truly seen in Saint Flour on the day." Then the questions started."How are you going to get the quota goods from the Col de Cere to Talizat?" asked Alexis. "And where are you going to hide the goods in Talizat?" asked Councillor Dechaux, "It's only a tiny hamlet." "I'm sorry but you don't need to 'know that at present." I said. "And only those concerned need to know." "When will we know the date of this hijack?" asked Mum. "You'll know the day before," I replied, "It's clearly a Friday so everybody involved will have to keep their Fridays clear until the day, it's not that far ahead." "How are you going to keep any hikers away from the scene of the hijack," asked Councillor Dechaux. "The maquis will take care of that and will use force if necessary stressing the extremely dangerous state of the road and paths." "What if the hikers report the matter to the Police or the Gendarmerie?" "By the time they can do that it will be too late and in the meantime the police and Gendarmerie will have had reports of very severe earth tremors as well as the roads being closed. We are counting on them to do nothing." I said. Alexis laughed,!"You obviously know just how to get the authorities to do nothing", Mum asked, "Who is going to choose the farmers to get the quota goods from Talizat?" As far as possible the farmers who were robbed of goods last week" I replied, "and we will take them to one side after next Friday's market and offer them the chance. They will have to agree to sell at bargain prices so they can sell out completely early in the day and agree to divide the proceeds with the farmers who have just been robbed" "So we know it's not next Friday." laughed Councillor Dechaux. "If they leave here at about two fifteen," said Alexis, "then the next bus to Aurillac will be only a few minutes behind them, and could be used to bring the Germans back to Saint Flour," "And if the Germans were late leaving, we could delay the bus by some minutes," said Manuel, "and the only other bus route to Aurillac via Pierrefort and Raulhac has to start from Saint Flour." said Dad. "I think that's a sound idea, I said, "The Germans will have to choose between staying at the Col de Cere or coming back to their base here. We will do our best to make them feel very uncomfortable at the Col de Cere"

It wasn't next Friday as Councillor Dechaux deduced but it was the one after

The matter of the bus arrangements was sent off to the Giborys next morning and we had their agreement later in the day. They also thought the Germans could be persuade to take the bus, "I'll even give them the money for the tickets in case they haven't got the change," said Pierre

We kept a close eye on the farms that were robbed on Wednesday and Thursday as usual and with the cooperation of the trusted police of Saint Flour told the farmers on Thursday what we hoped would happen to their produce. In most cases we were not believed. They were not given any details and were told not to mention the plan to anyone else

Christian de Boni was nominated to watch the barracks gates and report the departure of the truck. He had good reason to be there at the engineering works opposite the barracks. With a radio to transmit simple agreed 'en Claire' messages to advise the communication centre of the trucks departure and the time of departure As I was going to be missing from Saint Flour for most of the day of the hijack I arranged for many people to have seen me on the day here there and everywhere in the town. In fact I left very early in a police vehicle direct to the Col de Cere arriving just after six o'clock. I climbed the rock face at the point where we were going to block the trucks path. The maquis were there in considerable force and being detailed off to various tasks. Raymond had already prepared the holes for his rockfall charges and the Giborys had already loosened many clusters of rocks that could be levered to produce a rock slide large enough to frighten anyone on the road below without the sound of any explosion

It was a beautiful day in the height of the Auvergne summer. Just a trace of mist but, a clear sky. It was going to be hot out in the open when the sun was higher. Plenty of drinks were already there and food was promised for later. The resistance members began to arrive soon after eight and the positions for their deployment were soon allocated. Traffic on the road was almost absent until about seven-thirty and slowly built up but not to a level which would cause us a problem. The Giborys started a few rocks rolling soon after nine. "let's have a few reports of rock on the road nice and early but not enough to close the road." said Pierre. Some of the drivers stopped and rolled or pushed rocks to the side out of consideration for other vehicles. "The locals are quite used to having to clear this road at times." said Pierre. "We have sent a few rocks down over the past few days just to set the scene for a larger fall today."I expressed my thanks for his thoroughness

By eleven we were all hungry and thirsty. Food arrived and the maquis fed first before they went off to their positions to close the footpaths. Victor and Sebastian had checked all the weapons. I was somewhat alarmed to see all the maquis armed in this way but Stephan insisted they were ready for any eventuality. They had to start closing the paths early so as to get the hikers out of the area for our show later

Just before noon a Gendarmerie car came from the Aurillac direction and inspected the road clearing off lose rocks. They left after putting up warning notices of rocks on the road at each end of the pass. The reports of earth tremors had produced a result. The traffic slowed down noticeably as a result of the notices

Every now and again we sent down a few small stones to keep up the rumours of earth tremors. The maquis also rolled a few stones down on to the footpaths, just to give the hikers something to talk about as they passed each other. Stephan put one of his men on the highest point of the pass where all the hiker's routes were visible with instructions to signal every thirty minutes after noon with the number of hikers visible. By one-thirty they were all out of the area

Just after one o'clock two of the women from the farm arrived with five of the children. I was not expecting them. Pierre noticed my concern. "As soon as we have blocked the German truck the women and children will go down on to the road with one of the children 'injured in the rockfall' and ask the Germans for their first-aid box. They will make a big commotion about how dangerous it is here when we have earth tremors. Just to add a little pressure on the Germans," the children started to collect rabbit food from the roadside in the bags they had brought with them

By two o'clock we all moved to the positions prepared along the top of the slopes to send down the prepared loosened rocks as required. The tension was building up and so was the temperature. The rockets went up at ten past two. A few seconds later there was a minor explosion just audible and a dust cloud above the south-western bend of the pass. A green flag waved from the top of the cliff above the bend confirmed the road was closed. Two cars passed below us coming from the Aurillac direction having just missed the fall. Being lunch time there was little traffic. A 'policeman' or somebody looking very much like one appeared below us and was ready to stop any one entering the pass from the Saint Flour side. Raymond set off his second charge to partially block the road immediately below us. The women and children descended to the road ready to play their part. Again we were waiting

Only a few vehicles were turned back by the 'policeman'. Our estimate of the arrival time of the truck was two-fifty-five, with the bus due about thirty minutes later. Being Germans they were almost exactly on time. The 'policeman' had disappeared and so had the warning notice put up by the Gendarmes. Then screeching of brakes and tyres told everybody they had arrived. We peered over the edge. The lieutenant had got out of the truck and was surveying the rocks on the road, and kicking some of them to the side. He soon decided that they could not get through

At this moment Isabelle appeared running towards the truck. She was waving her arms and shouting that she needed first aid for her son who had been hit by a rock while collecting rabbit food. The lieutenant apparently understood enough French to understand. Jean Gibory now started to play his part. A well aimed rock bounded down the slope and hit the side of the truck. The other four Germans hastily got out looking at the damage. The lieutenant with the first aid box was being taken back along the road to where the children with Marrianne were clustered around the injured boy

A few more carefully loosened rocks came down all round the truck. "You ought to get your men out of here," shouted Marrianne at the Lieutenant, "We've had earth tremors all day and the whole of that ridge up there seems to be loose," she said, pointing at the top where we were hiding. A few more rocks emphasised her remarks. By now there were enough rocks on the road behind the truck to make it impossible to reverse. The lieutenant soon made up his mind, He shouted and waved to his four men to come back to him about a hundred metres behind the truck with the women and children. They were encouraged by a steady stream of rock and rubble further blocking the road. Several vehicles had arrived by now. The drivers left their cars and saw the state of the road. The 'policeman' appeared again and told everybody that the road was also blocked further on and it would take a day or so to clear it after the tremors had stopped. Two kindly car drivers offered to take the women and children back to le Lioran. They all went off taking the German first aid kit with them

Other drivers seeing the state of the road simply shrugged their shoulders and turned round one of them spoke enough German explain to the lieutenant that rock falls on this road occurred whenever there was an earth tremor but that he would be able to get through on the other road via Pierrefort and Raulhac. "But what about the truck," said the lieutenant, "That is for you to deal with," said the driver, but you will need more than the five of you to clear a way out"

A well timed bus arrived. Our well briefed driver got down from his cab. He walked some metres towards the blocked road. "No way through there today or tomorrow." he remarked. "Are you going back to Saint Flour? asked the Lieutenant. "Yes I've no alternative," said our bus driver. "Can you wait while we get our kit out of the truck?" "You want to ride with us do you? Have you got the money for the fare?" "We could always commandeer your bus," said the lieutenant

The conversation was interrupted by the arrival of Henri Gibory with several other farmers on horseback. All were armed. "Have you come to clear the road?" asked the lieutenant "We've come to look at how we might clear the road if the commune decide to pay us to do the job." said Henri speaking in Auvergnat. The bus driver translated. "Why are you armed?" asked the lieutenant?" "Because of looters." said Henri. Looking the lieutenant straight in the eye. "Your best plan is to get on the bus back to Saint Flour while you've got the chance, it may be summer but it gets very cold up here at night"

"I don't think we've got enough money for the fare," said the lieutenant. "I won't insist on you paying now said the bus driver, I'll ask Major Kempf for the fare tomorrow, but I've got to leave now because these other passengers will

254

have to take the later bus via the other road to Aurillac and I've only just got time meet that bus"

The lieutenant took the sensible decision. He ordered his men on to the bus. The other passengers moved away from them. "Aren't you going to charge them?" called out one passenger from the back of the bus. Our driver replied, "I'll get their fares from their commanding officer in the morning." Our driver told me the next day that it had been an uncomfortable journey for the Germans. Most of them knew enough French to understand the abuse being hurled at them, and he was sure that some who normally spoke Auvergnat deliberately used French so that they would be understood

Mum and Dad were relieved to see the Germans get off the bus at the Terminus without their arms or any other equipment. It was a clear sign that the day had gone well for us. Alexis had arranged for a police van to be available in le Lioran to bring me back to Saint Flour by a circuitous route and pull up at the back entrance of the Terminus where I slipped in un-noticed by anyone, slipped up to our room to change, and a few minutes later carried a case of beer bottles through in to the bar as though I had been there all the afternoon. I was tired but I dare not show it

The market was finished and most of the stallholders were crowded into the bar as usual. After some few minute Manuel put a hand on my shoulder as I was clearing a table looked straight in to my face with a raised quizzical eyebrow. "Not a shot was fired." I whispered. He smiled. I saw him later, talking with some of the farmers who were going to sell the quota goods next week. Smiles from them a discreet thumbs-up's confirmed he had passed the success news on It seemed an especially long time before the stallholders went home that Friday.

Immediately after the first hay harvest was sheep shearing time. Most of the farmers kept some sheep for wool and sheering had started during the past week. Wool quality and yields were being avidly discussed by those whose major single source of income was the wool harvest. There was general agreement that this year's price was going to be good

As the customers thinned out I was able to say a few discreet words to both Mum and Dad assuring them that no one had been hurt. "Keep the rest of the news until later," said Dad, "The Monday club will all be here after supper."Yvette took an early opportunity to hug and kiss me very thoroughly, "You're so brave," she said

Supper was late and I was ravenous after a day in the hills with only snack food between an early breakfast and supper. The Monday club had all assembled before my appetite was satisfied

As I joined them, congratulations were made that I had achieved the whole objective without a shot being fired and no one hurt. I demurred on the congratulations saying many people including all of you contributed to the success

I also praised the cooperation between the maquis and the resistance which had been exactly as planned and both sides must have gained confidence in the other as a result. "However I have to tell you there was one casualty," and went on to tell them about the injured rabbit food gatherer his mother and the lieutenant with his first aid box, and the other children. "Did anything occur that worried you?" asked Alexis. "Just one thing," I replied, "When the Germans and our bus driver were arguing about the payment of fares for the journey back to Saint Flour, Henri Gibory plus several farmers on horse back arrived all armed with rifles and looking quite menacing, arrived

The lieutenant in charge of the Germans asked them why they were all armed, and they said, to be prepared to deal with any looters, which could be interpreted in several ways. Fortunately the Germans decided to board the bus rather that stay and argue the point"

"Personally I thought the arrangements made by the Giborys were excellent especially the use of women and children to draw the Germans away from their vehicle. I suggest that any of you who meet up with of any of the resistance members who took part ask them about their impressions before we draw any final conclusions about the event." Everyone agreed. "However," said councillor Dechaux, "you achieved the objective without firing a shot. That is especially worthy of note. Now we must hope that the redistribution of the quota goods proceeds equally well"

"I'll make a point of meeting Valerie Hugot in a few days time and see what she knows about Major Kempf's conclusions of the event." "Good idea," said Alexis

During that night the Giborys, the maquis and the resistance finished the job. The quota goods all moved to a railway wagon at le Lioran, fuel tank on the truck emptied, wheels taken off, all German equipment confiscated for use by the resistance. The shell of the vehicle was left on the edge of the road for a tractor to push over the edge the next morning. I learnt all of this from Jean Chavent who stayed on to work through the evening and night

By Sunday midday euphoria was rife. Then the news of the invasion of Sicily was on the BBC French service and eclipsed our minor success completely. But once again Stephan's information and/or predictions were right

Chapter 35

Sicily Invaded

The landings in Sicily were derided by the Germans who announced that the Allies would soon be swept back into the Mediterranean. At the same time the jamming of the BBC French service was increased to unprecedented levels and reliable news was hard to come by. Cezaire would occasionally telephone from Clermont where he was able to filter out more of the jamming but such calls were likely to be tapped when both caller and recipient were likely to be arrested. We passed the Allies news by word of mouth to trusted listeners but many disputes arose over who was right

Cezaire arrived one day unannounced. He asked to be taken to our communication centre where he planned to install a filter to reduce the effect of the jamming. Our frequencies for communication with London were now also jammed. When I questioned Stephan about his radio links he finally admitted that he had radio links which were also jammed. We considered it essential that we could get the BBC news to counter the German version of the progress of the invasion of Italy. Calls to our centre from all of the surrounding groups reported the same jamming and need to counter the German version with the truth rather than fiction

So far our low strength local communications had not been jammed. We decided we could not risk losing those frequencies and dare not use them for passing the news. Cezaire had not recognised how remote our centre was and the risks of distributing the news via our telephone link to Bernice Rodot were too high.

The Monday club had another mid week meeting. "What we need is a good high point with no other high points too close," said Cezaire, "How high?" asked Alexis. Maps were produced. Cesaire and Alexis pored over them and finally homed in on a location just to the South of Saint Flour, just over a

257

thousand metres and nothing higher within a ten kilometre radius. "It will be only a receiver," said Cezaire, "and it will not be detectable by the Germans." "Who do we know near there, who we can trust," asked councillor Dechaux. Alexis thought for some minutes. "There's the Durand family at Vibresac," said Alexis, "they have no reason to love the Germans," Dad cut in on the conversation, "Yes that's where one of the Germans raped their daughter when they found her alone on the farm." "I remember that too," said councillor Leman, "It couldn't be proved because it was the word of the daughter against four Germans, but her parents are convinced she was raped"

Next morning Cezaire and I set off to Vibresac on bicycles. It was less than ten kilometres and we were there in half an hour. The Durand's farm was located on the southern side of the high point but only just below it. "Ideal," was Cezaire's only comment. Pierre and Mairie were shearing sheep when we arrived. It was another hot July day and they were sweating profusely

They were quite ready to take a break when I asked if we could talk to them in confidence on an important matter. "This is Cezaire from Clermont," I said in introduction, "He is an expert in radio matters and we have a proposition to put to you regarding receiving the BBC French news." Daughter Angelique joined us at this moment with a jug of their own cider, most welcome. Angelique taught at a Saint Flour school and normally travelled to and fro on the school bus. "I don't know whether you listen to the BBC news or not," I said. "We can't hear it any more because of the jamming said," said Pierre. "Cesaire here has something to suggest to you," I said

"Your location here should be good for receiving the BBC French service. Because of your location the jamming can be minimised with some equipment Cesaire can provide. What we would like you to do is to make a written precis of the war news each night and pass it to us in Saint Flour so we can spread the true news of the war to counter the German version. "There is no risk to you other than the usual one of listening to the BBC and you are so remote here that the only visits you get from the Germans are to steal your quota goods from you." Silence for some minutes. "I'm prepared to do it," said Angelique, "Can I Dad?" she said turning to her father

"Do you understand what might happen to you if you're caught?" asked Pierre. "But I won't be." "There is always some risk," said Cezaire, "but it's not a big risk." "I have all the equipment with me now, I could set up the aerials so you could try it and then make up your minds." "I'll agree to that," said Pierre. Cezaire and Pierre disappeared into the house. Mairie, Angelique and I talked about the war situation. The invasion of Sicily was regarded by this family as a clear sign that the eventual invasion of France would be in the South. "Corsica is effectively in the hands of the Maquis and Sicily will soon be taken by the Allies.

Then the Allies can ignore Italy and strike straight at France in the South. That's why the German army group H has been put into the South," said Angelique. "I think you're being too optimistic," I said, "I feel sure that the invasion will be in the North but there is now the possibility of an invasion in both Northern and Southern France, but not this summer"

If you take this task on you should be thinking in terms a year or more." "The schools are closed now for the summer vacation, so I won't be going into Saint Flour every day," said Angelique, "but after the vacation I could use the jelly duplicator at school to make thirty or forty copies of the news precis for the children to take home with them. In that way we could get the news to all of the outlying villages and hamlets by the evening after the news broadcast." "Now that is a very interesting idea," I said, "but my immediate reaction is a concern about what might happen to the children if the Germans got to know about how the news is being distributed"

Cezaire and Pierre returned. "Come and listen to the BBC," said Pierre. We went into the house and the family radio was tuned to the BBC and reception was remarkably good. "Now listen to it," he said, after he changed the aerial plug over to his old aerial. The sound of the BBC was barely discernable over the jamming. Pierre said, "I think we should do this. If we make sure the dogs are out when we are tuned to the BBC they will give us a warning of anybody approaching and we simply change the aerial plug and retune to a French station, takes about twenty seconds." Angelique clapped her hands in glee. "But you must understand, Angelique," I said, "talk to no one about outside this small group, everything must be on a need to know basis." Cezaire said, "The second aerial is very well hidden and cannot be seen from the outside of the house. If there is any problem with reception you should contact Henri and he can contact me." We thanked Pierre and Mairie for their cooperation and hospitality. Angelique walked with us to the road, "I've been waiting for a chance to do something against the Germans, and this is it." She said. "Don't let your desire for revenge make you careless," I cautioned her. "I can keep my mouth shut." And she did

We stopped at a small bar in Villedieu that still managed to serve some reasonable food at lunchtime. "That was a good morning's work," said Cezaire

"I'm worried about the involvement of the children," I said. "There is another way," said Cesaire, "Use your friendly bus drivers, simply let the children give the copies to them, the buses deliver parcels and packets to every village they pass through. They can equally well deliver the news"

A few trial duplications were made during the school summer vacation and were well received. Immediately after the vacation the service was six days a week

This duplication of the news precis from the BBC French service worked up to the liberation and was a significant morale booster as people recognised that the news was reliable. We heard later via Pascal that several similar schemes had been instituted where the right people could be found to do it

That evening talking to Mum and Dad about our success with the Durands I suddenly realised it was almost the fourteenth, Bastille Day. Manuel had arranged a special lunch as far as he could and expected to be sold out by one o'clock. I can't remember anybody leaving on holiday that year and the town was buzzing with excitement from sunrise onwards. Tricolours appeared as if by magic on many houses

The news of the invasion of Sicily was all over the town and morale had distinctly improved. Manuel reported from his ladies who pillow talked some of the German officers, that Berlin had described the attempts to land in Sicily had been repulsed with heavy losses to the Allied forces. Angelique had made a special effort and issued her first BBC French service news precis on the thirteenth and with the cooperation of the bus drivers had widely distributed copies during that day. She must have done a number of jelly printings. Copies were passed from hand-to-hand all over the town and not as discretely as they should have been. We started the rumour machine going again with the need to avoid the Germans getting a sight of these copies and to destroy them the day after they were issued

Much later in the war when the Germans started to withdraw eastwards as the Allied forces moved south into our region, the story was told of a German sergeant using a privy in one of the villages they were passing through. When he tore paper from the bunch hanging up in the privy, imagine his amazement at reading a handwritten transcript of the BBC news bulletin of a few days previously. After all paper was in short supply as well as everything else and nothing must be wasted

Until then I never knew what happened to yesterday's news

All the bars in the town were busy from mid-morning onwards. There was a determination of most people to 'have a good day out' The Maire called early on Major Kempf with a request to suspend the evening curfew for that night. The request was granted. "And what about the next day." asked Major Kempf. You needn't worry about the morning curfew next day, nobody will stir before about eleven, and they will be ready to be home by nine in the evening the Maire assured Major Kempf. The Maire announced the lifting of the evening curfew in the place de la Liberation outside the Terminus and again in the Place d'Armes

There was some derisory cheering and shouts of, "they couldn't arrest the whole town anyway"

Bastille Day was essentially French. Major Kempf had made a wise decision, we hardly saw a German all day and none at all in the evening

The Monday club met as usual in the terminus. Angelique had just issued her second news precis. And the success of this was apparent to all. It had been almost the only matter discussed in the bar that evening in spite of some Germans being present. It had to be assumed that they could not follow the mixture of Auvergnat and French in use. Dad had to assure many questioners that he had reason to believe that the news was genuine. Many questioners went on to say they were no longer able to hear the BBC due to the jamming and they did not believe anybody else could hear it, therefore the news precis must be fiction

We agreed that the news precis should be treated quite casually and if any of us were asked we would simply reply that we believed it to be genuine. A few days later Angelique's next precis reported that Palermo had fallen to the US seventh army thus cutting the main supply route to axis forces in Sicily. There was some taunting of the Germans in the bar that night. They were quite unaware that the invasion of Sicily was succeeding, and expressed their disbelief, but left the bar worried

Stephan had been in the bar that evening also. Before he left he took me to one side. "Do you know anything about these news reports?" he said pulling a copy of Angelique's latest precis out of his pocket. "I can assure you they are genuine but I must not tell you any details for obvious reasons." "I know they are genuine, I have my own sources as you must guess but we have jamming problems and many of my communications fail for that reason." "Where did you get this one?" I asked, "From a bus driver." he replied. "Then the best advice I can give you is to keep in contact with that driver and you might get further issues in that way. At present distribution is difficult but by the end of August there should be one issue almost every day." "By the way," I added, "I recognise that your prediction about the invasion of Sicily was correct, do you have any further news about the Allie's intentions?" "I do not expect any new plans until the liberation of Italy is established and successful. Can I pass on the information in your news precis to the rest of the maquis, they are especially interested in the Italian front now it is open." "Of course you may pass the news on to your associates, but I would prefer that you did not disclose how you get it," I replied

"When I am staying at the Rodot farm," said Stephan, "I could always telephone Pierre Gibory and get the news on that secure telephone line if you gave him instructions to tell me." "When you are staying at the Rodot farm Stephan, you can always telephone Pierre Gibory and tell him what is in the latest news precis that you have." I said smiling. He looked nonplussed "We have another reception point," I said to answer his unspoken question, "especially equipped to receive the BBC French service without the jamming. Please don't try to find out where it is, you might unwittingly disturb a carefully arranged operation." "I understand and I won't," he replied

We have a radio specialist, Cezaire," I said, "who has installed our reception equipment and who might be able to improve your reception at Mauriac for you, I could always ask him." "So you know about our radio at Mauriac," said Stephan looking surprised. "We've listened to your signals but obviously we can't decode them and it's none of our business anyway." "I dare not take advantage of your offer, I'm sorry to say, and I would beg you not to talk about the Mauriac operation to anyone else. In return I promise to tell you as soon as I have information about Allied future strategy." "I think it would be best if we stopped talking about this subject right now," I said, "before we find any more silly problems." "Agreed," said Stephan. "Now let me get you another drink"

The holidays that nobody could afford to take dragged on. The farmers were busy with the various harvests and their wives with the summer cheese making. People were getting used to the occasional news precis and the final cessation of the German/Italian resistance in Sicily was hardly considered noteworthy. Even the news of Mussolini's resignation and succession by Marshal Bagdolio was barely noted by the French, although Stephan got quite excited about it

On the third of September came the long awaited news of Allied landings on the Italian mainland accompanied by mass surrendering of Italian troops. Stephan got this news just before we did plus a hint of a total Italian surrender to the Allies

Evenings in the bar were devoted entirely to all the experts predicting what would happen next. Much to my surprise the idea that the Italians would soon declare war on Germany was used to taunt the few Germans who dared to use the bars in the evenings. Our late openings to serve the Germans exclusively were discontinued through lack of support. German morale had obviously fallen. Manuel reported from his pillow talk ladies confirmed this and the number of Germans seeking such comfort increased

As the summer drew to a close the prospect of renewed resistance activity increased. The Le Puy group, much less affected by farming kept the Germans on their toes with repeated successes against the electrical generators along the Rhone valley. Mathilde had cooperated with the Albi group following their successful cooperation over the David Turberville affair to provide their needs for a number of attacks on Albi's industry. Although our worthwhile potential targets in the Saint Flour region were few we had to do something to justify our existence without doing too much damage to the local economy. The Monday club talked a lot but decided little, they were too concerned about reduction of the fragile local economy. I asked Stephan what they had in mind. He wanted to have some more practice demolitions of roadside and railside cuttings so as to be able to more accurately assess the amount of explosive needed when the call came for total disruption prior to the invasion. Raymond strongly supported this because of the diverse rock structures involved

Between us we worked out a programme of disruptions to be made over the next two seasons avoiding the key points targeted for the pre-invasion total regional chaos scheme. Raymond was entrusted with the task of organising these and assessing the results. He promised to give us two days notice so we could all be seen to be in Saint Flour when the attacks took place

Following the successful attack on his own factory when over three hundred tons of tyres were destroyed Pascal's group had kept a very low profile. Their problem was transport. Making movements in the Clermont region was difficult. Roadside checks were frequent and the curfew prevented movements by non commercial vehicles after curfew. Despite all of these problems the Clermont group regularly exhausted their stocks and drew heavily on our reserves. Their most significant attack yielded a number of commercial vehicles. These vehicles were moved rapidly to a cooperative garage where the staff were ready to repaint them in different liveries and then immediately take them on the road to get them dirty before dawn

On the eighth of September General Eisenhower announced the surrender of Italy to the Allied forces, followed the next day by the landing of Allied forces at Salerno behind the front line at the moment of surrender. The Germans made it quite clear that they intended to carry on the war on Italian territory despite the surrender

Even though the schools were still on vacation Angelique made a special effort and issued precis on both of these days. People now expected to see these precis and their accuracy was recognised

There was widespread surprise at the surrender of the Italians and the taunting of the German troops in Saint Flour increased. There was no longer any belief in the statements of Major Kempf that the Germans were still containing the Allied landings. With access to the landing strips in Sicily the RAF and USAF were now dominating the airspace over mainland Italy

The Americans were pushing their way up the Western coast of Italy to link up with the bridgehead established at Salerno and the British were pushing up the Eastern coast of Italy against, now, only German resistance

Following the upsurge in resistance activity Clermont, Tulle, Brive and Mathilde were all clamouring for more supplies. We arranged two supply drops for our stock and a further one direct to Mathilde all during the first dark nights in October. All went smoothly

Raymond planned for Victor and Sebastian to work with Stephan and a mixed group of maquis and resistance to make trial road and rail blockages at suitable sites. He used the criteria that he would block roads used regularly by the Germans just to cause them some disruption plus a few rail blockages but not at any of the planned sites for the pre-invasion blockages. All of the blockages were carried out on the night of the second supply drop and just before it was due, we needed no other diversionary activity that night

All except one charge exploded Subsequent examination showed that both detonators had failed. A strange coincidence remarkably similar to the failure at the Montlucon tyre factory. "Are our detonators so unreliable that this could happen to some of the pre-invasion charges?" I had to ask this question of Raymond, Victor and Sebastian when we met to assess the results of our trial road blockage programme. Victor knew something of the manufacturing process for the detonators. He claimed that sometimes there would be a fault that continued un-noticed for some time which meant that some detonators did not work. "You can't test one hundred percent of them can you," he remarked. "Can you tell which boxes of detonators came with a particular supply drop?" asked Sebastian. "What is the shelf life of a detonator?" asked Raymond. "We can tell which detonator boxes came with each of the last two drops because they are still stored in separate locations," I said. "I've used detonators that I know were over six years old," said Victor, "and they did not seem to be any worse that when new"

"Then this is what we must do I said," We keep boxes of detonators from each of the last two drops and from our previous stocks on one side for the pre-invasion attacks and we increase the detonators to each charge to three, one from each of the three lots we have put aside for this operation. In that way we decrease the chance of failure as far as we can." All agreed. "Will you, Raymond, be responsible for this and I suggest we keep these detonators at the Rodot farm in one of their dry caves for the present." When we get nearer to the invasion we will place them in threes with each charge for each explosion site"

Italy's declaration of war against Germany and the axis powers passed almost un-noticed. "What difference can it make?" said Stephan when I asked him why he had not predicted it, "Germany is resisting all the way on the Italian mainland, playing for as much time as possible to bring their secret weapons into action to defend the fatherland." "What are these weapons?" asked Dad. "They wouldn't be a secret if we knew that," replied Stephan. "All I have been told is that long distance rockets are part of the technology they are urgently developing and a sort of bomb based on atomic fission." "How can you possibly split an atom," asked Alexis, "it's the smallest particle of matter that exists." "That's not exactly true," I said

"Work being done at one of the British universities has already split the atom and found that there are other particles called electrons neutrons and protons that make up the atom and probably some other particles as well. The various types of atoms that make up all the different elements of matter vary in the numbers of electrons neutrons and protons contained in different atoms. When you split and atom you start a chain reaction because each proton has enough energy to split another atom next to it, and so on. When you split a large atom with many protons the chain reactions it starts are so rapid the chain reaction becomes an explosion." "Well," said Stephan, "If you've already done it, why don't we have bombs based on atomic fission or is that what these new blockbuster bombs are?" "As far as I know blockbuster bombs are just big conventional bombs, believe me when an atomic fission bomb is exploded the whole world will know about it. We are talking about something resembling an earthquake."There was silence for some minutes while my bombshell was considered

"Is all of this really true?" asked Councillor Leman. "How big will these bombs be?" asked Dad, "Do we have aircraft big enough to carry them?" "When the British attacked that 'heavy water plant' in Norway," said Stephan, "that was supposed to be something to do with an atomic bomb but it was all hushed up." "What is heavy water?" asked councillor Leman

Everybody was looking to me for answers. "I know only a little about the questions you ask, an atomic bomb does not have to be very big so I feel sure our existing planes could carry it. The risk is in dropping it, the explosion could engulf the plane that dropped the bomb. Heavy water is water containing a heavy form of hydrogen called deuterium. All water contains a small amount of heavy water and there are processes by which you can increase the amount because the physical properties of deuterium are different from hydrogen. I do not know how heavy water could be involved in the production of an atomic bomb." I paused. "I feel sure this matter is under very tight security and all I know is what I remember from science lessons"

"The Americans have a highly secret operation going on in the Nevada desert." said Stephan, "and the Russians have highly secret operations in the Ural mountains. I've heard that both operations have the same objective," said Raymond. "An atomic explosion uses the fundamental forces that holds matter together to cause a chain reaction that might get out of hand, I think it's a highly dangerous idea and that is the sum total of my knowledge on the subject." I said

Chapter 36

Thieves

Our explosions on the night of the supply drop caused much disruption
Raymond, Victor and Sebastian had a good look at all the results and
noted the points of importance to the plans for the pre-invasion programme. The
railways reacted quite quickly and cleared the lines in two days. We were pleased
to see that no significant damage to the rails had occurred. The roads were
another matter due to the number of points that were blocked and the diggers to
clear the roads had to work progressively and there were not enough diggers.
However some of the smaller blockages were cleared by manpower alone just as
quickly as the diggers could do it, it was simply a case of enough men and shovels

We decided to discourage the shovel brigade by some precise sniping if
the Germans allocated troops to the clearance. Major Kempf was furious at the
disruption caused. Mass arrests of residents near the sites of the blockages for
questioning produced no hard information. The men who had laid the charges
had done it entirely at night and they were all locals anyway who could be
expected to be seen in the area

Two of the actual saboteurs were among those arrested but nobody had
seen anything of their actions and they were released with the others after the
questioning. Via Valerie Hugot we learned that Major Kempf now suspected that
the loss of his truck of quota goods was not simply bad luck but was a planned
operation using earth tremors as an excuse for the rock falls.   The SS were again
brought in. After they had heard the story of the happening as told by the troops
involved they set out to question the bus driver. Our driver performed
magnificently. He insisted that while he was standing there at the site that he saw
rocks falling on to the road and could feel the earth trembling. When SS Captain
Fieg suggested he was imagining the tremors he simply said, "Well I was there,
you weren't," which earned him a kick in the groin. He didn't know the names of

the women and children who were there but suggested they enquired at the doctors in Murat where the injured boy was taken. He didn't know the names of the farmers on horseback who arrived, but he had seen them all before and he knew they were locals. "Why didn't you wait for the troops to get their equipment out of the truck? was the next question. "I simply said that the bus passengers had to return to Saint Flour in order to catch the alternative bus to Aurillac and that to do that I had to leave almost at once

The road was difficult to walk on because of the fallen rocks and there were still rocks and debris falling without any warning. If you tried to dodge a falling rock you could fall over the already fallen rocks. Even today when I drove that route to Aurillac there were still newly fallen rocks on the road, the road has to be cleared every day." A notice posted throughout the town requiring persons travelling on the bus to report to SS Captain Fieg got no response

Next day SS Captain Fieg and his squad went to the Col de Cere. The Maire got a guarded message from Valerie Hugot asking if any of the bus passengers were going with the party. The Maire telephoned me asking the same question. I got an 'en Claire' message off at once to Raymond he should watch out for the dogs along the rocky cliffs while there were still so many loose stones falling. He reacted at once and Pierre and Henri Gibory arrived at the top of the Col de Cere soon after the SS arrived on the road

They watched as Fieg and one of his men climbed down to the rusting truck some fifty metres or so below the road. "They didn't find anything in or on the truck of course," said Pierre later, "We sent down a couple of rocks just to keep them on their toes." Later they came up to the top of the cliffs by one of the footpaths to inspect the top of the cliffs where the falling rocks originated and dislodged several pieces. Pierre and Henri were busy with two dogs inspecting the newly grown fleeces on their sheep. They ignored the shouted requests to come over to the Germans

Eventually the Germans came over to them. Of course Pierre and big Henri spoke only Auvergnat. Eventually Pierre tried some broken French and Fieg demanded to know if they knew anything about all the rock falls during July that closed the road and swept the German truck over the edge "The tremors we had then damaged our farmhouse as well," said Pierre, "The sheep were still heavy with wool then and we lost some of them too." "Where is your farm?" demanded Fieg. "Over there, about three kilometres," said Pierre pointing vaguely South."Were you here on the day when the road was closed?" Fieg asked, "No," said Pierre, "the sheep feel the tremors long before we do and cluster round the farm for safety." "I'm told there were some farmers about on that day," Fieg pursued his questions, "Could have been any of the farmers, there's six run their sheep up here. Big Henri spoke for the first time since Fieg's arrival, in Auvergnat, of course

Pierre translated, "My brother has just reminded me, about the truck, it wasn't swept over the edge; the morning after, all the tyres, wheels, fuel and contents had been stolen probably by the maquis, it was one of the diggers that pushed it over the edge, it was the only way they could move it." "Did you actually see it pushed over?" asked Fieg, Pierre and big Henri talked in Auvergnat. "Pierre said, my brother saw it pushed over he was called out to help clear the road, I didn't come here that day. Fieg wrote in a notebook from his pocket. He appeared pleased. "Now just one last thing." he said, "Could you and your brother write your names in my notebook, you've been very helpful," Pierre shook his head, "We can't write," he said. Fieg's smile vanished

Some days later we heard via Valerie Hugot, that Fieg's conclusions were, that the tremors were genuine, that it would have been very dangerous to attempt to get the contents out of the truck, that the maquis had seized the opportunity to rob the truck during the night. He considered it unlikely the local population were involved

Fieg questioned Kempf about the maquis, "How many of them are there?" We really have no idea, they are essentially itinerant workers, there is an extreme shortage of men to work the farms for reasons you know about, the maquis move from here to there wherever there is work to be done for little more than their keep. They are a mixture of French who are evading the draft, Italians who are evading Mussolini, and deserters from various armies including, I am told some Germans"

"What would happen if we mounted an operation against them?" "That was tried in the area round Vercours and in the Drome valley," said Kempf, "They simply disappear. We believe the increase in maquis in the Auvergne is a result of those operations." "I expect that there will now be more Italians crossing the mountains and joining the maquis, as Italy has declared war on Germany, said Fieg. "Some of my men have told me about that," confirmed Kempf, "Is it really true?" "Yes it is"

We were all surprised by the actions of Valerie Hugot, she may be sympathetic to the Germans but she is obviously very anti SS

We considered this combined operation a success and auguring well for future cooperation

Following our sabotage attacks on the roads Raymond, Vincent and Sebastian assessed the optimum charge for all Raymond's proposed sites for the pre-invasion attacks. This question emerged rapidly, Nobody had ever told us how long the roads and railways were to be closed. My original instruction had been to prepare plans to prevent any German troop movements South to North or vice versa, following the invasion landings. through the Auvergne and to cooperate with the groups in Brive and Tulle to deny use of the National twenty highway because this was the only road whose bridges could carry armoured vehicles. If Mathilde's group blew the bridge over the Tarn in Millau no armoured vehicles could enter the Auvergne road system. However the numerous small railway lines through the Auvergne were considered to be strong enough to transport armoured vehicles and in any event could transport infantry. Troop movements on the roads west of national twenty were to be prevented by air attacks as were troop movements through the Rhone/Saone valley

The Le Puy group were also to close the railways through their part of the Auvergne and now requested help from Victor and Sebastian to advise on their charge sizes. Francois Peillon suggested they should all meet at the previous rendezvous near Loudes He also confirmed that they had completed their collection of German unit types and numbers together with the senior officer's names, which reminded me that we had also been collecting similar data but so far Raymond, who I had not actually seen since the col de Cere attack, had not reported completion

We arranged to meet at the Mathis farm at la Cham where Simon and Patrice could also be present

Raymond confirmed he had over one hundred and eighty bits of information ready at the communication centre, "Much too dangerous to bring it here," he said. Simon and Patrice due to their close contact with the maquis had much more which they had kept hidden in a nearby cave for the same reason. There was of course some duplication inevitably but there were also some really good items especially on officers names and best of all a piece of paper, which Patrice had seen dropped by a German, with a reference to German Army Group G at present in the Auvergne, Raymond was nominated to contact Francois Peillon and get his collection and then to take a day or two to code it all prior to transmission to the UK

Victor and Sebastian returned next day from Loudes and we met at the Mounier farm near Saint Laurent de Veyres. I hadn't seen Fernand for several months but his welcome was as cordial as always. "Must be getting close to the great day soon I guess?" was his greeting. "Some months yet," I replied. "We are only just ordering our supplies "Don't leave it too long or the Italians will do it for you," he joked

We settled down to business "The Le Puy area is much simpler than ours," said Victor, "there's only one railway line to consider if we close it at Langogne, but if we also close the two branches north of Langogne at Le Puy and Alleyras that will give double cover." "The roads are a different matter, "said Sebastian. There is also only one North-South National route in the area until just to the south of Le Puy where it divides into two and just North of Le Puy into four"

"We took note of what you said about the Tarn bridge at Millau effectively closing the entry to our road system but your informant seems to have ignored the bridge over the Tarn just North of Florac, which the maps Francois Peillon has show, as the same strength as Millau. Then there is a second bridge over the Lot at Salsieges which is also strong enough for armoured vehicles. You need to close the road between Floreac and Salsieges very effectively; after Salsieges the road divides into a route into our area as well as the Le Puy area." Maps were produced obviously of a different vintage to those at Loudes. "And the next problem is that we would have to involve the Mende group to blow those bridges," I said. "Francois Peillon says the Mende group is almost non-existent," said Victor. "We will have to deal with these ourselves," I said, "and close the national 106 where it enters our area and insist Le Puy close the national eighty-eight where it enters their area, and do you think they will do that?" I asked Victor. "I am sure they will because they understand the problem." said Victor

"The Germans are no fools," I said, "they will sense the time of the invasion as it approaches but hopefully they will not know the location. When they sense the time is right I am sure they will have armed guards on key bridges tunnels and the like making it hazardous for us to attack those targets but they cannot guard every kilometre of road and railway. The bridge at Millau is a special case and we have to be prepared for some losses in blowing that one." "What happens if we can't blow it?" asked Fernand. "I know Mathilde has a contingency plan but it is not an easy problem and I'm not going to talk about it now. "When I returned to the Terminus I knew I had many hours of coding ahead of me Yvette had hardly seen me for the past few days and I needed to spend some time with her and Jean-Francois and I also needed some thinking time

Friday was the usual busy market day and I needed to be seen and talk to the stallholders Most of them were local farmers and frequently had snippets of information of value. Since our recovery of the quota goods at the col de Cere even those who did not support resistance were inclined to be more friendly and informative. The quota collections continued on a reduced scale and the routes and the times used to take them to Aurillac was being varied

Saturday was spent coding and I made good progress finishing the work early in the evening. Sunday was a family day. After mass we took advantage of a beautiful autumn day collecting chestnuts and just relaxing. Yvette knew better than to question me about what I was doing with the resistance. Sambo had finally accepted Jean-Francois' kitten even allowing it to share his patch on the bed

270

The baby rabbit was a baby no longer. He had out-grown his first hutch but Dad had kindly made another larger one and regularly supervised Jean-Francois' feeding and watering of the rabbit and the cleaning of the hutch

By the time the Monday club assembled in the evening I had confirmation from Raymond that he had passed all outstanding matters to London. Finally Councillor Dechaux had conceived a sabotage plan for Saint Flour. Valerie Hugot had alerted him that the whole of the Saint Flour wool crop was going to be seized by the Germans, when it had been degreased, as a reprisal for the loss of quota at the col de Cere. Major Kempf had at last made up his own mind that the theft by who ever it was, must be treated as sabotage against the German war effort. Therefore our next sabotage would be to raid the Lanoline/soap factory just as the cleaning of the wool was complete and ready to go to market. The quality of the local wool was high and it was the most profitable crop for many of the farmers. We could not attempt to sell the wool because the news of that would reach the Germans, but it could be stored in dry caves until the liberation and then sold. This idea got unanimous support, I thought it was brilliant

It was also bold. The lanoline factory was only four hundred metres from the German barracks. This would have to be covert sabotage. Alexis plus Councillors Leman and Dechaux were to plan the operation on an urgent basis as the wool would be ready in about two weeks time

I had only met Jean-Pierre Bourdet, owner of the soap and Lanoline factories, on one occasion. He never came in to the Terminus but preferred a more salubrious establishment in the upper town where most of the local business men met together

Many of his employees were regulars at the Terminus, always identifiable by the lingering smell of mutton fat. From spending a little time talking to them I found out they were well ahead with the wool cleaning programme. By chance I had some knowledge of the wool cleaning process from my chemistry studies in England before this assignment. I hurried up town to see Councillor Leman, to give him the bad news about timing, but with a suggestion as to how we might delay the final part of the process

"For the final cleansing of the wool they need vast quantities of soft water, they must have a water softener in their factory. If this were to break down it would stop the process completely." I told him hurriedly. "You can win some time if we can cause that to happen." "What would we have to do?" he asked. "I don't know which process they use but all water softeners have pumps and pumps are driven by electric motors. Sand in the feed water would cause the pumps to seize up, or an electricity failure would stop the pumps working." "It's a very old factory," he said, "I doubt if they have electric motors to drive their pumps, but the sand is a good one." "Then lets be kind to them," I said, "Sand in the pumps would probably mean new pumps, but if the pumps have diesel or oil fired motors to drive them, sugar in the fuel tank will cause them to stop quite quickly for no apparent reason, and it will take some time to diagnose what has caused the stoppage." "Leave it with me," he said, "I think I know just who to talk to"

Two days later one of our early morning customers brought the news, "The lanoline factory's just shut down." Next day the same customer said, "They say it's sabotage, the water softener pump is totally seized up." I felt sorry for 'Jean-Pierre Bourdet but this is war

The final plan for the removal of the wool was worked out but when Major Kempf heard about the breakdown he made contact with Jean-Pierre Bourdet firstly to find out when the wool would be ready and secondly to tell him that the wool was to be taken as quota goods by the Germans. Bourdet was furious "What price will you pay for the wool he demanded?" "Nothing," replied Kempf, "the wool is part of the quota goods France owes to Germany." "But I have to pay the farmers for their wool," protested Bourdet, "I suggest you do not pay them." said Kempf, and walked out of the office

By this time Councillors Dechaux and Leman had confidentially contacted a number of workers at the lanoline plant regarding the German's intention. Thus they knew about the Kempf/Bourdet confrontation within a few hours of the event. That same evening as Bourdet reached his home he found the two councillors waiting for him. They told him quite bluntly they intended to confiscate the wool and hide it until after the liberation when it could be sold thus providing Bourdet with his money and enabling him to pay the farmers."Isn't that better than letting the Germans just steal it?" said councillor Leman. Bourdet thought for some time. "Do you two represent the resistance?" "We have certain contacts," said Leman. "Who will actually have the wool?" "It's better that you don't know that," said Dechaux. "I assume you are going to hide it in some caves. If that is so then I will put extra packing on the bales to 'protect it en route Germany'

I've had to lay off the night shift because of the shortage of soft water and I will keep them laid off until you've have stolen the wool. I want you both to give me your word that you will do the best you can to keep the wool in the best possible conditions"

"We note your cooperative spirit and you will find this is the best way out of an otherwise impossible situation. You will doubtless get a vigorous protest from the farmers, but those who we can trust will be advised quietly of what has happened to the wool but not where it is." "Thank you for trusting me with your intentions, I rather look forward to seeing Major Kempf after this 'theft"

It wasn't going to be easy. The estimate of the volume was just less than the capacity of five railway vans. A railway siding line ran along the fence at the back of the lanoline factory but we had discarded the idea of using rail to move the wool because we did not know of a railway line that passed near to a suitable cave

Alexis went and talked to the superintendent at Talizat. He returned very pleased. "Our friend at Talizat can easily lose five wagons for us in a disused tunnel just to the north of his station. There is so little traffic on French railways today there are spare wagons everywhere. I've been to see the tunnel. One end is already closed by a landslip and if we think it advisable we could close the other end in the same way. Once we have decided on a date he will have five wagons ready for us and shunt them on to our siding just after dark and then collect them before morning. All we have to do is to load the wagons"

"Have you worked out how many bales that is?" asked councillor Leman. "Oh yes," said Alexis, "The railway staff know all about that, it is about nine hundred and fifty bales of fifty kilos each." "The bales will need to be moved about sixty metres from the warehouse to the rail siding and it will take two men to carry each of them," said Leman. Councillor Dechaux had been busy with a pencil and paper, "You are going to need about eighty men to do this job in a reasonable time in the dark and remember it will have to be done very quietly." "A bale of wool doesn't make much noise when it is dropped." I said to relax the tension

I liked the idea and I did not want it to fail. "I think all of us should make a point of looking at the area tomorrow independently of each other and think about where we are going to find eighty fit men without employing the Germans

As well as looking at the back of the lanoline factory Alexis went back to see our trusted superintendent at Talizat to seek advice on loading railway wagons. and jokingly said we didn't want to use Germans to load them. "Why ever not?. I've been thinking since your last visit. I'll get my opposite number in Saint Flour to go and see Major Kempf and say he's heard about this year's wool crop going to Germany and recommending using sealed railway wagons because the maquis cannot attack trains even if they knew the time when those wagons are moving. Then let the Germens load the wagons, seal them, label them for wherever they are going to in Germany. We would have to put them on a shunt to Clermont, which would happen to be after dark. As the shunt moved through Talizat it would stop, the labels and seals would be moved to another five wagons loaded to about the same weight. Your wool wagons go into the tunnel and the bogus wagons go to Germany. It would probably be about ten days before the Germans discovered they had been duped."

273

This was all related to us in the evening. The simplicity was attractive, the wagons would be loaded in daylight and they could make as much noise as they liked, and take as long as was necessary. "Then we'll get Serge Dartieu to meet Kempf as soon as he can," said Alexis

We heard all about it four days later from Jean-Pierre Bourdet Major Kempf had been to see him and told Bourdet that he had decided to send the wool to Germany by rail because it would be far safer that way. "That will ruin your plans to get the wool into caves and we will completely lose it" he complained

Having called at the Mairie to find either Dechaux or Leman, Alexis said, "we want you to cooperate with Major Kempf and do exactly what he asks about this and tell him he will have to use his own men to load the railway wagons because you have laid off your men and you won't bring them in specially to do this work when the Germans are stealing the wool. Those wool wagons will never leave France and you will have them back very soon after the liberation. If you don't know what happened to them you can't tell anyone"

Chapter 37

Pilgrims Again

At last London acknowledged our plans for the pre-invasion sabotage and requests for supplies. Arrangements for delivery will be finalised during a meeting in November. What meeting, where and with whom was not mentioned

The news leaked out that this year's wool crop was going to Germany as quota goods. From that moment on all surplus food disappeared from the farms and the Friday market ceased. Covert bartering and secret deliveries became the normal way of getting enough food

German patrols stopping cyclists and bus passengers looking for food being carried led to many ugly incidents. Regular quota collections ceased completely. That made it easier for people to make direct contact with farmers. News that a particular farmer would be at a cross roads between ten o'clock and noon meant that anybody passing could buy what he had available. Occasionally there was interference by a German patrol but they were usually out numbered and dared not interfere. Relations with the occupiers deteriorated fast. The day on which the wool was to be loaded became known. Angry farmers surrounded the lanoline factory and the Germans fired warning shots to keep them back. Jean-Pierre Bourdet made pleas to the farmers not to interfere and promised he would do his utmost to help financially but damaging the wool would only worsen the situation. Major Kempf was booed every time he appeared. When the job was complete and the wagons sealed an armed guard was changed every two hours until the shunt engine and train arrived. Major Kempf arrived some minutes later. All watched as the engine uncoupled it's existing wagons, collected the five wool-laden wagons, and re-coupled immediately behind the locomotive and then the rest of the wagons. He appeared satisfied as the train left on its way

Alexis was at Talizat with two of his trusted policemen to help speed up the detachment of the wool-laden wagons. It was an important part of the plan that the train did not take any longer than usual to get from Saint Flour to its next timed stop at Massiac. Saint Flour had recorded its departure time as ten minutes later than the actual departure and assumed that Kempf would not recall the exact time it left. At Talizat some very quick decoupling and re-coupling, and a rapid shunt of five wagons into the tunnel, ensured no time was lost. The shunting engine left with five bogus, re-labelled and sealed wagons immediately behind the locomotive plus the rest of its train as it had arrived at Saint Flour. The engineman and fireman made good time to Massiac and it was not necessary to ask for any time concession from the superintendent at that station

Alexis and his colleagues caused some small rock falls above the entrance to the tunnel on to the track to disguise the newly made marks on the rails, and the deception was complete. We never did find out what was found in those five wagons when they arrived in Germany

During July a supply drop planned for the Montlucon group had crash landed short of the drop zone near Saint Sauvier. The crew of five escaped only one of them with serious injuries. The Montlucon group had located them and hidden them until the injured navigator was fit to travel. Pascal had taken them over from the Montlucon group and now wanted to pass them through our zone to Mathilde for passing on to the 'railway to Spain.' The Germans had searched extensively for this group because no bodies had been found in the wreckage of the Halifax. Moving this group South was a problem. Five young men, one partly disabled, with only a smattering of French between them, spoken with an exaggerated English accent. Movement from Montlucon to Clermont made in the back of a goods lorry had gone well, and their hiding place in Clermont was secure

Pascal had discarded train travel with forged travel permits as unworkable. He had the possibility to move them to one of his safe houses in Issoire and was looking to us to take them over from there

The obvious next move was to the Le Puy group's safe house in Brioude which we had used before. Once again the police came to our aid. A number of sheep rustlers had been caught in and around Aurillac during October and had to be transferred to Clermont for trial next week. The prison van would be returning empty. A small diversion via Brioude would pass unnoticed. Le Puy agreed to the use of their safe house. I travelled to Issoire on the bus on the same morning as the rustlers went to trial, and waited for its return. My arrival at the Issoire safe house was expected. On making the agreed knocks on the door it was opened by a clean shaven obviously Englishman but dressed in second hand clothes typical of those on sale in French markets. "My name is Henri," I said, in

276

English, "you should be expecting me." "Oh yes, do come in," he said in quite loud English." I literally had to push him inside and close the door as rapidly as possible. "You may just pass as French in those clothes but only until you open your mouth." "You really should let Madame Guerin open the front door, you could ruin the whole operation if your voice were heard by an informer in the street." "Madame Guerin has gone to market to get food for lunch, she's a good cook, and your English is remarkable." I introduced myself to the other four. I could see why Pascal was so anxious to pass these five on. They simply could not be let out on their own

"After lunch," I said, "we have to wait until a van calls to collect us which will take us to another safe house in a different department where you will stay for a period until we have made arrangements to move you again. I don't want you to be alarmed at the van because it is a prison van. We are simply taking advantage of the van to move you into another area"

Lunch was quite a jolly affair. Madame Guerin lived up to her reputation, a truly tasty meal, and all the condemned men at a hearty lunch. They were all ready to talk about their experiences since the crash. "It's really better if you don't tell me all about this, if I don't know then I cannot tell anyone else." "Pascal has told me all I need to know about you." "This Pascal is quite a bigwig in Clermont isn't he?" One of them asked "So I understand," I said, "but we'd better talk about the weather." The conversation became very general. They were quite impressed with the way they had bee kept safe and accepted my assurance that they would not land up in a French prison that night

I made them prepare their small amounts of belongings ready to board the van as expeditiously as possible when it arrived. "Getting you into the van here is a risk we have to take we don't want more people than necessary to see you. When you arrive at your next safe house it will be dark. Please do not speak at all in the street either here or at the other end." The van was late arriving and already there were the first signs of dusk. I travelled in the back with the five. I jokingly pointed out to them that we were not handcuffing them into their seats and they could leave as soon as they wished. I'm sure none of them had ever been in a black Maria before

Pascal had made arrangements with Francois Peillon for a housekeeper to be at the Brioude safe house. There would be no dining out in the best restaurants of Brioude this time. The journey was uneventful, darkness fell, and the driver had some difficulty in finding the right street but he was able to pull up right outside the door of the safe house. Marie Christine, the housekeeper, opened the door and the five were into the house in less that a minute. I said a brief thank you to the drivers and the van was on it's way again

After dinner we tried to listen to the BBC French service but the jamming was completely effective. This was a new experience for them. "How do you get your real news of the war?" one asked. I explained we had one remote location where special aerials enabled the residents to always hear the news and they distributed as widely as possible

"You may be here for some days," I told them, "at present we don't know how we are going to move you on. You are quite safe here but you must not go out, and you are not to lean out of windows. The inner curtains are to be kept closed at all times and you may look out of the windows through these standing back from the window." "Are you staying here with us?" "Yes," I replied, "I'm your gaoler."And now what about some sleep, I started out this morning before seven o'clock." Alexis arrived with another man, dressed in casual clothes, immediately after breakfast. I introduced them to the five. The other man, Guillaume was unknown to me. "The first thing we need to do is to look at whatever papers you have been given by Pascal." said Alexis. Blank expressions all round, "We have never been given any papers." said the pilot. "So how were you moved from Saint Sauvier to Clermont?" Guillaume asked, "We were moved several times, always at night, and always in the back of some old truck or other, yesterday's ride in a black maria was luxury especially with out being cuffed." I was glad to see some sense of humour emerging." Please what is black maria?" asked Guillaume "A Black Maria is English slang for a prison van and without cuffs means no handcuffs."I interjected. "Ah now I understand," said Guillaume

Alexis and Guillaume moved into another room excusing themselves that they needed to discuss a problem. "Who are these guys anyway," said the navigator." Alexis is a member of the resistance, Guillaume, I have not met before but if Alexis has brought him he can be trusted." I said. "My nose says coppers," said the radio operator. "Oh you needn't worry about that," I said, "Many of members of the resistance are officials of some sort, and they are really quite useful"

"Are you some sort of official?" asked the pilot. "No I'm just a disabled person, unfit for military service." I replied. "How come you speak English so well?" asked the navigator, "Because I've been to school in London," I replied, and also in Belgium, Switzerland and Germany I added. "So you speak German as well?"questioned the pilot. "I can speak some German"

Alexis and Guillaume returned at that moment. "We are going to have to prepare some papers for you." said Guillaume. "That means we need photographs," he was holding a small Leica, "your present clothes will do, and we'll get you different outfits to travel in." he said."Where arc we going next," asked the radio operator, "South," replied Guillaume, "You'll have one more stopover before you go on the 'train to Spain' "First Class I hope," said the pilot.

278

"Wait and see." I said. Guillaume busied himself with the photography. Alexis tried his limited English on the crew. They appreciated this and the atmosphere relaxed again. Alexis tried to explain to them how difficult it was for us to find a way of moving them South and going South was the only way to the train

"Guillaume can produce papers for you that will pass any inspection, but if you are stopped and you cannot answer even the least bit of French, you may be arrested. We do not think the Germans are looking especially for you at present, but five young men together with fair complexions who should be in the services but can't speak French would be a target for even the dumbest Bosch"

Lunch relaxed the tension again. "Have you any thoughts?" I asked Alexis. "Not at the moment it's not an easy problem. You should come back with us tonight and we will brainstorm the problem this evening." It will take Guillaume four or five days to produce the documents," Guillaume nodded, "and longer still if there are any special ones required." he added

I asked Marie-Christine to join us. "Could you get some elementary French books and help these five get enough French to be able to answer simple questions within a week, do you think?" "I can try but it also depends on them." "We'll tell them that," I replied. "Think about it like this, if we were stopped and the official heard them speaking among themselves in French, a little rehearsed conversation with your sort of accent it would defuse the situation immediately "That would certainly help." said Guillaume

I explained to the five what they had to do and stressed the importance of it. They agreed but still seemed to me to be making very light of the matter. Guillaume drove us back to Saint Flour, leaving us at the back door of the Terminus to drive on to Aurillac. Alexis scurried into the house and changed his clothes upstairs and appeared a few minutes later in the bar. Yvette saw me return with Alexis via the back door and knew better that to ask me where I had been

The Monday club met urgently that same night. Alexis came early, "Exactly who is Guillaume" I asked. "Well I don't want to say too much but if the police need any forged papers he is the man we use, he can be trusted absolutely." "It's just about the most difficult situation imaginable," was Councillor Leman's summing up of our report. "But if we do nothing we have failed. We must find a plan." "Suppose we got them on to a bus packed with people we could trust, and simply drove that bus to Millau just ahead of a scheduled service the driver could then tell all the people at the stops there was an empty bus behind." suggested councillor Dechaux. "A lot of people would be aware of the unusual action and finding thirty or so people who could waste a day to help us might not be easy," I responded. "There are still some of the old twenty seater buses in the depot," said Dad, "but I don't know if they are in running order, and then you would only need thirteen other passengers." A germ of an idea was developing. I telephoned Christian de Boni at his home. "We could have one roadworthy within two days if you need it," was his answer. "So that could be part of our answer," said Alexis. "You've all forgotten what time of the year it is," interrupted councillor Leman, "listen for a few minutes. It is near to the patronal date for the Benedictine Monastery, you remember we used that last year. We could send only a small bus this year because nobody has the money available this year, tell Kempf about this and even get the Maire to advise him not to refuse permission for the journey because his theft of the wool harvest is why only twenty or so people can afford to go!" We all thought in silence for some minutes "It's got all the right elements," I reopened the talking. We talked more and refined the scheme slightly

Councillor Leman was to talk to the Maire tomorrow. Alexis was to confirm to Guillaume that only French identity papers would be needed for the five airmen, and that we would need about thirteen other sets of French identity papers for as yet unknown persons I was to telephone Christian de Boni immediately to get the bus ready, and to contact Stephan tomorrow re thirteen maquis to complete the busload, and to get them photographed for their identity papers. The Monday club would convene each evening until the operation was complete. After I had spoken again to Christian de Boni, I went to bed feeling quite comfortable about our plan. My first task the next morning was to find Stephan.   I left a number of messages to contact me urgently. Then I got advice that he was again at la Chaumette with no telephone. So on to a pushbike again; not so far this time but uphill most of the way. Managed to get him alone just before lunch. Told him I needed thirteen volunteers to be pilgrims for one long day, to go to a Monastery and back by bus

Within the next week, they would be provided with identity papers if they needed them and they would save the lives of five men. "Can you do it." he simply replied, "Yes, of course." "Then please have them all here the day after tomorrow with whatever identity papers they have. I will have a photographer here to take pictures for new papers as required and I will explain more to them then. Now I have to go, please give my regards to Madame Gourrier and apologise for my not greeting her this time." I went immediately to the Police station and found Alexis with Councillor Leman. Leman had just returned from an interview with the Maire. "I told him the lives of five English airmen were at stake, I and he had to get Kempf to agree to a twenty sweater bus pilgrimage to the Monastery "Did he agree to do it?" I asked. "He didn't like being told to do something, but I mentioned all the points we had to pressurise Kempf and he finally agreed. He called Kempf while I was there and is seeing him late this afternoon." "Well we have to assume he will be successful. Now I have some good news. Stephan has agreed to provide the lucky thirteen who will go on the pilgrimage to the Monastery and they will be at la Chaumette tomorrow lunch time can you Alexis get Guillaume there to take the photographs for identity where required?" Alexis picked up his phone and asked for an Aurillac number. When connected he said after the usual introductions, ""There is a most serious matter arising near Saint Flour which requires your immediate attention. Can you meet with myself and Henri at la Chaumette tomorrow at noon?"Guillaume obviously did not know the location of la Chaumette. Alexis gestured to me to show him on the wall map. I did so and pointed out the best approach road. Alexis relayed the detail to Guillaume and put the phone down. "That's done," he said

"So what have you told Stephan?" asked Leman. "Only that, if we can have thirteen volunteers to pose as pilgrims for a day trip to the Monastery we can save the lives of five men."   "I am impressed by his agreement on such a vague story," said Alexis. "We will have to tell him more tomorrow," I said. "and we must agree how much tonight." "When do you expect to hear from the Maire?" Alexis asked Leman, "He will call at my home early this evening before I leave for our meeting." "All matters are adjourned until later," said Alexis, "and now I must deal with some mundane police business" We left. Outside, councillor Leman put his hand on my shoulder and said "You've done well to get this arranged so quickly, it only needs Kempf's consent" We shook hands and parted

I arrived at the Terminus too excited to realise that I had eaten nothing for lunch. Yvette recognised my satisfaction and actually asked what it was about. "I will be going on a pilgrimage to the same Monastery as last year for a day or so in the next few days." I said breaking all the rules. "Can we come?" she responded immediately, "We enjoyed it so much last year." "Now listen," I said, "I've already broken all the rules by telling you where I am going, so I'll have to tell you more. On the coach will be some volunteers from the maquis with five English airmen who are escaping to Spain, it would not be safe for you and Jean-Francois to be on that coach." She was clearly disappointed "I had no idea you were so deeply involved." she said. I was impatient for the evening. Alexis arrived early, so did councillor Dechaux and we brought him up-to-date with our progress as well as Mum, Dad and Manuel. Councillor Leman arrived jubilant so we knew the news was good. In fact it was sensational. Not only had the Maire got a permit for the trip, he had the promise of a pass document, just in case, any spot checks were being mounted in the adjacent departments. Alexis counselled caution, "Its all been much too easy," he said, "Just suppose Kempf knows something about these airmen being moved South, he might spring surprise spot checks upon us on the day. After all he knows the date, he can easily find out the number of the vehicle, he can easily get the departure time, and he knows the route." "But there are still some things he does not know," I interjected. "He does not know we are going to pick up the five from Brioude and we could go from Brioude via Mende and not use national nine at all on the outward journey. The return journey doesn't matter"

We weighed the pros and cons. Councillor Dechaux found an excuse to telephone Valerie Hugot and talk to her about today's meeting. She already had instructions to draw up the pass ready for signature and commented that Kempf seemed quite happy about allowing the pilgrimage and was sorry that so few were able to go; after all last year I understand five coaches went from this area

That just tipped the balance and we decided it was a go situation. The date was fixed for four days ahead. And councillor Leman would confirm this date to the Maire tomorrow Before I went to bed that night a lengthy urgent message had to be coded for Mathilde, but I slept well and rose early to get off to la Chaumette

Stephan and some of the maquis were already there. Madame Gourrier said, "I hope I'm not expected to provide lunch for this lot." "No," I said but coffee when we've finished would be welcome," I handed the packet I had brought with me. "You think of everything." she said and after sniffing it, "it's real!"

Madame Gourrier had cleared her lounge for us to use. Stephan drew me to one side, "How far have you got with the arrangements?" "Virtually complete." I replied.

"Then you'll be able to tell us the whole plan?" "yes" I replied. The remaining maquis arrived. After securing their promises over secrecy I told them of plan to move the five airmen as part of a coach load of pilgrims to the next department ready to go on 'the train to Spain'. "Are they the five who crashed last July near Saint Sauvier?" asked one of the maquis I knew as Alex. "Yes." I replied,

"The injured navigator is now fit to travel." "If this Major Kempf issues a pass for the pilgrim coach he can still stop it and check the pilgrims, some of us have not got identity papers," asked another maquis. "Those of you without papers will have them before the trip, Major Kempf only thinks he knows the route we will take. We have a good reason to take an alternative but he does not know that." Stephan interjected, "I can assure you all that Henri is a careful planner and he will not be putting you into any danger of arrest." Alexis and Guillaume arrived at that moment in uniform. There was considerable unrest. "Most of you will have seen Alexis Lescaut before, he and Guillaume his companion are both exposing themselves to you as active resistance members, don't you think you can trust them?"

Alexis started his checks on those maquis that had some documentation. only two passed his eagle eyes. Guillaume got busy with his camera. How good will the documents be asked a maquis. Alexis showed them the documents for the five airmen, "I can promise you these will pass any inspection." Stephan said, "They look exactly like the real thing." "They are the real thing," said Alexis, "and they will be yours to keep after the trip"

After Guillaume and Alexis had left Stephan asked "When is the day, and where do we catch the bus? "Four days from now that is next Tuesday. Will you meet Alexis at the Barrat farm on Sunday at four o'clock in the afternoon, He will have the new identity papers for those who needed them and then he will tell you where you may catch the bus It will be somewhere on the Northern outskirts of Saint Flour and very early.   You'd better have a party on Monday night so you are all together." "I will arrange that." said Stephan. "When you get on the bus you must occupy all of the window seats so that any observer will get the impression that the bus is full. I will not be on the bus at that time I will join you when you pick up the five airmen." "Where will that be?" he asked. "I'm sorry Stephan, I said "but you don't need to know that

We were not able to meet until quite late on Friday evening. Councillor Leman arrived early, he winked and smiled as he entered the bar. So I knew he had the passes. Alexis and councillor Dechaux were late. It was after ten before we were all ready. But it was a short meeting. All the arrangements were made except for the departure time. "It must be very early," I said, "because the bus needs to have left the town before the Germans change guard at six. I suggest five thirty, a short drive out to pick up the maquis, and back through the town so that the guards see the bus full as it departs." "Sound idea." said Dechaux, and the point was agreed. "Do you have any confirmation from Mathilde yet?" Asked Alexis. "Not yet," I replied, "but I should hear by the morning, the only thing I might allow her to change would be the date, and that wouldn't matter because we are not committed to a date with Kempf." Mum and Dad had used the Friday market to get another set of clothes for each of the five, all now packed for me to take to them

Mathilde's reply arrived during the night and was passed through to me early. All was agreed. She would meet us at the Monastery and would have her own transport to take the five to her safe house after the religious services. The rest of her message caused me some anxiety. Two men have recently contacted her group claiming to have escaped from Corsica to join the maquis in the Auvergne. She had no proof that this was true. Could we collect them at the same time and pass them on to Stephan?

What a problem at the last minute. If they were genuine no problem; but if they were provocateurs?! Possible recognition of five English airmen on the last leg of the escape route; recognition of Stephan as a maquis leader; recognition of my involvement; and recognition of thirteen other maquis. I went to see Alexis at the police station. Luckily I found him alone trying to catch up with paperwork. He recognised the problems, but he had the answer. "Stephan will be there and he will decide. If they are bona fide then they come here and Stephan has two new members. If not then they are still taken on to the bus which now has spare seats, it will just be dark as they leave the Monastery, they shoot the two and divert via a bridge over the Tarn and drop them in." I was somewhat aghast at the idea. "This trip is supposed to be a pilgrimage," I said. "And how do you deal with traitors in wartime?" "Leave it with me I'll pass this on to Stephan tomorrow"

Chapter 38

By Train to Spain

Alexis had arranged for an unmarked police van to take me back to Brioude on Sunday. Marie-Christine answered to the coded knock. She was relieved to see me. "Its very hard work," she said, "They've got the words all right but it's the phrasing and intonation." It was quite a saucy bit of drama they'd put together. Marie-Christine blushed when I asked her, "Did you write this?" "In the plot two of the five were brothers and a third had twin sisters each of whom was being wooed by the one of the two brothers." That was the plot put up by Marie-Christine, but then the imagination of the five got the better of them and they had 'improved' it. I'm sure it would have been a riotous hit in any Parisian theatre

When they had finished rehearsing it for me and I had recovered from the laughter, I said, "it's a great pity you'll never have the chance to use it in France, but I'm sure the mess will appreciate it when you get home"

"So what's going to happen?" asked the pilot. "You are going to be pilgrims visiting one of our Monastery's for their annual patronal festival of Saint Gerard. After the various church services you will be passed over to Mathilde who is my equivalent in the next area, and who will take you to a local safe house. She expects to have you on the train to Spain within two or three days

The pilgrim coach will pick you up here before dawn on Tuesday. You will be travelling with a party of men who are all members of the maquis resistance. The local German commander has issued a special pass for the bus journey so even if you are stopped there should not be any examination of your papers. Now these are your papers," I said putting the five sets on to the table. "They look very official," said the navigator. "They are the real thing," I said, "not forgeries, you can take them home with you as souvenirs and France will lose five of it's citizens

"Now just a word or two about Mathilde," I continued, "Don't be put off by her appearance, she is exceptionally effective in everything she does and she is a very big girl." "O la, said the radio operator. "And before you get any ideas," I said, "She is my aunt." "There you are," said the pilot. "I told you he was French! You've lost your bets." I couldn't save his money for him

Dinner that evening was a cheery affair. The five seemed confident that they were on their way home at last. I explained to them that when they got to the Monastery they should stay close to the maquis group and follow them at all times. I will introduce you to Mathilde in the names you have on your identity papers and she will call you by those names. She speaks only a little English so be patient with her"

The five took over from Marie-Christine at the end of the meal and dealt with the washing up. "They are such charming young men," she said, "but so naïve and inexperienced." "Can you fly a four-engined bomber?" I said, "That's what they are trained to do." "Will they get to England do you think?" "The last group we passed through succeeded," I said, "But that was before the Germans occupied Vichy France"

Monday was spent sorting out their new clothes and clearing the signs of their occupation out of the safe house. I insisted they slept early as we had to be ready to leave by five thirty and no delay could be tolerated. The bus arrived only a few minutes late and parked at the end of the road

The five with their little packets of belongings moved smartly and quietly to the bus which left immediately. I doubt if anyone saw our departure. Christian de Boni had decided to drive himself. On the bus I introduced them to Stephan and they were pleased to find he spoke English and several of the maquis also spoke a little. After the first acquaintances had developed into friendly relations, the five insisted on performing their sketch

As previously it was a riotous success. Stephan even went so far as to say that if they had needed to use it the listeners would be so distracted by the plot that they would have got away with their atrocious accents. Had the sketch taken any longer there was a fair chance we could all have finished off the road. We made one stop on the way and arrived at the Monastery just in time for the High Mass at eleven

I did not see Mathilde until after the Mass. I left our group with Stephan and Christian in charge and went over to her. I gave her a quick briefing on the problems of the five, "They must not be allowed out, their French is minimal and we have not been able to induce any French idiom or accent into their speech." "Don't worry." she said, "they go 'on the train' tonight straight from here." "What about the two you have for me, I want Stephan to meet them alone first." Send him over to me and I'll introduce him. I pointed Mathilde out to Stephan"

Oh yes I remember her now, he said and walked over to join her. They disappeared into the crowd. We waited. Within ten minutes Mathilde and Stephan returned all smiles and in animated conversation. Stephan came over to me. "There is no problem with those two, I know one of them from my time in Corsica and he has vouched for the other, I'm glad to have them with me. They are first class fighters" After a small lunch we all went on the tour of the monastery, We kept the five well inside our group to avoid the chance of impromptu conversations from strangers. After meditation at four o'clock we all went to the bus. Within the bus I introduced Mathilde to the five and told them they would be 'on the train' tonight. I walked over with them to Mathilde's van and saw them safely on their way

There was much jollity among the maquis and their two new members on the return journey. After an hour or more I went off to sleep. We stopped twice, shortly before Saint Flour to let groups of Maquis get out to go to their farms. I sat up with Christian for the last few kilometres. "You were so fast asleep you never woke at the gendarmerie road check, the pass Kempf gave us worked perfectly they never even counted the number on the bus." It was just after curfew time when we drove into Saint Flour but nobody stopped us. Christian dropped me at the Terminus before driving to the bus depot

Yvette was relieved to see me back safely. I was tired and we went straight to bed. "Did everything go all right?" she asked. "Everything was perfect, and Mathilde was going to put them 'on the train' tonight" "That means they will be in Spain in the morning!" said Yvette, astonished. "I don't actually know what this 'train to Spain' means," I replied, "But I don't think it means a railway train." It was not until after the war that I read about the 'train to Spain' It certainly wasn't first class as the pilot had hoped

Wednesday morning I went straight up to councillor Leman's home. He was pleased to hear of the success of the pilgrimage. I asked him to be sure to remind the Maire to express the thanks of the pilgrims to Major Kempf. Alexis arrived as coffee was being served, "I found out you were here when I spoke to Yvette," he said, "and I understand every thing went well." "Yes," I replied, and there are now two more maquis in the hills, Stephan actually knew one of them, and he is very pleased to have them especially as they have experience of fighting the Germans in Corsica." "Do you think that's where Stephan comes from?" asked Alexis. "I doubt it," I replied, "Their accents are completely different but he may have been there to support them in a similar manner as he does here"

The maquis had increased in number by more than the two from Corsica. During the pilgrimage I had spent some time in general conversation with Stephan and told me that more than ten had arrived during the summer and he hadn't yet met all of them. He was becoming concerned that there may soon not be enough work on the farms to use them. I had also noticed that most of the maquis carried a recent copy of Angelique's news precis. The maquis had soon found out where the news was originating and reached an understanding with Angelique that they could pick up the latest copy whenever they passed Vibresac

Their assistance in distribution to remote areas plus the expanding help from the bus drivers meant this news was now reaching most of the people in our area and even further afield when the recipients talked to others at some of the smaller weekly markets in the villages39I felt I had to alert Stephan to the fact that whereas a bus driver if caught with a precis could always say he picked it up off the floor of the bus, a maquis had no such excuse, and may be in danger of his life. "If they saw a German approaching they could always screw it up into a ball and swallow it, if they didn't then it's their fault if they are caught, but thanks for the consideration," Stephan replied.

Chapter 39

England Again

Now I had to find time to go to England as commanded. It wasn't going to be easy to explain my absence again. Mum had mentioned that several of the regulars had commented that I was not around as much as I used to be, and Yvette was asking more and more questions about my absences. If I used the usual excuse about a visit to Mathilde, she would want to come as well

The first of our autumn supply drops was due in a few days time but it could be left to Raymond to manage that. A major part of it was 'farmers benefits' again for the winter and in dealing with that he could ingratiate himself with the farmers as he was soon going to need their understanding when we had to block the roads

The only reason I could think of that would satisfy Yvette was that I had to liaise with the neighbouring groups over who does what and where to close the roads and railways in the pre-invasion sabotage I explained to Yvette that there was now an Englishman in the area who had drawn up the plans for this area but had to liaise with the neighbouring groups and I was going along to help him "Oh you mean Raymond," she replied, "I don't mind you going with him he'll keep you out of any danger." I made a mental note to tell Raymond his cover was blown as far as Yvette was concerned. Thus I was able to say to London that I could spare them only three days in the next month but could probably meet their specific date request

Their reply by return was terse. Pick up Monday next, return Thursday night. Advise Lysander strips to use for outward and return flights. After consultation with Raymond we replied, Out Barrat Farm, In Mathis farm. Advise time Barrat farm and recognition codes for both. We can be terse as well

My pick up on Monday night went off without a hitch. It was the usual pilot I now knew as Jim. The profile looked different as the plane came in to land. It was a brilliant moonlit night and flying conditions were good I sat up in cockpit section as usual. "It won't be such a long flight tonight, we can now use Tangmere and then you'll go by car from there. The Luftwaffe leave us alone nowadays, "he told me

Our flight path was almost due nor-nor- west and we made good progress. I saw the Loire when we crossed it near Orleans and recognised Le Havre when we crossed the coast. There was some searchlight activity to the west "There was a raid going on over there as I came out," Jim told me

"Will we be taking off from Tangmere on Thursday night?" I asked. "You're going back again?" he asked. "Yes" I said, "I shall be there until after the invasion." "I don't have any instructions yet," he said, "but I don't have any other jobs on that night"

My instinct started telling me something might be going on. Terse messages and no return booking. There was the usual arrival procedure with a car to a London Hotel. Instructions waiting said 'Car at noon to take you to lunch with CO'. I didn't normally see the CO until everybody else had pulled me to pieces

The CO' plus a Major I did not know, both quite affable and I soon came to conclusion that the Major was some sort of psychologist. After the meal itself many questions to be answered and I eventually realised that this was an in depth review of the past year

"On the face of it you haven't achieved very much in the year and yet all the reports from adjacent areas speak very highly of you." said the Major, speaking directly to me, for the first time since he was introduced. "There is little scope for conventional resistance in the high country of the Auvergne. I thought this meeting was to finalise the plans for the pre-invasion disruption of the road and rail network in my region in conjunction with the surrounding regions along the lines of the plans submitted to you last September"

Both faces went blank. "Did you get an acknowledgement of that information?" the CO asked. "I am sure we did." I replied. I explained about our communication centre and the new message process we were using. They agreed that they had noticed an improvement in communications. "I coded all the information personally in view of its extreme importance. It had to be transmitted to you over a period of two days for the usual reasons, because of its length and complexity and at the end we asked for your guidance on the duration of the disruption we had to achieve." "Exactly when was this." snapped the CO. "I cannot remember the exact date, it was about the middle of the month, you should be able to isolate it because we used every minute of our air time for two whole days almost completely." "Peter," said the CO, talking to the Major "Get on to communications and find out why we have never seen these messages"

"If I had known there was a problem I could have brought the master copies with me." I said. It was more than half an hour before Peter returned. The CO looked at him quizzically, "Yes, on the sixteenth and seventeenth of September all the air time was taken up with a large amount of coded numerical data which the decoders put on one side because they could not understand it, and its still on one side"

"How much of it can you remember?" said the CO turning to me. There was a preamble saying that we were sending you details of the sites for blocking of roads and railways for the whole of the Auvergne followed by the map numbers involved followed by the map references for each site of disruption; each site with a note of which group would attack it and any special notes about that site. In all there were ninety-seven sites involved, I'm sorry but there is no way I could remember all of the map references"

"Peter," Get on to communications again and tell them those decoded messages are to be in my office within two hours. I held up my hand to stop Peter moving, "Have you got the standard Michelin road maps available at your office, because they are the maps we used." "Check on that as well" added the CO

"Well now we have to wait for a while." said the CO. He was surprised that ninety-seven sites were required. I explained that was why we thought the only way to convey the nature of the problem was by map work. "Although there are only four railway lines entering our area from the South there are so many small link lines that blocking the main lines only could be circumvented by use of these smaller lines. All of the rail lines are built to carry heavy goods wagons even where they are only single lines and as far as we can tell all the bridges are in good sound condition. The roads are another matter. There is only one road bridge over the river Tarn that can carry heavy vehicles, and that will have to be blown by my Aunt's group based in Millau. I am sure it will be heavily guarded and we will undoubtedly take casualties in doing that one. All major and minor roads can be blocked by landslips at convenient points, and should they be cleared by the Germans they can be blocked again else where, they cannot guard every kilometre of the road network. In general road bridges will only carry up to about twenty tonnes and the condition of some is questionable." The CO had listened intently to my explanation

"Let's go to my office now and wait for the decoded messages." We left the restaurant and walked the half mile to French Section headquarters. As we arrived he instructed an assistant to clear the conference room table and get all the Michelin maps of France out of the files. Another assistant was told to contact some others to join us and to cancel any engagements they had for that evening. "You're in for a late one too, even more so than us, the SGO will send for you some time tonight. So don't you make any plans either, By the way you are not to contact your family while you're here this time"

"You made some reference to your Aunt when talking about your plans, what did you mean?" "I assumed you would know that I replaced a young Frenchman who was killed in an air-raid but no body was ever found and I am in fact based with his parents, if I were really him, then Mathilde, who runs the group in the South of The Auvergne, would be my Aunt." "I must read your file again." he said. I retired to the conference room. One or two familiar faces came in to shake my hand and chat for a bit. Then the door opened with a rush and a guard from the front entrance came in with a case

"This has just arrived by motor cycle for the CO," he said. I didn't wait for the CO. I asked his secretary for a supply of coloured stickers, laid out the appropriate maps opened the decoded messages and began to plot the sites of each blockage on the maps. I completed the plots and sent for some coffee. It was going to be a late night. The CO returned. I had found out from his secretary that he was new to the French section, only appointed four months ago. He brought with him four familiar faces. Handshakes all round and enquiries after my health and welfare. You look very well indeed was the general view. "The mesdemoiselles must agree with you?" "Yes they do"

I replied. That'll give them something to think about was my thought. I talked them through the plans. There were of course a number of questions most of them were answered by the maps. I repeatedly asked how long we would need to maintain the blocks, but no indication. "You must have made some assumptions when drawing up these plans?" asked the CO. "I was originally told that the Rhone-Saone valley would be attacked from the air and the same information was given to the Le Puy group." "Alain Brenot and Regis Armengaud did not appear to have been told anything. So I had to assume that the original Western boundary was somewhat vaguer, although it was also suitable for air attack." "Yes that is still the plan." one of the aides confirmed

"The actual numbers of German troops in the central Auvergne region is not high. In Saint Flour just three hundred. In Aurillac, around four hundred plus a small contingent of SS infantry whose numbers vary; plus about another hundred in the remainder of my area." "You need not explain the numbers any further we've seen your reports and they are quite comprehensive." said the CO

"What we really want to know is what you have assumed about the troop concentrations to the North and South of your area." "There are larger numbers to the North, mainly centred around the industrial areas of Clermont and Montlucon. Pascal has the good up-to-date figures for that area and I think you should ask him. To the South it is much more difficult. Mathilde reports what she knows but the information is neither reliable nor complete, nor stable because the area is used as an R and R location for troops from the German Eastern front, and keeping up with the movements is not straightforward. Our thoughts were based more on the types of troops that we would have to deal with"

We considered Panzer divisions as one group who would need strong bridges for their armour. If we do not blow the bridge here in Millau," I said pointing at the map, "and they enter the high Auvergne it is very unlikely they will be able to cross the region." "Do you think they know that?" asked another aide. "I really don't know, some inspection of bridges has been reported but the information is not complete. We cannot watch all the bridges and it all depends who sees them and recognises that what they see is of importance"

"We also considered infantry with motorised transport. They could use either road or rail to cross the region which is why we have paid so much attention to blocking the railways. They are also the main reason for my question about the duration of the blockages. Lots of men with shovels could clear the blockages. We would of course take advantage of any opportunity for sniping. Simon and Patrice report that the sniping accuracy of the hillmen and the maquis is extremely high, but we do not have enough men to cover the whole area or to shadow columns of infantry on the move However we can always provide another blockage ten kilometres further on"

"The remaining matter is the Western side of our region which is in the hands of the groups at Brive and Tulle," I said again pointing at the maps. "The key to this area after the excellent railways is the French National twenty highway," the maps again used, "I am reliably told that all the bridges on this road are strong enough to carry armoured vehicles and being a continuous through route it must feature highly in any German planning of troop movements. It can however be attacked from the air as can the railways." Alain Brenot and Regis Armengaud have plans to ambush any columns on the roads as the bridges are already heavily guarded and they cannot guarantee to blow them

There are a number of points suitable for ambushes. They also intend to attack the loading facilities for railway transport of armoured vehicles which at present are not guarded at all and lend themselves to sabotage"

"Further West than the National twenty highway has not been considered. Logistically it would be better dealt with by resistance groups further to the west but we have no knowledge of those groups

More coffee was served. A few minutes later a secretary came in for the CO to take a phone call. It wasn't a long call. He returned, "A car will take you to the SGO at eleven fifteen." "Can you tell me why he always wants to see you when you come in from the field." "Yes." I replied, "I tell him a different story about the feelings of the French people from that which he is told by De Gaulle's

293

office and he seems to prefers my story." "He also calls for copies of some of your reports but not all, why is that and how does he know which ones to ask for?" "I think you should ask him," I said

I needed to excuse myself for some minutes. I tried to gather my thoughts. This was turning into an inquisition. I took the initiative. "This is almost certain to be my last return to the UK before the invasion and what I really need to know is the anticipated delay we have to achieve to German troop movements after the balloon goes up. Furthermore we need confirmation of the supply drops outstanding. Distributing these supplies to the adjacent groups needs time, and becomes increasingly difficult. I can't imagine the RAF will want to deliver anything in the couple of months before the event." "I will look into the matter and send a response within two weeks." said the CO

"The next matter we want to discuss is the information you report from this man you call Stephan. Who or what is he?" "The best description I can give is that he is the acknowledged leader of the maquis in my part of France." "How often are you in contact with him?" Sometimes almost every day at other time perhaps not for a couple of weeks, it all depends on what is happening." "So you are in fact cooperating with him." "That is putting it too strongly. He is always prepared to help in any activity where we need help. For example in the attack on the Germans at the col de Cere we needed people to keep the hikers out of the area during the attack, he provided those people and they were entirely effective." "How many maquis are there?" "It's almost impossible to answer and the number varies, some of the hillmen prefer to work with men under Stephan's leadership and some under our leadership and the split is not always the same. If you count the number of maquis without including any of the hillmen my guessed figure would be about eighty

Stephan himself is a man of his word, he is a communist I have no doubt. He has his own radio transmitter using a signal strong enough to reach Russia. The radio is located in the region of Mauriac," use of the map again, "and he is very well informed by whoever his superior may be. He predicted the American invasion of North Africa at least four months before the event," eyebrows were raised, "He told me about the SGO's painting holiday in Marakesh, he predicted the invasion date for Sicily, and the leapfrog landings at Salerno and Anzio, Italy's surrender as soon as mainland Italy was invaded, and even Italy's declaration of war on Germany. He is a far more important source of information to me than you are! And I almost forgot, the invasion date has not yet been decided

"I am sure he would not have told you about his radio transmitter," said one of the aides. "No," I said, "but he reluctantly admitted it when I told him we knew about it. Pascal's group traced it with the equipment in the Physics department at Clermont Technical College. They have given us much help with the setting up of our communication centre and more recently with avoiding the jamming of the BBC French service." "I understood it is no longer possible to receive the French service in France," one of the aides again. "I don't think we could do it without the special aerial arrangement set up by Cezaire from the college. We now have a regular precis printed each day of the BBC news of the previous evening distributed to trusted people by the bus drivers and the maquis." "Do you have any problems receiving our communications," One of the aides again. "Not now we have established our centre at very high altitude. "How high," asked the CO. "Just about six thousand feet."I replied. "Good heavens" exclaimed the CO. "Not quite that high muttered an aide"

The car arrived and I was pleased to get out of that discussion. I had about fifteen minutes to gather my thoughts. On arrival at admiralty arch there was the usual security checks, twice. I waited about half an hour before being called to the interview. A good thinking time, After the usual courtesies he got down to business. "You have clearly had a gruelling day and so I am not going to add to your worries." He told me that before today's discussions the CO had decided not to send me back to France because really nothing was happening. And now I know that there has been a communications problem and much has been resolved now that point is recognised. I interrupted him at that moment, "I consider it more serious than that sir, most of my information has simply not been read. I have spent several hours this today simply repeating information from memory." He complimented me on the messages I had marked for his attention and assured me that he had read them most carefully and found them essential to his understanding of the changing attitude of the French 'man in the street'

"Do you think you can stand perhaps another year in France? Before you answer, recognise that it will be a dangerous year for everyone in the field." "Yes," I said

"I recognise the danger but there is nobody as well placed as I am to get through that year unrecognised and therefore able to do what is necessary." "Thank you for your willingness to take it on, if the situation does not resolve itself to your satisfaction do not hesitate to inform me in the usual way

I expect you will know about the invasion date as soon as I do!." Take great care," he said as he stood up and shook my hand. The inevitable man at my elbow escorted me to the waiting room and I enjoyed the usual brandy. Considering the time of night the amount of activity was high.   There seemed to be three or four people yet to be seen that night. The car was late, the brandy did its work and they had to wake me on it's arrival.

I slept until nearly midday. I took a quick lunch at the hotel, paid a visit to the bank and transferred all my pay to a deposit account to get some interest on it. "You're not in London very often," remarked the manager. "No I'm on detached duties," the standard evasive reply. He looked at my shoulder, and glance at the date of birth on my file "You are very young to be a Major you must have friends in high places." I had to ignore the comment

When I returned to the hotel there was a message that I was expected at two to continue our planning. I took note of the change of tone and emphasis. During the morning they must have read all of the messages file again. Most of the questions were based upon getting a deeper understanding of the real problems

I mentioned in passing that we had recently received two new maquis members from Corsica and that they were known to Stephan who must have been active in the Corsican maquis. This involved mention of the five airmen who we had recently passed through our area. Again blank faces. "Have you reported this?" asked the CO. "Yes," I replied. "just over a week ago, they were the five from the crashed Halifax at Saint Sauvier near Montlucon. The navigator was badly injured in the leg and the crew wanted to stick together so they were hidden somewhere around the Clermont area while he recovered." "Nobody seemed to have seen that message"

"You'd better tell us briefly what happened. I related the story of the pilgrimage to everyone's amusement. "They were really quite a problem, five young men, fair complexioned, hardly a word of French between them, and that with English accents you could cut with a knife." "Where are they now?" asked an aide, "Probably they have just arrived in Spain. Mathilde's message file might have later information." "The rest of the discussion centred on the problem of how long we had to maintain the blockages coupled with a consideration of whether the invasion would be in the North or the South or both simultaneously or staggered. Simultaneously was ruled out because the RAF could not provide air cover for both areas together. More problems were raised than solved and I secretly resolved to rely on my own information via Stephan. The only point on which I did get a firm commitment was for ten days warning of the likelihood of an invasion by coded message and two days for action via the BBC personal messages

One of the aides was nominated to take me out to dinner that evening, the CO being otherwise engaged. We went to a night club after the meal. The floor show was poor. "Nothing like as good as you get where you are I suppose," suggested the aide. "There is not a single night club in the whole of the Auvergne," I said, "They are really quite a reserved people, it all happens at home." I went on to tell him how I had lost my bet over the German troops sleeping out. He was amazed

I went on to say that a few of the French women did it for the pillow talk and reported back any useful snippets of information. "They are the really brave ones," I said

The following day I had nothing to do until the car came for me at three o'clock to go to Tangmere. I dare not buy any presents. I did write a letter home in which I said a colleague was going to England and would post it for me

Jim flew in on time and while the Lysander was being topped up with fuel he pointed out the improvements on the IIIA version. I must say I didn't understand all of it. Once we were off and at cruising height I joined him up front. It was another fine night. "I didn't think you were going back again, you are a devil for punishment," he said

"It was not their intention to send me back again, I really don't know why, they had all the information they had asked for, but they did not appear to have read some of it and some of it had not been passed through because the decoders couldn't understand it"

"We have our problems with the French section too," he went on, "I am sure most of the problems arise because of the competition between the resistance controlled by de Gaulle and the resistance from the communist factions. Do you have any problems with the communists?" "No." I said "We help them if they need it and they work with us when we need extra help or people

We have done one combined operation and it worked out perfectly. We are going to need them when the invasion starts." We relaxed into silence. There was some searchlight activity chasing us as we crossed the French coast so we went to silent speed and came down low to avoid the searchlights

With the coast behind us we climbed again and increased speed. "I don't suppose you'll be going back again before the invasion,? He asked. "No, I shall be staying now until my area is liberated." "You seem very confident about your position in France?" "I have a very good cover story, I have replaced a young man who was killed in an air raid but no body was found, so with the collusion of the boy's family I have taken his identity." "Wow," he said. "But how have you evaded French military service?" "Both the boy and myself have the same physical defect that rendered us unfit for military service." "So how did you get into this outfit?" "When I registered for military service and applied for deferment to continue my studies, had the medical and was failed as expected, I was called to an interview and asked to volunteer." "I shouldn't have told you any of this"

"I can see now why you had to go back. Your disappearance would have been suspicious and put the family in danger." "Exactly." I said. "I'll never say a word." he promised We flew on in silence for some time

"Do you have any feeling for when the invasion might be?" he asked. "The date hasn't been decided yet." I replied. "You sound very confident about that statement," he remarked, "Is that what they told you in London?" "No," I said, "I get my information direct from the Kremlin!" "I can't believe that," he said laughingly

"You'd better." and went on to tell him about the previous predictions I had been given by Stephan. He was amazed. As we approached Saint Flour and confirmed our sighting of the Cathedral tower, Jim said, "I've enjoyed this flight more than any other, we've talked quite openly, trust me I'll never breathe a word of this to anyone."I learned very much later that Flying Officer 'Jim' McBride died from injuries when he crash landed at Tangmere in December. That would have been not many trips after the last trip I made with him

Raymond was waiting for me as we landed. Raymond and Jim recognised each other. "So you're still around too," said Jim, "It must be something special in the air." "It is," said Raymond, "I grew up only fifty kilometres south of here, so I'm at home." "I'd like to stay and join you," said Jim, "but I've got to get this thing back." He slammed the door, we stood clear, and he turned round, opened the throttles and was away. No more than three minutes on the ground

Laurent Mathis strolled over when the Lysander had gone. "There's a couple of hundred sheep ready to come on here." He had two dogs with him which were still nervous after the noise of the plane. "I take it you're sleeping here tonight, Raymond intervened, "There's been a tightening of the curfew while you've been away. You shouldn't try to get back into Saint Flour tonight. The Germans have got hold of a copy of a precis and are convinced somebody in the town is listening to the BBC." "Has anybody told Angelique about this? I asked. "Yes," Raymond replied, "Stephan had one of his men call and warn her"

On our way down to the farm we opened gates and the dogs started to move the sheep on to the landing strip area. Laurent stayed to see the move completed. It was quite cold that night and I was pleased to get in to the farmhouse. Raymond had collected my bicycle from the Barrat farm. So I could nonchalantly ride into town in the morning

Raymond was anxious to hear the news. I relayed the problems London had over our communications. "I promise you I have sent everything you have given me." "No Raymond you and your operators are not at fault, Firstly, they have not read the messages they have got and secondly the radio centre decoded the group of messages about the sites for landfalls but because they did not understand the data put it all on one side and forgot about it." "So we don't have any answers?" he asked

"No," I confirmed. "There is a new CO for the French section and I suspect they are all trying to score points off each other."So what are we going to do?" "I've already done it" I said "We will have our answers within two weeks""What did you do?" "I appealed to the highest possible level and certain decisions were reversed. Do you know they were not going to send me back because we had not achieved anything"

We had our answers within a week. Minimum four weeks road and rail closures, aim at six weeks. Delayed supplies will be dropped in about two week's time. Major supplies for pre-invasion sabotage will arrive in February next year. We are still studying the plans of the proposed sites of blockages. I could not understand how they might be altered by people so remote from the Auvergne

The following morning I was back on my bike in town as though I'd never left it. I was anxious to find out more about the precis that had got into the hands of the Germans. Mum and Dad had only heard about it in the bar. Yvette the same. I tried to find Alexis but without success. I went round to the bus station. Christian guessed why I was there, and indicated to me to wait while he finished allocating some work on a damaged bus. "Come and have a cup of coffee"

We went into his office. "It seems that a passenger on a bus picked up a precis off the floor and was reading it while sitting beside a German. The German understood enough French to understand most of it and took it from her. When he gave it to the sergeant who passed it to Major Kempf the soldier was put on a charge for not taking the woman into custody. There is a search on for the woman at the moment but I'm sure she has gone into hiding. The streets are swarming with Germans after curfew listening at people's windows and doors but no arrests have been made yet as far as I know"

"It sounds like an unfortunate coincidence," I said. Christian agreed. "Have the Germans been looking for people who have duplicating jelly available, they must have recognised the method of duplication?" I asked. "Not to my knowledge." he replied. "I wonder how many people have duplicating jelly in and around Saint Flour, the only people I can think of are school, teachers, some restaurants but they have not got enough food to duplicate anything

"It needn't have been in Saint Flour," Christian said, "The bus was the early service from Aurillac via the village route. So it could have originated in Aurillac or any of the villages en route." "Good that confuses the issue," I said. "Was it a current precis or some days out of date?" "I've no idea the precis' don't have any dates on them. So unless Kempf has been listening to the BBC he would not know how old it was. The jamming is as bad as ever and unless anyone has special aerials I don't see how you could hear anything of value," said Christian

It being my first day back the Monday club was assembling that evening, and I had to contain my impatience until then for any further news.   After supper, when everyone was present, I brought the group up-to-date with the news from London

'About time too' was the general attitude. I did not dwell too long on the message problems, but said I expected there to be a significant improvement. Councillor Dechaux had taken the initiative of contacting Valerie Hugot socially. He didn't have to ask, she was full of the news about that fake report of the BBC news that was found on the bus. She talked to him very openly. The first reaction had been one of amazement and this triggered the extra activity to find out if anyone in Saint Flour could be caught red-handed. No result so far. Kempf had several long telephone conversations with Aurillac and another location of which she couldn't get the name. The outcome was that Kempf himself tried to tune into the BBC and satisfied himself that the Jamming was completely effective. He reported this to Aurillac and was told to try again in the upper town because of the extra height. So he took his radio up to the bell ringing room in the Cathedral tower. The reception was better if he got the position of the aerial just right and he could understand some of the speech but not enough to take any notes of what was being said. His final conclusion was that the precis was a resistance propaganda stunt We decided to leave the situation alone but casually ask all recipients to destroy copies when they had finished with them

Chapter 40

The Way to a Frenchman's Heart

Good sabotage reports from all adjacent groups with the consequential requests for replacement munitions occupied much of my time. Two overdue drops came in the last week of the month which restored our position and made it possible to replenish our stock points during them long dark nights

At last we received London's agreement to the detail of our plans for the pre-invasion sabotage programme reiterating the need for minimum four weeks and to target six weeks. Provided we received our supplies in February while the nights were still dark enough to move them near to the points of use we could see no problem unless the invasion was much sooner than everyone expected

Stephan had been probing his sources and had finally been told that the middle of the year was now being 'worked towards'. So in spite of London's silence we had something to work towards also Christmas and the New Year prospects for the French population looked bleak. Although the Germans quota collections were not so intense or frequent the additional losses to them, local supply and demand situation, which was already stretched to the limit, hurt everybody. The loss of cash income for the summer's wool crop meant the majority of business was now done by barter, exchanges and promises

The slow down of the Anglo-American advance up the leg of Italy and the winter slow down on the Russian front influenced the French attitude to the war and the successes of the summer and autumn were soon forgotten

The Terminus was well enough supplied with wine but the locals had little cash with which to buy it. Valerie Hugot alerted us to the intention of the Germans to plunder our stock for the quota. Urgent action was necessary. We could not be seen to move any wine off the premises as this could also be seized

Fortunately the stocks had been delivered and cellared long before the Germans occupied Vichy France so they had no idea of the quantity we had in the cellar

We worked late into the night every day moving bottles from the cellar to the loft up to the maximum load the loft floor would support. The spaces under spare beds were filled, bottoms of wardrobes, and I was even able to excavate a small hole under my workshop for three hundred or so bottles.

We also had to make the cellar look as though it had not been recently emptied. Light bulbs were removed. Now the only light used in the cellar was an inefficient smoking oil lamp carried down by who ever needed to go into the cellar. Some buckets of river water were thrown in to make everything quite damp and generally unpleasant

Stephan came during the latter part of our preparations and we explained the situation. "Make sure you tell me when they come to take the wine," he said. "We might be able to teach them a lesson"

"What are you going to do I asked?" "I'm not sure we can do anything but if we can we will." Since the col de Cere incident the truck making the quota collections used varying routes to Aurillac and sometimes it even went direct to Clermont

The quota demand came on a Thursday. They arrived just after eight in the morning. Thursday was not a busy day for the Terminus and we had not even finished breakfast.

They demanded entrance to the cellar and to the outside food store in the yard. Mum gave them the keys to the food store Dad lifted the trap door in the bar which was the most difficult entrance to the cellar. Then Dad carefully lit the smoking oil lamp and handed it to them. I had hurried out and went to the bakers just around the corner to beg use of the telephone. I left a number of messages for Stephan and then I was lucky and found him. "Good," he said, in response to the news, "I'll get something moving straight away

The German who went down into the cellar was not at all happy. The water on the floor was several centimetres deep. He insisted Yvette went down into the cellar as well to hand him the boxes and crates which he then passed up to another German at the top of the steps for taking out to the truck parked on the bus stop

Yvette made a point of putting all the boxes and crates on to the floor before handing them to the German in the cellar so that they were dripping wet and the usually smart German uniforms became very soiled during the loading

They didn't completely empty the cellar. After the oil lamp went out for the second time Yvette refused to move any more wine and the German decided they had taken enough. The jeering crowds in the street may also have helped him decide. As the German went out he shouted to the crowd, "We've left you enough for Christmas!" but nobody understood him

The Germans robbing the food store fared better. They took every single ham, uncut cheese and all the cured meats. They ignored the vegetables but took most of the carefully stored apples and pears. Most of the conserves were ignored being home made and unlabelled

Mum was in tears. Many of the items taken were her carefully selected items for the year end festivities. Yvette tried to console her with little success. Jean-Francois had been frightened by the attitude of the Germans and was tearful as well

When the truck had driven off most of the crowd came into the Terminus to either commiserate with Mum and Dad or to slake their thirsts or to find out if we had any stock left for Christmas. We had the busiest Thursday on record

Alexis arrived after the truck had left he indicated he needed to speak to me. I took him through to the workshop. "They've done the same thing at most of the bars in town, if that's any consolation." he said, "In total there's four trucks of quota goods leaving Saint Flour this morning." "That means it will be quite a bleak Christmas and New Year." I commented. "Now I've got a question for you," he said severely, "Did you organise any thing for last Monday night? I looked at him blankly "No, I can see you didn't." "The Gendarmerie depot at Aurillac was broken into, the guard was bound and gagged and all the reserves of weaponry, ammunition and uniforms were stolen, and even two vehicles." I began to smile. "So you did arrange something," he said. "No," I said, "but I believe I know who might have done so"

I went on to tell him about Stephan's reaction to the warning we had received from Valerie Hugot. Then I told him I had contacted Stephan early this morning and the reaction of, 'I'll get something moving straight away.' "Something has already moved," said Alexis, "but I failed to recognise it. I have seen many maquis in town this morning and so have my agents, we even wondered if it was Friday. What are they going to do?"

"In the light of what you've just told me, I think they are going to intercept the German trucks but I don't know if they recognise that there are now five of them." "There were several maquis lounging about in the Place d'Armes watching the quota being taken from Chez Albert, and they followed that truck as it made it's way to the bars opposite the park and shortly after a truck from downtown joined them. So they must know there are three." said Alexis. "And now I must go, I expect it's going to be a lively afternoon and I don't want to miss the fun"

I went back into the bar to help relieve the pressure on Mum and Dad

I tried to speculate what Stephan might do with the arms and equipment taken from the Gendarmerie, but the possibilities were never ending

The following morning, market day, the town was alive with rumour and counter rumour. There was a Gendarmerie road check on the main road north about three kilometres and the four trucks were forced to stop. The Gendarmes were very friendly and one of them was fluent in German. So after the vehicles had been checked it was suggested that a little celebratory drink might be welcome on such an occasion

The event was watched by one of the farmers from Coren who was finishing his winter ploughing nearby. He said the drinking went on for nearly an hour

There were no Germans in the market that morning which was unusual. Then Christian de Boni arrived, "It seems the dogs are all confined to their kennels." was his contribution. A little elderly lady who lived almost opposite the gates of the old Gendarmerie barracks told how she was woken up late last night when a German truck was trying to enter the gates. "The men in the truck were very drunk indeed and the guards were refusing to let them in

After some time and even more noise Major Kempf with other officers appeared and all of the men in the truck were arrested. Extra guards were posted inside and outside the gates as though further trouble was expected." She was listened to avidly by everyone in earshot

"When I came out this morning to come to the market the guards were still there and there was lots going on in the main courtyard, they wouldn't let me stay and watch"

People coming in and out of the bar all had various ideas about what might have happened and wild speculation was fuelled by every new thought It was many months since we had experienced such a busy and amusing market day. The one person who could have told us everything was conspicuous by his absence

Councillor Dechaux came into the bar in the late afternoon. I took him through to the workshop

"Major Kempf has been to see the Maire, there will be no German troops on the streets for an indefinite period while disciplinary matters are being taken. Do you know what has happened?" "If you go and visit the market you will hear the most fantastic rumours but I don't suggest you believe them. The only hard information I have comes from Alexis and it is that the Gendarmerie barracks in Aurillac was broken into on Monday night"

"Oh yes I know about that," he interrupted me. "Well my thoughts are that Stephan and his merry men robbed the Gendarmerie barracks. The four German trucks of quota goods that left Saint Flour on Thursday afternoon were stopped by a Gendarmerie check point near Coren and that event turned into a drinking party that went on for about an hour. The liquor consumed was that stolen from here and other bars"

"An interesting connection he mused." "The other piece of hard news comes from Madame Perot, who you may remember lives almost opposite the barrack gates, she was woken up in the night by a number of drunken Germans attempting to enter the barracks They were eventually arrested and this morning she tried to see what was going on inside the gates she was forcibly moved on by the guards.

If you can find her in the market she'll be pleased to tell you all about it." "Could the maquis have done all of that do you think?" "I don't actually know very much at present." and I went on to tell him about Stephan's thought that he might be able to 'do something about it' and his comments that 'I'll get something moving straight away'

Speculation continued throughout the weekend. One further fact emerged

One of Christian de Boni's bus drivers who was on the last service of the day from Clermont to Saint Flour found one way working on the main road around the Massiac bends. Southbound traffic was passing normally but northbound was diverted on to the tiny road via Sargues. His concern was that the northbound bus service could not possibly have got through on the road via Sargues

Christian checked with the driver of the northbound bus who said, there was a Gendarmerie control on the main road near Saint Mary le Plain diverting the northbound traffic via Sargues because of an overturned vehicle blocking the road. But when the driver argued he was allowed through and saw no sign of any problems on the road

Yvette and I took Jean-Francois to Mass as usual on Sunday morning. Gossip amongst the congregation was rife. There were no German personnel at the Mass, compared with the usual twenty or thirty. Alexis was waiting for us at the Terminus. While Mum and Yvette prepared lunch we tried to make sense of the facts we had. In spite of the advice from everyone else, Nobody had seen Stephan for more than a week. Alexis had failed to reach him by phone. The Maire was concerned by the 'disciplinary action' of the Germans taking so long to resolve

We convinced ourselves that Stephan was behind the events.

One communication from London relieved the tension for an hour or so

'Five airmen safely returned to UK via Spain send their grateful thanks to Marie-Christine, Henri and his Aunt, Christian and the pilgrims.' please explain pilgrims?' A loaded question, I replied 'ask the airmen.' and the matter was dropped

The Monday club met as usual after we closed. Alexis had spent most of Monday trying to find out what had happened on the main road to Clermont on Thursday afternoon. No breakdown or accident had been reported. His agents had contacted some of the regular users of the road and eventually found that at about dusk there had been a Gendarmerie control point near Saint Mary le Plain. Small vehicles were being advised to use the small road via Sargues because the main road was partly blocked at the Massiac bends although some saw southbound traffic coming through apparently normally. The small road had been clearly marked with the usual Deviation signs

A driver of a large truck was stopped and told he could proceed with caution but must expect to find a delay at the Massiac bends. He found no such delay. He had also left messages for Stephan everywhere he could think of but had no response. His agents had also instructions to quiz any of the maquis they encountered but the maquis were all missing from their usual places of work and had been since last Thursday

The Maire had received no further communication from Major Kempf and the Germans were still 'confined to barracks'. None had been seen on the streets since last Thursday. Councillor Leman reported a number of house parties on Saturday night were held to celebrate the occasion. We asked councillor Dechaux to maintain contact with Valerie Hugot and find out as much as she knew about what was going on in the barracks

Early on Tuesday morning contingents of SS arrived from Aurillac and Clermont. An observer at the barrack's gate said the officer from Clermont was an SS Colonel. In total about thirty SS men were said to have arrived. By the evening we had learnt via Valerie Hugot that the SS had taken over control of the barracks. Certain men were in isolation and they had been intensively interrogated by the SS

Major Kempf was also isolated and had been under interrogation all day. Valerie Hugot had been told that her services would not be required for some days. The last snippet of information she overheard was that when the five wool wagons arrived in Germany there was no wool in them

Although Valerie's German was not perfect when she actually repeated the phrase she had overheard there was no doubt regarding her translation. "It appears that Major Kempf is in it up to his neck," said Dad

On Thursday morning Alexis received a telephone call from Stephan. He was apologetic but had been otherwise engaged. Could we meet him at the same place as our last meeting, in the afternoon. All was still quiet in the town, so

Alexis agreed and came down to the Terminus out of uniform and with a bicycle from one of his agents

We left the Terminus separately having agreed to meet on the road to La Chaumette. "Under these circumstances you never know who you can trust," Alexis said as he left. I left by the back door some minutes later. We met as agreed and when we arrived at La Chaumette. Madame Gourrier was ready with a nice lunch for us. Stephan looked very tired but his attitude was triumphant. "I expect you've worked out some of the story already but it's much bigger than you could have guessed

The Gendarmerie headquarters in Aurillac was raided by two groups of Maquis. We worked with the group from Tulle because they were desperately in need of ammunition and weapons whereas our need was the uniforms and vehicles. As far as we know the Gendarmerie has not yet discovered who raided them." He looked expectantly at Alexis. "I have no information nor have I heard any rumours." Alexis answered the implied question, "How much do you know about what is happening in Saint Flour?" I asked. "I know what happened when the highly inebriated Germans arrived back at the gates. One of my men drove them as far as the outskirts of Saint Flour and then handed over to the least drunk of the drivers. He followed on foot just out of sight and heard the uproar at the gates. Do you know that four or five Germans absconded during their trip and are on the loose somewhere around Massiac? "No," we both replied. "Do you know the SS have taken over the Saint Flour barracks?" "Yes," he replied "Do you know the wool wagons were found to be empty when they arrived in Germany." "No, "he replied. We all seemed to have run out of questions

"Well," said Alexis, "We've all got some catching up to do. Why don't you start by telling us what happened near Massiac on Thursday." "You know about the road block and the deviation we set up. Well after the four German trucks had gone into the diversion we removed all the signs on the main road and let the normal traffic flow resume

We followed the German trucks at a distance until, they got to the hijack point at the bridge over the river. The bridge was blocked by another Gendarme vehicle and they had to stop. And we closed up on them from the rear. They were of course still quite drunk and the suggestion that we all had a drop or two more was acceptable but this time the drinks were fixed with some hallucinatory drugs we had prepared and they got very dopey indeed. That's when some of them took off into the woods. We got a number of them back but we didn't really know how many there were to start with. While all this was going on one truck was emptied into the other three so that we could put all the Germans into one truck which Guillaume, that's our German speaker, drove back to Saint Flour, and you know the rest of the story"

307

I broke into the conversation at that point, "So we don't know why the SS are there. It could be for any of the reasons, the theft of the quota goods, the deserters, the empty wool wagons, or just the outbreak of drunkenness." "By the way," said Alexis, "Where are the quota goods?" "I thought you'd never ask," joked Stephan. "All the perishables are in a cold store where we have a good friend in charge at Murat. We will have to work out a plan for dispersing them again and recompensing the people from whom they were stolen. All the wine and cognac and other alcohols are in two trucks nicely tucked away in a cave near La Cham from where they can be quietly returned to their owners although I have to say the amount is somewhat depleted." "You took a risk in moving those trucks didn't you," said Alexis. "Why," exclaimed Stephan, "They had a Gendarmerie escort!"

We spent an hour or two exchanging minor pieces of information to bring all of us fully up-to-date. I suggested that Dad could quietly contact all the bars raided by the Germans and getting a statement of the alcohol they lost I said I would contact the shopkeepers and get similar statements from them.

We agreed that we would say that resistance activity had resulted in the recovery of some of the stolen items which we would return to them as and when possible. We would not enter into any discussion about the events because we didn't know any detail

It took a long time to return all of these quota goods covertly. We made extensive use of people's extra movements over the Christmas and New Year period to deal with some of it. Finally it worked out that those who lost perishables got back over eighty-five percent of their losses but the bars only got back about eighty percent. The resistance as a whole improved their status quite significantly and at last was respected as a result of these events. Perhaps a good way to a Frenchman's heart is via his stomach!

Chapter 41

Strengths and Weaknesses

Valerie Hugot having some time on her hands went visiting friends and relatives. Returning one day on the train from Murat she was surprised to meet one of the SS officers from the Barracks but not in uniform. In a brief conversation he told her that Major Kempf had been under suspicion of somehow stealing the wool crop However he had completed his investigation of the matter and could say that the disappearance of the wool must have taken place after it left the area of Saint Flour

Thus Major Kempf was exonerated and reinstated in command. He added that this was a fortunate meeting because he could now also tell Valerie that she should return to her duties tomorrow. When she arrived in Saint Flour and parted from the SS man she went at once to the home of Councillor Dechaux to bring him up-to-date with the news

The SS departed the same evening and local Germans returned to the gate duties at the barracks. German troops reappeared on the streets two days later. Slowly we were able to piece together what had occurred. There were many witnesses to the loading and sealing of the wagons at Saint Flour and the SS were satisfied that the wool actually left Saint Flour. They had then followed the route of the shunt train as far as Vichy where the wool wagons were uncoupled and attached to an express goods train to Munich. The SS had studied the time and movement records at the various stations en route where the shunting engine stopped. and reached the conclusion that there was no possibility for the wool wagons, which were fastened right behind the engine, to be detached from the train. They had completely overlooked the fact the possibility that the actual start time of the journey from Saint Flour was earlier than on the recorded time of the shunt engine's departure

Major Kempf's problems with drunken troops were beneath the dignity of the SS to involve themselves. Now he was restored to his command the normal disciplinary procedures would take care of that problem

The fact that the barracks had just lost three motor trucks did not emerge in the presence of the SS. "Where are the three missing trucks?" was my first question to Stephan when the Monday club next met. "Do you know I have completely forgotten about them." was his reply

"They are quite valuable as a source of motor fuel, tyres and other bits of equipment." "Well we don't want them said Alexis, I can just imagine Kempf's reaction if one of them turned up on the streets of Saint Flour""Leave it to me," said Stephan, "I'll find out and do the necessary

Next Friday's market broke all records for high cash turnover and minimum goods on show. The dark evenings concealed so many movements of goods that we actually wondered if the German troops were turning a blind eye because there was not one attempt at a search

One of Manuel's pillow talk ladies came up with the news that five German soldiers had disappeared in the course of the party at the road block. Nobody was sure whether Kempf had reported this loss or not. So far none of them had been found but who was looking? The police would only look if they were told officially, unless crimes were reported and attributed to German troops. In general terms the crime rate in the Auvergne was about the lowest in France, so any increase would be recognised quickly. Alexis instituted some searches in the area with questioning of local agents and instructions to ignore the men if they were identified. None were. There was clearly some agreement amongst the Germans to keep the matter quiet In due course Kempf would have to account for these five or had he already done so in a manner we knew nothing about

We decided to ask the Maire to test the delicate situation. The Maire called on Major Kempf to say that he was concerned about repeated reports from the Massiac area of a German soldier begging for food from remote farms. Kempf denied any of his men had been anywhere near Massiac and that his command was at full strength. So that was the way Kempf had decided to play it. Alexis came up with one incident to taunt Kempf further. The remains of a German uniform partly burnt were found near a farm at Rezentieres, a small village due north of Saint Flour. The remains included enough of the badges to identify the uniform as that of one of Kempf's command. Kempf appeared unconcerned, none of my men are missing and no new uniforms have been issued for over a year." he stated, adding. "Are you going to do anything about it?" "No, I don't need to do anything," replied Alexis. When Alexis reported this to our next meeting, He added that he thought there was now an understanding, "he does nothing and neither do we." "Well then," said Stephan, "If I find any of them I'll sign then up for the maquis"

Christmas was fast approaching and it was going to be a bleak one. There as nothing worthwhile to buy in the shops unless you went to a major city and then the price was beyond the reach of the average Auvergne resident. One relief was that the weekly quota collections had ceased and a few extra food goodies were to be had on a barter basis. We were slowly getting some of our stolen wine back so we could always barter with that. It was not unusual for a customer to come in with a cheese and go out with a few bottles

It was not going to be children's Christmas. There were simply no new toys to be had at any price. Jean-Francois was lucky. Charles Pelletier his grandfather came in to see me. "I've brought you some of Philippe's old toys. I can't think of a better home for them than with his son, he was now weeping, and I know you are trying to be to him what my son can never be, God bless you both." And he was gone before he could be thanked or even see his grandson

The toys were in two large boxes. I smuggled them past Jean-Francois and out to my workshop. There were enough for many Christmas's and birthdays. I sorted out those suitable for a three year old boy and got to work cleaning them. repairing and repainting to make them look new. I showed the results to Yvette. She was thrilled for Jean-Francois. "I think you should tell him these are from his father." I said. "Not this year," she said "wait until he is old enough to understand, I'll make a special point of taking him to see his grandfather several times over the holiday period and explain my point of view"

Major Kempf lifted the curfew over the Christmas and New Year period and the Germans put on a party for the children but this year the attendance was poor. The German officers came out and tried to mix with the French people with very little success. Just a few lonely ladies succumbed to Germanic charm. We rather got the impression that there was an attempt to improve relations but any such success was minimal

Progress of the Anglo-American forces up the leg of Italy had ground to a halt against the German winter line, although the Russians continued to make some progress on the Eastern front in spite of the winter weather

I spent some of my time over the holiday period preparing more of his father's toys for his birthday. This time I concentrated on building bricks. There was a large box of coloured stone bricks with only a few chips out of them. All they needed was a good clean. Additionally there were many wooden bricks made to fit in with the stone ones. They looked to me as though Charles Pelletier may have made them himself for Philippe to increase the range of models the bricks could build. These had been well used and a number were broken. So I replaced the broken ones and repainted the whole lot. When Jean-Francois got these all over the floor constantly building things up and knocking them down again, Sambo was inclined to join in the fun. In the end we had to stop Jean-Francois throwing bricks at Sambo whose idea of when to knock something down was not the same as his

Further copies of Angelique's news precis fell into German hands. Major Kempf questioned Valerie Hugot about the origin of the precis, "I see copies quite regularly but I have no idea where they come from." she replied. "Do you think they are the news from the BBC French service?" he asked. "People believe the news is true because it agrees with the news on Voice of America." she replied. "Oh that's just the same propaganda machine," he retorted, "and how many people in Saint Flour understand English especially when the Americans speak it?" "Not very many I suppose but it doesn't take very many to confirm the news." "What I don't understand," Kempf continued, "is how they can hear the news when the French are jamming the radio wavelengths so efficiently." I don't really know about all this jamming," she said, "but I thought it was the Germans who were doing the jamming

"That was quite a difficult conversation," Valerie said, when she told Councillor Dechaux about it. "You can take it from me that those news precis are a true report of what the BBC is saying." said Dechaux. "Then the Germans are losing the war?" "Yes, and I believe that France will be liberated later this year, and that Kempf also knows that." "Then I'll be out of work before the end of the year?" "I think I can say that the Maire will recognise that you have been of significant service to the town and will find a position at the Mairie for you." Thus we acquired an informant inside the German barracks

Early in the New Year a leading German official stated he wanted another million French workers for the German war effort to work in Germany. This of course was in addition to more than two million prisoners of war retained in Germany after the capitulation of France and the skilled Frenchmen compulsorily transferred from their work in France to similar work in Germany. There was an immediate reaction from the Frenchmen who thought they might be one of those to be transferred. Many changed their jobs several times in quick succession, with the connivance of their employers so that the employment records became muddled and out of date

Others gave up work and joined the maquis especially in areas like the Auvergne Stephan was very selective of the potential new recruits he took into his force and some of those disappointed formed new groups based in a town or a prefecture

The news that the American fifth army had landed at a place called Anzio had everybody searching the maps again to see what this meant in the Allie's advance up the leg of Italy. The advance on the western side of Italy had been halted for some time by the resistance of the Germans at and around the monastery on Monte Casino. "Now they have outflanked Monte Casino and the winter line they will go straight for Rome," said Dad. "They have still got to break the Gustav Line," said councillor Leman who was in the bar at that time, "and that is the strongest defensive line the Germans have constructed so far in Italy"

Late in January Mathilde reported that German SS troops from the Eastern front were arriving in Herault. They were said to be in very bad condition and were under strength. Some days later we were asked to find out exactly which units were involved and which German army group they represented. Mathilde must have spent much time on this problem. In spite of regular reminders it was over a month before she was able to reply.

During this time the news of another summit conference at Yalta was reported by the BBC. Within a week Stephan came to talk to me. "France is to be invaded this summer from the North by an Anglo-American-Canadian force with free French participation, and when certain objectives have been achieved a second landing will be made in the South by the Americans." was his opening pronouncement. "The date will depend on the weather patterns but the intention is sooner rather than later."

That sounds like June to me. I said. "Yes," I agree he replied. "So we should soon have our supplies for the pre-invasion disruption." I said. "I hope so too." said Stephan

"What are you going to do about all the new resistance groups being formed?"I asked. "I'm quite concerned about them," he replied, "I've rejected some very good men who approached us, but I decided I must protect those who have proved themselves already in preference to taking risks with men of unknown other affiliations"

I understood Stephan's point of view and said so at length. "If I get requests for arms for these men I will have to fulfil those requests, as far as I can, but I promise you your supplies will not be reduced as you have already proved your effectiveness"

"Now we have another problem," Stephan went on, "Two German deserters are trying to join in with the maquis." "This is a very delicate matter and at present I have to veto any such thought, and I went on to explain about Kempf's problems over the deserters and his indifference to the loss of the five men. I also told him of the unusual attitude of the Germans over the holiday period and he confirmed that he had similar reports

"If Kempf could penetrate the resistance, this would perfectly justify his attitude over the deserters and win him approbation from his superiors. I agree," said Stephan, "I will tell all of my men to ignore and reject any German deserters they encounter. We don't need them"

The total strength of the maquis in France as a whole was something to be considered despite their disparate composition

I asked Stephan straight out if he had any idea. "I hear various figures quoted," he said, "but not everybody thinks the same way about who to include. I won't have anybody in my group who I don't completely trust, so that limits our group to say one hundred and eighty. But if I put out a call to the hillmen of the Auvergne we would become over two thousand but they would be uncontrollable. In France as a whole there are about eight thousand committed members but if you then add on the support available on call it would be over one hundred thousand and even less controllable. And you can't try to fight the Germans with such a disparate force, they would massacre them"

"Have you heard about what happened in Bergerac last week?" Stephan asked. "No," I replied. "Bergerac had formed a very large and apparently efficient resistance group with no political affiliation," Stephan explained. "They had shut down almost every factory working for the Germans in the Bergerac region. They had a secret headquarters from which they ran their campaign. They accepted German deserters as members but they were not all deserters and the SS raided their headquarters, totally destroying it, and all the occupants of the mass meeting in progress at the time. They lost over one hundred and forty men mostly from that small town. You can imagine what that has done to the morale of the local population"

During February De Gaulle's office in London announced the formation of the French Forces of the Interior, the FFI. This was said to bring all the diverse resistance groups in France under one centralised command. This news came completely out of the blue. I immediately contacted Stephan again. He had just got the same news. "I will have nothing to do with it," he said, "for reasons you will clearly understand.   We work well together in this region, we can't fight all of France's battles and I advise you to ignore De Gaulle's group absolutely"

I contacted Pascal on the same subject. He said he had heard rumours of an attempt to centralise command of the Gaullist controlled groups, but he considered it impractical simply because of the communication problems. He also claimed to know that the Germans had broken the code system used by the Gaullist groups and were making the whole situation unworkable by false messages in reply to instructions from De Gaulle's office before the French group, who were the addressees of the instructions, had time to reply. For the moment he intended to ignore the FFI

The bombing of the Monte Casino monastery was heavily criticised by the Catholics in France as being unnecessary even though the Allies had been stuck there for months. The final assault by the Polish brigade won them much admiration for such a determined effort and the heavy casualties they suffered.

The American fifth army had yet to break out of their bridgehead at Anzio. When this was accomplished only the Gustav Line was between the allies and Rome

Late in February and early March we received all our necessary munitions for the pre-invasion sabotage and I was able to demonstrate to Stephan that I meant what I had said. Raymond had plenty of problems dispersing the supplies to the locations near where they would be used and welcomed the help from the maquis so freely given

The extra air activity over the Auvergne and the surrounding regions led the local Germans to the conclusion that the invasion was soon to come. The talk in the bar of an evening from the Germans was that they would soon repel any invasion and then their secret weapons would take over and win the war for them

Mathilde finally got the details of the German SS infantry arriving in Herault. They were the SS Hitler Brigade, with one of the toughest records in the German army. The army group so formed was H. This was passed to London, and acknowledged with the comment that the other main part of army group H was the Das Reich armoured brigade. Just a few days later Mathilde reported that her informants in Herault said an armoured division was starting to arrive but they were in bad spirits and short of every sort of equipment. Then within a week they were confirmed as the Das Reich SS armoured brigade

London was very interested in German army group H. They sent through an extensive list of questions, none of which could be answered from our present knowledge. We could only pass these questions to Mathilde and hope she could elicit some of the answers. In view of London's attitude I asked for weekly updates even if there was no new information. Mathilde first weekly report answered nearly a quarter of London's questions with good quality information gathered from her contacts regarding the ancillary corps of the German army attached to group H. She had reasonable information about the strengths of the major units based on ration issues

The Hitler Brigade was twenty-two per cent under strength. Men from other SS infantry brigades were arriving daily transferred from presumably heavily mauled units. The state of the new arrivals was stated as pitiful. The problem of the Das Reich was different. The men were in reasonable spirits, only seven per cent under strength, which was said to be the result of their tradition of never leaving anyone behind. Armour and support vehicles were however over thirty per cent down

I thought Mathilde had done a remarkable job knowing the conditions she had to work under to get the information and all this was in addition to her sabotage activity. She had even got the name of the new general appointed to take command of the Das Reich brigade following their mauling on the Russian Front for which the previous General Hauser had been moved elsewhere. The new SS General, Heinz-Bernhardt Lammerding, had a reputation for brutality in his management of his staff and expecting them to be just as brutal with their subordinates. London's response was immediate. We need all the information requested. In view of the slow progress so far we are parachuting in a German army specialist to speed up the gathering of the answers. His code name is Hector and he will arrive at your Southern drop zone on date to be advised soonest. Please afford him every assistance and facility. He is fluent in French and German. He is to communicate through the usual channels using his own codes

Chapter 42

Hector and Benjamin Arrive

The sabotage activity of Pascal's groups was now at a high level. In the past months they had stopped production at all the major steel works in and around Clermont each for many days at a time. Add on the start up time for the furnaces and each shut down lasted at least ten days. At another factory making anti-tank guns production was stopped for overt two weeks. The specialist precision engineers making cylinder heads for the Luftwaffe were also shut down for some weeks on two occasions. At last the French trade unions were prepared to accept the consequent loss of earnings as part of the price of liberation

The German controlled French radio news service minimised the results of the sabotage and maximised the effects of the loss of earnings on the families of workers. The few workers who were arrested for involvement in sabotage were treated very harshly by the French authorities. In spite of these activities the increase of support for sabotage grew steadily

As a result of the sabotage of the steel works many of the specialised processors of steel in the area were short of raw materials and this knock-on effect added to the workers hardships. Attempts were made to purchase special steels from Sweden. A representative of a Swedish steel consortium arrived in the area to discuss the local specifications needed by individual companies. He was escorted everywhere by a plain clothes SS officer When he was about to visit Clermont itself, and specifically Pascal's company, I was asked to be available in case there was the possibility to speak to him. So I joined the bus early on a Monday with the weekly Clermont commuters. I was smuggled into Pascal's main premises as a new employee. The Swede was due on Wednesday

At dinner on the Tuesday evening the SS escort was suddenly taken ill and was still quite ill on Wednesday and thus unable to be present at the meeting with Pascal. Pascal had undoubtedly arranged for something to be added to the

SS mans dinner the previous evening. He had also decided that he could not speak anything other than French which the Swede did not understand well. Thus he was able to say to the Swede "Do you understand English?" to which the Swede replied, "of course." "We have several young English speakers on our staff because, as I am sure you know, we have two manufacturing plants in England" Then of course he asked me to join the meeting

I described the applications using special steels about which I had been briefed during the previous days and asked the Swede which of the specifications he could meet. In fact he could meet all of them and thus I asked him to quote prices and conditions. Pascal intervened at that time and asked the Swede if he really wanted to supply. The Swede stated that he was under instructions from the chairman of his company to do so because the chairman was an ardent supporter of the present German government. Pascal took the opportunity opened up by this reply. "Do you personally want to help the Germans prolong this war?" he asked and I translated."I feel I am among friends," replied the Swede, "I consider the present German government one which has to be defeated at all costs"

"Now you have to tell our Swedish friend what you know," said Pascal addressing me. I spoke to the Swede. "The invasion of France by the Allies is imminent, you may have time to make one delivery before the whole of the transport services in France are disrupted, and I can think of no way in which we could pay you for any delivery you made"

This rather brought proceedings to a standstill. "I suppose the payment position is much the same for all French companies," said the Swede, "My instructions on that point were to only accept payment in German marks guaranteed by a bank in the Hanseatic League." "I can think of no way in which we could arrange that under today's conditions in France." was Pascal's reply

"My chairman is convinced that the secret weapons Germany is preparing will win the war for the Germans. He was entertained at Peenemunde recently and shown a demonstration of a flying bomb, for which we are supplying some special alloys. He was also told about a rocket development that could deliver a huge explosive charge supersonically and which could not be intercepted by any aircraft

Information of that sort was the last thing I had expected to hear about in Clermont. Pascal sensed my concern and immediately ordered coffee to be served to break the tension. Conversation about the war became more open. Both Pascal and I detected that this man was an ally. "Could you please excuse us for a few minutes while you enjoy your coffee?" asked Pascal in broken English. "Certainly" was the reply

We withdrew. How far can we trust this man was the unspoken thought in both our minds. In Pascal's office we exchanged thoughts hurriedly, the same thoughts, this man could be trusted and would work with us rather than against us. "I'll reserve the private dining room for lunch and have the conversation recorded." said Pascal and picked up the phone to make the arrangement. "I have a further thought to test him, you know we have those duplicate photos for document preparation in the UK for 'twin personages'. We could ask him to take these back to Sweden and post them to the UK. If he did that for us he would have proved himself to me." "Agreed," said Pascal

"I've just organised lunch for us in the company's private dining room," were Pascal's opening words when we rejoined the Swede again; it's the safest place in Clermont to talk." "I'm amazed that I should find such a situation where you clearly have to do some work for the Germans and yet you are creating a situation by which you may be unable to do anything for them at all." remarked the Swede

"Like you we all regard the German regime as one to be destroyed as rapidly as possible and that time is very near." replied Pascal. "Do you have any idea how near the Germans are to using these weapons."I have no firm information, but I believe it to be months rather than years"

"There is a significant resistance force already in France to act as soon as the Allied forces land, which we expect to be in the next few months." I said as soon as we were alone in the dining room." "When will you be returning to Sweden?"asked Pascal. "At the end of this week," replied the Swede. "Would you be prepared to take a small envelope with you and post it to England when you get to Sweden?" I asked. Silence while our Swedish friend considered the point

"I think I have the right to know what will be in the envelope." "A few photographs of heads and shoulders of a number of men" I replied' "and nothing else?" "Just a number on the back of each photo," "and who do I send it to?" "I can either give you a name and address to remember or a separate slip of paper with the address on it." I replied. "Where are these photos now, could I see them?" asked the Swede. "Henri lives in a small town away from Clermont," said Pascal, "but we can arrange to get them here quickly." "Tell me the address." "Personal for CO French Section, 64, Baker Street, London, W.1"After some further consideration he replied, "Yes I'll do it," I'm sure I'm talking to people I can trust"

"Shall I send Cezaire over to fetch the photos?" said Pascal, "No," I said better that Raymond brings them over here but you could get Cezaire to send a message to Raymond to ask him to bring them here top priority today if possible and to confirm time of expected arrival." Pascal picked up the phone and asked the operator to find Cezaire. Before coffee was served Cezaire responded to Pascal

319

and got his instructions. As we were preparing to leave the dining room Cezaire called again to say Raymond expected to be on the last bus this evening

The Swede was clearly impressed" I expect our SS friend will have recovered by this evening and will be with me at dinner, I don't want you to give me the envelope while he is around." "Of course not," I replied. "There's a bit of a problem there," said Pascal, "Does he go everywhere with you?" "Normally yes," "When you leave on Friday does he go with you to Paris?" "No he will leave me at Clermont station to catch the Paris express." "Good." said Pascal, "Then Henri will be on the same train as far as Vichy and will give you the envelope discretely." "That sounds good." replied the Swede. We filled the rest of the afternoon with a tour of the main factory in Clermont. As the Swede was ready to leave the receptionist called to say the SS car was waiting for him

The SS man had recovered sufficiently to resume his escorting duties

Raymond duly arrived that evening and joined us for dinner in the discrete restaurant Pascal always used for such occasions. We bought him up-to-date on our day's discussions. "That was a remarkable piece of luck." was all he could think of to say. Raymond got on well with Pascal it was the first time they had met face to face.   We talked widely about the war situation and then about our expectations when it was over. Raymond wanted to return to France and find some employer for his civil engineering skills and Pascal offered to help him in any way he could

Raymond was also given the grand tour of the factory the following day while I was coding a long message to London re the photographs and the urgency of the need for the documents to be prepared using the photographs. I made it quite clear to the CO that even if he could identify the sender in Sweden he must not make any contact with him. Raymond left on the last bus back to Saint Flour that evening having promised to transmit without fail that night

The Paris express was due to leave at twelve twenty but was invariably somewhat late. I was at the station early. I wanted to see the behaviour of the SS man and the Swede together before they parted. The relationship was clearly cool

I dare not get close enough to hear any of the conversation. Then the train arrived only a few minutes late and the Swede boarded at once and the SS man departed. I boarded the train and found the Swede in the dining car. We lunched together as two fellow passengers. I discretely passed him the envelope and told him very quietly that I had told London not to make any contact with him in any circumstances. I had to leave before the lunch was finished and we shook hands very warmly before I left the train at Vichy

I could not help remembering my previous 'arrival' at Vichy. Now I was acclimatised to France and getting another train back to Clermont and then the bus to Saint Flour seemed to me like just going home

Our Swedish friend must have acted very promptly on his arrival home. By the end of the following week London confirmed receipt of the photographs. More importantly they said the documents using the pictures would be sent via the German army specialist shortly leaving to assist Mathilde

London also cautioned us about using the Swedish route for documents to the UK because some such communications had been opened en route probably in Copenhagen. They had examined the envelope from me exhaustively and were confident it had not been opened. I was surprised to learn that some other people had used the Swedish route

An exchange of messages with Francois Peillon confirmed the increase in sabotage in his area. Both he and the Drome valley group had concentrated on the Valence factories to such an extent that the Maire of Valence had complained to the FFI headquarters in London about disturbing of sleep of the Valenciennes. On a more serious note the Germans had increased the guards on the bridges, road and rail, over the Rhone. All persons using those bridges were stopped and checked before being allowed to cross. Traffic delays were horrendous during peak hours

Whilst in Clermont news came in from the FFI groups Correze about the pressure being put on them by the occupying Germans. As in Cantal there was a quota to be fulfilled every month for shipment to Germany, and the Correze farmers were apparently just as reluctant to meet their quota. The terrain was rather easier for the Germans to collect the quota but the FFI resistance were quite active in aiding and abetting the farmers, even to the point of skirmishes taking place on quota collection days. During April there had been several actions resulting in a loss of about twenty-two of the FFI. Six were killed in combat, and the others tortured and shipped to concentration camps in Germany or shot in front of the local inhabitants to terrorise them

The SS were involved in so far as they insisted on these reprisals being acted upon by Wehrmacht personnel. The local German commander had protested to the SS especially as farms providing shelter to the FFI were subsequently burned down thus imposing a greater quota on the others

The tempo of message communication built up quickly. Answers were demanded in a few days to questions needing weeks to collect the information required

Then the arrival of Hector was announced within two days time. Fortunately Mathilde was able to accept his proposed arrival time. Additionally London wanted Hector to move North when he has assessed the real strength of German army group H and check up on the data we had supplied regarding our army group G

I had to arrange for Victor to be present at Hector's arrival to collect the identity documents prepared from the photos delivered via our Swedish friend. On his return with the documents he said Mathilde and Hector started arguing within an hour of Hector's arrival and he could not foresee any serious cooperation between them He also brought the news that the Das Reich armoured division had started to relocate around Castres and Albi and were now up to full strength. The Hitler Brigade were expected to follow soon when they had completed a retraining programme

I showed the identity documents to Alexis for his comments. He was quite enthusiastic about them. "They will pass any inspection." he said. I told him they were to be used mainly by the people who were placing the explosives for the pre-invasion sabotage to provide cast-iron alibis for anyone who was visually identified doing their work

Allied air activity over France was increasing. Mathilde had some difficulty with Hector's arrival in identifying the plane dropping him. It was quite clear that the invasion date was approaching. Repeated night raids on the Toulouse aircraft establishments, and the daylight raids by high flying American planes on the Marseille region oil industry

London commented most favourably on the news sent by Mathilde regarding the relocation of the Das Reich armoured brigade saying this was the sort of information they really needed and now that Hector was in place they expected improved and prompt advice. Their message did nothing to improve the relations between Mathilde and Hector

Hector chose to operate entirely independently and moved about in the Herault Aveyron and Tarn departementes with total disregard for any security and simply passed his messages to Mathilde already coded and refused to discuss their content with her. I sent him repeated requests for details of his findings which were ignored. I finally sent him an order to report his findings to me directly, copied to London

London apologised assuming Hector was communicating with me. They sent me all his reports recoded into my codes. What a waste of time. I was now spending more time coding and decoding than doing my job. Raymond stepped in to relieve the pressure. But his time was now getting short as well

I was barely getting four hours sleep a night and spending very little time with Yvette. Her birthday was approaching." The best present you can give me this year is just two days of your time, one for me and one for Jean-Francois." I promised, and we took two days with Angelique and her family at Vibresac. Quite remote, no telephone, good but undemanding company, even the BBC to listen to in the evenings

322

Angelique had done a remarkable job with her news precis. She had hardly missed a day. She guessed as well as anybody that the invasion was imminent

"I have brought some of the duplicating jelly home here for invasion time. I expect most things will stop but I'll do the best I can to get the news to the people"

"You do realise the risk you are taking?, I asked. "I think everyone will be too occupied to worry about where the news is coming from at that time," she said. A very brave girl

On the way back to Saint Flour Yvette asked, "Do you know how soon the invasion will be?" "I think it will be within the next two months," I replied. "What will happen?" she asked, "Very little in Saint Flour itself," I said, "Wars are not won and lost in the mountains." She seemed relieved. "I expect the fighting will be all around the Auvergne and at some time the German garrison will have to withdraw or be cut off When that happens we will simply wait until the Allies arrive."

"What will the resistance actually do when the invasion happens?" "Make life as difficult as possible for the Germans." I replied. She had to be content with that answer. "I shall be quite busy then," I added. "Will we be safe in Saint Flour?" She asked, "I doubt if there will be any battles in or near Saint Flour"

I had been waiting to see Stephan again to pass over the 'twin documentation. He finally responded to my messages when I was back in Saint Flour. He was delighted with papers. "I will announce to the world that France has another nine legitimate citizens but don't tell the government," he said

Next day I received London's news that Benjamin would arrive on eighth of May to organise the maquis in the Auvergne. I had to go and find Stephan again, this was urgent. It was always worth trying Jean Chavent for information about Stephan, this time was no different. "He's training men hard with Victor and Sebastian at Saint Laurent de Veyres." That was a difficult place to get to without any transport. I begged the use of a police van and driver from Alexis

"What do you know about Benjamin?" I asked Stephan when I eventually reached him. He looked blank. "Well he's arriving in a few days time to organise the maquis in the Auvergne."Stephan handed over the rest of the training to Victor and Sebastian. "I need coffee, lets go back to the farm." We sat down in comfort in the Mounier's lounge. "Do you mean to tell me that London is now sending someone to train us after all the instructions they gave you about not supplying us with any equipment." "I simply don't know," I replied and showed him the message

"I suppose he's got to be coming from the UK," said Stephan, "but we are probably only weeks away from the invasion, how much training do they expect to manage in that time. We've been training now for over a year and I find the results quite good considering the conditions these men live and work under. Victor and Sebastian have worked hard but there is still some language problem, because we are such a mixture"

"I suppose I shall have to meet this man on arrival," I said, "but I don't know how he is arriving or where yet. Frankly I have no use for him." "I'll tell my superiors and ask if they know anything about him, I can always use an extra pair of hands if he is trained, but I will have to satisfy myself he can be trusted"

We went on to other matters. ""Do you know about army group H who are just moving into Tarn near Albi?" He didn't so I explained about Mathilde's and Hector's findings. "That all makes sense," he said, "My people have told me that German troop movements northwards or southwards in Western France must be prevented at all costs after the Allies land and the National highway twenty is the key to those movements. So a concentration of German troops around Albi makes sense"

"Do you know the main elements of this army group are the SS Das Reich armoured division and the SS Hitler Infantry Brigade Headed by a new SS General Lammerding who has a reputation for brutality?" "No," he replied, "and that's an especially nasty combination. I wonder if Benjamin is a specialist in attacking such troops." "Perhaps you ought to be with me when he arrives so we can decide then exactly how we are going to use his talents, if any." "I agree," said Stephan

"By the way, have you found those three German trucks your lot hijacked yet?" "I forgot to tell you about that," he said, "We've decided to keep them until the Allies have landed and then use them to move our men to wherever we are going to attack the German troop movements. We reckon that German trucks with drivers in German uniforms will be waved through any check points. They are quite safe where they are. Remember it's a good few kilometres from here to the National twenty

We are relying on you to prevent any movement through the Auvergne and we feel sure your plans are sound. We think our best role is to help the maquis groups to the West of us"

"One other thought we had was to change the plates on the vehicles, do you think Mathilde's group could steal some plates off some army group H vehicles. Nobody would want to upset that lot would they." "I like that idea," I replied

"I'll get a message to her tonight." "If she succeeds we will arrange to collect them." said Stephan. Stephan had decided to stay with the training programme at Saint Laurent de Veyres until the invasion. It was remote and difficult for me to get there. "I think we need to have regular communications, would you are prepared to use our communications centre, I could authorise Vincent to code and send messages for you and to decode the replies?" "I accept that idea with pleasure"

As soon as the training had finished for the day I gave the necessary instructions to Vincent. Before I left I took both Vincent and Sebastian on one side and asked for their frank opinions of the maquis personnel they had been training. Both were enthusiastic. "They are a real tough bunch, most of them are better marksmen than I am," said Vincent, and they all very quickly master the Bren and Sten guns but they are not so comfortable with grenades and road mines. We will finish training this lot next week and then there's just one more group to be trained unless more turn up." said Sebastian. "Ever since the Italians declared war on Germany we have seen new faces every week, mostly Italians, but the best, their camaraderie is also such a strong influence on their determination to succeed." added Vincent. How are re the Mouniers feeding them all?" I asked Vincent. "With some difficulty," he replied, "but they have a new voluntary quota system with lots of other farmers in this region and nobody goes hungry. Madame Mounier has help come in each day from other wives and the food is much better than field rations"

The Police driver had spent his time watching the training. He was very enthusiastic and spoke almost continuously about it during the drive back to Saint Flour. "I've seen shooting today far better than anything I've seen on police training courses." he said. He also liked the camaraderie he had seen. "They could do an awful lot of damage in an ambush situation." he added. I pointed out to him that they were likely to be attacking SS troops. He went silent. "Then the best plan would be to attack hard until the Germans were organised and then disappear into the hillside and attack again at a different location." He didn't convince me

Hector succeeded, very quickly, in getting the plates for Stephan's trucks. In fact he got two sets for each vehicle. You never know when you need a change of identity, was his comment. He would not say how he did it, but. Stephan was very happy with the result

My reply to London regarding Benjamin stated that the only possibility to receive him was at Saint Laurent de Veyres, with its map co-ordinates and accepting 8th May with a fallback on 9th if needed. I stressed the need for this location as a result of increasing German activity at night in the region. I asked for details of then training he would be giving to the resistance to avoid duplication of effort as I had recently witnessed training sessions already in progress, adding that both Victor and Sebastian had also witnessed maquis training and spoke highly of their efficiency

Raymond reported he had now deployed all his explosive charges ready to add the detonators and timers at short notice. He submitted a revised plan of action based on an assumption that the Germans succeeded in preserving the Millau bridge from Mathilde's planned attack. He had studied the reports from Francois Peillon of how the Germans were guarding the Rhone bridges and anticipating they would do the same in Millau thus reducing the chance of Mathilde blowing the bridge to almost impossible.

He therefore now proposed to allow troop movements over the Millau bridge and to travel some distance on the Auvergne roads and then to close the roads both in front of them and behind them. Thus whatever they decided to do they would have to dig their way out. thus causing them to lose time which was the real intention of the exercise. He was also going to try and split them into smaller groups by blocking the road and railway in the middle of their columns if they moved in that manner

Opinions were very divided as to whether the Army group H would try to move as one group or as several smaller groups reassembling nearer the battlefield. We had to cover both possibilities

There was increased uneasiness among the German troops in all areas. Night patrols increased as did spot checks on all transport.   The other factor that was increasing was German desertions. Our effective communications enabled us to exchange information on this subject. It was especially bad in Francios Peillon's Le Puy area and attributed to a very demanding senior officer who clamped down on all personnel sleeping out. Mathilde's area was the only one not to report an increase. She must have frightened them all off

The deserters were a nuisance. Nobody trusted them. Where there had been a relationship with a French woman, they dare not return. Nobody wanted them

Benjamin arrived on time but not on target. He appeared to be dropped from too high an altitude and there was a fair north-west wind that night. We guessed where we would find him but it took time and there was light in the sky when we did. Nobody had thought to tell us that three containers were to arrive with him. So we had a rush job to find a hidey-hole for his special mines he had brought for dealing with the Das Reich armour

On these fine early summer mornings the Storch spotter planes were up early to try and catch anyone breaking the morning curfew. They seemed to know something had happened last night and we frequently had to dive for cover. I don't think they saw us, and they gave up after about an hour

Having been up all night followed by some early morning exercise all our people were tired and barely refreshed by a large breakfast at the Mounier farm

Benjamin on the other hand must have store slept for some nights and he wanted to get on with the job. He didn't get much attention. I had to stay over another night and hope I would not be missed from Saint Flour. Most of the next night had to be spent recovering those special mines from their hidey-holes. and getting them back to Saint Laurent de Veyres.

Getting Simon and Patrice to Saint Laurent de Veyres was first priority when I got back to Saint Flour. Alexis was sensing the build up to the invasion and readily placed a police van and driver at my disposal. Off went Simon and Patrice

Raymond was missing from his usual haunts but I knew he was very much engaged with his revised plans to deal with the Hitler Brigade if they decided to move North via the Auvergne

Our communication centre was getting overwhelmed with messages Mathilde was concerned that she had heard nothing from Hector for many days, London wanted to know if Benjamin had arrived safely Regis Armengaud from Tulle reporting all bridges on main highway National twenty now guarded and advising similar news from his neighbours to the North and South. Francois Peillon had lost a number of containers on his last supply drop and, "had we ammunition to spare?"

London asking again for confirmation of all information about German troop locations and movements. But we still had no news from London, as promised, of two week's warning of likely invasion date

Chapter 43

German Unrest

Stephan arrived late in the evening having risked the curfew. He had just received news that the invasion was to be in the North of France at a number of locations between Le Havre and Cherbourg but no date had been fixed because of disagreements between some senior officers. He also brought news of the test firings of Benjamin's new mines. "They are many times more powerful than our other mines but much more difficult to conceal. Unfortunately the noise they make attracts attention and questions are being asked about our new weapons." he said, "I think we will have to stop the testing because of the attention we are getting from the German spotter planes"

"What does Benjamin have to say about it?! I asked. "He says he needs more blasts to complete the training of enough of us to be effective against such opposition as the Das Reich division." Dad was sitting in on this conversation "How long will it take Benjamin to complete the training?" he asked. "just a day," replied Stephan. "Then why don't you wait until the invasion and finish the training on the first day of the invasion, a few extra bangs then are not likely to attract so much attention and I guess the spotter planes will be otherwise engaged"

"Benjamin has been asking about another agent dropped in on the same night as him near Clermont Ferrand to do a similar job as himself with the local organisation, "said Stephan, "do you know about this man?" "No." I replied, "but Pascal is responsible for that region and he reports to De Gaulle's office in London"

"This man has a code name of Cardozo and is supposed to be working with the maquis in Clermont," said Stephan. "I am in regular contact with Pascal and I can enquire but I understood that the maquis in that area is made up almost entirely of men from the communist trade unions and as such I believe Pascal is not supposed to work with them"

The long awaited message arrived at last, immediately recognised by it's special code reference, only I could decode it. That is where our communication centre was a weakness. It was immediately recognised as something very special and secret and of course everybody wanted to know what it contained. In view of the timing combined with other indications only its length was deceptive. "Surely it doesn't take a message that long to say when the invasion will start." That was Dad's remark when he saw the coded text. Because I was not experienced with that particular code, decoding was a lengthy process

It was a complicated message and needed careful reading several times to recognise all the implications. It detailed a number of personal messages to be broadcast by the BBC French service with details of the action we had to take on hearing each message. There was an absolute requirement to listen to the BBC French service at the times detailed to see if any of your particular messages were included, in which case you were to take the actions indicated by this message. And just case that was not enough, 'Please confirm your completion of instructions at each stage

I immediately had to involve many people in order to carry out the instructions. The first priority was to get a second listening post with the special aerials to beat the German jamming in case our single receiver was out of action for any reason. I sent a request to Cezaire for a repeat of the job he had done for Angelique. I called all my men plus Stephan to a meeting at Jean Chavent's farm for two days hence with lookouts to cover all the approaches Cezaire replied to my request but he could not help for at least ten days because he had other priorities

Excitement was running high on that Monday morning at the Barrat farm

Stephan was early and had posted all the lookouts before I arrived. As everybody came in it was the same question Jean Chavent was posted up on the roof from where he could see all of the lookouts and alert us if any danger was signalled by the lookouts

"Before we get down to business," I remarked, "to answer the question you have all asked in one form or another, we have to assume this is the start." We rapidly agreed that the first priority was a second listening post for the BBC French service. We knew we had to wait at least ten days before Cezaire could help us and during that time we had to have a second person located at Vibresac to support Angelique. "That person will have to make sure she does not include any of the messages in her news precis." I said very firmly. "It appears Major Kempf is an avid reader of the precis whenever he gets hold of a copy." "I could

329

move from la Cham to Vibresac," volunteered Simon, "Good," I said, "please do so today and you may explain to Angelique why. If you pick up one of the messages you should telephone me first and then as many of those here as you can find. All you need to say is to repeat the message itself and nothing else."

"Next point has to be the location of the second listening post Victor will you see if you can persuade Fernand to accept Cezaire's help in establishing our second post and be the ears yourself?" "I'm sure he'll cooperate and I'll follow the same procedure as Simon"

"Next, Sebastian, how far are you with the distribution of supplies to the various groups?" I asked. "We've completed all of the movements to our regular customers last week, but I'm getting new requests almost every day from new groups. I check them out as well as I can before they get anything, and there are probably four lots outstanding today, but it changes every day." "Good," I replied, "But don't be overgenerous, we should not expect further supplies in the near future"

"Raymond, you are going to be very busy at short notice when the action plan for the roads and railways has to start. Is Pierre now capable of dealing with the communications side?" "Not really," he replied, "and I don't think he ever will be, but one of the 'wives' up there has learnt reasonable English from listening to the BBC and she is now perfectly capable on the Morse key. She has in fact been handling over half the message traffic for the past two months. without any problems whatever." "But can she work twenty-four hours a day? I asked. "because my instinct is telling me that we are likely to get messages on the emergency frequencies at any time of the day or night when the invasion starts." "We have set up an alarm system that everyone understands when it flashes Anne is to be told at once so she can go to the Morse room. She has a bell in her bedroom for the same reason. So far this system has worked well, "Raymond explained."Have you had many messages on the emergency frequencies,?" I asked, "because they should hardly have been used up till now?" "Mathilde is the usual one who uses them, she obviously thinks every need of hers is an emergency." "I'll try and stop her from doing that," I said. "but she'll probably expect to be thanked for testing the system."   Typical Mathilde again!

Mathilde's next message on the emergency frequency was to tell me that the guards on the vital bridge over the Tarn I Millau had been quadrupled, now eight at each side of the bridge with full searches being carried out at all times. She concluded by saying that she could not guarantee to blow the bridge on demand under such conditions. A house almost adjacent to the bridge had been requisitioned by the local German commander for reserve guards, who were standing down, but available in any emergency. This was duly reported to London with the suggestion that this was an indication of a potential German attempt to pass troops Northwards through the Auvergne. London agreed with our suggestion and confirmed that similar action had been advised by Francois Peillon regarding the bridges over the Lot at Mende

Then Hector reported further infantry units apparently from the Russian front arriving in the Herault area but not appearing to be any part of army group H. he was seeking further information. This was the last report from Hector, his fate is not known. Troops assembled in Herault have only two possible routes Northwards, up the Rhone valley, already heavily guarded, or via Mende and Le Puy, now also guarded. I gave instructions to Raymond to liaise with Francois over his planned rock falls and to have details of those caused by the Le Puy group

Army group H was now in the area between Albi and Castres South of the Tarn and heavily guarding the Tarn bridges at Albi and Gaillac. Mathilde reported that their behaviour towards the local French was typically German but correct, provided they got their own way!

The curfew was strictly enforced resulting in curtailment of resistance activity in the towns

There was a sudden increase in air activity over France both night and day. Official reports of this activity by the French were evasive. When you listened to the BBC French service the targets being attacked led one to the conclusion that the invasion was imminent. We still had no news from London regarding our personal messages requiring us to act

Piecing together the various reports we received was difficult. We could understand the concerted attacks on the roads and railways through the Rhone-Saone valley and attacks on the larger cities. Attacks on Marseille and Toulon by planes from the South did not make sense if the invasion was to be from the North, or was this just a 'ruse de guerre'? However we interpreted the facts, all of the potential groups that had been restraining their more hot headed members, now began their planned actions against factories working for the Germans, and even outright attacks against smaller and isolated German depots

These attacks brought reprisals from the Germans. The new resistance groups were generally not maquis but groups acting under the umbrella of the French Forces of the Interior (the FFI). The technique of these FFI groups was to attack fast and hard and withdraw rapidly. Thus few members were ever captured and the vengeance of the Germans was applied to the local population who were accused of harbouring the FFI

The French news service ignored the resistance activity and only minor mention of the incidents was included in the BBC French service. Angelique was being given local reports of the retribution meted out by the Gestapo and SS troops. She therefore added a few sentences to her precis reporting the actions of the Germans in nearby towns

It was not long before the reports of the atrocities came to the attention of Major Kempf. His response was a leaflet circulated throughout the town absolutely denying such actions would be taken by the occupying Germans. He tried to get the bus drivers to distribute the leaflets more widely. They took his leaflets and simply threw them out of the bus when they had left the town. "Well isn't that what he wanted." one of them was heard to remark

The situation became more serious very quickly. A German SS General based in Tulle announced that for every German soldier wounded by the resistance, three maquis or their accomplices would be hung; and for every German soldier assassinated by the resistance, ten maquis or their accomplices would be hung. This announcement was part of a leaflet he had printed blaming the communist inspired maquis for all the terror aided by the police and gendarmerie.   Copies of this leaflet were soon in our hands via the bus service and were prominently displayed on all Church notice boards throughout the town

The information was immediately passed to London. We broke the rules and quoted the text of the leaflet without coding, as our codes were not designed to handle the French language. London was slow to respond. Have you actually seen this leaflet? A question directed to me personally. Yes, I replied, we have copies on every Church notice board in Saint Flour. So far no reaction from local Germans

I added that resistance activity was at an all time high with many new groups emerging, most of them communist trade union led. But no real links to the FFI in this region

Stephan saw copies of these messages some days later. "It appears to me," he said, "that if we kill any Germans it is the French civilians who will suffer because none of my men are going to volunteer to be hung and I am sure we will not fight in such a way as to be captured except in really extreme circumstances"

On my return to Saint Flour I called on Councillors Leman and Dechaux to enlist their support in pressing the Maire to meet Major Kempf and finding out if he had any specific instructions regarding casualties to his men caused by resistance forces. Both were disturbed by the threat of the German commander at Tulle and readily agreed

In all five members of the town council accompanied the Maire to meet Major Kempf. "I suppose it is the imminent invasion of France by the Allied forces that brings you here?" said Major Kempf as soon as the meeting started. "It is more the consequences of the invasion and in anticipation of greatly increased resistance activity when the invasion starts," said the Maire, "and we would like to reach an understanding with you regarding what might happen in this sub-prefecture of Saint Flour. We cannot believe that there will be any violent attacks on any installations in the town. but the resistance now unified under the FFI by General de Gaulle have a duty to act in support of the liberation of France"

"The German High Command do not recognise the existence of the FFI and thus any action in their name will be treated as a direct attack on the sovereignty of the German Reich. Consequently those persons involved in such attacks will be treated in accordance with German Law"

"Have you seen the leaflet issued by the German General commanding your forces in Tulle?" asked the Maire, "Yes," replied Kempf, "Does German Law allow such retribution against civilians for casualties caused by insurgent militia? "asked the Maire. "In the case of uprisings such as I have been informed about in the neighbouring department of Correze, I believe the German commander will have declared a state of emergency under which he has absolute authority to take whatever actions are necessary to restore order.""Would you take such actions in this area?" asked the Maire. "I understand the German commander in Tulle is an SS General. The SS are more ruthless in their actions than the Wehrmacht commanders and as you have rightly pointed out parallel actions in Saint Flour to those in Tulle are not foreseeable. I can say no more in this matter"

In everybody's mind this dilemma had to be the main topic for the next Monday club meeting Stephan took a chance and evaded the curfew guards to be present. I had also asked Jean Chavent and Fernand Mounier to be present to represent the hillmen who were the main group of the non-maquis resistance forces in our area. Both arrived in the early evening and were staying overnight at the Terminus

The meeting started with the report of the two town councillors. After the Maire and councillors had returned to the Mairie they convened an emergency meeting of the whole council and it was the feelings of the whole council that were expressed by Councillors Leman and Dechaux. Saint Flour wanted to be rid of the German occupiers as soon as possible. Saint Flour was not a strategically important place for either side and resistance activity should be less intense for that reason. The real reason that we had such a large number of German troops present was simply because there was a suitable barracks for them to occupy

Stephan proposed, "Suppose we say to Kempf, keep your men in Saint Flour town and we will not take any action against them." "Can he do that?" asked Alexis, "he has to obey orders from his superiors." "We could cause plenty of unrest in the town such that he needs all his men to keep order without the use of violence," said Dad. "How long do we think it will be after the invasion before

Saint Flour is liberated?" asked Raymond. Too many questions with no answers was the conclusion

"When the Allies land in Normandy," said Stephan, "they will try to consolidate their bridgeheads into one large conclave in which they can accumulate sufficient manpower and armaments to support a drive on Paris as a first major objective." "How do you know that?" interjected councillor Leman

"Listen to Stephan carefully," I interjected, "he has already correctly predicted the US landings in North Africa, the invasion of Sicily and the Italian collapse. Either his information sources are better than ours or his knowledge of strategy surpasses our own." Many nods of agreement

Stephan continued, "While the drive on Paris takes place there will be other important objectives, capturing Le Havre and Cherbourg must be high on the Allies priority list. A drive to the South will have a much lower priority or perhaps none at all. If the Allies either land in the South or enter France from Italy the possibility of our part of France being cut off is very real. By then Germany would be fighting on four fronts. I see our most pressing problem as being this, German army group H and where they are going to try to enter the battle. My first priority is to make life as difficult as possible for them to enter the battle area of the North. Quite clearly we cannot stop them completely but they are such a powerful force that even some days of delay could influence the outcome of the initial landings in Normandy." Pausing to collect his thoughts, he continued,

"Even after they have passed through our area they have to cross the Loire and only some bridges are strong enough. I hear the RAF has been paying a lot of attention to those bridges but with little success so far"

"We are rather getting away from the purpose of this meeting," said councillor Dechaux, "we are concerned with Saint Flour." This remark brought the meeting to a silence. Mum didn't often say anything at these meetings but now she spoke quietly and effectively."It seems to me that if we could cause just enough unrest in the town and surrounding area to keep our local German troops fully occupied they could not be deployed elsewhere and provided we don't go so far as to necessitate Major Kempf having to call in other forces we might just be ignored by those forces." The two councillors clearly liked this idea and supported her

Late as it was by this time we got down to the detail of what we should do. After Raymond had fired the initial rock falls to close the selected roads and railways only a few further firings would be needed to keep the through routes closed if any clearances of the initial blockages were achieved. Just sufficient resistance men were to be left behind to do this. The rumour machine would let it be known that those who had fired the first rock falls had left the area

Stephan and the maquis supported by the main force of resistance men would be ready to move against army group H as soon as they made a move.

We would increase the number of copies of the BBC French news so that copies could be seen everywhere in the area. Removing these would occupy a number of Germans. Alexis volunteered his police agents to post these precis after dark working in groups so the Germans could not catch them red handed. During the daytime groups of townspeople would taunt the Germans in the streets, perhaps an occasional egg might be thrown. Tyres would be punctured on any unattended vehicles, Nails scattered at the entrance to the barracks with the same intention. Absolute refusal to supply any thing at all to any attempts to collect the Quota. It was likely that supplies to the Germans from Aurillac would not be able to get through so the shopkeepers would refuse to sell anything to the Germans except medical supplies. Similarly bars and restaurants would refuse to serve them "How long are we going to go on with this?" asked councillor Leman to all of us in general." Alexis proposed, "Let's start slowly and progressively increase the pressure as we see the allies succeeding. It's likely to be some months." General agreement. "We are fortunate in being a self sufficient area as far as food is concerned," said Dad, "all we lack will be the variety"

Chapter 44

Nearly Ready

I sent a brief summary of our intentions to all the surrounding areas in case our ideas were of use to them. Pascal replied promptly saying our approach would probably be successful in country areas. He also finally answered about Cardozo, who arrived unknown to Pascal, and was received by the communist resistance and was working with them on plans to take control of the major industrial plants in his area to prevent the Germans from destroying them as they withdrew. So far he had not met Cardozo and the communist resistance was acting entirely independently

I made a point of going out to Saint Laurent de Veyres and confronted Stephan with the independence of the communists around Clermont. "The problem is," he said, "they are under orders from communist headquarters to secure as much control as they can of the industrial sites around Clermont so that the Germans cannot sabotage them as they withdraw, and they do not trust the De Gaulle resistance groups to protect the industry as well as they can," he continued."Pascal's company is an exception, but they do not trust him either

Remember over eighty percent of the employees in most of the companies around Clermont are members of the French communist party and they have been well supplied, thanks to your efforts, with the means to protect the factories from the Germans. Pascal has only released small lots of his stock pile to them"

At last the long awaited personal messages started to come through. None of the first batches involved action by us but the listeners at Saint Jacques des Blats had to follow every broadcast in case our expected messages were included. This was when we really benefited from the efforts of Cezaire in positioning the aerials, the German jamming hardly affected our reception

The increase in the number of personal massages alerted the Germans During the times of the transmissions we saw many Germans out on the streets listening at doors and windows of houses suspected of resistance involvement

At daybreak every morning the Storch spotter planes were up looking for any unusual activity and this continued until nightfall. With the long summer days, sixteen hours of daylight, and more spotter planes operating, we had a problem. Although Raymond had prepared his plans very thoroughly he could not carry out all he had to do in the eight darker hours of each day

"We could set up some firing points to discourage them" said Victor, "I'm thinking about three or four of our marksmen each firing about twenty shots rapid at them and then going to ground." "Some of the Storch planes have a machine gun at the observer's cockpit," interjected Patrice. "Yes I know," said Victor, "but even if they accurately spot where the firing is coming from it would take them some minutes to get into the right position to return the fire"

There was only one solution to this matter and that was to try it. "Can you organise a trial for later today or first thing tomorrow? I asked, "and I'd like to be one of the guns please"

Victor came back to me later in the day. "We've noticed that one of the first places the planes inspect every morning are the dams on the Truyere, we are going to have two firing points, one on each side of the Grandval dam up on the hills again and see if it works better than last time, "Good," I replied, "I'll be one of the guns on the north side." "You'll have to be there by three-thirty a.m. said Victor, and what weapon do you want?" "Who is going to be with me?" "Simon and Patrice." replied Victor. "Then I'll join them at la Cham this evening, and I'll get Alexis to use a police van to move us all to Grandval by three a.m"

The dam at Grandval is the highest dam on the river containing a lake over twenty kilometres long and terminating at the dam between two spurs of high land so that each firing point was about three hundred meters above the dam and less than one kilometre apart. There was a small German garrison in the village of Grandval providing guards for the dam in conjunction with the Gendarmerie.

The orientation of the dam is almost North-South and the planes flew West to East when making their inspection

We were dropped at the roadside in darkness and had to climb steep paths to get to the firing point as the first signs of daylight appeared. We exchanged torch signals with the southerly firing point confirming our arrival. We heard the noise of the Storch plane almost as the sun rose approaching the dam from the East and at about two hundred metres above us. The observer must have been looking in our direction. He got off a short burst from his machine gun just as we finished firing and then had to rapidly swing through one hundred

337

and eighty degrees when he received fire from the southerly firing point. We cached our weapons as arranged and set off on our withdrawal route all through pine forests to a road where we could rendezvous safely with our police van

We all thought we had hit the plane with some of our shots but not in a place to cause any serious damage. The plane climbed and left the area Later we heard similar remarks from the guns at the southerly fire point. What was really interesting was that within twenty minutes three other Storch planes were in the air over the dam and lake but at much higher altitude out of range of any weapons we had. and they continued to scan the area for over two hours

Luckily both the firing groups were withdrawing through forested areas and could not be seen from the air. The guards on the dam itself closed ranks and the roadway by the dam. Both of the firing parties reached their rendezvous points without further incident

All involved assembled at la Cham later that evening. What had we learnt? All six guns thought they had hit the plane at least once. The rapid response from the observer/gunner on the northerly firing position was considered fortuitous as he did not fire at the southerly firing point and two of the guns from the southerly firing point said they saw him struggling to get his gun round

The rapid arrival of three other Storch planes was the first question dealt with. We concluded that the first must have had radio contact with the other Storch planes in the air at the time of our attack because there was not time for planes from their base at Clermont to have arrived. "I think the most important conclusion," said Raymond, "is that within some minutes of your attack all the Storch planes in the area had been directed to the site of the attack"

"The latest advice we have from Pascal." I interjected, "is that there are now eight Storch planes at their base, four in the air with four to replace them when they return for refuelling. That sounds just like a Germanic approach to a job like this." "I agree." said Raymond, "and we can use that tactic to our advantage, are working"

"We are planning to work in the Causse de Severac tomorrow afternoon, "said Simon, "let's try the idea then." "According to Pascal the second flight usually takes off about eleven o'clock which means they would be overhead Saint Flour about eleven forty-five," I said. "And if we have our best marksmen all round the ramparts we should get his attention," said Alexis. The discussion was getting frivolous

"We need to know where the afternoon flight start their observations," said Raymond, returning to the problem of tomorrow. Sylvie Mathis had come into the room to replenish the supplies of Coffee, "They pass over here every day soon after noon," she said, "they come from the direction of Saint Flour and turn

338

towards Moissac, they always come down low to look at the landing strip." Maurice Blin, one of Alexis' sergeants, had special responsibilities for the main roads in the area, "I've often seen them flying down the national nine as I go home for lunch, your best plan is to have all the police force look out for them all day long and record every sighting, place and time, and if possible the identification marks of the plane." Alexis agreed to do this for the next four days

It really only took one day. Each of the planes operating from Clermont had a regular circuit and a number of points for special low level inspection, and each of the three flights per day followed the same routine. We never used the same firing points or the same number of marksmen and we could rely on bringing all of the four airborne planes to an agreed area at an agreed time so that Raymond and his team could complete their priming of the explosive charges undisturbed and unobserved, at least by the Germans

The number of personal messages on the BBC French service increased still further but so far none of them had been on our list. There was a distinct chance that our listening lady at Saint Jacques des Blats was suffering from listening fatigue because there was nothing for her to report. Fortunately Angelique able to be a second pair of ears and by a strange coincidence it was only two days before our messages were included Raymond and his teams were in instant action completing the priming of all the charges for the roads and railways. By the first of June he was ready. Two routes out of the high Auvergne to the West had been left open to allow for the resistance to move to the National twenty highway as soon as any Northwards movement of the German army group H was reported. Stephan recovered the three German army trucks taken from Major Kempf's command. The appearance had been changed somewhat and the new plates identifying them as belonging to army group H

He ensured their free movement even though more control points were in operation. He had also negotiated a deal with Christian de Boni to requisition four buses as soon as he needed them to move men to the West Regular times were established for the resistance groups in neighbouring areas to exchange messages via the communication centre at the Gibory farm

Victor and Sebastian took over command of the resistance volunteers other than Stephan's maquis and had established an excellent rapport with him during the training period

The troops under Major Kempf's command were more on the alert than ever before. Usually there were at least sixty moving about in Saint Flour night and day watching all key points, listening in to groups of local people conversing, attending all Church services and visiting even the meanest of bars. They arrested several persons for listening to the BBC French Service who were held prisoner in the barracks pending trial

Pascal advised us that another flight of four Storch had arrived at the Clermont aerodrome and the area being patrolled from the air had increased to cover all of the departments of Aveyron, Cantal, Correze, Haute Loire, Lot and Puy de Dome. There was also a rumour that they could call up a squadron of Messerschmitts to intervene if needed, but he could not name the base from which the fighter planes would come. This was important information and reinforced the idea that our attacks on any German troops would have to be short, swift and followed by a quick withdrawal, as well as being effective

Use of fighter planes against resistance groups had not been considered a likely course of action

This information was passed to London. The reply was comforting. 'The RAF and the USAF will take control of all the airspace over France and any other countries where our ground forces are involved. Any airborne enemy aircraft will be destroyed

The first alert message for all resistance forces was followed only two days later by that requiring Raymond to block the through road routes. We coupled the final training for the mines with his activity although the sounds of the two types of explosion were quite distinctive

The plan to divert the Storch spotter planes worked well for a day or two after which the Germans realised they were being played with. Raymond had two groups working and by using the first and last hours of the day, when the light was too difficult for the Storch planes to spot activity in areas being prepared for road blocks. Before the road block plans could be completed the message to block the railways came through. As soon as the first rail blocks were reported German occupation forces were alerted to start clearing the lines and patrols were introduces along the major routes. All tunnels and bridges were guarded. We took this as confirmation of the German intention to use the railways for troop movements and so reported to London. The reply was terse and to the point, 'essential you complete your plans on time

But what time. It was already apparent that the timetable originally proposed was not being followed. We had to assume that the invasion was imminent

Messages exchanged with our neighbouring groups confirmed they were making similar assumptions

The limited weather forecasts we could receive indicated that conditions in the South were good for an invasion whereas conditions in the English channel were unreliable and expected to continue so for many days. The consensus opinion was that the first landings at least were to be in the North

There was no way the Germans could win the competition to keep the railway lines open. Raymond reported that it took a squad of soldiers up to six hours to clear an average rock fall, whereas he could cause a replacement some kilometres away in about an hour because there was so much of the track laid in cuttings

However the line patrols were becoming a nuisance. They appeared to have radio contact with the Storch planes who were now concentrating their efforts on the railway lines

No attempts were made by the Germans to clear rock falls on the roads. Thus all our efforts were put into closing rail tracks. Victor and his group were working on the main North-South Line which roughly followed the route of the National nine highway. This was by far the most important rail route in our area and the Germans knew that too. The Storch planes regularly patrolled the line whenever they were in the vicinity. On a Sunday morning three points had been targeted for blocking, all close to their depot at Saint Laurent de Veyres. They set out before dawn intending to be ready to blow all three falls at daybreak

They heard aircraft but never saw them and continued their work. Diversionary activity was being done North of Massiac Just before sunrise a flight of four Messerschmitt machine gunned the diversionary site making three passes and wounding two of our men. They then followed the line of the railway southwards and attacked the groups round Saint Chely d'Apcher

Fortunately they had been heard approaching and all our men took cover. Again they made three passes in line astern so the area was heavily sprayed with machine gun fire and again we took casualties, fortunately only slight. A lucky shot triggered one of the charges already laid and primed and neatly finished that blockage for us

German troops were also alerted to this operation and arrived within minutes of the planes departure and captured one of the wounded at Massiac. The remainder of the day was quiet and no further air activity was noticed. Victor personally returned to Saint Chely d'Apcher and finished the other two blockages in spite of the presence of German troops The remaining seriously wounded man from Massiac was treated at a Mauriac surgery and carried up to The Gibory farm to recuperate

The man captured at Massiac was brought back to the barracks in Saint Flour and imprisoned. His wounds were treated and he was held pending SS interrogation. Subsequent events ensured this did not happen

That Sunday night there was intense air activity all over France. Francois Peillon confirmed that the Rhone-Saone valley roads and railways had been hit very hard and that daylight attacks were continuing with planes coming from both North and South, as he was making this transmission. In Saint Flour we could only hear the planes and see the vapour trails criss-crossing the sky

341

All of this activity was clearly the prelude of some action. The French radio news on Monday morning made only vague references to the high level of enemy air activity; and the BBC French service did not mention it at all. After departure of the early buses who hoped to get through to Clermont

German troops were active throughout the town. The situation felt tense

Storch spotter planes flew over Saint Flour at least every hour and Raymond reported that attempts to divert them didn't work any more. Victor and Sebastian were using the noise of Raymond's rock falls to mask the last training exercises with the special anti-tank mines. Early in the afternoon Alain Brenot from Brive la Galliard reported air attacks thought to be aimed at bridges throughout his area but so far not one had been hit. "The planes fly too high, I don't think they could even see the bridges, the Germans would use dive bombers for that sort of attack." Again the sky was full of vapour trails

Tuesday morning started early. Before six Angelique was on the telephone with the news that the BBC had just announced that Allied forces had landed at a number of points on the Normandy coast. I asked her to also call Bernice Rodot so that she could pass the news to our communication centre for onward transmission to all other areas

Chapter 45

Murder on the Streets

So the long awaited invasion of France had started. It didn't feel any different. The Germans were still there. They did not seem to know about the invasion until around lunchtime, when Major Kempf sent for the Maire and informed him that the 'Allies had tried to land troops at several points on the Northern coast of France but they were steadily being pushed back into the sea.

By this time a number of other reports from the BBC had been heard by Saint Flour residents who had seen the notices put on the buses by Angelique, 'Allies land in Normandy.' Whenever a bus stopped any nearby German troops would immediately remove the notices but that was really too late

As soon as the communication centre knew of the landings they listened continuously to the BBC French service so they could update any of their contacts who wished to hear the real latest situation

The long evenings of early summer caused many of the local people to congregate together at street corners and in bars to discuss the latest news in spite of the curfew. German troops enforcing the curfew had little success, as fast as they broke up one group another formed at the next corner, or just round it

On Wednesday Major Kempf issued a new notice. "The changing situation of the war entitles the officer in charge of a town to take emergency powers in order to keep public order. Such powers include arrest and detention of any person who does not comply with an order of a German soldier

"Within an hour or two over thirty Saint Flour citizens were imprisoned within the German Barracks. At curfew time in the evening every other Saint Flour citizen was out of doors talking to others in large groups defying the German troops unfortunate enough to be on duty. Some of the outlying villagers came in to support the town dwellers and the situation was stalemate

The Maire went to see Major Kempf the next day and pointed out to him the unreasonableness of the situation. After several hours of talks the thirty or so citizens of Saint Flour were released with a caution and the troops told not to arrest anybody unless a crime was involved. I missed all the fun of that day as I had left with the maquis and resistance groups to move towards the National highway twenty We imposed yet again on the generosity of Fernand Mounier and his friends

In total it was quite a large assembly. The maquis outnumbered the resistance by more than two to one. All of the heavy munitions had already left on the three German trucks. And were hidden away in a forested area close to the places where the attacks were planned on any troops moving North. They were passed through control points without even stopping with the drivers in German uniforms and their plates identifying them as part of army group H

It was not so easy for the maquis and resistance men travelling in commandeered buses. Almost all of the bridges over the Truyere were either over the dams or bridges very close to the dams and well guarded by better trained Germans than the occupation troops. We had selected two bridges which seemed the most isolated and most distant from the dams

Our cover story if we were stopped was that we were volunteers who had agreed to assist the bus company in keeping their routes open after the blockages caused by the resistance. To support this, the baggage space was well filled with spades and barrows which nicely concealed our rations for the journey, after which we expected to live off the land

The latest report from Mathilde was that the Hitler brigade and the Das Reich armoured division were in a high state of readiness but no signs of any movement yet. One coach went ahead to test out the planned crossing point over the Truyere. They passed the bridge without problems so the following two buses went the same way.   Before nightfall we were joined up with the trucks of munitions, the maquis and resistance groups from Brive la Gaillard and Tulle

The point for the first blockage and attack on army group H was chosen by the Brive la Gaillard and Souillac resistance groups. Stephan, Raymond, Victor and myself went to look at the point. It was indeed well chosen. The charges for the rockfalls were already in position and guarded. If the National highway twenty was blocked at this point the only alternatives for South to North movements were via narrow departmental roads with bridges of unknown strength

Victor said "Just one broken down vehicle will effectively close those roads. We'll mine both, to be ready for any attempt to use them." We returned to our base feeling satisfied with our plans

Within an hour news came that the army group H were moving towards the National twenty highway. Before we could take any action a second message told us units were passing through Caussade and leaving in the direction of Cahors

Raymond left at once with the necessary men to arm the rockfall explosives and mine the two minor by-pass roads. We had made contact with a local man near our base who was a regular listener to the BBC French service. The latest news from the Normandy landings indicated they were going well and being constantly reinforced. That was why army group H was moving North. The Cahors resistance group was mainly maquis but the local police were not sympathetic to resistance activity so they did not have as much freedom of action as other maquis groups. Neither did they have any geographically advantaged spot on the main road for a blockage. Thus they could only offer to harass the Germans while they were passing through. Thus we worked out that the first German units would reach our rockfall at dawn

Nobody had any sleep that night. We had established our base in the ruins of an old chateau with a forward base just a kilometre from the rockfall. Firing points were set up on each side of the main road with a plan that firing from one point would attract return fire which would be countered by fire from a completely different direction and so on. Any of the firing groups could withdraw if their position became untenable taking any casualties with them

As dawn lightened the sky we could see the full extent of the rockfall. I had hoped for a greater volume of debris to be on the road.   Raymond was also disappointed with the result and was booby trapping the debris with some of our less effective mines as a deterrent to those clearing the blockage. Some of the local population were concerned about the war coming to their villages. We could only assure them that this was not going to be a battleground but simply a delaying tactic. I'm not sure they understood

One small man took an exceptional interest in what was going on. He insisted on talking to Stephan, in English, saying his name was Monty, although I'm sure he was French. He did, however, have something important to say, "You've mined two of the diversion roads from the South but you've not mined the best one! This was just before the lookouts reported the first German units in sight. Monty pointed out the start of this road to Sebastian. It didn't look as though it went anywhere but Monty insisted it completely by-passed our rockfall and was less than two kilometres long. Sebastian and Raymond and a number of other men immediately took a supply of mines and with them to see what they could do in the short time remaining. This small road way was not shown on any of our maps. Fernand Mounier said that was often the case with 'C' category

345

roads which were the responsibility of the local commune, but this turned out to be a remarkably good 'C' road

Before the sun was up our lookouts sighted the first units of army group H on the National twenty highway. The Germans were clearly expecting trouble. The lead vehicles were a number of scout cars. Some were used to close off side roads feeding on to the National twenty and three were running ahead of the convoy checking the route. When the first of these rounded the bend at the top of the steep ascent of Crezelade and saw the rockfall it stopped and was clearly advising the column by radio of the blockage because our lookouts reported the convoy as stationary and deploying infantry to cover the armour

A second and third scout car arrived, one with an officer on board. Maps were produced and a rock by rock search of the cliffs on each side of the road was being made with field glasses

Raymond reported that no possibility of blocking the 'C' road existed and that he had mined the road but any blockage by disabled vehicles could be easily cleared. "We will need all of the maquis from the Western group to have any effect on an infantry supported opening of the road to the armour and only a few hours of delay could be achieved. I will try to cause a rockfall on the Southern slope of the Belvedere de Lanzac but no guarantee of success." If he could cause a rockfall at the Belverdere de Lanzac it would also effectively close the National twenty but there was no cover for any sniping activity on those clearing the rockfall

The Germans detached a scout car and it went immediately to the start of the 'C' road and disappeared into the side road. The Germans clearly had better maps than we had. Our lookouts reported mustering of infantry in the stationary convoy ready for some offensive action

An explosion from the direction of the 'C' road followed by a smattering of small arms fire we assumed to be the destruction of the scout car and its occupants. Numerous truckloads of infantry were reported moving north from the stationary convoy. An urgent message was sent to London giving the precise location of the stationary convoy and proposing an RAF attack

The start of the infantry movement towards our positions bolstered up with several light tanks coincided with the arrival of a Storch spotter plane from the South Whereas we had good cover from ground observers the terrain provided little cover from airborne observation. And withdrawal was perilous for the same reason

A fortunate coincidence provided a chance to move from the close vicinity of the rock falls. As the light tanks and infantry tanks passed through the Belverdere de Lanzac Sebastian's charges exploded. He must have used every bit of his explosives. And the result was clearly successful. There was also an immense cloud of dust which provided us with a chance to withdraw from our front line position along the crests of the cliffs into the more wooded lower land where there was some cover to be found

The Hitler SS Infantry brigade was moving up each side of the National twenty highway with the apparent objectives of protecting the road and dispersing any resistance close by the road. A second Storch spotter plane arrived from the North so we had two observers to hide from. It was not our objective to stand and fight the Hitler brigade. We needed to move further North where we had some further opportunities to delay army group H

It had been in our plan to blow the bridge over the Dordogne at Souillac which would have caused the Germans to make a huge diversion over poorer roads, but the Germans knew that too and the guarding of that bridge made any attempt impossible without huge causalities and only a minimal chance of any success

At least we knew that. Our communications were working well. When we knew the Souillac group could not destroy their objective we moved them north to work on our next target for delay, just South of Noailles

We managed to move our transport vehicles empty, the spotter planes ignored them. Having swooped low over two of them early in the day they seemed to assume they were part of army group H, which of course is what their markings said. Raymond and Sebastian lost contact with us after the destruction of the scout car and causing the rockfall at the Belverdere de Lanzac and their radio had been put out of action by a lucky shot from the Germans. Nevertheless they made it to the rendezvous point by dusk having used a ferry to cross the Dordogne. They had three casualties two of them serious. Our trucks set off immediately fully laden for Noailles and would make several journeys during the dark hours

Next matter was for Stephan, Raymond, Regis Armengaud, Alain Brenot and myself to decide on our next actions. Raymond reckoned the Germans would clear a way through to Souillac during the night. After crossing the Dordogne there was nothing to stop them unless we could delay them further at Noailles or just north of Brive la Gaillarde where Alain Brenot had charges ready laid at Donzenac. Unfortunately it was possible to by-pass any blockage at Donzenac going via Tulle on which route there was no further possibility of delaying army group H unless the first bridge in Tulle could be blown

Raymond and Alain Brenot left with the next trucks to organise all possible activity at Noailles. Sebastian and Victor went with Regis Armengaud to go on to Tulle where his resistance group were in reserve to explore the possibility of blowing that vital bridges North from Brive la Gaillarde and Tulle the responsibility for delay passed to another resistance group based at Oradour sur

Vayres. This group maintained a very independent attitude and both Regis Armengaud and Alain Brenot had problems in liaising with them. They claimed they had plans to close the National twenty highway at several unspecified places. "Tell us your best estimate of the time army group H will arrive at Uzerche." was all they ever really said to Alain and Regis

By two in the morning we were all assembled at Noailles and established our base in the caves nearby. The location was not as favourable as Souillac. The road was narrower but there was not such a large volume of rock available to bring down. Raymond had decided to destroy the road and bring down as much rock as possible. The Germans would have to clear enough of the rock to let the armour through and let the trucks either try to drive over the rubble or by-pass the blockage in some way

There were numerous possibilities, all very narrow country roads. We mined them as far as possible. The tortuous course of the road just south of Brive la Gaillarde was itself quite a problem for the armoured vehicles

Numerous supporters from Brive la Gaillarde were joining us. They were of the opinion that the armoured vehicles could only pass through the city by knocking down some of the buildings because the roads were so twisting and narrow. They claimed they had blocked the inner ring boulevard on both the East and West sides of the city with the local buses. They had not been able to blow the one bridge over the Correze because of the heavily armed guards of both the Germans and the Mlice

North of Brive la Gaillarde their blockage of the National twenty was said to be complete and would take days to clear a way through. There was only one possible way to by-pass the blockage and that was now also blocked and mined

Our charges all went off at about half past four in the morning and the results were disappointing. Sebastian and his team set to work to booby trap the fallen rocks as fast as they could. The German infantry were reported as passing through Souillac town at five o'clock and we could expect them by five thirty. As soon as the light was good enough Victor set up ambush points for the infantry trucks to cause some small delays and also alert everyone to their arrival.

Before we had set up our ambush points the Storch spotter planes had taken off. Today there were three of them scouting ahead of army group H. One persisted in low level inspections of the rock falls at Noailles despite intense small arms fire from the maquis and we did not seem to get a single hit. The other two Storch planes worked with the head of the German troops and we could make no safe interference with their steady progress. Before they reached Noailles the armour came to the head of the convoy, and to everyone's surprise they left the National 20 highway and took to the open country on both sides of the road.

We learnt later that they used a rail bridge on the eastern side of Brive la Gaillarde to cross the Correze and in Tulle there were so many bridges over that river, destroying them all was not possible especially in view of the strong presence of Germans, including SS in the town which was the home of the MAT, (Manufacture d'Armes de Tulle), working exclusively for the German war effort

North of the Correze the land was much hillier again and the same dispersion of armour and infantry carriers over the country roads was not practical. They now had the advantage of spotter planes surveying the route ahead of them. Thus they concentrated on use of the National road from Tulle to Uzerche and Limoges because the blockage of the National twenty a few kilometres north of the Correze which was really very effective and the Germans made no attempt to clear it

We suddenly felt isolated at Noailles. With the aid of their spotter planes the Germans had neatly and effectively negated our efforts at Noailles and Brive la Gaillarde. Our supporters from Tulle and Brive were concerned over what might be happening in their towns and left us, en masse to see what they could do to help their own people. There was time to catch up on the news from Normandy. It was now the third day of the invasion

All the BBC reports were enthusiastic about the progress and stressed that the second and third stages of the invasion were progressing well. There was no longer any doubt that this was the creation of the second front for which Stalin had been pleading, for so long. The communists of the resistance were delighted

Our little contribution to the delay of army group H's entry into the battle did not seem very great. The most optimistic assessment of the delay was only two days. Perhaps the Oradour-sur-Vayres group could achieve some further delay but the terrain in their area was not so favourable. Further North of Limoges there were no geographical features to delay army group H until the Loire and a choice of good roads all the way to the Normandy battlefield

Shortly before we were ready to leave urgent news arrived from Tulle that the Germans were planning a massacre of the towns folk in retribution for the delays and casualties we had caused them. Regis Armengaud stated that men of all ages were being taken by the SS for an examination of their papers. However he claimed" he knew that they intended to execute them as a reprisal for the delays and attacks on army group H. He put his safe house at our disposal

In view of the previous threats by the German commander in Tulle about executing civilians in retribution for German soldiers killed or injured, this news was a serious matter. In a rapid exchange of messages it was agreed that Stephan, Raymond and I would meet him at his safe house that night arriving just before curfew. Regis replied that we should meet him at the back entrance of the safe house so that we could use the secure entrance. He gave us very exact instructions about how to approach the area

Fortunately I remembered the way to the bus station from where Regis instructions started. We left our truck on the outskirts of the town with two guards. There were clear signs that there had been fighting in the streets as we entered the town. The open square where both the rail and bus stations were located was littered with debris and many of the houses were seriously damaged. Raymond was engaged in conversation with several elderly men trying to secure their houses for the night. It appeared that a squadron of heavy tanks had been attacked by the local maquis in the square as they stopped for some reason. The Germans simply got back into their tanks and fired with heavy machine guns at anybody who moved. Many were killed and injured and the damage to the houses was considerable. We were recognised as resistance and the locals pleaded with us not to provoke the Germans any further

There were few Germans left on the streets. They were trying to clear the roads of the debris so normal vehicles could operate. The main problem was the burnt out buses and those vehicles alone were enough to occupy them and we were not questioned at all

Regis was quite agitated when we met him because we were ten minutes late. "It's been a bad day for Tulle" he said, "there are scenes like this all over the town. It seems the communist resistance groups tried to get control of the MAT works, and the Germans diverted tanks into the town to counter their move"

I saw that we were not at quite the same house as I visited before. "This is our real safe house," he said to me. "The other one," he said, pointing to the mansion where I last met him, "is the German officer's bordello." We descended into the cellar of a small cottage at the bottom of the garden of the mansion. "Nobody ever comes here nowadays. The Germans are occupied with other matters in the evenings and all night. In the daytime the place is deserted, the locals avoid the place because of its use by the Germans and that suits us very well"

Alain Brenot followed us into the cellar. He had been watching to be sure we had not been followed. "Nothing to be concerned about," he said, as we gathered round the table

"Earlier today the SS with other German troops began calling on men at their homes and taking them into the MAT factory for an inspection of their papers, and they are still there," said Regis, and continued, "I have information from my contacts that these men are going to be murdered in retaliation for the casualties we have inflicted on army group H." "How many men are involved?" asked Stephan. "No reliable information yet," said Regis, "but well over a thousand." "Who is in command of the Germans?" asked Raymond. We are not

350

sure," said Alain, "but SS General Lammerding has been seen in Tulle and he would be senior to any other officer in this region"

"What do you think is the total number of Germans in Tulle at present asked Stephan. "Our normal complement of Germans is about one hundred and sixty," Regis replied, "but with the extra men from the Das Reich division and the Hitler Brigade probably over six hundred now." "There is no way we could or should attempt any interference with what the SS choose to do," I said, "any further casualties we inflict would only result in the murder of more civilians." Nods of agreement all round. "I was not expecting any intervention," said Regis, "what I do want is independent observers of what happens and immediate reports sent to London so that the BBC can broadcast the actions of the SS worldwide." "We can certainly do that," I assured him. "I will also send details to Moscow," said Stephan, "but by comparison with the massacres carried out in Russia it is unlikely that any serious attention will be paid to what happens here"

"Do we know what is happening to the North?" asked Raymond, "are the Oradour group in contact with the Germans yet?" "There is no information yet," replied Alain, "but they should be in contact by now." "What will happen as a result of any German casualties they cause?" asked Stephan, "my information is that the Oradour group are very aggressive and ruthless,"   I interjected. We seemed to have reached a dead end. "Is there a radio link here?" asked Raymond. "Yes, in the next cellar," replied Regis, "but we only use it in emergencies, we don't want the Germans to find this place." "I think this is an emergency," I said, "We are now three days out of date with the overall situation, let's send the shortest possible message asking Pierre Gibory to relay all radio traffic in and out since our last contact."   "Who's fastest on the key?" asked Stephan. Everybody looked at Alain. "I'll code the message in a private code so that Pierre knows it's is my request." I said. Alain was fast, he was only on the air for six minutes. "There's very little chance the Germans could locate us in six minutes," he said after he switched to receive. "Nevertheless we'll put a watch outside for the next half an hour," said Regis. He and Stephan disappeared into the night. I went outside briefly and could hear the continuous noise of heavy vehicles and occasional bursts of gunfire in the direction of Brive

We were busy for the next couple of hours with the incoming messages. Much of the content was either known or guessed at. Considering we were just a few days into to the largest military operation ever mounted the content of the messages was really trivial. Pierre clearly recognised this fact too, Angelique's news reports are far more interesting, he added, after sending all the requested traffic, Would you like me to send them to you? We declined his offer it would have taken much too long. Amongst the trivia were two private code messages for me. "What do you think they are?" asked Raymond, "I don't know," I replied, "and I can't decode them, I never carry those codes with me anywhere." I stuffed the messages into a pocket

Regis and Stephan returned having moved about very quietly outside and talked about all the German activity in the town. It seems as though many more Germans have arrived. Distant cheering had been heard, and Regis said there was now intermittent light artillery fire .as well as small arms. We all settled down for a few hours sleep but not much sleep was had by anyone that night. Although we were well below ground level the noise was almost continuous

One of Regis' men was hammering at the door soon after dawn. He brought news that the Germans led by SS officers were calling at the homes of employees of MAT in the rue Victor Hugo and taking the men into custody for a 'check on their papers.' The men were all being taken in to the MAT factory area. We were all puzzled by this action. Before any conclusion was reached there was a similar event in the next street to us when one of Regis' men was taken in a similar manner from his home in the rue Marbot. Madame Pierre who came at once to Regis for help told us that the Germans said, "There are terrorists everywhere"

Regis made a number of telephone calls. "It seems this is going on all over the town," he reported, hundreds of men are being arrested for a check on their papers and being taken into the MAT factory enclosure which is now sealed off by the SS. It also seems that the operation is being directed by the officers of the Das Reich division."

There was no way in which we could stop German activity in Tulle. Regis commented on the activity, "It is all done by the communists organised through their trade unions," he said, "They have drawn heavily on our supplies so they were prepared to act as they are now doing without any reference to us. or respect for the other inhabitants of Tulle," Stephan agreed, "There is no point in fighting an enemy when you are outnumbered by several hundreds to one"

We risked one more short transmission to the Gibory farm explaining our position. A reply told us that the Oradour resistance were heavily engaged with the tanks of the Das Reich division and had finally had some success with the new mines against even the main German battle tanks. This was good news and we wondered what action the Germans might in Tulle as a reprisal for that success

The day continued with ever increasing German activity. Regis was almost continually on the telephone with his contacts throughout the town. The numbers being taken in to the MAT enclosure increased steadily and some reports were as high as a thousand. Then the telephone service ceased

The schools had all been closed as soon as the news of the Allies landing in Normandy was announced. There was a fire causing a very dark column of smoke over the town which we later heard was the main girl's school for the town. A number of Regis' men collected around the safe house simply because they had nowhere else to go. Their families were in the cellars but they were not inclined to pass through the main roads for fear of the Germans acting in an unpredictable manner

We got a better sleep that night. And the streets were much quieter next morning. Regis and Alain arranged for their men to find out what was happening. It didn't take them long, and the news was so shocking that the first messenger was not believed

The German SS troops were said to be hanging men from the lamp posts in the main street. The regular German troops, were keeping the French population away from the corpses already hanging there dead. Whatever the risk, we had to see this for ourselves. As we neared the main street we separated as a group was more conspicuous and each one of us arrived at different points on the main street

I saw two bodies still struggling for life, I saw a woman being refused permission to recover the body of her, already dead, husband. "He will stay there to remind you!" was shouted repeatedly at her. Stephan saw an SS officer taking pictures with a Leica camera, of the corpses. Raymond, who was the nearest to the town centre, saw more prisoners being force marched towards already prepared ropes on lamp posts. I had to withdraw from the street to be violently sick at what I had seen

We regrouped at our rendezvous and made our way back to the safe house in a shocked silence at what we had witnessed

Chapter 46

Massacres

Our departure from Tulle became a matter of urgency. Our batteries were low and we must keep some power for real emergencies. It was too risky to try and find charging facilities in Tulle. I also considered it an emergency to distribute the news of the atrocities we had witnessed in Tulle. The similar atrocities we had heard about in Brive, which, because of the facts we knew of events in Tulle, we also had to believe

Although the main force of army group H had moved on North into another region, the resident SS in Tulle were encouraging all German personnel to act far more brutally than had been usual. Patrols were more numerous, more active, and more demanding. For us, being stopped by a patrol under these conditions would almost certainly have resulted in detention and worse. The fate of our waiting truck and guards was unknown

Regis decided to trust the few members of the town police who were sympathetic to FFI activities with the job of getting us to the truck, tracing our two guards, and getting the truck plus us out of Tulle. We all considered it of great importance to get the news of what had actually happened at Tulle and Brive known to all throughout France that the threats of retribution for killed and injured Germans had become reality in our region

Sergeant Roy was the senior policeman involved. He was known to Alexis Lescaut, who had once told me that if I had a problem in Tulle, he could be trusted. Regis fixed a meeting at the police headquarters which were only a few hundred metres from our safe house. He returned very quickly with an assurance of complete cooperation after mentioning we were friends of Alexis Lescaut

The plan was that six of his officers who had curfew passes would be outside the safe house at dusk and would sweep the route in front of us as we made our way to the truck. In the meantime two further men would go to where the truck was parked, find the two guards, and advise them of our plan to leave that night

Regis reported that the atmosphere in the town was still extremely tense

Permission to remove the hanging corpses for burial were still refused. Several wives, attempting to claim their husbands, had been taken into custody for defying the ban. Many of the original men collected for the examination of their papers were still incarcerated in the MAT works complex. The situation was desperately tense

The six policemen arrived early and immediately started to explore our route to the truck. They acted as though they were on duty stopping and questioning people in a friendly manner. Our two guards were found without difficulty. They had been sheltered by a family who were hard core patriots but whom were now suspect because they had accommodated "German personnel"

"You must expect some reaction from the local people when you all get into that truck." said Sergeant Roy, "they will take it you are collaborators"

Sergeant Roy had also seen two of the local SS officers during their excursion. "That truck has been parked there for a long time," said one to Sergeant Roy, when his interest in the truck was noticed. "Wasn't there a report, some months ago, of several trucks of that type being stolen by the resistance?" queried the other, "But the plates are army group H," said the first Sergeant

Sergeant Roy interjected, "If they belong to army group H then they will be leaving almost at once." "I think we should keep an eye on that truck," said the first. "Yes, I think you are right to be cautious, "said Sergeant Roy, "I and Bernard will stay with you, just in case there is a problem"

Sergeant Roy took his second in command, Jean-Michel to one side and explained what he was doing, Jean-Michel and the other policemen then left to carry on and make their way back to the safe house

Regis, Alain, Stephan, Raymond and I listened intently to what Jean-Michel had to say. "Those two SS men are suspicious of the truck and are going to watch what might happen. Sergeant Roy and Bernard are going to 'help' them

The only way you can leave in safety, is to take the SS men with you as prisoners." There was a stunned silence. "You will have to imprison them somewhere until the Allies arrive or the Germans withdraw from this region. It should not be for more than a few weeks. Even if they escape in those weeks you will be safely back in your own territory." The silence continued while we digested to boldness of the idea. "I was planning to stop off at the Gibory farm on the way back," I said, "and that would be a good place to confine them." "I don't want to know where you imprison them," said Jean-Michel "I think that is a brilliant idea," said Stephan, he turned to Jean-Michel, "How do you propose to capture them?"

Sergeant Roy says we should take some bottles of beer and some sandwiches with us and when we are all relaxed to suddenly disarm them handcuff and gag them, ready for you to take them with you"

Alain was sent off to get the beer and sandwiches while the rest of us talked to Jean-Michel. "The four of us will return to the truck ahead of you and make sure there are no extra Germans about and then rejoin Sergeant Roy and Bernard, then we will all climb into the back of the Truck to eat and drink in comfort, three of us to each of the SS men will make lots of bawdy laughter as we handcuff and gag them. When all is quiet you can arrive get your two guards from their house and leave as quietly and quickly as possible"

I wanted to go via the Gibory farm to ensure that the news of the atrocities the Germans had perpetrated in Tulle and Brive was properly sent out to the world at large even if we broke all the rules about limited transmission times. I felt confident the Gibory's would be pleased to confine two of the perpetrators in one of their underground caves. So we worked out our route to avoid main roads and minimise the chance of being stopped. There were only two problem points in the route. We had to cross the Dordogne at the dam at Chastang, which was bound to be guarded, and much later we had to cross the main road from Mauriac to Aurillac at a point in a small town where there might be a German presence. We agreed we would shoot our way out of any problems

Navigation was not easy. We left Tulle on the right road but there were many turns off our route not shown on our map, and we took several of them!

Eventually we encountered a lonely Gendarme on his bike. Telling him we had urgent supplies for the guards at the Chastang dam he offered us help and rode with us through the next village and ensured we were on the right road for Chastang

The minor roads were tortuous and we were much later than planned at Chastang. The noise of our truck roused the guard at the dam and four very sleepy individuals raised the barrier as soon as they recognised our plates and were too tired to think of any questions

Our prisoners in the back of the truck were restive and we had to stop to allow nature to be satisfied. We used this stop and the last of our battery power to tell the Giborys we were coming and to meet us at dawn at the head of the track from Super-Lioran. By this time we had little faith we could make it by dawn. We crossed the Mauriac-Aurillac road without incident and entered the volcanic region. Although the land was more rugged there were fewer possibilities of making mistakes, and we caught up some lost time. We made it soon after dawn. All three Giborys were waiting for us. We hid the truck and started the climb up to the farm. When we came to the really steep part we had to either take the blindfolds off the prisoners, or carry them. They protested at having to stumble

356

along behind a horse. Jean Gibory said let them go free and drive them in front of us. We took the hand cuffs off them and without any common language with them Jean made it very clear that if they tried to make a run for it, what he would do, un slinging his rifle, to drive the matter home. Although they continued their protests they allowed themselves to be driven. When we all stopped for a breather Pierre explained to them that after what they had done in Tulle, "they could consider themselves lucky not to be shot on sight"

When we all arrived at the Gibory farm, there was both alarm at the sight of the two SS men in uniform and surprise on the part of our prisoners at the place where they were to be detained. They were now handcuffed together so each had one hand free with which to eat breakfast. After the meal Stephan sat down in front of them, "You will be held prisoner here until the Germans start to withdraw from this part of France, and then you will be released to withdraw with them." he said. "We will never withdraw from France," retorted the SS men. Stephan continued, "When the Allies start the assault on Paris, a further invasion in the South of France and an advance up the Rhone -Saone valley will cause the withdrawal of all German troops from western and central France, otherwise they will be trapped and isolated by the pincer movement." Once again I was astounded at Stephan's knowledge of the whole plan of the campaign

After breakfast the SS men were stabled in one of the vacant barns in full view of all passing through the enclosed yard. "The women can shoot nearly as well as I can," said Pierre as he fixed their chains. I spent the whole day catching up with the news and the messages. There was not as much traffic as I expected. "I reckon they have enough on their plate with the war in the North to spend much time on us." said Raymond.

I spent much of the day composing the details of the atrocities in Tulle and Brive. I was tempted to send the report 'en claire so that any listener would be informed of what had happened in those two towns. But eventually it was all coded and sent with instructions to immediately copy it to De Gaulle's office

The news from the Oradour group was interesting. They claimed they had disabled fourteen German battle tanks and numerous lighter armoured vehicles

However the Das Reich division had used all their might to force a way through and they only achieved about 36 hours delay. Their casualties had been heavy and they had also lost some men as prisoners

The news from the Mathilde's group detailed a great deal of activity. With the departure of army group H Northwards the occupiers were thin on the ground and vulnerable. There had been no attempt to cross the Tarn and enter the high Auvergne. A number of maquis groups were active and annoying the Germans immensely while not actually killing or injuring them. In spite of that those maquis or FFI who were captured were being tortured to get names of others who could then be arrested, and similarly treated. Consequently all had taken to the countryside, and any Germans venturing out of the towns were likely to be captured unless they moved in considerable force. Mathilde reported she was now holding sixteen Germans at a secret location

Similar reports from Francois Peillon in Le Puy but with many of his men arrested and tortured, He suspected some of the prisoners had informed under torture. There was no hard news from Clermont, but some rumours of similar actions by the Germans to those of Tulle

As the news of the atrocities spread among the Gibory extended family their attitude hardened. The children were forbidden to go anywhere near the SS men. The women reduced contact to the bare minimum and it was made clear to the SS men that if they did escape they would be hunted down and shot with no compunction whatever

The British news from the North was encouraging. Troops and equipment were continuously being landed and small gains made. The control of the airspace over the battlefields was complete

We left on the morning of the third day. I had to be able to explain my absence for several days longer than I had anticipated. I had prepared the ground by having lots of people having seen me at various times and saying so in public but these statements must be wearing a bit thin by now

I went first to the Barrat farm with Raymond. Jaen Chavent was relieved to see us both. I spent some time on the telephone having light conversations with various people who could then say quite honestly they had, 'spoken to me the other day'. Then I took my bicycle and went to spend the rest of the day with Angelique. I gave her copies of the reports I had sent to London on the atrocities of Tulle and Brive and asked her to put out a special newsletter. She had some difficulty now in distributing her news because of the disruption to the bus services. This brave young lady said she would distribute this news personally if need be as it was so important. She also told me that there had been no mention so far of the atrocities on the BBC French service. Then I cycled to Saint Flour and slipped into the back door of the Terminus at dusk

Dad was resting in the room behind the bar. He was both relieved and worried at my return. "You must be careful how you explain your absence, those who know what you have been doing have done their best to have 'seen you' in various places, but I can't remember all of them." He went into the bar and Yvette came, straight into my arms. "Shush," I said as she raised her voice, "quietly now, my return must be as unremarkable as possible, I'll tell you all about it when there is no possibility of being overheard." "Have all the others come back," she asked, "Unfortunately no," I replied, we lost one killed plus four slightly injured," "Who was killed?" she asked, "One of Fernand Mounier's men, I've never seen him in here, I doubt if you know him." "But where have you been?"

"I'll tell you later. How is Jean-Francois?" I asked to change the subject. "He's fine," she replied, "but he's been asking for you too."

There was a scratching and miaouw at the back door and Sambo came in. He simply wanted a fuss and a nuzzle. "He has slept in your place every night you've been away," said Yvette,   "Fortunately he can't count time or ask questions," I replied. Yvette went back to the bar and Mum came in

After the embrace I gave her the same news as Yvette, and asked that my return should be completely unremarkable, she understood. "What has happened to the one killed and the injured men?" she asked. "The Souillac group took the body and it will be buried with military honours as soon as an opportunity arises. The injured men are all at a doctor's country home near Noailles, they will probably be able to travel home in about two weeks time

The doctor is a trusted member of the Brive FFI group and Alain Brenot will keep us informed of their progress"

The curfew could not be enforced Saint Flour in the summer months and it was almost ten o'clock before the last clients left the bar. Mum closed up and we settled down to a long talk. They were horrified when I told them about Tulle and Brive. "You actually saw the bodies hanging from the lamp posts?" questioned Dad, "How many?" asked Yvette. "I couldn't stop to count them," I said, "perhaps a hundred." What has happened to the rest of the men they took?" asked Mum. "I have no idea," I replied, they were still in the MAT factory when we left"

"Don't you think you should keep those two SS officers you have at the Gibory farm for trial in France?" said Dad. "Do you think I have the authority to hold two German Officers for a trial in France?" "Should I hand them over to the FFI or the Maquis? I hope De Gaulle will take the decision out of my hands"

"You said Stephan told them they would be released when the pincer movement from Paris and the South started," said Yvette, "But how does he know that?" said Mum

"I think he knows," I replied, "He was right about the occupation of Vichy France, the invasion of North Africa across the Atlantic, and the invasion of Sicily." With that final thought we all went to bed, but Yvette kept me talking long after two in the morning, before I went to sleep in protest

It was Jean-Francois who woke me in the morning. Yvette had slipped away to cope with the early bus departures, fewer now because all the routes were not operating. I had not realised how short I was of a real good night's sleep. It was past ten and I could easily have slept again

After some coffee I let myself be seen in the yard of the terminus busy with a number of jobs outside the workshop. Some acquaintances stopped for a gossip and I gave the impression I had been busy for some days catching up on a mixture of tasks. The progress of the Allied invasion was always the first topic in everyone's mind and it was clear that most people were ignoring the ban on listening to the BBC French service. The jamming was still bad but somehow the news was getting through

The most important event for some days was the link up of all the Normandy landings to form a continuous beachhead of nearly seventy kilometres following the capture of Carentan

A message from Alexis Lescaut via one of his men called for a meeting of the Monday club that night in spite of it being Thursday. Dad decided that the only way he could get the Terminus empty early enough was to run out of beer about eight o'clock. Bad for business, but a necessary sacrifice

Members arrived at various times during the evening. There was an aura of urgency in their attitude. Some quietly disappeared into the backroom early. I let myself be seen but declined any conversation. Angelique had kept her promise about personal distribution of the news and this had clearly triggered the urgency of the meeting. Alexis Lescaut was, unusually, the last to arrive

He was accompanied by another man, disguised and not recognisable. For the first time the Maire of Saint Flour was attending one of our meetings! It was the liveliest meeting I had ever attended.   Normally   it   was   either Alexis or Councillor Leman who led the meeting. Now the Maire wanted to be in charge

"Before I start this meeting," said the Maire, "there is one important matter to settle, I know all of you, except that gentleman there," he continued, pointing at Stephan. "Stephan is the leader of the Maquis in the Auvergne," I replied to the Maire. Some moments of silence while the Maire digested this information, "Did you know about this?" said the Maire addressing Councillor Dechaux. "I became aware of it since the German occupation," prevaricated Councillor Dechaux

"Stephan and his compatriots have been key players in almost everything we have achieved."Nods of agreement all round visibly noted by the Maire "I know about your exact status here," said the Maire addressing me, "and I understood you had orders not to assist the maquis." "That is true," I replied, "but I also had a job to do, and it is much better to do it with the cooperation of the maquis instead of in rivalry or in competition with them." Again under wartime conditions one has to make some allowances," he conceded

"What really concerns me is the news letter distributed in the last few days about the atrocities in Tulle and Brive, I have been inundated by people asking me if it is true, and if it is true it will cause the Saint Flour residents to react, perhaps violently, against Major Kempf and his men." "You must answer that Henri," said Alexis, addressing me

"Stephan, Raymond and myself were in a safe house in Tulle on the nights of seventh and eighth of June together with the FFI leaders of the Tulle and Brive groups. During the day of the eighth we began to get reports of men being detained by the Germans in the MAT factory for an 'inspection of their papers'. The total number detained was many hundreds. A very small number were released and these seemed to be those with some highly specialised skills. Many of those detained were taken almost from their beds on the morning of the eighth

Then on the morning of the ninth we got early reports of men being hanged from the lampposts of the main street of Tulle. We did not believe the first report, but within the hour we had so many independent reports we had to go and see for ourselves. We saw many men, some already dead, some still struggling. We did not count them but perhaps a hundred were hanging there. This was also witnessed by Alain Brenot and Regis Armengaud and others.

Wives and mothers attempting to recover the bodies of their men folk were driven back by armed SS men"

"We did not stay long in the area," said Raymond, "but I can confirm every word Henri has reported is true." Stephan spoke next, "If I may be permitted to speak at this meeting then I also confirm Henri's statement. You must believe it. It is only a repetition of the type of atrocity that the Germans committed in Russia"

"I think you must now believe Henri's statement," said Alexis to the Maire "Angelique's news letter is based on the reports sent to London and which should have been copied to De Gaulle's office. Even if they do not believe these reports, there must be others from other sources, and it can only be a short time before these atrocities are included in the news services"

The Maire was not well pleased with the situation. "If I confirm the reports, and major Kempf hears that I am confirming he will demand to know the source of my information." "You could simply refer him to the news letters," said councillor Dechaux. "He will also surely have heard that several of the local women who have been entertaining Germans in their homes have kicked them out on the strength of the news letters," added Alexis. "You could also confront major Kempf with what you have heard, and ask him to confirm or deny the reports, mentioning that you did not expect the Germans to repeat their treatment of the Russians in France." said Stephan

The Maire and councillors Dechaux and Leman left together at this stage

They all went to see major Kempf the next day and did confront him as Stephan had suggested. Kempf admitted to knowing about all of the reports but expressed the view that they were highly exaggerated and he was sure that no German commander would allow such things to happen

That same evening the BBC French service reported the massacre at Oradour-sur-Glane and made a passing remark that reports of further atrocities committed by the same German army units were under examination

Details of exactly what had happened at Oradour-sur-Glane were difficult to establish. The first reports were that the women and children of the village had been herded into the Church and the Church set on fire. Then we were told that the men of the village had been machined gunned to death

After some days the facts emerged. Some villagers had escaped the massacre. Some villagers, who were absent at their work, during the time of the massacre, were banned from returning to Oradour that evening and had to seek shelter in neighbouring villages. Five men had escaped from the machine guns. They all told a similar story

When the guns started they all fell to the ground feigning death. After the gunfire had ceased and the SS had shot again anyone who still moved, straw was spread over the bodies and set alight. The five survivors extricated themselves from the mass and moved to a corner of the inferno and finally managed to escape to nearby bushes where they hid until dark

The women and children in the Church had heard the machine guns and were fearful for the safety of their men folk. Eventually the church door opened and two Germans came in with a large container with fuse cords protruding from it. This container was placed near the communion table, the fuses were lit and the Germans left locking all the doors behind them. The container exploded filling the Church with black acrid fumes. The women and children panicked and when they tried to escape through the windows the Germans machine gunned them from the outside. Eventually the Church was consumed in fire. In spite of the efforts of the Germans, one woman did escape. Behind the altar she found the ladder used to light the candles and climbed up to a window from which she jumped almost three metres to the ground. Although wounded, the woman managed to reach a garden where she collapsed among foliage which concealed her body. She remained there semi-conscious for many hours until found by rescuers

When the SS searched the village for inhabitants trying to evade the massacre some did manage to hide and thus could bear witness to the brutality of the Germans towards the villagers. They could also report on the drunken revelry that followed the massacre. Many of the houses in Oradour had well stocked cellars and larders. The Germans soon found those houses and spent most of the night in debauchery before finally setting fire to those homes as well before they left on the following morning. Nothing remained of Oradour-sur-Glane. Six hundred and forty-two people had been exterminated

The story of what happened at Oradour came through to Saint Flour by many routes and with some distortion, but the horror dwarfed what happened in Brive and Tulle. It was not until after the sermon preached by Parson Chaudier in Limoges on 18th June that the news was broadcast in France. From that moment the people of Saint Flour, en masse, hardened their hearts against the occupying Germans

Chapter 47

The Martyred Village

Almost all of the Germans who had enjoyed being entertained 'at home' in Saint Flour found the doors locked against them. People who had spoken freely with the occupiers now crossed the street to avoid conversation. Getting any service in the shops and bars became very difficult for the Germans

Following a tense meeting between Major Kempf and his adjutant, at the barracks, with the Maire supported by Councillors Dechaux and Leman, Major Kempf issued a notice which was posted all over the town saying he felt sure that the reports from Oradour-sur-Glane had grossly exaggerated the facts and he would seek out the real facts and advise the people of Saint Flour what really happened

A hastily convened meeting of the Monday club, after this meeting at the barracks, decided to make a response. The atmosphere was electric. No members of the Monday club, any longer had any doubts about the truth of the reports from Oradour. Something dramatic had to come out of this meeting

The Monday club was split. The majority wanted instant decisive action. The minority of the Maire and councillor Dechaux, were continuing to urge care and caution. Very late into the night the majority had its way with the following plan. An offer was to be made to Major Kempf to transport him, two of his officers, and three councillors from Saint Flour to Oradour-sur-Glane, to see first hand what had happened and to talk to the survivors of the village. The offer was to be made in the name of the FFI who would provide transport and armed escorts for the party. No weapons were to be carried by any of the Germans or the councillors. Major Kempf was to use his authority to obtain permission of the German commanders in Aurillac, Tulle and Limoges through whose areas the party must pass. The Maire with councillors Dechaux and Leman were to convey this offer to Major Kempf

364

Since the start of the invasion by Allied forces much more interest was taken in Angelique's almost daily news letters. She did her best but there were simply not enough copies to go round. The loudest complainant was Mathilde. She was the most remote recipient and if she got two copies for her whole group she was lucky. Mathilde, being Mathilde took the matter into her own hands. The first person to get her copies was now one or both of two school teachers who also had jelly duplicators. So within a few hours two copies had become about one hundred and twenty which completely solved her problem even though some doubt as to the authenticity by some recipients because the handwriting was different. It was of course summer and the schools had shut for the summer vacation with school teachers much less busy than usual

Even in Saint Flour it was not always easy to see a copy. I went to see Angelique. "I'm doing the best I can, I write two copies every day now so there are twice as many copies going out each day." she said defensively. "The bus drivers are taking them further away because people who have seen one copy want to continue seeing others." "I think the best we can do is to recruit some other teachers, most of whom have access to jelly duplicators, and for you to get first copies to them to rewrite and distribute in their locality." She liked the idea. I know teachers at all of the schools in the Saint Flour sub-prefecture," she said, "I can think immediately of at least six who could be trusted to do it if they have the duplicator"

If I arrange for one of our local police sergeants to drive you around to see these teachers, it will keep the matter completely confidential. Telephone conversations are not safe and this must be stressed to the teachers. It may mean the news is a day later getting to some people but it will reach more people that way." I said

"Now I am going to ask you to do something else on an occasional basis which is probably more dangerous than simply reporting the BBC French news." She looked apprehensive."You probably know that the FFI are active in this part of France." She smiled. I continued, "The brutality of the SS in Tulle, Brive and now Oradour is likely to be explained by the Germans as a reprisal for the attacks on their forces by the resistance as a whole and causing them casualties. They are sure to say also that the reports exaggerate the facts." The FFI have no voice to tell the true facts." I went on to tell her about the proposition being put to Major Otto Kempf by the Maire and the likely outcome that he would reject or ignore the proposal."Could you actually do that?" She asked. "Yes we have the necessary transport and personnel." I replied, "but I want to make it impossible for him to reject or ignore the proposal. Therefore I want a news letter to go out in the name of the FFI telling everyone that the proposition has been put to Major Kempf."

She thought for a few minutes. "I'll do it," she said, "after all, I'm telling the truth"

We settled down to write the news letter Number One of the FFI in Cantal

It was quite brief and simply stated that the offer had been made to Major Kempf by the Maire on behalf of the councillors of Saint Flour because he had issued a notice saying he would find out the facts and report them. The FFI felt sure the best way to find out the facts was to go to Oradour and see for himself

When we were both satisfied with the draft, I said, "tuck this away in a safe place and when I know that Major Kemp has rejected the offer, I will telephone you to say 'your wine order is ready for you to collect' and then you can go ahead and issue the FFI news letter for distribution exactly as the news reports"

It was the same day as the US army reached the outskirts of Cherbourg when Major Kempf finally agreed to receive the Maire and councillors. The Maire started by asking Major Kempf if it was true that US forces had reached Cherbourg. Kempf didn't know but considered it unlikely. After all it is a major port and the Germans need to keep control of it." he said. "How will you provision the troops when it is surrounded?" asked councillor Leman, "by sea?" The Maire went on, "We want you to be completely confident in the statements you make regarding the martyrdom of the village of Orator-sur-Glane so we have the following proposition to put to you." The Maire then explained in full detail the proposition from the Monday club. Major Kempf's face became redder and redder and his adjutants increasingly fidgety as the Maire went on

Kempf finally stopped the Maire with a crashing blow of his fist on to his desk."I have never had such an outrageous proposition put to me in all my military career." he said

One of the adjutants rose and ushered the Maire and councillors into the outer office. "You should wait here until the Major gives you permission to leave," he said, and fetched a sentry for the outer door. "You should consider yourselves lucky he has not taken you prisoner as collaborators with the so-called French Forces of the Interior"

Madame Person, the Maire's secretary became anxious as the day wore on without the return of the Maire and councillors. At seven in the evening she could wait no longer and telephoned the police. Alexis Lescaut was still at the station as he was also waiting for news of the meeting. And of course there was to be a meeting of the Monday club later that evening. Alexis telephoned his superiors in Aurillac for advice.   Eventually the result was that Colonel Schmidt, Kemp's CO, proposed that Kempf should release the Maire and councillors as it was really, "quite impossible to believe that the FFI could actually do what they proposed"

The Maire "preferred not to attend" the Monday club meeting but councillor Dechaux speaking for the Maire said he intended to be seen not to be at any meeting that night "just in case." It was a lively meeting. We don't actually have to do anything now to embarrass the Germans," said Mum. I read over the text of the FFI News Letter One and it was agreed that we should let it stand as an offer with no comment on Major Kempf's reaction. I left the meeting to let Angelique know that her wine was ready for collection. When I returned there was an animated discussion as to what Major Kempf's reaction might be. "We must wait and see," said Stephan, "he is probably going to do nothing and that will mean we have to consider our next move very carefully."

We agreed to meet again in three days to see what had happened up until then and to receive any new ideas about the content of FFI News Letter Two

Angelique reacted immediately. By nine o'clock next morning the town was buzzing with the news. German soldiers were being asked, "What is your CO going to do? It's a very reasonable way to get at the truth." In fact none of the German soldiers knew anything about the offer. It was the next day before the average German in the street had been told that, "Some offer had been made in the name of the FFI but it was too preposterous to even consider." By that time of course some of the German soldiers had seen the FFI news letter and those with enough French to translate it told others of the content. In the meantime news was filtering through, mainly via the bus drivers, with details all of which confirmed the news precis issued by Angelique, and a new term was being used, The Martyred village

When the Monday club met again the change of attitude of the people of Saint Flour was one major concern. The other was the taunting of German patrols with such phrases as, "Do you specialise in the massacre of women and children," or "why did you set fire to Oradour, to hide the evidence?" Stephan was at pains to point out that this sort of event had occurred frequently at the time of the invasion of Russia and that there was a second 'Martyred Village' in Czechoslovakia, Lidice. The concern was that if the tension continued to build some incident might arise in our town. With the apparent success of the Allied invasion of France, liberation was something we could anticipate, in due course, and there was nothing to be gained by provoking the Germans into some violent action

This lead us to the subject for FFI News Letter Two. We all agreed that we should point out that Das Reich division was an SS division noted for its brutality wherever it had been engaged. The people of Saint Flour should not assume that the occupying Germans in our town would act in the way the SS Das Reich had behaved in Tulle, Brive and now at Oradour. While I was actually working with Angelique on the text, the news of the capture of Cherbourg by the US Seventh Corps, with most of the port facilities intact. We rounded off the news letter with this point and said this could only bring our liberation nearer.

Chapter 48

Progress

Within the next few days the news continued to encourage people to follow the advice. Avranches fell thus completing the liberation of the Carentan peninsula so that the Allies could turn their effort more to the East which led to the capture of Caen on the ninth of July after a long bitter battle in which most of the town was destroyed

It was now increasingly important for the Allies to push hard to the East. Since the middle of June the South-East of England and London had been targeted by the first of Hitler's secret weapons. The V-1, also called the Doodle Bug, was a pilotless rocket propelled aircraft with about a tonne of high explosive in the nose. These were being launched from ramps in the Pas de Calais region of France. They did not seem to be very reliable; many crashed into the channel and some more were destroyed by the anti-aircraft defences that were moved to the South coast. They flew so fast that even the Spitfire could barely catch them and the time they were in range of the anti-aircraft defences was short. Nevertheless those that did get through to the capital caused considerable damage and casualties

The Maire had been notable for his absence from the Monday Club meetings. "It is better that I have always been seen elsewhere when you meet, I cannot be seen to have any involvement with the FFI." was the message conveyed by councillor Dechaux at our next meeting. He also asked that he should always receive an early copy of the News Letters so that he was not left waiting for somebody else to tell him the latest news. Alexis Lescaut volunteered to send a copy as one of his men always met the bus to get copies

The feelings developed that we must use the FFI to have an impact on the local community and at the same time discredit Major Otto Kempf's remarks that he doubted their capability of doing very much. The Germans were still actively trying to collect some quota for shipment to Germany. "They usually go out in patrols of four or five including a sergeant in charge," said Raymond, "Now that we can see the liberation looming closer do you think we could get the Giborys to hold another four or five prisoners on a short term basis?" "It shouldn't be a problem," said Stephan, "they have plenty of supplies during the summer and I could spare the necessary men to act as additional guards." "Could you get up there and ask?" I said. "I'll go tomorrow." replied Stephan

"On the assumption that the Giborys will cooperate lets plan what we will do. We don't have to get involved in a fire fight with a German patrol, if we simply let them see that they are surrounded by about a dozen armed men they ought to have the good sense to surrender." "But what if they don't," interjected councillor Leman

"Then we simply shoot the sergeant in the leg and repeat the surrender demand." I replied. "And then?" We disarm them and load them into their truck, transport them to prison." "Remember this is the height of summer, you'd better use the Prat de Bouc approach to the Gibory farm; there could be too many pairs of eyes at Super-Lioran said Raymond, "Good thinking," I replied

Stephan came to see me the next evening. "Yes it's on, the Giborys will do it

He went on, "They have used one of their warmer caves as a prison and have put up an iron grid across the entrance which is quite secure, there's room for about fifteen prisoners in there. They've been making those two SS men work for their keep carrying hay harvest, with guards of course, four legged ones backed up by a marksman"

"Two men working under armed guard is one thing," I remarked, "six would be a different situation." "I agree." replied Stephan. "but they could work shifts"

We'll mention it to the Giborys," I said, "but they are not fools" "I'm going to be losing some of my men soon. Now that the North of Italy is slowly being liberated some are ready to go home and try and pick up their life again." said Stephan. "Also there is another matter of which you should be aware and that is German deserters from the Brive and Tulle garrisons are turning up on the hill farms around Aurillac seeking work in exchange for their keep. Most have discarded their uniforms and weapons." "If they were to get information about FFI men working on farms they might try to buy their way back into the Wehrmacht with that information," I commented. "Exactly" agreed Stephan. "As a matter of urgency we must alert all the farms who do, or have ever supported us to this and ask them not to take on anybody they even suspect of being a German deserter," I said

"Especially as with the sheep shearing time coming up there is bound to be a demand for extra hands," said Stephan, "Can I use your four sergeants to do this?" asked Stephan, "You can have three of them," I said, "but leave me Patrice, I need his skills with a rifle"

"When do you think you will take your prisoners?" asked Stephan. "I will have to work out when the Germans are likely to go to a convenient farm, and which farms are convenient. My first thoughts are that any farm to the West of Saint Flour could be used because it would be a shorter journey on minor roads to the Prat de Bouc." Stephan nodded thoughtfully. "Once we've secured our prisoners an agreed phone call to Bernice Rodot who can then pass the news to the Giborys via the landline"

It was only a matter of days before our opportunity came up. This was a time when the German methodology exposed them to our attack. As soon as they had called at their first farm of the day we knew exactly where they would be going for the rest of the day

The little hamlet of Buddies with it's one farm employing almost all of the locals who were typical Auvergnat and intensely anti German and their quota demands. We arrived in Buddies as quickly as possible. It had one great advantage, it was at the end of a minor lane that went nowhere else. We explained to the locals that they were not to get involved and if they could all suffer from blindness and deafness that day it would be most helpful

The quota gatherers arrived soon after lunch. They parked their truck in the usual place completely blocking the lane and went on foot to the farm, about three hundred metres. The sergeant led the way as usual along a narrow track with good cover on both sides. The first shot rang out. This was the signal for the truck guardian to be seized by our group, and the loud warning shouted to the four men on the track that they were surrounded and were invited to surrender when they would be treated as prisoners of war. There was a period of silence. Patrice fired again just at the toes of the sergeants boots and shouted that the next shot would be in his thigh.

The party laid down their weapons. They were searched for any concealed weapons, none found, and were handcuffed. By this time the locals could contain their curiosity no longer and we had quite an audience as we loaded them all into the back of their truck after unloading the quota they had collected already for the locals to return it to the rightful owners.   "Where are you going to hold them?" asked the farmer, "That's a closely guarded secret," I replied and you don't need to know"

The truck was comfortably full by the time we got our five POW's settled in and guarded by Patrice and myself. Within the hour we were handing them over to the Giborys for a hard climb up to their farm.

I dropped various people off at convenient locations for them and then left the truck hidden just outside Saint Flour. After dark I drove it with Patrice to the old Gendarmerie barracks. The Guard on the gate recognised the truck and started to open the gates. At that moment we both quickly got out of the truck and took to the small back streets. Within five minutes we were in to the Terminus via the back door, a little out-of-breath but with the satisfaction of having done exactly what we had planned

Angelique's second FFI news the next morning reported that five German soldiers collecting the quota had been taken prisoner by FFI forces and were now imprisoned as POW's. "They will be returned with all the other prisoners to the command of Major Kempf when he surrenders to the FFI and is ready to withdraw Eastwards"

Chapter 49

Time to Go

As well as our local successes the BBC French service was detailing the continued successes on the Normandy front for inclusion in Angelique's daily news sheet. The Falaise gap was now closed with huge German forces entrapped. Caen was finally captured and the Allies were poised for the drive eastwards toward Paris

The unsuccessful attempt to assassinate Hitler was almost disregarded by the news services

The Germans in Saint Flour were aware of the successes from reading Angelique's news letters as well as the increases taunting in the streets. Quota collections almost ceased after we took the POW's. Then Major Kempf started to send much larger collection parties of up to twenty or more men with two trucks

We could not see any way of capturing such parties without a significant fire fight in which farmers and civilians were likely to be injured, and we could not accommodate the POW's but the Germans did not know that speculation was rife among the local population as to how long it would be before Saint Flour was liberated and with what consequences.

The Allies southern advance had stopped at the Loire. All of their effort was now in the thrust towards Paris

On the 15th August Stephan's long predicted invasion from the South made steady progress

One French, and three American divisions had landed in the area of Saint Tropez and immediately started a push towards the Rhone valley. As soon as we were sure of this news Angelique produced her masterpiece.

The heading was, 'Time to go, Otto' In a week or two's time the Allied forces approaching Paris and those fighting their way up the Rhone valley will meet and then it will be too late for you to escape back to Germany and we don't want you to stay here either

The FFI therefore make you this offer. You must surrender all of your weaponry and equipment to the FFI. In exchange you will receive a document confirming your surrender and requesting the FFI commanders in the districts you traverse to allow you to pass unhindered and unmolested. You will be permitted to take two of your trucks with sufficient fuel, food and water to get you over the river Saone and in which you may carry any wounded or sick personnel. The POW's we hold from your command will be returned to you when you depart together with the any other prisoners and deserters we have taken in the meantime. Timing of your withdrawal is critical. We would therefore suggest that you start negotiations with the Maire of Saint Flour as soon as possible

The FFI will cooperate with you and the Maire to achieve a fair conclusion to your stay in our town. We will not permit other contingents of German troops withdrawing from the west of Saint Flour to pass through our town. So you can have an unhindered journey for at least the first two hundred kilometres. If you take the route via Le Puy and Saint Etienne the local FFI commanders will respect the documents we will give you. After Saint Etienne your route will depend on how far the invasion from the South has progressed. It would probably be better if you did not try to pass through Lyon as that city is heavily garrisoned by your compatriots

The effect of this FFI news bulletin was stunning. Before the end of the morning the Germans had almost disappeared from the streets and as far as we could tell were all in the barracks

Matthilde reported all the German troops South of the Tarn were being moved to the East to regroup around Avignon. Francois Peillon from Le Puy reported all Germans moving to the Rhone Valley and control of the town handed back to the local gendarmerie. Alain Brenot and Regis Armengaud both reported plans for a withdrawal to Clermont but so far no movements taking place. Perhaps the most interesting news from them was that the SS personnel had all left some days ago for unknown destinations

It soon became apparent that the fighting spirit of the Germans had largely deserted them. In spite of the large numbers of troops deployed to defend the Rhone valley every day progress was reported by the BBC French news service, now listened to so openly that Angelique's daily precis were no longer necessary. For four days Major Kempf took no action. The Germans who did come out of the barracks were taunted on the streets about 'when are you going then?', and, 'where are you going?' New deserters appeared almost daily, mostly from other areas because there was work to be done on the farms now that the maquis were steadily returning to northern Italy. Some of the men from the Saint Flour Garrison were also finding ways to get out of the barracks and take to the hills. Finally the Maire and councillors requested a meeting with Major Kempf to settle the matter of the German withdrawal

It turned into a delicate situation. Major Kempf stated he had no orders to withdraw. We pointed out the withdrawal of other garrisons towards Clermont and in the South towards Avignon. Seeing the weakening position of Major Kempf the Maire next said that he was awaiting the surrender of all the German weaponry in accordance with the demands of the FFI and then the Germans could withdraw safely. Major Kempf's response was that he could only surrender to an officer of equal or higher rank from the allied forces, he would not surrender to irregular forces like the FFI There was an immediate meeting within a meeting. The Maire and his councillors made some rapid exchanges in French while Kempf and his fellow officers looked on nonplussed

The Maire spoke directly to Major Kempf, "We may be able to help you in this matter, there is a British Major in this area, but of course his work here is of a covert nature and he is only known to a very few people and I am not sure if he is empowered to take your surrender." "I don't know whether to believe you or not," was Kempf's reply, "I cannot believe that a British Major could arrive here the Auvergne and it not be known to the occupying forces," he blustered. Major Kempf. Councillor Leman intervened, "I hope you will believe me, I know this British Major well, he arrived here nearly a year before you did. He was already part of the community and I know that he is known to you." The German officers now had their separate meeting, and finally Major Kempf conceded, "If he is empowered to take my surrender, then I will surrender to him." "We will find out and come back to you," said the Maire with an air of finality, and the Maire and his consorts left the meeting

The Maire told councillor Leman to find me urgently. He found Raymond who was able to contact me by radio as I was spending that day with the Giborys and we were having prisoner problems. A number of deserters from regions to the West of us had seen our POWs working on the Gibory farm and had sought work for themselves, only to find they were immediately made POWs themselves to prevent the location of our POW camp being leaked. Thus when Raymond's message reached me I was able to contact London at once on the top priority emergency frequency

I didn't get an immediate answer to my question. Instead I was asked why I was still in the Auvergne ignoring London's message to return via Lysander at first opportunity as instructed on fifteenth of June. An assumption had been made that I was out of action, injured or a prisoner. On checking the message log I was able to tell London that their message of fifteenth of June was not included in our message log and that our radios had been in use on that day with no recorded problems. Having wasted an hour or two sorting that out I got an answer to my question En Claire! 'Yes, take their surrender with as many witnesses as possible. The surrender agreement need only be in English. It must be witnessed by Raymond as your two IC, and by at least three of Kempf's senior officers with their names rank and identity numbers, also by the Maire of Saint Flour, the most senior police officer and as many of the councillors as are available

Disarm the Germans at their barracks and make them leave the barracks to all attend the surrender ceremony. As soon as they have left the barracks have the FFI place a well armed guard over the barracks. The Germans should leave Saint Flour immediately after the surrender is completed

We agree with your allowing two trucks to be used for humanitarian purposes although you should insist that the group move with white flags clearly visible just in case any stray aircraft should see them. This will become very important as they get nearer to the Rhone Saone valley

Although it is not necessary, your idea of a document to show to the FFI groups through whose areas they pass could do no harm. What might happen to them if and when they join up with any other German forces thankfully is not our responsibility

With reference to your POW's, by all means hand over all of your Wehrmacht personnel and any other deserters you may detain to Major Kempf. The two SS officers you hold and any others you detain must continue to be detained until you can transfer them to the first Allied forces to reach your area. This instruction must also apply to any German personnel who you even suspect as being members of the SS even if they are in Wehrmacht uniforms. The Americans will doubtless cross the Loire in the next few days and it can only be a week or two after that until they reach your area. In other areas surrender of the local occupying troops has led to extensive desertions. It would be appropriate for you to employ FFI members to reduce desertions as far as possible

This message is sent 'en claire' in view of the urgency of your actions It should not be necessary to use code any longer for our general communications unless it is essential in your opinion. If you transmit in code you will be answered in code and vice versa

What a relief, all of those hours of coding and decoding finished. The above en claire transmissions would have wasted so much time if coded. So I mustn't waste any time about getting back to Saint Flour. Alexis sent a car to Prat de Bouc to wait until I could get down there. It was a warm evening and I was running with sweat by the time I got to the car and I must have broken all records for the descent. Maurice Blin was driving. "You daren't put in an appearance looking like that," he said, "did you fall or were you pushed?" I laughed, "I was in a hurry"

"We must get you to the Terminus as fast as we can, you've got to clean yourself up, you're meeting the Maire officially. Major Kempf has agreed to surrender to you""I gathered that from the messages that have been exchanged in the past few hours," I replied. "We've got to try and make you look about ten years older," Maurice said "Well I can help," I said, "I feel about twenty years older, I've heard today that I was supposed to have left here in the middle of June, but the message was never received"

Maurice made a record time to Saint Flour. As we drove into the Place de la Liberte, Raymond was watching out for us and waved us round to the back entrance of the Terminus. The Maire is already waiting for you in the bar, so get yourself cleaned up and join us as quickly as you can. I went up to shower and change. Mum was waiting for me as I came back into the bedroom with her make-up bag. She said she only managed about eight years as I went down to the Bar

"Although I knew you were an English substitute for the son of this family, I had no idea you were actually an officer in the British army," was the Maire's opening remark. "Do you know how to arrange the surrender of our German occupiers?"

"I have received very exact instructions on the procedure," I assured the Maire. "It is actually quite a simple matter and it seems to me that the most important aspect is to have as many official witnesses as possible to the actual surrender and their signatures on the surrender documents.

It is unfortunate that we can only make limited use of the FFI in the actual surrender process because they are regarded as irregulars. During the drive back to Saint Flour I have prepared in my mind a plan that I believe will work, provide the security we need, and which can be witnessed by as many people as we can get into the Place de la Liberte"

"Don't you think the Place d'Armes be a more appropriate venue," asked the Maire. "That would mean marching the disarmed Germans up into the centre of the town and down again which would increase the opportunities for desertion and I am under instructions to limit desertion as far as possible." I replied

Fortunately almost everyone else agreed with my view and the matter was closed

"Nomination of the signatories to the surrender is an important aspect and must be settled now," I said. "We can dictate to the Germans who should sign and it will be, Colonel Bruno Schimdt from Aurillac as Major Kempf's superior officer, his two Captains, and any other officers of rank of Lieutenant and above, and we need to know the name and number of each signatory in advance," I added. Without allowing any discussion on the point, I went on, "Myself and my second-in-command, will sign on behalf of the Allied forces." "You have a problem immediately," interrupted Alexis, "Colonel Schmidt has not been seen for several days and the rumour is that he has been recalled for some reason, Captain Mohr is his deputy," "Then we must have the most senior of the two whoever is available," I replied

"As far as witnesses are concerned," I went on, "The Maire must be a witness and so must Alexis as the chief police officer for the town and from the canton we should also have the commandant of the Gendarmerie, Lieutenant Borotra, even though he is said to be pro-German. Do you think you could arrange that Alexis?" If it is any help you can tell him that as a superior officer I require him to be a witness"

"I feel sure that the SS actions at Oradour-sur-Glane will have modified his sympathies," replied Alexis. "After those persons we could allow any town councillor to add his signature. Are there any questions?"

"Who is going to prepare the surrender document?" asked the Maire. "I have to do that," I replied, "It will be in English only, authorised translations can be made at a later date, if there is any dispute, and the meaning in the English language will always take precedence."I continued, "I will need the use of which ever of your secretaries has the best command of English." "Mademoiselle Hugot has the best English in the Mairie," replied the Maire. "Then I will need her undivided attention until the surrender documents are ready

I decided a good night's sleep was necessary before tackling this task. I arrived early at the Mairie and found that Valerie Hugot had been briefed by the Maire and was ready although apprehensive of what lay ahead. I tried to put her at ease by using Christian names between us. We settled down to type the first draft. Valerie's spoken English was quite good but her spelling was atrocious. It took all the morning to get a correctly spelt first draft on paper. The second draft went much better and I was satisfied with it. As a courtesy I took it to the Maire's office and read it over to him in French.

Fortunately he agreed. I returned to Valerie's office and asked her for twenty copies of which ten must be original top copies. She settled down to the job. After the first two typed copies it became obvious I was going to have to check every one for spelling. I found a second typewriter and supplemented her efforts with the extra difficulty of a French keyboard. We finished about five in the afternoon, so I was able to send the Maire off to see Major Kempf to arrange for the actual surrender to take place three days later

The Monday club met again that Friday evening. We arranged for Stephan's men to collect all of the weaponry as the local occupying Germans left their barracks. Captain Mohr was instructed by telephone to arrange for the smaller forces of Germans from Aurillac and Mauriac bring all their armaments and trucks with them to also be surrendered at the Saint Flour barracks. Simon, Patrice, Victor and Sebastian were to assist Stephan in the disarming of the Germans and after locking up the barracks, would supervise the march from the barracks to Place de la Liberte. Notices were to be posted throughout Saint Flour informing everyone of the surrender location at twelve noon on Monday twenty-first of August.

During the intervening day the Wehrmacht Germans from the Gibory farm were to be brought to Saint Flour and reunited with their comrades, plus a further nine deserters from other regions. The two SS men were to remain at the Gibory farm until the allied forces arrived in Saint Flour. Stephan and his men were to round up as many of the deserters in our region as they could find to be handed over to Major Kempf before Sunday the twentieth. When all the business of the evening was over we celebrated. With all the extra people in the bar it was not possible to see everyone who was there. When the party finally broke up, long after curfew, I found my way up to bed. To my surprise our room was empty. When I tried the door of Jean-Francois' room the door was firmly locked, even though I could hear some movement from within the room. On going back to our room I found most of Yvette's clothes and other possessions had been taken out of the room. I went downstairs again and found Mum and Dad. They told me that Yvette had now discovered that I was an English officer and not Henri Dufour. Mum had tried to convince her that I had to conceal my real identity from her but Yvette said very forcefully, "If he can't trust me, I can't trust him, he might have a wife and children in England for all I know." Nothing Mum or dad could say would change her idea

I spent a restless night. In the morning neither Yvette nor Jean-Francois came down for breakfast. Mum said Yvette had taken some food upstairs the previous evening. The bar was busy from an early hour. The news was out in the town that tomorrow would see the Germans surrender and leave the town. Angelique's FFI news letter had arrived early in the town. She must have made a special effort to get the copies to the very first bus. I tried several times to get Yvette to open the door of the room but she was adamant. Jean-Francois was crying and whimpering at being confined on a beautiful warm summer's day

The news was also out that Henri Dufour was not Henri Dufour. Reactions ranged from congratulations on deceiving the Germans effectively to castigation for deceiving Lisette and Robert and putting them in danger of execution if the deception was discovered. I had decided to ride this criticism. I did not think it was my place to disclose that the substitution was their idea. Mum eventually took me in the back room and said she was going to use the master key to get in to the room with Yvette and Jean-Francois and try to resolve the matter. "Is there anything you want me to say to her?" she asked. I had already spent much thought on what I had to say to Yvette when my identity was revealed."Tell her I love her deeply and sincerely. I want to marry her as soon as it is confirmed that she is free to marry. I will accept Jean-Francois part of our family and be a father to him on whatever terms Yvette wants. Say I am sorry I had to deceive her but I was under strict instruction to disclose my identity to nobody who was not approved by my superiors. Tell her I sent details of her identity to General De Gaulle's office in London asking for approval to include her, and that approval was refused. Tell her again I love her." Mum went upstairs

There was some brief shouting and screaming as Mum and Dad forced their way into the room. A few raised eyebrows in the bar at the noise but I did not explain anything. I was too upset myself to talk about it. Dad came down again after a short time, and ignored enquiries as to where Yvette was today. "She's calmed down a little," he whispered to me at a suitable moment. Manuel arrived as usual to prepare the lunch food. "Talk to him," said Dad, "and tell him as much as you can because he will need some help with the food." "I worked that one out for myself after the Monday club meeting," said Manuel. "I had forgotten that we had so many extras at that meeting," I said," and helped him as much as I could until Mum came down again

Yvette brought Jean-Francois down for a late lunch after most of our customers had departed. She ignored me. After the meal Jean-Francois came to me and wanted to play. Yvette was busy on the telephone

Mid afternoon and father Albert came in to the Terminus to see me. We went through into the back room and Dad came too. "You are now reaping the reward of your disgraceful deception." he said addressing me. Dad answered, "The idea originated here in the Terminus after we lost our Henri in the air raid on Lille and when we heard that French identities were needed for Allied officers to get settled in Vichy France before it was occupied. Our new Henri is obeying orders from his government and the deception is theirs, not only of Yvette but of most of the population of Saint Flour, and most important of all, of the occupying Germans"

"Is this true?" said father Albert, addressing me again, "Yes I was recruited specifically for this work. I had a reasonable knowledge of French, I had spent several periods of time in France and other French speaking countries, I was reasonably like the real Henri Dufour, and I have a corrected club foot on my right leg." "I suppose there are others like you in France as well?" questioned Father Albert. I made no answer. "Can you confirm this?" said Father Albert to Dad. "I can only tell you that after we had suggested our dead son as an identity

380

we were told that an English officer would be sent to us to replace him." "Who told you this?" asked Father Albert. "You must not answer that." I intervened. "You can't give orders like that to a French citizen." said Father Albert. "I am sure that Robert will recognise that confidentiality is an essential part of the work the FFI do and after all he is an old soldier who has completed the oath of loyalty to France." Dad nodded

Father Albert spent some time with Yvette while I amused Jean-Francois. He had recognised there was something wrong and was trying to tell me all about it

His attempts to console me brought tears to my eyes and I began to recognise how much he now meant to me

Valerie Hugot came in the mid-afternoon with all the copies of the surrender documents. She must have made a very special effort. I couldn't find a single error, and complemented her. "I think those papers are about the most important I will ever type," she said. "The Maire and councillors will be coming to see you this evening to check the procedures again." she said. "Tomorrow will be a triumph for you"

Chapter 50

Surrender

I was up very early next morning. I was not the first to be out on the Place de la Liberte. Alexis and his men were marking out places where the townspeople could stand to witness the event and where the troops could be drawn up. The actual surrender was timed for noon. and the troops were expected to leave about one o'clock

The celebrations started early. The bar was full from eight o'clock onwards and the luncheon tables that had been put out on the terrace soon filled up as well. A large table with tricolour flag as a cover was laid out with all the documents ready for signature in the middle of the Place de la Liberte. Everything was going according to plan. Even the Maire was early

Exactly on time at eleven forty-five a bicycle messenger from the barracks arrived to say the disarmament was complete and the troops were about to leave. When the troops were in position and the German officers who were to be the signatories lined up on one side of the table, I read the surrender document in English. The Maire then read an unauthorised translation in French and Councillor Leman an unauthorised translation in German. I then requested Major Kempf and his officers to accept and sign the documents. I then added my signature followed by the French signatories. Then a seemingly endless stream of witnesses completed the procedure

Major Kempf was given two copies of the document. Plus one copy each for each of his officers who signed. I also gave him letters addressed to Francois Peillon at Le Puy and Gabriel Deforge at Saint Etienne confirming the surrender and suggesting they should afford reasonable assistance to the troops in transit

"Beyond Saint Etienne I have no contact and I am not even aware of the name of the FFI officer in that region. I would avoid Lyon because there is a large and very active FFI group in the city and outbreaks of violence occur on most days. You are in no position to take any part in such events"

I think Major Kempf was pleased to have the letters to Peillon and Deforge, because he did not know either what had happened to German troops in those areas. Before they left most of the German officers were prepared to shake hands with me and the other signatories

I am pleased to say that as they marched out of the Place de la Liberte the local population exchanged waves with the Germans. After they had left there was an almost uncanny silence. Then quite suddenly, almost en masse, the people recognised that they were no longer constrained. No limits on the number of people in a group talking together, nobody to stop you and demand to see your identity card, no curfew, nobody to search your shopping bag. Now they really had something to celebrate and they did

The group of us around the table used for the signing of the surrender documents were their first target. Everybody wanted to shake everybody else's hand. I received many congratulations and expressions of surprise at my real identity

Just a few asked what really happened to the true Henri Dufour and when they were told went on to both commiserate with and congratulate Mum and Dad. Strangely enough that is how I still thought of them

I slipped away from the crowd and into the back door of the Terminus and up to my room. I wanted to be alone, and I wanted to find a way to win back Yvette's love. I lay on the bed for some hours. I could do nothing unless I could be face to face with Yvette, preferably, on her own. Neither she nor Jean-Francois were in their room nor anywhere in the Terminus

I wandered across the Place de la Liberte avoiding people as far as possible. I heard singing coming from the Church. I quietly entered. There was an impromptu thanksgiving Mass in progress and I took a seat at the back so that I could speak with Father Albert after the service. Father Albert saw me there as he greeted the departing participants of the Mass, and when the last had gone came and sat with me

"I suppose your job is over now," he said. "By no means," I replied. "My desire now is to find a way to marry Yvette as soon as she knows she is free to marry again, I love her deeply and I know she loved me until she found out that I was not Henri Dufour. I can understand her feeling of not being trusted with the truth." "Perhaps she does not want to go and live in England?" suggested Father Albert. "That is not a point at issue," I replied, "I am perfectly happy to return and live in France

I have no emotional attachments in England, and I think I have proved I can live in France." Father Albert thought for some minutes, "You will find her

383

and Jean-Francois at her home in Murat and I think that answers the question you were going to ask me. But don't expect her parents to welcome you, I know they very strongly disapproved of you as a new partner for their daughter and potential guardian of Jean-Francois, before these latest revelations"

On the way back to the Terminus I met Simon Laert, a shopkeeper from the upper town, where I regularly bought supplies for the Terminus. "You must be a very brave man to do what you have done; Lisette and Robert must have agreed to have you of course?" "In fact," I answered him, "the idea came from Lisette and Robert, they are the brave ones, and I was chosen by the authorities in England simply because they judged I had a chance of passing as Henri Dufour with the full support of Lisette and Robert. Think what might have happened to them if their involvement became known to the occupying Germans"

We reached the Terminus and I had to use the front entrance this time. The bar was packed tight with people. We forced a way through to the bar and Mum and Dad who were rushed off their feet. Simon insisted on announcing to everyone in the bar that Lisette and Robert deserved the Croix de Guerre with Palms for what they had done

I am not quite sure how many understood; an awful lot of alcohol was being consumed

Mum took me on one side into the back room. "Have you seen Yvette?" She asked. "She's taken Jean-François and gone to her parents at Murat." I replied, "Father Albert told me so. I'm going up to lie down. I can't stand all of these people just getting drunk"

She returned to the bar and called Simon Laert, "I need to go to Murat and I can see your van is outside, can you take me to the Deville home, Yvette has run away from here and I need to talk to all the Devilles urgently." Mum told me all about this the next day They drove to Murat. Yvette's two younger sisters were out with Yvette and Jean-Francois celebrating the departure of the German occupiers. Auguste Deville had been recruited into the Tricolour brigade, and wounded in fighting on the beachheads. He was thus not favourably inclined towards the Allied forces. "I've come to talk to you about Henri and Yvette, there is so much you need to know." "We don't even know who Henri is," interrupted Francine, "other than that he is an English officer, we don't want our Yvette going off to England with our grandson, we may never see him again."

"That's why I am here to talk to you," said Mum, "they have lived together in my home for two years now and I believe that I know more about their relationship than you do. They are a perfectly matched couple and Jean-Francois could not have a better father than Henri, I still call him that because, even now I, do not know his real name." Simon intervened, "There is a lot more to know about this than I ever dreamed of, and I've only found out about it today. Lisette and Robert volunteered their real son's identity to the resistance because he was dead but not so recorded because no body had been found. The English officer, I must still call Henri because I do not know his real name either, was chosen by the British Army because he had a chance of being passed off as Lisette's dead son. You can hardly blame him for falling in love with your charming daughter." Mum interrupted, "nor blame Yvette for falling love with Henri, when they were thrown together by the war. I saw Yvette falling in love, it happened under my roof, I know they are well matched, it doesn't matter that they were born in different countries." The temperature of the argument was rising. Auguste entered the argument

"We don't want our grandson going off to England and perhaps we see him only once or twice as he grows up." "It won't be like that," said Mum

"The war will be over in a year. Then Henri will have to return to England to be demobilised. Then they can marry. Henri has told me he has no sentimental attachments in England. He enjoys the French way of life. He is ready and willing to come and live here. He has a promise of employment from a man who I know represents a huge organisation in Clermont. He wants, and I want him to marry Yvette. My dream is that they will marry, have further children, and when Robert and I give up the Terminus, Henri will retire, and with Yvette take over the Terminus which we will bequeath to them: they are in effect our family too." Mum paused for breath. "There and now you know it all," she added

There was a long silence. After everyone had gathered their thoughts, Auguste said, "This places the whole situation in a different light, of course we did not know anything of this and we must thank you for opening up your heart to us in this way. I think you should leave us now to our thoughts," said Francine, but of course nothing will change Yvette's mind, she simply will not trust him because he did not tell her of his real identity and even now she only knows he is not Henri Dufour but a British officer with no name." Simon drove her back to the Terminus where the celebrations were still going on, just more boisterously and more noisily

I stayed in my room until the partying subsided, by which time it was dark. I wandered out into the Place de la Liberte and breathed the cooler night air. What was I going to do now, my task was almost over. My plans had been to get out of the army at the first opportunity, take up Pascal's offer of employment and further education in France. Marry Yvette at the first opportunity, and settle down somewhere in the area between Saint Flour and Clermont

I heard midnight strike from the Cathedral tower Somebody had worked very quickly to have the chimes restored. There were still a few hardened drinkers

385

in the bar of the Terminus. I wandered in Dad immediately set up a Pastis and water for me. I consumed it rapidly followed by another. After that everyone was buying me a drink I don't remember going to bed that night other than waking up with Sambo beside me at first light.

Saint Flour did not wake very early the next day. I was the first to be up and about until well past nine o'clock. Some early buses left almost empty, others did not leave at all. I set about clearing all the glasses from the night before. Then both the terrace and the bar and restaurant area had to be swabbed and dried

The breakfast coffee was put on and breakfast prepared before Mum came down. She looked around, poured coffee for both of us and said, "I want you to sit down and let me tell you about yesterday." She told me of her visit to the Deville family including her dream, and their reaction. "At the very least I have removed their objections to Yvette marrying you."

"Did you see Yvette?" I asked. "No she was out celebrating with her sisters

I do not know how much or when or even if they will tell her about my visit. It was Simon Laert who drove me there and back and he thus knows what was said, but I am confident he will be discreet."

After breakfast I went out to the workshop. I had a delicate repair job to do. by hand for a local pharmacist who had dropped his fine scales. The concentration took my mind off my other problem. When I had fine tuned them to the required accuracy I delivered them back to his shop. By this time the town was awake again but there was lethargy everywhere. The pharmacist was busy selling his hangover cure. No news from Yvette all day

I attended to my incoming messages. The war news was good. Many German troops plus a huge number of armoured vehicles had been trapped by the closure of the Falaise gap. I had to look at the maps to understand the significance of this.   The Americans had reached the Loire at many places but there was still now hard news that they had crossed the river, and no news about how many bridges remained intact. There was also a major thrust towards Paris. The Franco-American thrust up the Rhone valley was meeting little resistance. Thus the gap through which the Germans might leave Vichy France was narrowing. A message from Francois Peillon confirmed that Major Kempf and his force had passed through the Le Puy area without incident although a number of his men had deserted

Alexis Lescaut knew of a number of deserters remaining concealed in our area, on farms where in general terms they worked for their keep, in homes where a woman was concealing them for her own purposes, and some on the loose working here and there so that at any one time nobody was aware of exactly where they were. "What are we going to do about them?" was Alex's question at the next Monday club meeting. The Maire, who had now decided to become a member of our club, said "Arrest them and put them in jail." I don't have enough cells," said Alexis, "even if I fill all the cells in the whole of Cantal, there are not enough cells"

"Then perhaps we should do nothing," said councillor Leman, after all if they are working, the farmers need all the help they can get."

I hear there are plans to tar and feather the women in the town who have Germans living with them," said Dad, "and we still have no idea how long it will be before the Allies get this far South, they seem to be stuck at the Loire."What sort of number are we talking about?" asked the Maire, "I actually know of one hundred and fifty-six," said Alexis, "and I expect there could be another thirty I don't know about." "Could we get the FFI involved," asked Raymond, "and where is Stephan tonight? It's not like him to miss a meeting"

"Stephan has gone," said Angelique to me, "He has left a note for you with my father on the understanding it is only to be given to you or destroyed," "So who is now in charge of the FFI in Saint Flour?" asked the Maire. "Most of them have left with Stephan," said Angelique, "I saw them go yesterday." "Then you must take charge of them," said the Maire to me. "I can of course accept that responsibility, but only on a temporary basis, I will doubtless be recalled once I have completed my orders here, which should be only a week or two from now." Raymond speaking to Alexis said, "If you are so short of cells perhaps the smaller number of Germans who are co-habiting with local women could be arrested and imprisoned, this might reduce the feelings about tarring and feathering." "That's a sound idea," said councillor Dechaux. "What are you going to charge them with," asked the Maire, "No problem," said Alexis, "No identity card, illegal residence in France, and if I read the law books I am sure we can find enough to keep them in custody for several months." The meeting became quite rowdy

"What about the women and their loss of conjugal rights" said somebody." "They never had any," shouted another. "Well now they have a choice," yet a third voice. Nevertheless several women were tarred and feathered on the Place d'Armes a few days later, before the police could intervene

The BBC French service on the twenty-fifth August announced the surrender of Paris to the second division of the Free French Forces under General Leclerc. The German Commander, von Chlotitz, defied Hitler's orders to destroy the city. General De Gaulle entered the city in triumph on the same day. This news was cause for further celebrations on the Friday evening and most of Saturday before the people had enough

Father Albert had arranged a special celebratory Mass for the Sunday as had all the other Churches in Saint Flour. With the liberation of Paris as an extra cause the Churches had never been so full. On Sunday evening Yvette and Jean-

Francois returned to Saint Flour. She apologised to Mum and Dad for deserting her during such a busy period and asked if her job was still open. Mum generously welcomed her back. She was polite to me but there was no expression of affection She rebuffed any attempt I made to talk to her about our relationship

A message from Pascal on Tuesday advised that all German personnel had now left Clermont Ferrand and the Canton of Puy-de-Dome. He suggested that I should visit him before I left for England. Two days later the telephone service was restored and I could speak to him directly. Eventually he decided to come to Saint Flour to lend his advice on the situation with Yvette

Chapter 51

Orders from London

London made contact again. When I had completed all matters in Saint Flour I was to bring all of my men with me to Angers, Tours or Orleans where arrangements would be made with the Americans occupying those cities to fly us back to the UK. You can expect to be liberated by American forces moving South from Tours, timing not known yet

Officers in charge have been told that Germans have withdrawn from your area and that they should establish contact with local FFI forces as Allies. Please advise your latest information re location of any German forces

It was quite a simple answer. Officially the German forces occupying Cantal surrendered on twenty-first August and left here to move Eastwards to the German lines under white flags. We know of one hundred and fifty six deserters in our immediate area and probably another thirty we don't know about. Both of these figures include deserters from other cantons especially those to the West

In general terms the Germans are leaving as quickly as they can. We have definite information that the canton of Puy-de-Dome is free of all Germans. On the other hand in the Cantons to the South the German are harassing the Allies advance up the Rhone valley from Saint Tropez with little success but there is no sign of their withdrawal. Definitive numbers and locations other than those above vary from day to day and are unreliable based in many cases on hearsay. We do not intend to arrest those Germans who are working on the farms at present. The farmers need the extra manpower because the Maquis have entirely withdrawn from our area, and all areas to the West of Cantal. Please ensure that the advancing Americans have our radio frequencies so they can advise us of their progress. All contacts can be en claire

In addition, in code, we requested details of the American identification codes and asked London to advise them of our recognition procedure.

We received a rare message from the Oradour-sur-Vayres group. They stated that a large number of the SS troops responsible for the Oradour-sur-Glane massacre had changed their uniforms for the standard field-grey wehrmacht uniforms and were trying to travel Eastwards through the northern part of our Canton so avoiding the Puy-de-Dome Canton because of the success of the liberation and the absence of any regular wehrmacht with whom they might mingle They obviously did not know of the surrender and departure of our Germans. However there were a number of deserters working on the farms with whom they might find some comradely connections This gave us a real problem. The first part of their move would be through the high volcanic area of the Auvergne. The farms were remote and we had little knowledge of them. There had been a number of Maquis working there but the area was considered poor and even the Germans did not try to collect quota from them. This was essentially a job for Alexis and the police. The sub-prefecture of Mauriac would be the first part of our Canton they would enter. Accordingly Alexis sent over half his personnel to reinforce the Mauriac force

I spent some time studying the map of the region and immediately recognised the problems. If the SS personnel, who were reportedly using the standard German trucks retained their use they would immediately be recognised as an unusual troop movement and might be intercepted by the use of road blocks. However if the trucks travelled in a convoy there would be too many soldiers for even the reinforced Mauriac police to effectively arrest them if it came to a fire fight

On the other hand if they abandoned their vehicles and tried to cross our territory on foot via the farms we did not have enough personnel to cover all the possible routes through the region. I immediately placed all five of my personnel at Alexis' disposal with Raymond in charge and he left for Mauriac within two hours. The telephone service was now almost back to full working order which would help the situation considerably. Lieutenant Borotra from Aurillac with over half his men also moved to Mauriac with all their transport also within two hours

The gorges of the Dordogne to the west of Cantal formed the border with the canton of Charente. with only six crossing points. All of these were manned by police controls within four hours of the start of the operation

It was a relief to hear from the crossing keepers of some of the roads that crossed dams that no German trucks had passed over those crossings. Further enquiries among the population of Mauriac and nearby farms revealed that German deserters were at work in the area and had been for some time. Some had left going East and more had arrived generally from the west and on foot No reports of Germans in trucks. The estimate of German deserters in the area was around sixty. We pressed the resistance group at Orator-sur-Vayres for their estimate of the number of German SS in wehrmacht uniforms and they eventually replied, "about forty men in four trucks, fully armed and with enough fuel, food and water to get them to Germany"

It didn't sound as though they were going to work their passage."We've got to act quickly." was my opening remark at an early meeting of the Monday club that evening after I had explained the position. "I think you've already done the most important preparation," said the Maire. "We need all the help we can get," said Councillor Leman, "you should ask Pascal to provide more FFI members, the route they will likely take borders his canton and he has far more men than we have." Nods of agreement all round. "Let's see if the telephone is working"

I said and went into the back room. I eventually got through to Christoff, Pascal's deputy, who until now was only a name I knew. I explained at some length what we knew, and he too slowly recognised the need for extra help and the urgency. "I know where Pascal will be at eight o'clock and I will talk to him urgently, I am sure he will do what he can" he said. I returned to the Monday club and advised them of the position. "What about your man in Le Puy? Shouldn't he be told also, because that is where the Germans will go when and if they leave Cantal." said councillor Dechaux. Another telephone call, not so successful. I spoke to some body who I did not know about and who did not know me. A lengthy conversation to explain the whole situation eventually led to some sort of action. He agreed to contact François immediately but said their resources were stretched because of the numerous deserters trying to pass through their canton

Shortly after the meeting dispersed, Pascal was on the telephone in a very business like mood. "I've heard some rumours about these SS people but nothing so concrete as you have now told me." We must work closely together on this and capture all these impersonators if we possibly can. I will arrive at Mauriac tomorrow morning at eight o'clock, can you be there by then also?" "Yes," I replied. "I will arrange for all available FFI men to be at Bort-les-Orgues as soon as they can get there, you are absolutely right to base the operation on Mauriac, controlling the crossing points on the Dordogne is the key to catching these Germans"

I rang the police station. Fortunately I spoke with Franchoit Frachot a senior clerk. "I have to be in Mauriac before eight o'clock tomorrow morning and need a car to get me there, who have you got available?" In his position he knew all about the situation. "I'm sure Felix de Boni would be delighted to drive you," he said. "Then can you ask him to pick me up at six o'clock from the Terminus"

Mauriac woke up to find the war had returned! Pascal had also acquired a number of German vehicles and with those from Saint Flour in a small town like Mauriac plus lots of police and FFI in evidence, all that was missing was the enemy. Pascal had already sent patrols off to all the river crossing points to the North which with those we already had in place left no place for the Germans to cross the Dordogne without our knowledge. After crossing the Dordogne the next continuous line to be crossed was the departmental main route from Aurillac to Clermont. Pascal had already arranged for one observer to be placed at every road junction from the west along the length of the road with instructions to report the route taken by any of the trucks going Eastwards. We at once made the same arrangement. In theory it looked good. We would get news from the river crossings that the trucks had entered our area and again the route by which they were moving Eastwards

We did not have to wait long. Our communications centre heard again from Oradour-sur-Vayres, that the four trucks left Oradour-sur-Glane yesterday evening heading towards Limoges. Pascal had good contact with an active resistance group at Bugeat and had already asked them to report any information re these trucks. Just after noon they intercepted four trucks travelling in convoy on the route from Limoges and going towards Ussel. The Germans were belligerent and threatened the FFI if they did not let them retreat to the East. They added that there were still many German deserters moving in groups some with transport of the same type as the convoy of four but usually only one at a time. We were now receiving reports from the river crossing patrols. Single German deserters and small groups were now crossing the Dordogne, some motor transport also and several single lorries of the type we were seeking. Many of the deserters were trying to buy food and or fuel

The distance from the river to the main road left little scope for deviation and all of the single lorries were intercepted and judged to be innocent deserters making the best they could of their situation

Late in the afternoon we got a report from the bridge in Bort-les-Orgues itself that, two trucks of the type we sought crossed after stopping the town trying to buy fresh food. The shop keepers refused them and they actually asked our bridge patrol where they could stop for the night. He sent them south down the main road with instructions to turn on to the Departmental route three for Antignac where they would find common land to stop overnight. This sounded too good to be true.

"If they actually stop there overnight," said Pascal, "to surround them before dawn and take them just at daybreak would be the ideal tactic." "Could you arrange for a bicycle patrol to approach the site at dusk and report?" asked Raymond. "I'll provide the men and the bicycles said Pascal if you will lead the patrol." All agreed

No sooner than this arrangement was made a report from the Pont de Project that they had stopped a truck of the type we sought and diverted it to the bridge at Aigle because it was too heavy for their bridge. There had been much argument over the matter. The Germans said there was no warning signs about the weight limit on the bridge, the French Police said the bridge had been closed to al traffic over two tonnes since before the war. Eventually they persuaded the Germans that it was unsafe to cross. They managed to see inside the truck and reported much weaponry including machine guns, mortars and what looked like road mines Their estimate of the gross weight was almost six tonnes. One of the police offered to show them the way to Aigle as it was now dark and road signs were not frequent. The offer was accepted and the intention was to take a very circuitous route to Aigle. The bridge at Aigle was narrow and limited to twelve tonnes and of course was patrolled by our men.

Pascal immediately sent off extra FFI men to Agile taking advantage of the delay due to the circuitous route to reach it. His idea was to try and provoke the Germans into some violence and if they responded to give way to their demands. "Lets make them show their hand." he concluded It was going to be a lively night

Three trucks pinpointed, where was the fourth?

The bicycle patrol reported from Antignac. The Germans had stopped for the night. One of the patrol men approached close enough to be stopped by one of the German sentries who was fully armed and aggressive wanting to know why he was approaching their camp. Our man claimed he was looking for sheep lost from his flock and he could hear where they might be better at night and common land was often where they might be found. "The German clearly didn't understand about sheep," he said. "Where are you going? He asked the sentry, "Back to Germany," replied the sentry. The FFI might stop you," They'll get a bloody nose if they try, we don't want to fight them any more but if they start it we'll retaliate and wipe them out"

The common land where the Germans were overnight was almost entirely enclosed by roads although some were in very poor condition. "There's no way we can use vehicles to approach the site," said Pascal, "they'll hear a truck two kilometres away, "so its back to two wheels each," said Raymond. The FFI made a fine effort

Before daybreak the German encampment was surrounded at a distance of some two hundred meters. As the first light was in the sky a single shot started the operation. Following the single shot, flares were fired and lit up the German vehicles and surrounding areas and a single shot volley over their heads indicated they were surrounded by armed troops

The Germans had the good sense to recognise they were trapped and after a brief exchange of shouted words agreed to surrender as prisoners of war. The contents of their trucks were left under guard and the trucks used to transport them to a disused barn on the outskirts of the village where they were kept under heavy guard

The reinforcements sent to Aigle arrived before the Germans were able to reach the bridge. Victor and Sebastian were put in charge of this group. On arriving they found that the FFI had already staged a bus breakdown in one of the tunnels on the approach to the bridge. The breakdown crew had just arrived and were working on an alleged broken rear spring. Victor strolled over the bridge to the broken down bus and engaged the German driver in a friendly conversation. The driver was initially not friendly but warmed to the friendly conversation especially when Victor criticised the maintenance of the bus and the local roads. "Not nearly as good as in Germany," Victor remarked. "No," agreed the German driver, "I wonder if you could tell me what the road from Mauriac to Riom-es-Montagnes is like" "Rather better than this," Victor replied, "No big rivers to cross and no bridge problems but some very steep gradients, beautiful views though all the way." "How long do you think this repair will take?" questioned the German." "About an hour I expect, you'll be on your way before dawn, and by the way don't linger in Mauriac. It was full of police and FFI this morning, but they should be fast asleep when you go through." Victor walked away towards the breakdown crew with a shouted thank-you following him

Victor did not stay long with the breakdown crew but triumphantly picked up the phone to give us the route of this truck and a reasonable idea of the timing

Raymond and Sebastian were given the task of trapping this truck.

No sooner than allocating that task than a call from a FFI group in Neuvic via our communication centre to say that a German truck answering the right description was in the town and causing problems by demanding that shops should open to sell them fresh food especially bread. Nobody had bread at that time because the bakery just starting work. If they wanted bread they had to wait for some hours. While waiting for the bread to be made the baker was asked for the way to the Pont de Vernejoux, and the baker marked the route on the German's map. He stressed that the roads were very narrow and marked some steep gradients saying, "If your truck is fully loaded you might not make it," and added, "there is a weight limit on the bridge but I can't remember what is the limit" One of the FFI members was a witness to this exchange, and soon the news was with us

The bridge at Pont de Vernejoux was not one we had considered of much importance and there were only two FFI men there plus the guard who was responsible for checking the weight of vehicles using the bridge. The next problem would arise if this truck was also bound for Rion-es- Montagnes the most direct route would take them past the site of the German encampment near Antignac when there might still be some action going on. "How soon can we get more men to the Pont de Vernejoux," asked Pascal, "How many men have we got left," I replied. "Eleven, if we include ourselves, replied Felix."That's not enough to confront them," said Pascal. "Eleven of us against say a dozen SS trained and armed Germans is not a battle we should fight." "We've got to delay them until we can free up some of our bicycle army at Antignac," I said, "We've got the odds right there but once they are captured and disarmed we won't need eighty men to guard them"

"If we blow the bridge we could delay them by at least two hours," said Felix looking at the maps, "but we've only got an hour to get the explosives there, laid and fused, before they could arrive." I replied. "Too costly and too risky," concluded Pascal

"If they were buying bread, it must be for breakfast," mused Felix, "Suppose we could find somebody to offer them breakfast,' as a gesture of good will' for withdrawing with out fighting' If it were done right we could gain at least a couple of hours." "Make it a place difficult to find and maybe we gain "three hours,"I added. "Unconventional, subtle, definitely not in the rule book, but I think it might work." said Pascal. We called back to our FFI man. "We have to delay them without arousing their suspicions," said Pascal, "Find someone who will offer them breakfast, because they are leaving without fighting and causing mayhem."

About six o'clock when the last baking was in the oven, the baker started phoning around his most trustworthy clients. He finally remembered he had one client with distinct pro-German feelings who had even been heard to say, 'France should have joined the German side in the war.' "Who's paying," was the first, response to the proposal and the Baker put the FFI man on the line. He explained we had to delay the Germans to avoid a bloody battle when they were intercepted, and finally the breakfast was on provided the FFI guaranteed to pay "Now the baker had to sell the idea to the Germans."I have just been speaking to one of my regular customers who has always been sympathetic to the German cause, and he would like to offer you and your men breakfast at his farm as a gesture for not causing mayhem in our village." The German looked astounded, but he went and talked to his men. "We put it to the vote," he said, "and it was seven to four in favour of French Breakfast"

"If you wait twenty minutes you can even deliver the bread for your own breakfast, and our friend here," he said indicating the FFI man, "will have to take you because now I've got to do another baking." It all looked and sounded so innocent

It appears that the Germans enjoyed their breakfast, they spent almost two and a half hours over it. By the time we knew this, we also knew of the successful incarceration of the two truckloads from the Antigenic common. Pascal now used his influence with the Maire of Clermont to send all of the prison transport vans to Bort-les-Orgues to take the Germans into custody as suspected members of the SS involved in the massacre at Oradour-sur-Glane

Simon and Patrice with another twenty FFI men had set off in trucks to block the road to Riom-es-Montagnes at a suitable point.   Fortunately   some of the FFI men knew the road and were unanimous about the best place to close it. "It's the highest point on the road, very isolated, no where to go if you leave the road."They made directly for that point. Simon agreed it was a good point. Two men were sent further on to prevent any stray locals coming from the other direction from being involved. The road was mined past the place where the truck would be stopped by stones and tree branches on the road.

Then Simon would approach the truck and tell them that they would be picked off one by one if they attempted to leave the truck without giving up their arms first, and telling them that the road mined further on of the managed to force their way through the blockage. He then called to the marksmen to show themselves, and then the Germans surrendered

Simon kept the Germans under guard and sent Patrice back to Trizac where there was a telephone to advise us of the successful capture of the Germans. Pascal immediately diverted one of the prison vans collect them. So by ten o'clock in the morning three of the four truckloads had been captured

Never having been in a prison van himself Pascal had no idea of how many places they had or even how many prison vans there were in Clermont.

Each van finished up making three round trips during the day. The fourth truckload having breakfasted negotiated Pont de Vernejoux after satisfying the guard that they were not over the weight limit and continued on their way. They crossed the main Aurillac to Clermont road and took to the lanes leading to Antigenic. As they approached the village they caught up with a party of cyclists who did not give way to them. After all it was a Saturday afternoon, the sun was shining, the harvest was almost in, and they were out to enjoy themselves. They passed through the village and were driving alongside the common land, and there was another of their trucks parked at the roadside. The truck stopped and the officer got down and looked inside the parked vehicle. He saw a handcuffed German

"You've arrived at last," said the handcuffed man, "I should accept the chance they will give you to surrender, there's far more of them than you could beat." At that point a single shot followed by a volley from all points of the compass, broke all the lights on the truck and punctured all four tyres. "Is this what they did to you?" asked the officer. "More or less," replied the handcuffed man. A cyclist appeared, a German speaker. "Do you accept our offer, you will be arrested and treated as prisoners of war." The breakfast had done it's job, they surrendered. More cyclists appeared, this time they were armed and escorted the Germans to the barn to join their comrades. Back at Mauriac we were jubilant. We mustn't forget the two SS men at the Gibory farm, "I reminded Pascal."If you will hold back the last prison van until I go and get them, and that will solve a problem for me." "Agreed"

I used Felix de Boni as a chauffer having got a message to the Gibory Farm via Bernice Rodot. The steep climb up to the Gibory farm from the Prat du Bouc was difficult, I'd had no sleep for over twenty-four hours. The message had only just got through to Pierre Gibory so I had the chance to relax and with a fine ham salad and half a bottle my energy level improved. Pierre said he'd had some good work out of the prisoners and he wondered if he might offer his service to the local prison governor. "They've not made any attempt to escape. They still don't know where they are in France, and sometimes I wonder if they even think they are in France" I laughed, "We'll soon change that, they are off to prison in Clermont to await trial for the offences at Tulle and Brive, and we've just captured four truckloads of suspected SS in wehrmacht uniforms that are said to have been at Oradour-sur-Glane"

"This may be the last time I see you Pierre, I've had a recall order when I have tidied up matters here, which will be only a matter of days." "What about Yvette?" he asked, "I thought it was common knowledge she's rejected any idea of marriage. It was my intention to return to France and marry her as soon as I could get out of the services." "Any time you return to France, and whoever might be with you, you will always be welcome here

The three brothers all accompanied us down to the car, the two Germans, now back in SS uniforms, were handcuffed before getting into the car. I stood for a few moments of long handshakes with the Giborys, then I had to get in the car in a hurry before my feelings got the better of me

It was a straightforward drive back to Mauriac. The last prison van was waiting on the forecourt of the Mairie. I had a thought during the drive back to Mauriac. The prisoners taken from the four trucks had all been in field grey wehrmacht uniforms and now we were going to confront them with two men in full SS uniforms. Before allowing them out of the car I brought Pascal out of the Mairie to witness any reaction explaining my thoughts on the way. When we opened the doors of the prison van six wehrmacht uniformed men were locked in their seats. The first of our SS men greeted one of the six as follows, "Hail Hitler Herr Lieutenant, Ich bin uberascht, bitte enschuldigen, Ich kann nicht salutieren." showing his handcuffed hands.

The two SS men were locked in their seats and the van left for Clermont. Back in the Mairie Pascal was delighted. "He greeted a wehrmacht uniformed soldat as a Lieutenant to whom he was known and had possibly served with. That is just the sort of evidence we need to hold all these Germans as suspect SS members. I don't know what it cost you to hold these men for the past three months but it was worth every centime just to see that incident." I laughed, "It didn't cost us a single centime, the Giborys made them work for their keep, doing heavy manual work outdoors." "Was that safe?" questioned Pascal. "Pierre Gibory said it was worth getting several men's work for one armed guard plus three dogs to watch them

You've never been up to that farm I'm sure, it is such a remote location in a quite terrifying terrain. Until we sent our wehrmacht prisoners back with Major Kempf the Giborys were getting seven men's work for no pay for almost three months. They rebuilt two barns that needed serious attention and walled in an area of good grass for new born lambs. They are very happy with the result"

"The news from the war is good too," said Pascal, "It is expected that Lyon will be captured in the next few hours and the drive South from Paris has got as far as Auxerre. I should imagine they will meet up within two weeks, and we are going to celebrate tonight with an early dinner at the local inn which somehow can still put on a good menu for special occasions and then an early nights rest for me, you youngsters can keep going longer." I didn't say how tired I was

Over dinner Pascal commiserated with me over Yvette's attitude. "Perhaps she hasn't recognised how difficult it might be to find another partner after a major war like this one. Those men returning after the fighting can afford to be very choosy over who they court. I'll have a word with your mother and make sure she says all these things to Yvette." "None of those points however change her sole point that, although I had to deceive her, I didn't break the rules and tell her." I replied

"I believe this could be our last face to face meeting before you go back," he went on, "I want you to know all the offers I have made to you still stand and will continue to stand. France is not at all generous with it's recognition of outside help but I can act as I choose. You know we have a manufacturing unit in England. I will make sure that the boss there will recognise you if you turn up there or call him using the name of Henri Dufour and the same will apply to all of his successors for as long as I am in charge here." At last I felt I could put a real name to Pascal. We finished early and returned to our lodgings in the Mairie. In spite of my fatigue I could not sleep

A late morning start as all the Mauriac gathering sorted themselves out and to go their separate ways. Too many goodbyes to be said to so many people with whom a close trust had been developed and who I was now unlikely to see again

Felix was quiet on the drive back to Saint Flour. He recognised my distress at parting from so many people and the parting from Saint Flour would not be any easier

Chapter 52

Our Allies Arrive

With the telephones now working and improving daily, news of our deeds preceded us. Angelique had put out a special FFI news letter even though it was Sunday and she had to bring the copies in to the town on her bicycle. So everybody was looking out for our return. Lyon had now been liberated and that was also cause for celebration. In our absence, the trucks of last year's wool harvest had been rescued from the tunnel, and soon it might be sold so the farmer's cash position would improve. The wool had not suffered any damage

This year's wool harvest was still at the farms but soon it might be possible for Jean-Pierre Bourdet to reopen the lanoline factory to process this year's wool, and soon afterwards, the soap factory as well

Although we were receiving much more news including the progress of the Americans, who had finally crossed the Loire, in some force, The Germans were retreating as rapidly as they were allowed to move by the concerted air attacks. We had not received a single message from General Bradley's third army group who were supposed to be headed in our direction. Poitiers was liberated on Tuesday and South of that City there were no reports of any remaining Germans

I considered the journey we will have to make to either Tours or Orleans. It soon became apparent that Orleans would be better than Tours. Accordingly I sent a message to London asking them to send the uniforms for all six of us to General Bradley's headquarters in Orleans await our arrival

Next day we heard that the gap between the Southerly thrust from the Paris area and the Northerly thrust up the Rhone-Saone valley was ever narrowing and was expected to close in the next few days. General Bradley's southerly movement from the Loire valley had now liberated Gueret and Montlucon. It looked as if it would be the force that had liberated Gueret would be the troops that liberated Aurillac and Saint Flour. I sent a courtesy telegram to

General Bradley's headquarters advising him about the uniforms that would arrive shortly. I added a reminder of our radio frequencies and that I expected to hear from his group approaching Cantal in the near future. I added the information that we had many German deserters in the area with SS men in wehrmacht uniforms amongst them. I telephoned Pascal to check with him some of the details of our journey to Orleans. "I really don't know why they haven't arranged to send a plane for you

We can't have you travelling on buses and trains, arriving tired and probably scruffy, unannounced, You tell me when you are ready to go and I'll send two of our cars to collect you all and deliver you in comfort and with some ceremony to Bradley's headquarters," I thanked him profusely, but wondered what the 'some ceremony' might involve

I didn't feel like spending much time in the Terminus. Yvette almost ignored me, Jean-Francois didn't understand why whenever he came to me he was soon removed and taken upstairs. Mum and Dad tried to stop this attitude but with no real success

And then on Friday night Mathilde arrived, unannounced, and clearly with something on her mind. I was in the bar but in just the right position to see her getting off the bus

"Mathilde's just arrived," I said to Dad. "I can guess what she wants," Dad replied, and went to get Mum from the back room. Mum welcomed her sister-in-law as she pushed her way through the throng towards the door to the back room using her case as a battering ram. She clearly expected to stay. "We didn't know you were coming," was Mum's greeting, "you weren't intended to know," Mathilde replied, "Where's Yvette?" "Putting Jean-Francois to bed," Mum answered. "Don't you go off anywhere" Mathilde addressed me, as she went towards the stairs leaving the three of us apprehensive of her return. Many of the bar's patrons heard all or part of Mathilde's diatribe. One joker was heard to say, "Some one is in real trouble"

I remembered Mathilde's warning to me that if I ever let Yvette down she would follow me to the ends of the earth. Bar patrons tended to linger late that night, waiting I suspect for Mathilde to come down stairs again. She didn't come down and at our normal closing time; some persuasion was necessary before we could close up for the night

As soon as we had closed Mathilde did come down, "I wasn't going to give those drunken sots the satisfaction of seeing me have to apologise." she said. "The story in Millau is that you were only impersonating an English officer and were going away and leaving Yvette behind after you had taken advantage of her." "It is Henri Dufour I was impersonating," I replied, "I am a Major in the British army on detached duties to liaise first with the resistance and subsequently with the FFI

My plans after I left Saint Flour were to leave the British services as quickly as I could, return here, marry Yvette, adopt Jean-Francois, take up the offer of employment from Pascal, and live somewhere in this part of France." Mum and Dad were both nodding in agreement with what I said. "So what are you going to do now?"

"When I leave here I have to return to England and await any further orders. I am still in the British Army, I am also still deeply in love with Yvette, but I have some understanding of her feelings about my deceiving her. I did try to get clearance to disclose my identity to her but it was not given"

"Even we only knew that he was an Englishman posing as our son Henri and was here to help the resistance." said Dad, and went on; "Until I saw his name on the surrender document I knew neither his name nor rank, said Dad "Although Pascal knew he was a British officer he did not know either," added Mum

"I came here especially to make you marry Yvette before you went off to wherever you are going," said Mathilde. "I would marry her tomorrow but she will not even think about it." I replied. "I know," replied Mathilde, "I am desolated for you both," she said hugging me. I could see no way forward, I was tired so I excused myself and went to bed

Sambo was waiting for me but it was little consolation that a cat could detect one's feelings. From attitudes the following morning, I guessed that Mum, Dad and Mathilde had talked late into the night

Saturday mornings in the summer holiday period did not start too early. Many of the employers in the area had not yet returned to full working and there were no weekly commuters to return and nobody to make it fun doing the job anyway. Bar and terrace cleaned, floors washed, Sambo fed and the breakfast coffee brewed, well before any one else was up. Dad came through into the bar and we were both surprised to see a large Citroen pull up outside and Pascal come into the bar

"Is that sister of yours up yet," he asked Dad after the handshakes. "After that telephone conversation last night I am going to take Yvette and Jean-Francois over to her parents at Murat and add my weight to the argument against Yvette marrying you." he said. She and possibly her parents obviously don't believe you tried to get clearance to tell Yvette, but I know you did because the question was referred to me for an opinion. I did not know the young lady concerned and could get no opinions as to her trust worthiness, and there fore could offer no advice." "She simply does not understand the extreme danger Henri would have been put into if she had let anything slip, and none of us knew

402

how the relationship was going to develop, and I am really quite surprised we all managed to keep the information from her for so long." added Dad

Mathilde came down, and introduced herself to Pascal, "Thank you for honouring your promise so promptly," she greeted him. Both of them were large people. "If you two cannot change her mind, there is no hope for me." I said. Eventually Yvette agreed to be taken to Murat for the day. Late in the day Pascal telephoned to say he had made no progress and Yvette was going to stay in Murat because she felt pressurised in the Terminus and that he was returning to Clermont

In conjunction with Mum and Dad I arranged for Raymond and the four sergeants to move into the town, Raymond in the Terminus and the sergeants in the Saint Jacques with Manuel. This made more work for Mum and she insisted Yvette returned to her job, which she did reluctantly

When I checked with the communications centre late in the day, I was surprised to find that the progress of the Americans to liberate us was moving faster than anticipated. We had only very occasional contact with the resistance group in Creuse but they considered it necessary to alert us and other Cantons to the actions we could expect from the advancing Americans

They target the principle towns and when they have established some agreement with the local Town Halls they move on using only major roads and always with a squadron of tanks in the lead. At the least sign of resistance they tend to shoot at anything that moves, and that includes the FFI unless they have already established contact. Most of the German deserters they encounter are shot on sight if in uniform.' Attempts we made to contact the senior American officer in Gueret were all rejected because we were not yet liberated and, "Who the hell are you anyway"

We told the Creuse resistance group that the Americans had been given our frequencies and told to contact us before they arrived in our Canton, by General Bradley's headquarters in Orleans. "The armoured ground troops don't obey their local officers here and they are much less likely to obey officers who are 200 kilometres away." It was not a reply we could ignore especially as we had received no information from them

They may have succeeded in bulldozing their way so far but they are not going to enter Cantal in that manner," I said to the assembled group on Monday morning. The news had just come through that the Southerly drive from Paris and the Northerly drive up the Saone valley had joined each other finally closing the trap on any Germans remaining Vichy France. "And this latest news will make them more bullish than ever." I continued, "the problem is that after Ussel there are two possible routes to Mauriac and we have no way of knowing which they will take." Raymond came over to the map. "I think it's quite simple," he said, "we either declare the bridge at la Forsse or the bridge at Antigues as unsafe and they are forced to use the other route." "But how do we make them take any notice of us?" said Patrice. Some nods of agreement. "We could avoid the problem by making them stop on the departmental road leaving Ussel, "said Victor. "There's a steep up-gradient just before la Serre with plenty of cover and rocks to block the road if we wished," I said. "With a nice little by-pass through the village of Mestes," said Sebastian. "We should get the Maire of Ussel and his staff to all be saying there is only one safe route to Mauriac and that is via Bort les Orgues. Then if we use one or more of those Four German trucks we won, to block the route via Neuvic at the la Serre junction. This will make sure they take the Bort les Orgues route." said Raymond re entering the discussion. And that was what we finally did. The FFI group in Ussel cooperated well and I don't think we really needed to block the route via Neuvic

We selected a location just before the border of Correz and Cantal. At that point the road wound round the side of a belvedere viewpoint looking over the lake formed by a Dordogne dam. We could block the road by a rockfall backed up by mines if necessary. There were numerous excellent points for locating the bazookas to be aimed at the tank squadron which were an essential part of my tactics in dealing with the Americans. Based on the rate of advance of the Americans we could anticipate their arrival in Ussel on Wednesday or Thursday. They normally lingered for a day in a sub-prefecture so we could reasonably expect them to move into our canton on Thursday or Friday. In the meantime Pascal advised that another spearhead of General Bradley's force had entered Puy de Dome from Vichy where they had stopped for some days. Their behaviour was much the same as reported from Creuse. He was having their progress monitored by a German Storch spotter plane repainted in French colours and they still fired at it "We've also got a second Storch ready so we can monitor the progress of the spearhead approaching your canton as well, and they will be able to advise you by radio of their exact position" I accepted gratefully

By Wednesday evening Raymond completed his preparation. All the mines and charges were in position and only needed fusing. Traffic diversions were in place so the Americans would have the road to themselves. Pascal was to be advised when the Americans left Ussel and thereafter would be monitored from the air. The Americans left Ussel just after dawn on Friday, and when the morning mist had cleared our first report from the air put them at Chabanade thus having covered only about eleven kilometres in ninety minutes. This report also confirmed that they were on exactly the right road for Bort-les-Orgues and our planned hold-up. Raymond busied himself with the fusing of the mines and charges. The bazookas were all in position and the men to use them nearby. A radio report from the air reported small arms firing from the tanks at Margerides and people apparently hit. The tanks were moving in line ahead with about twenty metres between them, their speed was only about twenty-five kilometres per hour. At just before eleven Patrice who was looking back down the road they were using signalled that they were in sight. He climbed down from his viewpoint carrying his Bren gun at the trail and crossed the road just in sight of the lead tank. There was a burst of automatic small arms fire from the lead tank and he was hit. Raymond detonated the first charge for the rockfall and it was an adequate blockage. The lead tank stopped with the others behind him at intervals. The officer in the lead tank was obviously talking over a radio with those behind. The last tank in line started manoeuvring to turn round. We were ready for this and Raymond detonated another charge closing the road behind them

Two large white flags were raised and I stepped out into the roadway and approached the lead tank. The officer in the turret was a Captain. I shouted out over the noise of the tank engines. "Captain please shut off your engines you are not going any further until certain matters of your behaviour have been agreed"

"I am not stopping for you or anybody." was shouted back, "we can soon blow those rocks off the road and drive through." "As soon as your first shot has been fired a bazooka shell will hit your tank. I shouted back, now let's have those engines off." He spoke into his handset and one by one the engines went off

I approached the lead tank closer. "You are interfering with the American Army doing its job and that's a serious offence." "You have just shot one of my men and that's pretty serious too." Simon ran out of the covering rocks and told me Patrice was dead. "I've just been told he's dead, so that's a Court Martial for you. Get down from that tank." "Like hell I will and you can't give me orders." "I am a major in the British Army on detached duties as a liaison officer to the French resistance and the French Forces of the Interior. Now get down from that tank or we might just shoot you up anyway." He got down and confronted me. He was a young white man aged mid-twenties, he slouched towards me and almost saluted. "You will stand to attention in front of a superior officer." He just about made it

"You are just about to enter the canton, you might say county, of Cantal and based on the reports we have had from the other cantons you have passed through we will not tolerate certain of your activities here. Any German deserters you encounter, in uniform or not, are not to be shot. Most of them are working on the farms at a peak time of the year. A few others not so usefully engaged will be dealt with by the civil police as they are discovered. Secondly there is to be no random use of weaponry unless you are fired upon first. I cannot believe that there will be any need at all." "I suppose your bazooka threat is a myth." he interrupted me. "No," I replied, "at this moment there are eight bazookas trained on your squadron, we don't do things by halves." I gave a pre-arranged wave and eight Bazookas were held up from their positions in the hillside. "You were also given our radio frequencies and ordered to contact us as you approached our canton and you have not done so, why?" "Yeah, our Colonel said something about that, transmissions had to be 'on Claire' and I guess we don't have the gear for that." "For your education 'en Claire' simply means not in code"

"Now I need to know the name and rank of your superior officer in order to initiate your Court Martial for the killing of one of my men." "But he's French and not your responsibility." "I assure you he is an English sergeant." "The Colonel in charge of this group is Gregory Painter and he is still at Ussel

He probably won't leave there until we hit Aurillac." "When are you going to start the Court Martial proceedings?" "I'm seeing your General Bradley in about a week's time and that will be the start, I expect, but these matters take time"

"Your next destination is Mauriac where I understand you will be stopping for one or two days. The Maire of Mauriac has orders to report immediately on any breach of the instructions I have given you and also on any matters of lack of discipline by your men or those support forces who are moving South later today. You will convey my instructions to your superiors." "What have we got to do about this lot," he said pointing at our rock falls. "Raymond and his men will assist you but you must wait until he has defused the mines that are in the road." I waved for Raymond to come over. "I think we have an understanding" I said, "When you've cleared the mines work with the tank crews to clear the road and make sure they do their share. Then the rest of you can go back to Saint Flour and you can meet me at the Mairie in Mauriac"

We released the Storch spotter plane with thanks to the pilot. "You certainly put the fear of God into that lot, I could pick up some of their conversations between the tank crews." he replied

I went off to Mauriac. I intended to be seen on the streets that evening. The Maire welcomed my presence as he was also aware the problems when the 'yanks arrived'. The tank squadron had been caught up by the support infantry at our rock fall and they had travelled together to Mauriac. I watched their behaviour as they drew up in front of the Mairie. I noticed they let their Colonel introduce himself to the Maire first. I remained on the balcony overlooking the area in front of the Mairie. Gregory Painter was certainly a more amenable man than his tank Captain. The Maire had one of his councillors to act as interpreter so progress was slow. Finally their vehicles were all parked at the railway station, the officers accommodated in the local hotels and the other ranks roughed it round the vehicles at the station where enough restaurants were open to feed any of the men who chose to eat there I came down from the balcony at the end of these arrangements and the Maire introduced me to the Colonel as Henri Dufour the resistance leader for the canton of Cantal. We conversed for some time and the Colonel complemented me on my knowledge of English. "I have been told there is a British Army Major in Cantal as a liaison officer to the resistance forces, I need to talk to him." "You are doing so now," I replied. He took a step back from me, "But your name is Henri something or other," "That is my French identity." "Then I need to know your name rank and number, you stopped and threatened my tank squadron this morning." "I am afraid your name is not on the list of persons authorised to know my real identity

You can always apply to the British Army intelligence headquarters, but I feel confident you will not receive an answer. Please remember your lead tank shot dead one of my men this morning. He was no threat to your squadron and that is a Court Martial offence. There were more than a dozen witnesses of the incident. The proceedings will commence tomorrow when I return to my base"

"I told your tank Captain this morning that the sort of behaviour your unit has indulged in during your advance from the Loire will not be tolerated here in Cantal, we can either work together with you on a friendly basis or make your time in Cantal completely unrewarding. We liberated ourselves from the Germans some weeks ago, we don't actually need you here at all. If you cannot accept the situation you might as well turn your vehicles around and go back the way you came." "Who is your commanding officer in France?" He demanded. "I don't have one, I sometimes report directly to British Army intelligence headquarters and sometimes to De Gaulle's headquarters and I have received instructions from both"

"The police throughout the whole of Cantal and the high Auvergne have instructions to treat any misconduct by your men in the same way as they would for local people and all reports of misconduct will also reach me. I shall be seeing your General Bradley in about a week's time and I shall simply add any such reports to the list I have already." At that point I left him and returned to the Maire's office where Raymond was waiting

I told the Maire of our talk and reiterated the instruction to report all misconduct. The Maire, Raymond and I had dinner together later in a restaurant overlooking the station forecourt. Our instructions had been effective. The G.I.s were enjoying the fine evening, the local girls were enjoying teasing the G.I.s and getting drinks off them. What local men there were, were not enjoying the girls teasing the G.I.s. There was a small police presence. Later the Maire, Raymond and I walked round the town and all of us felt comfortable with what we saw. As we returned to the Mairie we passed the tank Captain. He stopped us briefly, "I think I understand you a little better now, this is the best reception we have had anywhere." I translated this for the Maire and we all shook hands goodnight. Raymond drove me back to Saint Flour on a soft balmy September night spoilt only by the loss of Patrice to a trigger happy yank

I advised London next morning about Patrice adding that Court martial papers would be prepared when I was back in London. Time was running short. I tried again to talk sensibly to Yvette with no success. Jean-Francois was in tears when she snatched him away from me at the end of this talk. I remembered I had to collect the message Stephan had left for me with Pierre Durand and I also wished to especially thank Angelique for her work on the news distribution

As she was now back at school after the summer vacation, I went to meet her as she left for the day. I had commandeered Felix de Boni again and he drove us to Durand farm. Only the dogs were at home. Felix waited in the car. "I think I know where my Dad put it," she said. A few moments later she returned with a plain envelope simply marked 'Henri' I pocketed it

"Thank your father for saving it for me." She came and stood straight in front of me, "During the long summer holidays I do not hear any of the news from the town, and I was devastated when I heard about you and Yvette, I simply do not understand the girl unless she feels her husband might not be dead and she should not have encouraged you if that was the case"

"It's not that," I replied, "She is convinced he is dead, but I did not, and could not disclose the fact that I am not the Henri Dufour she helped at school. Therefore she cannot trust me or marry me." She put her hands on my shoulders "Unfortunately you met her before you met me. In spite of my war experience, "I would marry you tomorrow and if I had known about Yvette's attitude sooner "I would have been on your doorstep, and quite quickly into your bed" she moved closer, "Angelique, you are a very brave young woman, I admire you immensely, but please understand I am not in a frame of mind to indulge in any further romance for some time. I will be leaving Saint Flour in a few days. I do not know where the war will take me next, or how long the war will last. If you had ever been discovered by the SS as the source of those news bulletins I dread to think what might have happened to you. You have been braver than any one else I know." I kissed her fully on the lips, "but this has to be goodbye

"During the drive back to the town I read Stephan's note. He thanked me for the wonderful cooperation we had together saying that such cooperation should continue when peace came but he doubted of it would 'It is unlikely we will ever meet again and that is unfortunate for both of us. I would like to see the way you live, and to show you how my wife and family live I have spent quite a lot of my time at the Durand farm because I always wanted to see the news before you got it. Now, this is the main reason for my note to you

408

Angelique is in love with you. She is a very brave person as you well know. Her bravery matches yours, and you two together would have a wonderful life. She will make you a much finer wife than Yvette who will now let you down"

It was simply signed, 'your true friend, Stephan I wondered exactly when he wrote that note and when he expected me to read it. It must have been about the time of the surrender as Stephan had gone by the twenty-second of August when I had tried to find him

Back at the Terminus life seemed very flat. I had done everything I had been ordered to do and the time for packing up and calling Pascal was imminent. All my group were quite anxious to be on their way. One last task I had to arrange was for Patrice's body to be embalmed and returned to England as soon as it could be arranged. Pascal also promised to co-operate in this task. I did not know how I could face the task of saying goodbye to all the people of Saint Flour and the region with whom I had contacted in my time with them. I eventually decided to limit the personal goodbyes to my parents and Mathilde

I wrote a final news letter for Angelique to distribute using my 'orders' as an excuse for a hasty departure. I telephoned Pascal and asked for his cars the day after tomorrow and told my colleagues to be ready at eight in the morning

The only witness to the conversation with Pascal was Sambo. From that moment he hardly left my side, and they say cats don't understand humans! The Terminus closed the day before my departure. It was the most difficult day of my life to date. I was leaving people whom I had come to love as real parents who had risked their lives for me to do a job

The cars arrived on time, suitably decorated with Union Jacks and Tricolours. That gave the game away. People poured out into the Place de la Liberte from all over the town. We stowed our bags as quickly as possible and were cheered all the way out of the town only being able to crawl through the crowds. My last view of the Terminus included a disconsolate black cat sitting on the corner of the terrace. Some of us, including myself, were in tears

Pascal intended to make this a day we would remember. The journey was inevitably slow, numerous delays by damaged roads, bridges down, repairs in progress and diversions. Christoph and Cezaire had been volunteered to drive us and we soon found out why.

On passing through Clermont it seemed to me we were not taking a very direct route

We finally stopped at the Hotel du Departemente where a lengthy speech from the Maire was witnessed by the Puy de Dome FFI and the resistance groups of the local trades unions. And we were cheered on our way again the roads improved somewhat as we left the higher parts of the land. Our next unexpected stop was at a very pleasing chateau on the outskirts of Montlucon, where an excellent lunch awaited us. Pascal had gone to considerable lengths to make this day one to remember.

"Do you know who Pascal really is," asked Simon as we got under way again. Christoph was suddenly seized by a fit of coughing. "No," I lied, "the contact was arranged by De Gaulle's office in London because we had no British intelligence officers in the area until I arrived." "That's not quite true," said Christophe, speaking for the first time, "several had been parachuted in before you arrived, but Clermont is such an important strategic location that Vichy French intelligence was strong and active here so they did not survive for very long. When the opportunity to put you into Saint Flour with a very reliable cover story we decided to work with and through you"

General Bradley's headquarters was in a park on the Southern outskirts of Orleans. As we arrived and passed the controls at the entrance a military band struck up Rule Britannia followed by La Marseillaise. We did just manage to stand at attention after that inebriating lunch and on a warm September afternoon. The local French resistance leaders were all present and introduced them selves, Petro seemed to be the leader. "We have organised a farewell dinner for you all tomorrow evening and we hope you will do us the honour of joining us. We will certainly have much in common to talk about. We hope you will be in your uniforms which we are told await you here." I turned to the others and saw nods all round "With great pleasure." I replied. "We will have taxis here at six-forty-five to collect you." said Petro. An American officer had turned up in the meantime at my elbow. "Can you arrange for those taxis to be admitted to your base?" I asked, "No problem," he said. "Your uniforms have been pressed and await you, but General Bradley has asked that you, Major, meet him as soon as possible before you change into uniform

"Not the ideal location," Bradley said soon after I was introduced to him, "the only two airstrips are on the other side of town. I see and hear that your group must be something a bit special." I don't know what you regard as special, we all arrived in Vichy France before the Germans occupied it but I am not at liberty to discuss what we have been doing." "Sure I understand. But the fact you've survived tells me something." "I'm afraid we did lose one man, Shot dead by a trigger happy American from one of your tanks." "That's what I wanted to talk to you about," replied Bradley. "There is not much to discuss," I replied, "Patrice, that's his code name, was crossing the road carrying his Bren gun at the trail, he was no threat to your tanks, and your gunner shot him dead with a burst of machine gun fire." "I understand that you had closed the road with fallen rocks." "We closed the road with fallen rocks just after Patrice had been shot but I admit we were ready to do so, if necessary." "Did you actually witness the

410

killing of this man Patrice?" "No, I did not actually see him shot, I heard the burst of machine gun fire, and heard the shouts that Patrice had been hit. Several of my men were nearer to the incident and saw more of the action, and probably another twenty or so of the local FFI also saw the incident." "FFI?" he looked quizzical. "French Forces of the Interior," I explained. "You controlled them as well?" "When they assisted us in one of our plans they accepted our command. We also frequently supported them in joint ventures as well as supplying them with the necessary munitions" "Most of our attacks on the Germans involved both organisations and sometimes from neighbouring cantons as well." "I want to talk to you again about this tomorrow, now you'd better get changed into something better than those duds."He dismissed me All of us found it strange to be back in uniform and having to salute so many unknown American personnel. We all found we had need of a tailor to adjust the uniforms to fit having acquired a few extra kilos especially in the past month. We agreed that we would stay in and recover from the celebrations and the magnificent lunch

In the morning we discovered that the tram service into town passed the gates of the American base. On the trams any attempt to pay was refused and we were shown pictures in the newspapers of our arrival yesterday. Similarly in the city coffee was never paid for nor any admission charges to anywhere

The taxis arrived spot on time and we left again for the city. By comparison with the lunch we had eaten yesterday the meal was not remarkable but the talks we had with our counterparts in the local resistance made the evening and a good part of the night a time to remember. We all slept quite late the following morning. I was woken early by one of Bradley's aides to confirm a meeting with him at three in the afternoon

When we were all assembled I instructed all to be available in case I needed them during this meeting with Bradley. In fact the meeting with Bradley was over in minutes. It was simply to tell me that any attempt to Court Martial any of the tank crews or command officers would be resisted with all the force at his disposal. Everyone was wanting to know why such a short meeting and I felt I had to tell them. I told them I would be initiating Court Martial proceedings when we were back in England and as soon as I had found out how to do it. To a man they all agreed to support the action

The next day I approached Bradley's aide again. "We have reported your arrival to London as they requested. They are making arrangements and you will hear shortly." Food at the American canteens was surprisingly good and we lacked for nothing. No mess bills were presented and the hospitality of the city was used to the full. Then the news we were all anxiously waiting for, "A Dakota will collect you all during the afternoon of Monday twenty-fifth September. Be ready at the airstrip of Chateaudun from fourteen hours"

We spent the morning packing and acquiring some real duty free goods, from the store at Bradley's headquarters but nobody knew what the limits were. Transport was laid on by the Americans and Pietro and some of his colleagues came with us to the airstrip. It was not a happy departure, the plane was delayed by three hours and what do you find to talk about for all that time. When we were finally airborne our feelings were a definite sadness and a wish to return to France under happier and less stressful circumstances

We landed at Tangmere some two hours later. No customs control so we could have brought more. A car awaited me and after some very hasty farewells I was whisked away to London without ever knowing the real identities of any of my companions

Epilogue

One Friday early in March 1972 the export director, of a major chemical distributor, visited Clermont Ferrand accompanied by his wife. Business being completed in the morning led to a lunch party at the top of the Puy de Dome. Unfortunately the weather was not kind so the views were restricted. Lunch over and the guests were driven back to their place of business. The weather had deteriorated into a steady drizzle. After leaving their clients the couple set out to drive to Barcelona where they had further business engagements on Monday. As they left Clermont behind and began to climb up into the high Auvergne the weather deteriorated even further and visibility was poor to the point of being dangerous as it became darker. "I don't think I want to drive much further tonight in this lot," said the man to his wife. "Remember you've had a fair lot to drink as well, "said his wife. Another fifty or so kilometres and the weather had not improved

"You know I've just had a thought," said the man, "It is exactly thirty years since I first travelled this road." "Why should you remember that?" said his wife. He ignored the question. "It was on a bus one Sunday afternoon and I was travelling from Vichy to Issoire to catch another bus to Saint Flour." "That's where you were during the war isn't it?" asked his wife. "Yes, let's, stop there for the night. It's only about another sixty kilometres and there's quite a decent hotel right on the main road." "Well there was thirty years ago," replied his wife. "Things don't change very fast here," replied the man. After crossing a very high ridge they descended into a river valley and continued for some time. The mist was not so troublesome on the lower road. In the small town with some street lights it was better for a few kilometres. Then a steady climb, "We're getting quite high, I've just seen an altitude marker of over a thousand feet." "They use metres here, we're approximately three and a half thousand feet up." said the man

The descent came quite quickly and they left the worst of the weather behind. The lights of another small town came into view, over a railway bridge, round a bend and into a large area with shops all round and a smart looking hotel on the left."There it is said the man triumphantly, Hotel St. Jacques, but it looks as though it's changed hands. Madame Belmont was never one for outside appearances." They turned into the car park. Only two other cars, "I hope they are not closed for the winter season," the man said

They weren't. A young receptionist took their passports and checked them in. They reserved a table for dinner at seven. The dining room was large with a log fire at one side and they took a table close by. "This is nice and cosy," said his wife. A neatly turned out waiter took an order for two Kir de Mure and left the menu with them. The meal was good, freshly cooked to order, and tasty. At the end the man said, "They used to have a speciality here you will never have tasted before, smoked walnuts, would you like to try them with a liqueur? She nodded. He summoned the waiter "Do you have any smoked walnuts this evening?"Certainly sir," said the waiter and fetched the basket and two pairs of crackers from a side table. "They are as good as they always were." said the man after the tenth one or so

After coffee the couple strolled into the reception area and looked out into the night. The rain had cleared completely and the moon was just visible. "Shall we take a stroll to the upper town," said the man, "It's not far and you can find out how I got my exercise," "our coats are still in the car, I'll get them." said his wife

They walked across the Place de la Liberte. "I see the Terminus is no longer the Terminus and has changed hands," said the man, pointing at a bar and restaurant across the Place. They crossed bridge over the river and turned right up a small road. "This doesn't go up to the Cathedral," said his wife. "Wait and see." just as the houses stopped a flight of stone steps on the left clearly did go up to the Cathedral. "I used to run up these steps all the way said the man, I was fit in those days." They climbed steadily and emerged through a narrow gap between buildings on to the Place d'Armes. The Cathedral front was impressive in the moonlight and the bells struck the half-hour. "If you come over here," said the man leading the way over to the North side of the Place, "you can see how this was such a good site for a town in medieval times." She looked over the wall and saw the rocky outcrops on which the upper town had been built. "And if we go over here," said the man, leading her across to the South-West corner of the Place, there is the gatehouse that was the only entry point to the upper town in those days." The width of the gate would have allowed a horse-and-cart to pass or a small car

The gatehouse formed the end of the more modern Town Hall. They strolled down the rue Marchande to the Place de la Halle-aux-Bleds with its market hall and on down the rue des Lacs. The town was almost deserted, but the bars were quite busy. They reached the Pompidou gardens. "So that's where the buses stop now," said the man, "I wondered why there weren't any down by our hotel, and that will be why what was the Terminus is no longer the Terminus"

They walked along the side of the Pompidou gardens as far as the rue du College. "If we go down here," said the man, "it brings us back to where we started and then you will have done the grand tour of Saint Flour by moonlight"

People were beginning to leave the bars and goodnight calls were directed at us as well as the real locals Christian de Boni had spent his usual Friday evening at the Riviere Bar playing cards, he didn't win or lose any significant amount of money and left shortly after ten-thirty, walking along the side of the Pompidou gardens to his car. A couple of strangers were walking towards him. He wished them 'Good night and got the same response. A few metres further on he stopped and looked back at the couple as they turned into the rue du College. "That was Henri Dufour," he said out loud, but there was nobody to hear him. It troubled him all the way home so much that before he went to bed he called the now retired, Alexis Lescaut. "I'm sure I saw Henri Dufour tonight." Some moments of silence, then Alexis said, "Where and what were the exact circumstances," "Along the side of the Pompidou gardens with a lady, we exchanged good night greetings." "So it was dark, you heard him speak two words, he was with somebody you didn't recognise and I assume you had been drinking. How can you be so sure?" "Everything was right, his accent, his posture, that very slight limp, his age." Alexis thought for some minutes and thought about the date, March Nineteen-seventy two, thirty years after he arrived? coincidence? "I don't think I'm going to do anything about it," said Alexis, "If it was Henri, then he shouldn't be here, he was banned from returning for fifty years." If it wasn't Henri, then I don't need to do anything, I'm sorry Christian I'm not thinking you were right"

At breakfast in the morning, the couple were served by the same waiter. He acted as though he knew the man. Later he obviously called the chef who came to the door of his kitchen and also inspected the couple

Shortly after the couple came down from their room, packed and ready to depart. The young receptionist took their payment, receipted their bill and they went to their car. The Chef looked out of his window and saw them putting cases into the boot of an English registered car. He looked more intensely, Yes it was.

The couple were standing talking and the man was pointing out certain things to the woman. They were in no hurry. They walked back into the Place de la Liberte and continued to look all round. Manuel, the Chef, rushed back into the reception area, "Are they leaving?" He asked the receptionist. "Yes they've paid their bill." He grabbed the telephone and called Alexis Lescaut. "I'm sure Henri Dufour is at the Hotel," he didn't even say who was calling. Alexis was dumbfounded, Christian must be right after all. "Keep him there until I get there," he said. Manuel went outside but could not see the couple although the car was still in the car park. He looked at the register and got their room number, went up to their room but it was empty. As he got back to the reception Alexis Lescaut got off his bicycle and entered the hotel, "I think they've just gone," he said, "a bronze English registered car has just pulled out of the car park and turned South on to National nine"

Everybody stood nonplussed for some seconds. "Have they collected the registration slips yet?" Alexis asked the receptionist, "No" she replied, "we only had five guests last night, but I'm not supposed to let you see the slips." He snatched them out of her hand. Picking out the two with British passport numbers on then he pronounced, "Yes it was Henri Dufour and his wife. I shall have to report him this time just in case anyone else makes the connection when these slips go to the records office."

Now I know why I felt the way I did when I served them." said Jean-Francois, the waiter, "and when the man asked for the smoked walnuts and the liqueur I knew they must have been here before." I only saw him from the back last night," said Manuel," but when I looked at them putting their cases into the boot, I recognised Henri's characteristic limp

"I would like to have spoken with him much more," said Jean-Francois, I remember him vaguely being very nice and kind to me. Do you think I should tell my mother?" "Probably better not," advised Alexis. "She refused to marry him because she said she could not trust him, which I always thought was nonsense." "I remember he came back several times after the war to see her and tried to persuade her," said Manuel. "I don't remember that," said Jean-Francois." "She wouldn't let him see you," said Manuel. "Did you report him then?" Jean-Francois asked Alexis. "No but he didn't stay in a hotel so there was no registration slips to worry about"

The young receptionist was obviously concerned and forcibly took back the registration slips from Alexis, saying, "What's so special about Henri Dufour anyway"

About the Author

Born in Sussex he was educated by an international Catholic boys teaching order and he qualified for university entrance in the early days of the 39-45 war. When registering for miitary service the author was tempted by a proposal from the SOE to take a French identity and be put into Vichy France as a liaison link with to French resistance organisations. After his war service he completed a first degree at London University followed by employment in industry and also a government research organization. Later studies and experience led to diplomas in macromolecular and bio-chemistry from European universities.

At 36 years of age he abandoned a purely scientific career and was engaged in support of the worldwide sales activity of a major chemical supplier to industry. Extensive travel and occasional location abroad caused a marriage break-up and a period of lost contact with his children. Later with a business partner he established a manufacturing company of special products eventually selling out to their major customer.

While on business in Vienna he met his second wife without knowing she was the daughter of a by-then deceased officer whom he had met on a previous occasion. They have subsequently spent time together in France and Belgium. After retirement they returned to the UK and have settled in Sussex.

Restrained by the official secrets act from disclosing any information about war service for many years the author finally wrote down the story of his time in France at the behest of his second wife for the benefit of his family. It read rather like a scientific report; although much of the content was far from scientific! His biography of that time is now published as *Within the Shadows*.

Lightning Source UK Ltd.
Milton Keynes UK
UKOW04f0326220917
309664UK00001B/126/P